CATHERINE DE' MEDICI

and the Lost Revolution

CATHERINE DE' MEDICI

and the Lost Revolution

BY

Ralph Roeder

SECOND EDITION, ABRIDGED

VINTAGE BOOKS
A Division of Random House
NEW YORK

9664

Catherine de Medici
Caught between two world

Contents

CHAPTER   I   Youth   3

CHAPTER   II   The Reign of François I   30

CHAPTER   III The Reign of Henri II   49

CHAPTER   IV   The Reign of François II   129

CHAPTER   V   The Reign of Charles IX   186

CHAPTER   VI   The Reign of Henri III   391

               Bibliography   477

               Chronological Table of Principal
                  Events   479

               Relationships of Principal Figures   483

               Genealogy of the Medici   486

               Genealogy of the Valois-Angoulême   487

               Index   489

CATHERINE DE' MEDICI

and the Lost Revolution

CHAPTER I

YOUTH

- 1 -

Money is sterile. Of all the teachings of the primitive Church none was more stubborn: it lasted well into the Renaissance, when the giant infancy of Capitalism rose on all sides to confound it. Everywhere the evidence was overwhelming; everywhere the teeming fertility of money was transforming the world; but still the old prohibition stood. *Pecunia pecuniam non parere potest.* Money cannot breed money; money is a medium, not an agent, and by its nature unproductive. To profit by its fruits is an abuse of nature, a perversion of function, a sin against God and man, and the wages of sin is death. For the doctrine was not so much economic as moral. It was stubborn, it denied blindly the facts that refuted it, because it preserved the economic ethics and was constant to the original virtue of Christianity. The command of the Founder coupled two principles: "Love ye your enemies, and do good, and lend, hoping for nothing." The moral law and the economic law were one, human solidarity, mutual assistance. But when, with the rise of Capitalism and the transformation of the world by a money economy, the moral law and the economic law came into conflict and the world passed under a double dispensation, the moral law commanding co-operation and the economic law dictating competition, and the one as essential to salvation as the other to survival, the doctrine became impotent except as a protest.

But it was doomed. The Renaissance was an age of moral and economic transition, which a creed so unworldly could not survive. The usurious civilization of the modern world, which it stigmatized, submerged and undermined its economic, and hence its moral, foundations. It was obsolete. It harked back to the monastic communism of the Middle Ages and to the simple secular economy which favoured it. For there had been a day when the doctrine was not unworldly. The economy of co-operation flourished for a thousand years in the simple and static conditions and the isolated and self-sufficient communities of the Middle Ages. But with the growth of towns, the development of nations, and the expansion of life, the old household economy no longer sufficed for a world which had become interdependent, unstable, and competitive. The medieval economy of subsistence yielded to the modern economy of exchange; the catalytic agent of this change was commerce; and money, as its medium, was transforming the whole social structure and revolutionizing an entire view of life. Life was no longer being but becoming; all that had been fixed was fluid, all that had been static, dynamic, all that had been certain, speculative. Nothing was certain but change, and the Church, in common with all the institutions of the past, was compelled to adapt itself to it. But it contested every compromise. Reluctantly conceding the legitimate profits of commerce, it continued nevertheless to denounce trade in the medium of exchange, and would not admit that the medium was itself a commodity, involved in the same risks, and entitled to the same profits as any other trade.

For never had the formidable fertility of money been more manifest. It stimulated, it transformed, whatever it touched. It conquered and penetrated and developed every domain—commerce, culture, politics, art. It had produced the Renaissance, it was about to produce the Reformation. The times were ripe for a new advance, and in the first years of the sixteenth century it came. The latent power of

Capitalism mustered its energies and, precipitating its course, suddenly penetrated to the apex of Christendom. In 1513 Giovanni de' Medici was elected Pope.

- 2 -

Other Popes had owed their election to money; his was untainted by simony; that only made it the more momentous. Its very legitimacy marked the advent of a class and the canonization, as it were, of its power. Leo X personified it supremely. Other banks had waxed and waned— the Frescobaldi, the Cerchi, the Bardi, the Peruzzi—but none had scaled so many spheres of influence, none so clearly epitomized the indomitable capacity of capital enterprises as the Florentine firm of Medici and Sons.

The origin of the family was obscure, and its heroic age, like theirs, was also its period of obscurity. It emerged from the masses as their champion. In the fourteenth century it was a Medici—Salvestro—who supported the weavers and carders, the lowest class of Florentine labour, in their successful riot for improved living conditions, remission of debt, and the franchise. In the fifteenth it was a Medici —Bicci—who backed the popular struggle for a tax reform which antagonized the patricians. The ruling class retaliated on his son. An attempt was made to uproot the family in 1431 by banishing Cosimo de' Medici. But its roots were too firmly entwined in the economic structure of Florentine life, and the blow rebounded on its authors. The Medici had in the meantime gained control through the guilds of the silk-trade and founded a bank to serve it. True to their traditions, however, the bank catered to a needy popular class which depended on it and which was so numerous that widespread distress followed the exile of Cosimo. When he proposed to transfer his bank to Venice, the popular reaction was strong enough to compel his recall. To avert a repetition of such accidents, he took the step which earned him the title of *Pater Patriae* and launched the family on its political career, and gained control of the State. It was the logical consequence of his control of the guilds, and he administered the government by the same methods—by forming a political syndicate, distributing its shares among his friends, and making of it a closed corporation. He occupied no official or recognized position and employed no force but financial influence. It was from the till that he manipulated elections, appointed his partisans, disciplined his competitors, and formed a Medici faction from the clientele of his bank; and never before had the power of money been so systematically or so fruitfully employed in politics. For Cosimo brought into politics the commercial spirit and directed the policies of the government to what he considered the only proper end of statecraft, the promotion of his own trade interests and the economic welfare of the community as a whole. The result was a period of halcyon prosperity and an experiment of considerable significance. For in Florence the world saw, not an oligarchical republic like Venice or Genoa, but a semi-democratic and wholly commercial State, ruled nominally by the elected representatives of the guilds and actually by the financial manipulation of one man.

Cosimo took measures to avert it, governing himself on the principles which he left to his successors as the safe-guards of the system: dissimulation of power, popular partnership or the semblance of it, personal simplicity, and commercial success. The necessary capacities, however, were not easy to unite in one man or to transmit to another; and at best the system represented merely a compromise with the inherently imperialistic tendency of capital enterprise.

The system functioned for three generations. Three generations was the average life of a great bank. The Medici firm was no exception: it was already weakening under the grandson of Cosimo, Lorenzo de' Medici, a notoriously bad businessman, who left its management to his subordinates. Toward the end of his life, under the lash of Savonarola, whose eloquence and success in denouncing the fleecing of the people revealed how far the Medici had outgrown their popular origin and support, it was generally expected that Lorenzo would take the next step, appropriate the government, and proclaim himself dictator.

In the next generation the crash came. By some the reverses of the family were laid to their women. Lorenzo was the first to marry out of his class and country. His wife was a Roman Orsini. His son Piero married another mem-

ber of the same baronial family, and both from his wife
and his mother he derived more than his share of the
overbearing spirit of a feudal race. Without commercial
training, without political ability, young, inexperienced, he
began life under many handicaps. Within two years he
had broken all the rules of the system and forfeited the
popularity on which, because of its ambiguous position,
the power of his house depended. In 1494 the city rose,
the Medici were expelled and proscribed. At the instigation of his wife Alfonsina he made a half-hearted attempt,
at the last moment, to seize power by force; but he failed,
and she never forgave him.

There followed an exile of eighteen years, eighteen
years of depression and restlessness which revealed how
precarious the Medici system had been, how much of a
compromise. The restoration of the family, constantly
planned and intermittently attempted, was a matter of
two alternatives: finance or force. The former was impossible. The family property had been confiscated, the bank
was on the verge of failure, the exiles commanded no
credit. The Medici brothers, Piero and Giovanni, living in
a shuttered and mortgaged palace in Rome, passed
through a period of acute penury, from which Piero sought
relief at first in debauchery and then, returning to his wife
and falling under her peremptory influence, in a series of
futile attempts to return to Florence by arms. He died in
1503, an obscure soldier of fortune, fighting in the ranks
of the French. He left a widow nursing her memories, her
ambitions, and a son named in honour of his grandfather
Lorenzo.

The headship of the family now passed to the Cardinal
Giovanni, who should have had it by right, for he possessed the true Medici temperament, ingratiating, cautious,
and oblique. For seventeen years he pursued the restoration of his family in the patient spirit of the Medici motto:
Le Temps revient. Half fatalist, half opportunist, and
wholly diplomat, he cornered all the chances. In 1512 he
drew the right one. With a threat of force, he re-entered
Florence peacefully, requested permission to reside in the
city as a private citizen and to buy back his property, and
quietly recovered the government by the old half-forgotten
system of his ancestors. After the steady rise and abrupt

fall of the family, it was necessary to begin over again at the bottom, and he did so. But one essential element was lacking: the bank. Fortunately, six months later, Giovanni de' Medici became Pope Leo X.

- 3 -

The Medici had recaptured the State, they had attained the Papacy, and in their rapid development they had embraced the whole social scale. It was remarkable that, with the infusion of feudal blood and the habits of inherited power, they had preserved so much of their mercantile temperament intact. But with the decline of the bank they had lost the organic basis of their power; they were now a race of footloose adventurers, compelled to maintain themselves by political expedients; and there ensued a psychological change. "Since God has given us the Papacy, let us enjoy it," the Pope said to his brother Giuliano. The spirit in which he accepted it was one of devout gratitude. The Pope, who passed in the eyes of the world for the supreme consummation of commercial power, was in reality nothing of the kind. He illustrated none of the constructive phases of capital enterprise; he had no commercial instincts, no interest in accumulation, organization, or investment; he was a spender. Years of privation had whetted his appetite; the Papacy itself was no permanent tenure; and he proceeded to cash it.

Exile had done its work: the Medici were morally uprooted. The only use which Leo made of the enormous resources at his disposal was to dissipate them with the reckless extravagance of those in whose veins runs the congenital taint of insecurity and the fatalistic aimlessness of a race that had missed or outlived its function. The fatalist squandered what the opportunist won. It was as if the only capacity that remained to the Medici was to consume themselves, to accumulate and to dissipate, with the restlessness of a family that felt itself, in the very flush of fortune, without a future. Not that Leo was improvident. On the contrary he was far-sighted. He exploited his position conscientiously. He fortified, with the resources of the Holy See, the dominion of his family in Florence. And he gratified himself. He had missed his vocation in life: he was a dilettante, a patron of arts and letters, a musician, a gourmet, a munificent lover of life. "He would have been a perfect Pontiff, if with these amiable qualities," wrote one of his contemporaries, "he had combined some knowledge of religious matters and a little more inclination to piety, in neither of which did he display much interest." But he understood perfectly the mission of the Church as an agent of civilization; he made a religion of art, and he devoted himself with exemplary public spirit to the embellishment of Rome.

It was surely an irony that the innocent hedonist who occupied the Papal Throne should be disturbed in the pursuit of his amiable mission by anything so irrelevant as religious dissension—the one thing that left him cold—but there he was, the symbol of a system, and there was a propriety in the fact that under a Medici Pope the long-gathering protest against the power of money should at last make itself heard. Vast forces were at work which, suddenly seizing on an insignificant incident and magnifying it, hurried the Pope and the world into a movement the consequences of which those who initiated it were far from foreseeing.

- 4 -

The year 1517, in which [Luther's] Theses appeared, was memorable in the annals of the Medici for a very different reason. It marked a new stage in their climb. To climb had become a matter of necessity as well as ambition. The power of the family had been re-established in Florence but it was precarious, as the past had shown, and when the prop provided by the Pope was withdrawn, who could foretell what might follow? It was not too soon to provide for the future with its incalculable hazards and lurking reverses. *Le Temps revient.* Prosperity today was almost a guarantee of adversity tomorrow, and the Medici were consumed by a pathological craving for permanence and stability. For years the Pope had planned to place his younger brother Giuliano in one of the minor Italian States; for years he had hesitated because of the political complications. His hopes settled on Urbino, which was small, isolated, and without political ties, and in 1516 he began his preparations. At this juncture Giuliano died. The loss served only to deepen the determination of Leo, whose affections were not for persons but for posterity, and who was distinctly alarmed to see his line shrinking. The last legitimate male descendant was now Lorenzo, the son of Piero and of Alfonsina, and to this nephew he transferred all the ambitions which he had nursed for Giuliano. Lorenzo succeeded his late uncle as Capo di Stato in Florence and as Gonfalonier of the Church and led a victorious expedition into Urbino in 1517. The ducal title cost the Pope more than he could afford, but he created thirty Cardinals at one sitting and was satisfied. He prepared for the next step. For a next step there must be: Alfonsina had decided it. Lorenzo was Duke of Urbino; that was something, it consoled her for many mortifications in the past, but it was nothing unless it led further. Giuliano had married a distant connection of the French King; why should not her son do as well? She was determined, the Pope was willing, and François I was agreeable. The capture of Urbino had impressed him, officially at least, and the letters of congratulation which he addressed to Lorenzo were couched in a tone of flattering familiarity, without a trace of condescension. In private his tone was apt to be different. Discussing the exploit of Urbino, he observed that Lorenzo had indeed taken Urbino, but that it remained to be seen whether he could keep it. "For, remember," he said knowingly, "he is only a trader." He suggested as a suitable match for the young man an heiress of great wealth and a distant connection of his own, Madeleine de la Tour d'Auvergne.

Lorenzo journeyed to France, and in the spring of 1518 the marriage was celebrated at Amboise in the presence of the King. The bridegroom took part in a tourney and, in the words of a French sportsman, "did as well as he could" —an unfair judgment, for he was suffering from a wound in the head and not from his ancestry. The King, however, paid him the compliment of inviting him to sponsor the new-born Dauphin. The summer was spent in inspecting the estates of his wife and the autumn in bringing her home to Florence. There, complying with the customs of the Medici, she became very popular by adopting Florentine fashions, which she found extremely becoming.

Alfonsina was supremely happy, and so was the married couple. In the superfluity of their good fortune, they were in love with each other and played like children. The days slipped away. Lorenzo was frequently absent. His journey to France had brought him into contact with a society in which caste-feeling was far more pronounced than in Italy, and he returned with a desire to accumulate titles. He made a trip to Rome for the express purpose of requesting the Pope to sanction his assuming the style of Duke of Florence. But his uncle read him a lecture on the family traditions and sent him home with a recommendation to keep his head and, above all, to secure control of the municipal bank, for "that is the heart of the city." On his return, he neglected affairs, fell ill, and retired to the country. He sank rapidly. The doctors struggled with a complication of ailments—nervous irritation, pleurisy, syphilis. Consternation spread through the family. In the hey-day of triumph it was now on the verge of extinction. Their failing hopes fastened on the Duchess, who was pregnant. On April 13, 1519, she was delivered of a female infant. Two weeks later, the mother died of puerperal fever. Among the envoys who arrived in Florence to condole with the Duke was Ariosto. He arrived on the very day that Lorenzo himself died. At a loss what to do or to whom to express his sentiments, he addressed an ode to the frail little life, hovering between birth and death, which was the last tendril of the Medici. *Verdeggia un solo ramo. . . .*

> *A single branch buds, and lo,*
> *I am distraught with hope and fear,*
> *Whether winter will let it blow,*
> *Or blight it on the growing bier.*

- 5 -

It was indeed a growing bier that followed the birth of the orphan. Her grandmother was stricken and unable to care for her, and the Pope sent Cardinal Giulio from Rome to wrap the infant in his robes, to nurse it in the childless lap of a churchman, and to coax it into existence with the mighty name which was as yet its only identity: Caterina de' Medici. On Leo the blow had fallen with the weight of fatality. It was as if he laboured under some curse. He was not superstitious, but he became suddenly pious. "God has given, God has taken," he repeated in dazed decorum, bowing to the inevitable; and to his familiars he apologized for a life that had not been entirely blameless.

The death of Lorenzo left Leo with two alternatives: to pass on his inheritance to the younger, collateral, and commercial branch of the Medici, which he had always relegated to the background, and that solution he refused to consider; or to commit it to the illegitimate offshoots of his own family. Of these there were three: Cardinal Giulio, his factotum; Ippolito, the bastard of his late brother Giuliano; and Alessandro, a boy born to Lorenzo. These bastards were all more or less likely, but the solution was distasteful to a man in whom the dynastic sense was so strongly developed, though it was preferable to promoting his remote commercial cousins. But it required some gloss, at least, some graft of legitimacy. Then, at last, hope dawned on him. He saw some use for Catherine. She was a link: he would marry her to one of the bastards and legitimize him. His fertile brain began to teem, and he shifted matrimonial combinations as neatly as diapers. The choice was soon made. Giulio was too old, too cold, and a Cardinal: Alessandro was the infant's step-brother; the only possibility was Ippolito. Ippolito it was, Ippolito it should be; and in due time the Pope planned to confer on him the title of Duke of Florence for which Lorenzo had so pathetically pleaded. In due time even that might be possible.

But these plans were premature, and they were tempting Providence, for the little life upon which he speculated was feeble and had to be saved before it could be invested. For a time it seemed as if the curse which had carried off her parents were about to claim her as well. Born in April, in August she was dying. All the care, all the coaxing of Cardinal Giulio were wasted; all the potency of the name she bore, Caterina Maria Romola dei Medici, was lost; she failed to respond; and it was after all her grandmother, Alfonsina, who had to rise from her sick-bed and nurse the child back to life. In October, Alfonsina brought the result to Rome. The Pope inspected it gravely, studying it with his eye-glass and deciphering it like a codex; and the verdict was a triumph for her grandmother. The child was a credit to her care. "Fine and fat," he declared. Profoundly relieved, he felt that he could now afford to be sad. A lugubrious and elegant line occurred to him. "*Recens fert aerumnas Danaum,*" he said of his sister-in-law and her charge. "She comes bearing the woes of the Greeks." The appositeness of the text brought tears to his eyes.

The suggestion of classic fatality continued to hover over the infant. She continued to gain, but to gain, as it were, merely a little advance upon death: death dogged the growing life and hugged it with sullen persistence. Six months later, while the Pope was attending a comedy, Alfonsina died. She was buried, according to her own directions, quietly and inconspicuously: her ambition was dust. She left her estate to the Pope on condition that he refrain from celebrating her demise—a condition with which he readily complied, for he had never been fond of her. The child, being of an age that required the care of women, was entrusted alternately to her aunt Clarice Strozzi in Florence and to her great-aunt Lucrezia Salviati in Rome, and both women proved admirable substitutes for the mother and grandmother she had lost. Meanwhile, the influences which were to determine her destiny grew as she grew.

- 6 -

For she was the child of an age. No Medici could henceforth escape it. The future which they inherited was that movement which began when she came into being and matured as she developed, and which revolutionized the world into which she was born. The movement developed far more rapidly than the man who precipitated it. Luther himself was hurried on by forces which compelled him to advance, if he was not to be outstripped, and to outgrow himself, if he was not to be outgrown. It was only in 1519 that he reached the revolutionary stage of challenging the Papal authority.

[The next year,] Luther published his *Appeal to His Imperial Majesty and the Christian Nobility of Germany, concerning the Reformation of Germany.* With this pamphlet, of which 4000 copies were sold, Luther transformed himself into a movement and made his first political stride. Plunging into the ferment of national feeling and economic opportunity excited by the election, he rallied that immense motive power to his cause. The appeal was built on the economic argument and repeated the same goading complaint: Germany is priest-ridden, Germany is poor. In Rome the *Appeal* created yet more excitement than in Germany. Published on the eve of the imperial election, and addressed to an impoverished people, an impecunious nobility, and a debt-laden State, its import could not be mistaken. It was one more manifestation of that growing and schismatic spirit of economic nationalism against which the Church had to contend, and from which it was beginning to suffer in France. Luther, in fact, cited as a precedent the Concordat of 1515, by which François I had wrested from Rome the reservation of annates and the right of appointment to benefices in France. "If the kingdom of France has been able to defend itself, why should we be mocked and scorned?" Yesterday France; today Germany; tomorrow . . . ?

Even Leo realized that Luther could no longer be neglected. A bull of excommunication had been prepared, which, still averse to extremes, he revised, tempered, and laid away against further provocation. It came with the violent tract on *The Babylonish Captivity of the Church,* in which nothing, perhaps, was more effective than the recapitulation which Luther made of his progress: "Two years ago I attacked indulgences, but with such faltering indecision that now I am ashamed of it. No wonder, though, since I had to roll the rock away alone. Then I denied that the Papacy was from God but admitted that it stood by human right. Now, however, having read all the sophistries by which the pundits support their idol, I know that the Papacy is nothing but the reign of Babylon and the violence of the mighty hunter Nimrod. I beg all my friends and my booksellers to burn the books I have written on this subject before and to substitute for them this one proposition: The Papacy is a general chase, led by the Bishop of Rome, and having for its object the snaring of souls." Accordingly, the bull was launched; the students of Wittenberg burned it; Luther appealed to a General Council; the Legate Aleander appealed to the Emperor [Charles V] to arrest Luther; the Emperor referred him to the Imperial Diet; and the secular arm came into action.

It soon appeared that the secular arm was lame, unwilling, unwieldy. On his way to the Diet of Worms, in January 1521, Aleander found a new Germany, tense, sullen, hostile, wherever he passed. He found the Electors cold, and the Emperor evasive. The appearance of a condemned heretic before a lay court was itself an implicit recognition by the highest authority in the land; and, if conceded by Rome, it constituted a tacit admission of civil jurisdiction in an ecclesiastical cause. Luther, relying on the secular arm, insisted on appearing at Worms. All that followed was like the culmination of a national march: the crowds on the rooftops approving his boast, "Though there be as many devils in Worms as there are tiles on the roofs, I shall come"; the crowds in the streets seething at his heels; the crowds guarding him all night with mysterious expectation; the crowds waiting in the morning while he was smuggled by a back way into the palace; the boost of the old soldier who clapped him on the back—"Little monk, little monk, you are making a fight the like of which neither I nor many a man has made in the worst battles, but go on, in God's name, if you are sure of your cause, He will not forsake you"; the silence of the Diet as he entered; the overpowering hush of two hundred princes waiting for the word of a little man who, in his agony, began to sweat violently; the regulations to forestall his speech; his evasion of them; the speech, first in German, then in Latin; and the ringing conclusion, "Here stand I. God help me, I cannot do otherwise." The result was that he left Worms as freely as he left Augsburg three years before.

- 7 -

In 1522, Leo X was gathered to his forefathers. Though his death was unforeseen, it had been systematically prepared for, and it did not materially affect the fortunes of his family or of the little girl who, in three years of life, had lost her guardians in such rapid succession. There seemed to be a sinister system in the elusive regularity with which death played about her, but none of the Medici was superstitious, and she was in safe hands. System for system, that of the Medici was organized to protect her. She continued in the care of her aunt Clarice Strozzi and under the custody of that remote and left-handed relative who now became the head of the family —Cardinal Giulio. The change was imperceptible except to Clarice Strozzi, who disliked the Cardinal and considered his promotion a funereal one for the family. She would not allow that he was one of them, though he was obviously nothing else, for he was not a man but the Medici system incarnate. He was the familiar family slave. All his life had been spent in its service, all his waking hours he had drudged for Pope Leo, and the result was that, without will or initiative or a life of his own, he had become a consummate subordinate and a confirmed inferior. This was what she could not forgive him and what she regarded as so fatal for her family. High-spirited herself, despising his illegitimate birth and his nerveless nature, she was humiliated by the half-Medici. Like a lonely seer, she nursed her prejudice with tenacious superstition, for no one shared it. For nothing had changed. Cardinal Giulio followed Pope Leo in the administration of the family, of Florence, of the Church. With the same long gliding step with which he had trailed him in life— shadowy and discreet and deferential, like some eminent ecclesiastical flunkey—he glided after him toward the Pontifical Throne. His first attempt failed, but the second succeeded. In 1523 Giulio de' Medici became Pope Clement VII.

- 8 -

The constitutional inferiority of the new Pope, which Clarice Strozzi was so quick to detect, appeared in his conduct of public affairs only in times of stress. He conducted them skilfully, so long as they remained a normal routine, along the conventional lines laid down by Pope Leo. But his lack of initiative, amid the growing complexity and the increasing pressure of the problems confronting him, slowly laid bare the decaying enterprise of his race and exposed it, and the State, and the Church, to the mercy of events which the Medici had helped to produce, which they were incapable of controlling, and of which they could only suffer the consequences.

Assuming the inheritance of the Medici, Clement VII had but one aim, to preserve it as a faithful steward. Where Leo had squandered and enjoyed, he suffered and saved. It was the final phase of the family. What he contributed to it was conservatism. He was on the defensive. It was in this spirit that he approached all his problems. As a trustee, he made it his duty to maintain the *status quo*. In the field of international politics this was difficult. The rivalry of François I and Charles V, whetted by their competition for the imperial crown, continued in a military and diplomatic struggle for the partition and plunder of Italy. The vicissitudes of this struggle were a constant strain on the Pope, but in spite of increasing pressure, he followed the example of his predecessor and pursued a policy of isolation and neutrality, while this was possible, and when it was not, of vacillation and duplicity. But in the religious conflict it was impossible to stand still. The indecision of Leo had allowed the Lutheran schism to develop, to spread, to entrench itself. The indecision of Clement VII allowed the schism to mature, to multiply, to ramify, to make more and more radical progress. He appealed to the Emperor for assistance. He warned him that the social character of the movement made it as dangerous to the secular as to the ecclesiastical State. But no help came from the Emperor. It came instead, and inadvertently, from Luther himself.

- 9 -

When Luther disappeared after the Diet of Worms, he became a legend. He captured the imagination of the people —an enormous source of power. But a legend was the last thing which Luther desired to be. It was too remote from reality. During his retreat he saw the movement which he had launched in danger of disintegrating through the undirected zeal of his disciples, who, like all disciples, failed to distinguish between the trivial and the essential, broke into doctrinal disputes, beclouded the real issue, and endangered the remarkable cohesion which he had given to the movement by appealing to the economic complaints of the nation. It was to check this friction that he left his legendary retreat and returned to the battle. He brought with him his translation of the Bible, which, literally interpreted, he gave to the movement as its guide. "Luther," said the Emperor's confessor, "wants to argue from the Bible. The Bible is like wax, you may stretch and mould it to any shape you please. I myself would undertake to find authority in the Bible for doctrines far more extravagant than those of Luther." And, in fact, it precipitated the Peasants' War.

The risings of a pauperized peasantry were endemic in Germany; not a decade passed without them; but the outburst of 1525 was bolder than previous revolts because it derived, or believed that it derived, from Luther. The leaders invited his alliance and claimed his support. Was he not a peasant himself? Was he not known to the nation as *Der Mann—der deutscher Mann?* Was he not shaking the yoke of the priests? Why should he not shake the yoke of the landlords? These questions occurred to many who studied the Gospel according to Luther; for the good book, like all good books that are not written but rewritten, was rewritten by everyone who read it. Thomas Münzer, one of those disciples whom Luther found it necessary to discipline, professed to find authority in it for social justice; and though he could not locate the text, he did not need it, for he was a Bible reader only because he was a revolutionary. In April 1525, when he was dismissed by the Town Council of Mühlhausen, which refused to recognize his pastorate, he deposed it, organized his followers, and proclaimed a community of goods and an equality of conditions. The same ferment was at work elsewhere; Thuringia, Saxony, and Franconia were aflame; and the revolt spread from Swabia to the Rhine. Spontaneous, scattered, and unconcerted, it yet had a common inspiration: the Bible of Luther.

The rebellion of the *Bundschuhe* shook Germany with an upheaval which, though short-lived, was so startling that the nobles were at first paralysed and unable to rally. The peasants swept on unchecked, undisciplined, unorganized, unled, driven by rage, by despair, by confusion, in blind destruction. Münzer, failing to raise Mühlhausen, though he frightened the Town Council into feeding the poor, carried his promise of common property, compulsory labour for all, and the abolition of authority, into the country. At the head of eight thousand peasants, he terrorized Thuringia. After a month of brotherhood and butchery, the rebellion was crushed. The atrocities on both sides were ghastly, but it was those of the peasants which appalled Luther. Shocked by the choice they had made, he could find no words to express his horror of their conduct. They were mad dogs, they should be placed under the ban of the Empire. He fully approved their punishment. "The peasants," he said when they were massacred, "deserve no mercy, no toleration, but the indignation of God and man." But when the danger had passed, he apologized for the violence of his abuse. They were, after all, his own people, and they bled in him, and in himself he had to crush them again and again. How deeply he was shaken he admitted when he said: "I mourn over these calamities. Often I have asked myself whether I should not have done better to let the Papacy go its way unmolested rather than to see such commotions."

Germany was asking the same question. Though the rebellion of the *Bundschuhe* accomplished nothing else, it shook Luther's position. Despite his repudiation of the peasants, the nobles held him responsible for the rising, and the upper classes began to cool toward him. The masses also had learned their lesson. Disillusioned, they understood that Luther had nothing to offer them. To the Church of Rome the rebellion of the *Bundschuhe* was a godsend: it provided the most telling illustration of the orthodox axiom that a division in religion invariably breeds a division in the State.

- 10 -

The desperation which drove the peasants to revolt was an excess of, and a relief from, their normal condition. In the repression that followed, thousands were put out of their misery; thousands more returned to it satisfied; while for those who still found it unbearable, there was always the army. The mercenary armies of the German princes, their primary source of revenue and the principal export of the country, provided a regular outlet for these conditions, absorbing and draining off the restless, needy, and shiftless outcasts who could not earn a livelihood in any other way. The social security provided by this institution was its most valuable feature; but it was not the only one. It happened, not infrequently, that for long periods the armies remained without pay; then, the old hereditary spirit reviving, the mercenaries mutinied with a violence which no authority, no discipline, could control but which an able commander could sometimes turn to account. These accidents, if they caused many calamities, were responsible for some of the most memorable battles and brilliant victories of the day. A striking instance was the Battle of Pavia. In February 1525, while the Peasants' War was culminating, a combined Spanish and German imperial army lay before Pavia, besieging and besieged by the French, besieging that glittering host which François I had assembled, and besieged by their own desperation and poverty. They were already deserting when their commander induced them to gamble, against overwhelming odds, on the plunder of the French camp; they charged; and they won that victory which decimated the flower of France and sent François I a prisoner to Madrid.

Two years later, a yet more memorable accident occurred. Charles V was in arrears to the Fugger, [those Medici of South Germany,] who, though they had obtained the silver mines of Guadalcanal, the quicksilver mines of Almadén, and a lease on the revenues of the Orders of Sant' Iago, Calatrava, and Alcántara, had to contend with the antipathy and the tariffs of a people who, despising and neglecting industry themselves, resented that of the aliens who exploited their rare natural resources. Harassed by the Fugger, harassed by the chrysotic fallacy of Spain, harassed by the economic antagonisms and internal disorders of his vast and heterodox empire, it was not surprising that Charles should fall in arrears in his payments to the armies in Italy. In the winter of 1527 there were two of them: one in the Milanese which it had cropped to the ground, under the command of a French deserter, the Constable de Bourbon; the other fresh from Germany, filled with the dregs of the Peasants' War and the overflow of the Lutheran movement, led by the soldier who had sped Luther on his way at Worms, Georg von Frundsperg. The latter, debouching from the Alps, found hospitality for a time in the State of Ferrara, but this was only temporary relief. The peninsula was feebly defended. The Pope approached the Duke of Ferrara with a proposal of alliance, political and matrimonial, renewing a suggestion which he had already made that his little ward, Catherine, might be a suitable prospect for the heir of the House of Este. The proposal had lapsed, partly because of the parsimony of the Pope, who haggled over the dower, and partly because of his incurable obsequiousness. He understood, he said, that "the House of Medici was not to be compared to that of His Excellency, although, considering that the child was nobly born and in legitimate wedlock, and a Papal niece, and with the capital which she possesses, the match did not seem too much to expect." He waived his objections to the dower; but too late. With the coming of spring, the Germans mutinied, captured their commander, and with the imperial cry of plunder or pay pressed him forward. At the same time the Spanish army in the Milanese rose, besieged the Constable de Bourbon in his tent, beat him out of it, and advanced. The two armies merged and rushed on in that torrential progress which, swerving at first toward Florence, veered and plunged on unerringly until it broke into the headlong cataract that ended in the Sack of Rome. The apocalyptic cataclysm that overwhelmed the Eternal City, as it settled and foundered in its ruins, submerged and ravaged by hordes of invaders exploring and violating the venerable sanctuaries that contained the accumulated wealth of the centuries, draining the marrow of empire and rattling the bones of dead Popes in the streets, in an orgy of sacrilege and extortion, carnage and vandalism, with horses stabled in the Vatican, with the Pope a prisoner in Sant' Angelo, with priests paraded in lock-step, with Lutherans mocking Anti-Christ, lasted for nine months, amazing and appalling the world, and wringing from Luther himself an expression of sympathy for the Pope.

One calamity begetting another, the sack of Rome precipitated the revolt of Florence. Cardinal Passerini, who administered the city, fled with his charges, Ippolito and Alessandro de' Medici. In the family council which preceded their departure, Clarice Strozzi rose to denounce it with that scathing tongue which the revolution in Florence set free. Flight!—what else could be expected of the education of two bastards by another? She railed at the pusillanimity of the Pope, of the two lads, of their tutor; she contrasted the character of her ancestors, who were true Medici, with those of their degenerate offspring; she blamed Clement for all the misfortunes of the family; and she dismissed the fugitives with the parting sneer that the Medici Palace was not a stable for mules. They might abscond with the family name; she would remain to preserve the family honour, for in the hour of misfortune it depended upon her to defend it. She was still scolding, still fuming, when the mob invaded the Medici Palace, grown too large now for so shrunken a race, and hustled her out of the rooms which were henceforth public property—the rooms where she had spent her youth. They did her no further harm. It was enough for a woman who lived on her memories. The years of the locust had come, and her only satisfaction was that she had foreseen them.

She retired to the Medici villa at Poggio at Cajano, and she carried Catherine with her. But the republican government claimed the child as a hostage, and Catherine, accordingly, was placed in the Dominican Convent of Santa Lucia, where it was felt that she would be surrounded by salutary influences, as it was the sister house to San Marco and equally sacred to the memory of Savonarola, the apostle of Florentine liberty. In consequence of an epidemic of plague, however, she was subsequently transferred, at the request of the French ambassador, to a less salutary but more salubrious house, the aristocratic convent of the Murate. The politics of these nuns were suspect. Here she remained for a year. The movements of the little girl, as she was shifted from convent to convent and from party to party, focused an unhealthy attention upon her. When her aunt Clarice Strozzi died, in May 1528, she remained completely alone, and her isolation and helplessness were feeble guarantees of safety in the faction-ridden city. She was a public charge—a responsi-

bility and a danger—and the authorities treated her with
the consideration due to gunpowder. They secluded, ignored, and never lost sight of her. But she was not without powerful protection. The French ambassador applied
to the government, in behalf of her mother's family, to
send her to France and marry her there. He took the opportunity to visit her and to report to her maternal uncle,
the Duke of Albany, on the rudiments of her nature, for
she was now nine years old and a person. "Madame your
niece is still in a convent, leading a good life, but rarely
visited and little regarded by these Florentine *signori*, who
would gladly see her in Kingdom Come. She expects you
to send her some presents from France for the Seigneur de
Ferraris. I can assure you that I have never seen anyone
of her age so quick to feel the good and the ill that are
done her."

The government, despite its eagerness to be rid of her,
declined to surrender its hostage, and changing conditions
lent her an increasing political value. The Pope survived
the sack of Rome and rose from it with wraithlike tenacity.
Unable to live, unable to die, he revealed an impersonal
vitality which was that of his race, for it was not his own,
and he was galvanized by it. He had been sacked, but he
was still a trustee, and with remarkable enterprise he set
about to recover what had been lost. He recovered the
ruins of Rome, and by the grant of a *cruzada* or concession
to sell indulgences in Spain, he obtained the support of
Charles V and the services of the army which had sacked
Rome to besiege Florence. In October 1529, the visitation
appeared in the valley of the Arno. The siege became, on
both sides, an obsession; and obsessions moved, as conditions became more desperate, about the inmate of the
Murate. The little life which had begun so frailly was hard
pressed to prove itself imperishable, although the good
nuns, who fondled her, fed her religiously on the faith
that she was a true Medici and would survive. But even
with her little store of knowledge she was not one of those
half-educated minds that swallow everything whole, and
she was nervous. She knew that she was an object of controversy, of passion, of partisanship. Proposals had been
made in the Town Council to expose her on the city walls
or, better yet, in a brothel. The protection of the nuns was

a prejudice the more, for they were divided into factions; and when her friends were so indiscreet as to send gifts to political prisoners worked with what appeared to be the Medici emblem, a public scandal ensued, an investigation was made, and her removal was demanded. An official arrived to return her to Santa Lucia. He found her hugging the knees of her beloved nuns in stubborn terror. No coaxing could move her, no patience pry her little hands loose. They were pretty hands, and he admired them, but in vain. When he insisted, she met him with a dodge which he found it difficult to credit to her unaided intelligence. She showed him her cropped hair and announced her engagement to Christ. He smiled, an intolerable adult smile, of which she felt, however, the comfort as well as the insult, and she still refused to stir. Before such a battery of obstinacy, wiles, and fear, he desisted. On the next day, however, he returned with strict instructions to remove her. She was ready for him; she waited for the smile; then, giving him her hand, she followed him with imperturbable childish dignity to Santa Lucia.

The quick susceptibility to sympathy of the impressionable little girl served the official in good stead after the fall of Florence. She interceded for his life when the Pope, in retaliation for a siege which lasted nine months and cost the lives of twenty thousand men, punished his opponents by wholesale reprisals. And she interceded successfully, for the Pope could refuse her nothing, not even the permission to return to the Murate before he called her to Rome. She flew to the sisters, who received her with transports of joy, and together they lived over and laughed over the past and all its foolish fears—the folly of her fear when the official came to fetch her; the folly of thinking that she would ever be a nun; the folly of taking anything to heart when everything always turned out well for the Medici. For the nuns of the Murate she always entertained a fond memory: they were identified in her mind with the days when she could still believe that life was a fable with a happy ending.

- 11 -

For the ending was fabulously happy. In the summer of 1530, when Catherine arrived in Rome, she was an interesting figure, the survivor of a long and trying experience. The Pope received her with a display of feeling which convinced everyone that "she is what he loves best in the world," and of which few thought him capable, for he was considered cold. He embraced her with tears in his eyes, and listened to what she had to say with manifest pleasure and pride in the propriety with which she expressed herself. He behaved himself like a nun. Naturally, it was of her experience that he encouraged her to speak, and she needed no urging. "She cannot forget," someone noticed, "the maltreatment she suffered, and is only too willing to speak of it."

Gradually, however, the painful memories faded. She was only eleven, and everything was done to efface them. She lived in the Palazzo Madama, under the care of her great-aunt Lucrezia Salviati, and in the company of Ippolito and Alessandro. She was allowed to ride out with them, on a large horse, with a bishop and a large escort. Alessandro she disliked, but she was soon relieved of his presence, as he left for Florence, the Pope having decided to groom him for government. Then not a cloud remained. Ippolito had her heart. A handsome, hot-headed, spectacular young man, with a fancy for exotic clothes—Hungarian toques and aigrettes, Turkish scimitars and swaggers—he was generally regarded as rattle-brained and unbearable, but not by her. She saw no fault in him. He never treated her as a child; stooping gently, he listened patiently to all her confidences. There was a sympathy between them, and a secret, which the world soon suspected. "People are whispering," a diplomat noted, "that the Cardinal intends to lay aside his Hat, and marry Catherine, for whom he has the liveliest fancy and by whom he is tenderly loved. She trusts no one but him and addresses herself to him alone for whatever she desires, and in all her personal affairs."

The Pope had other views. He sent Ippolito as his Legate to Hungary, and as the marriage of Catherine was too persistent and premature a topic of speculation in Rome and created an unwholesome curiosity about her, he sent her to Florence. She was still very frail and could not be mated for another two years.

The Pope had other views. The match which Leo had

settled no longer satisfied him. After following his predecessor so long and so faithfully, he surpassed him. The
sack of Rome had emancipated him from the past. He
had suffered the utmost calamity, and survived it, and
being now a man of the most accomplished misfortune,
he gained confidence in himself. The match at which he
aimed was more ambitious than Leo himself could have
dreamed, a match which, if he brought it about, would
absolve all his failures, heal all his humiliations, and efface
in the innermost recesses of his being his congenital sense
of inferiority. The last act of his stewardship would be a
personal triumph, if he, the underling, the illegitimate
Medici, proved to be the one to redeem his race from
that insecurity which was its nemesis and which made its
progress more precarious, the higher it climbed. Before he
passed on, he was determined to attempt the unattainable,
to scale the last inaccessible summit, to twine the frail
little tendril of his family on a perch far beyond the
reach of chance or change, and to bequeath to Catherine
and her posterity the one blessing which the Medici had
never known—the assurance of permanence and security.

How high he reached the Pope revealed by the ease
with which he discarded what he would have formerly
considered very promising proposals. A match with the
della Rovere would have settled the question of Urbino,
of which Catherine bore the title, though the State had
been recovered by its original owners. A match with the
Gonzaga of Mantua would have been as flattering as one
with the Este. But he eliminated all Italians, and he picked
his foreigners. He would have nothing to say to the Duke
of Richmond, who was a son of Henry VIII, but illegitimate. He considered, but only to discard, the King of
Scotland, with whom the expense of a regular correspondence by courier would be ruinous. Minor or morganatic
royalty was not enough; he would be satisfied with nothing less than an alliance with one or other of the two major
powers in Europe.

A confidential proposal was made to him on behalf of
François I in favour of his second son, the Duke of
Orléans. Then what had been a vision that sustained became a reality that tormented him. He was consumed with
anxiety lest it elude him. When he consulted the oldest

living members of the family, Lucrezia Salviati and her husband, he was discouraged by an argument which he had not completely outgrown. They opposed the proposal, insisting that the Medici had never prospered when they aspired above their station. The old sensible superstition stirred in him, stopping progress. It appeared to be tempting Providence, he suspected himself of presumption, he could not believe his incredible good fortune, and in discussing the proposal with the French ambassador he assumed an attitude of false humility which amused that diplomat, who described the Pope, in his report, as "repeating over and over that his niece was not worthy of so lofty an alliance but ready, nevertheless, for every sacrifice and any concession to secure it." A delusion it was not: the Duke of Albany arrived in Rome with an official offer. The Pope was still diffident, though on different grounds. He told the Duke candidly that "he wished his niece to make the greatest match in the world but that, neither for that nor for any other reason, would he ever consent to anything contrary to the welfare of Christendom." He dreaded the political complications which his temerity might produce and was unwilling to antagonize the Emperor. His feelings by now had reached such a pitch that the Duke thought it necessary to send a word of caution to François I. "His Holiness marvellously desired this marriage; if we raise his hopes as we have done, and if by chance we should not keep our promise, I doubt whether we could ever win him back again." It was time to call a halt. The French proposal was, in fact, a diplomatic feint made by François I to oblige Henry VIII, who wished to block the prospects of the King of Scotland. It had never been meant seriously. The Pope suspected as much when he learned that the Duke of Albany was about to be recalled and replaced by another negotiator, and he became highly indignant. He had only one word to describe such conduct. It was Venetian—the technical term for the diplomatic device which consists in shifting agents in order to reopen a negotiation on the point of conclusion.

Tantalized, suspicious, unsure, he continued the negotiations without confidence, for the purpose of impressing the Emperor, from whom he hoped to provoke a counter-proposal. When it came, it was mortifying. The Emperor put forward, not a member of his family, but one of his political puppets, the Duke of Milan. He attached less importance to the French marriage than the Pope had expected. His attitude was so tolerant as to be indifferent, and so indifferent as to be insulting; and the slight rankled in the spirit of Clement VII more deeply than anything since the sack of Rome. Nevertheless, the offer of Charles V had a decisive effect. François I, haunted by the vision of Italy, the memory of Pavia, the captivity of Madrid, and the daydreams of the defeated, dreamed of returning to the peninsula and recovering Milan; and to prevent an alliance between the Pope and the Emperor he was prepared to go to great lengths. The offer which he first made as a feint he now renewed seriously. A secret contract was signed at Rome, in the summer of 1531.

The marriage was settled. The contract was signed. But what was a contract? What were the promises of princes? It was two years before the union could be consummated, and for two years Clement lived in suspense and uneasiness, in a twilight zone between illusion and reality. When the existence of the secret contract became known, the Emperor pressed the suit of the Duke of Milan. His ambassador attempted to destroy the confidence of His Holiness in the sincerity of the French, assuring him that "they are not seriously considering this alliance, they are thinking only of troubling the peace of Italy." The Pope professed to agree and evaded the question. There was a time, indeed, when the question was almost reopened. François I attempted to revise the contract and to make it contingent upon the consent of the Pope to the divorce of Henry VIII. For two years the diplomacy of Clement VII was severely taxed to preserve that marriage which represented the culmination of Medici ambition, and which was constantly in danger of being involved in the most treacherous international questions of the day: the English divorce, the Lutheran schism, the balance of power.

At the end of two years Catherine had reached nubile age. As she developed, and her features became more pronounced, the generic charm of childhood disappeared and her heritage emerged. "She is small and thin; her features are not delicate, and she has bulging eyes, like most of the Medici." What she lacked in physical charm she made up in mental endowment. She was ready for marriage: she had reached the age of discretion. Discretion, indeed, was her most pronounced trait. The orphan, who had passed through the hands of so many foster-parents and in her most impressionable years had formed so many fleeting attachments, had acquired a precocious prudence and reserve. She had learned the difference between fable and fact, and the French marriage indeed was more dazzling, more fabulous, than any future she had dreamed with Ippolito. She prepared for it breathlessly. She learned French, hastily and imperfectly, without grammar or spelling, picking up a language as she picked up life, by ear, like all the Medici, who always improvised and never grasped the rules.

The last commission which Vasari executed for her marriage was an imaginary picture of the celebration itself, conceived as a political allegory: an enormous canvas, crowded with famous figures, focused by the bridal couple joining hands under a rainbow, and illustrating the device she had chosen for herself: *J'apporte la lumière et la sérénité*. It was completed after the event. On September 1, 1533, she left Florence, followed a few weeks later by the Pope. On October 12 the look-outs at Marseilles sighted, and the guns saluted, the Papal flotilla sweeping the sea like the gulls in long patient flight. He landed amid a jubilation which he shared. His lifework was over, he had brought his trust safely to port. The marriage was celebrated on October 26. As he blessed the nuptial rings, the Pope could not conceal his elation: he beamed like a Holy Ghost. Yet, even in the unimaginable triumph of that hour, he could not be sure that it was not all a delusion. Late that night, and early the next morning, he entered the bridal chamber, trembling with secular anxiety, to see with his own eyes the daughter of the Medici covered by the son of the Valois.

CHAPTER II

The Reign of

FRANÇOIS I

- 1 -

The bridegroom was a robust, taciturn, and morose lad of fourteen. The years of captivity which he had spent in Spain, with the Dauphin, as a hostage for François I, had marked him for life. Both boys resented them bitterly. When they were released, and the Constable of Castille asked them to forgive their maltreatment, the Dauphin had the grace to accept the apology, but Henri was too deeply hurt. He broke wind. He had no command of speech. Stubborn, vindictive, he nursed an undying hatred of Spain and a deep-seated grudge against his father. While the Dauphin showed some inclination for study, his brother had no aptitude for anything but violent exercise, and remained mentally backward.

In the days preceding the ceremony, he treated Catherine with courtesy and consideration, but with complete indifference. They met, exchanged a few words, and inspected each other gravely. The curious eyes of the young

girl met the bruised eyes of the young man, and that was
all. Their acquaintance was no further advanced when, at
the marriage supper, she sat between him and the Dauphin at the head of a long table lined by Cardinals, while
the King and the Pope presided over another, and a third
was occupied by a galaxy of ladies chaperoned by the
Grande Seneschale de Normandie, Diane de Poitiers. The
laughter and the talk flowed about them, but he hardly
uttered a word and, her natural liveliness subdued by
decorum, she was too discreet to take the lead. She was
no longer a person, but a personage. Nor did the marriage night turn their acquaintance into intimacy.

Morning came, and with it the long wizened face of
the Pope peering through the bed-curtains, and the long
satyric face of François I behind him. Then came the
lever, and the routine of her new life began. She had prepared for it, and the transition from one world to another
was easy. There was no abrupt change. Italian culture,
Italian art, Italian styles, had been assimilated by this
French civilization, which, however foreign, was not unfamiliar to her. The ceremonial and splendour of the Papal
Court had prepared her for the etiquette and magnificence
of royal life, and she adapted herself to it without difficulty. Her distinguished manners, her innate dignity, her
schooled self-possession, allowed her to assume her exalted
station without criticism. But she was not fully prepared
for the worldliness of the French Court. She met it, however, with the knowing smile of a young person who
knows enough to learn more, slyly observing the impression she made. Above all, she studied her husband. She
soon understood that, in spite of his obstinate reserve, he
responded to influence, that he guarded himself against it
but was completely swayed by it once he was won. He
was blindly devoted to and ruled by his friends. They
were men friends—the Grand Master Montmorency, the
young Saint-André, and five or six others. There were no
women except the Grande Seneschale de Normandie, who
was twice her age, and to whom he was attached because
she had mothered him when he returned from Spain. Discreetly, Catherine cultivated them all.

The Pope lingered for two weeks after the marriage,
longing for the first signs of conception but unable to wait

for them. After his departure for Rome, the Court left Marseilles on that routine peregrination from château to château, never settling long, always on its way to the next, which was also one of the foreign but not unfamiliar features of her new life.

The marriage contract contained, in compensation for the generosity with which François I subsidized his daughter-in-law and consented to her renunciation of her rights in the Medici inheritance, a set of secret clauses in which the Pope pledged his assistance and the surrender of certain Italian towns in the event of a campaign against Milan by the French. Her personal dowry had been left to the discretion of Clement VII. The French ministers found it shockingly inadequate when his provisions were examined just before the wedding, and there were some sharp discussions with Filippo Strozzi, the broker who had advanced the Pope the bulk of her *dot*. Strozzi referred them, with expressions of surprise at their ignorance, to the secret articles. The great expectations which they contained were hypothetical, however, and the Pope, upon returning to Rome, denied their existence to the ambassador of Charles V and assured him that he would never make the marriage of his ward the occasion for ruining Italy and embroiling the world anew. It was a family match, nothing more. These declarations obtained credit and created a scandal at the French Court, and a cloud of unpopularity gathered about Catherine. She weathered the storm, however, by sedulously effacing herself and courting her father-in-law, who protected her, partly from pity, partly to pique his son, whose antipathy he had come in time to reciprocate. But a year later, a far more serious situation developed. In 1534 Clement VII died. All the projects based on his signature and longevity vanished. He died, as Madame d'Etampes said, thirty years too soon; it was the culmination of a life of ill-faith. The Medici marriage was a swindle, a misalliance of which the French Crown had borne the whole cost and which had proved a mockery and a delusion. *"J'ai reçu la fille toute nue,"* the King remarked wryly. Nor was this all. Papal sharp practice had done its worst; it remained for Divine Providence to complete the terrible trick. A suspicion had been growing, which was now a certitude. The bride who had been bought with such barren gold was inwardly warped and through some radical organic disorder could not even conceive.

- 2 -

The grim fact had to be faced. The Italian woman, who had only her sex to recommend her, was sealed in the source of life. To all the disabilities under which she laboured—plain, unpopular, parvenue, a foreigner, a marital foundling, and a fraud—was added the final one: she was a woman disqualified. Such an accumulation of mishaps might well have crushed anyone but a Medici, but she showed her breed and her youth by meeting final defeat as if it were merely a passing impediment. She consulted her father-in-law, who, himself a veteran of many reverses from which he had not recovered, was willing to encourage her illusions, to advise her to take medical treatment, to extend credit to her constitution, and time to her lively temperament. The doctors disagreed. Their probings ended in hypotheses and their diagnoses in conjecture, and where their science faltered, gossip positively traced her condition to the syphilitic infection of which her parents had died. Without waiting for analysis to determine the cure, she accepted indiscriminate prescriptions and submitted to every experiment, but with negative results. The impediment was unyielding. She tried prayer, but she tired of it, perceiving clearly that a Diety who could afflict her, through no fault of her own, was indifferent to her welfare. Without faith in the doctors, without confidence in divinity, she veered from one to the other and finally sought relief in those psychic realms where the material becomes spiritual and the spiritual material. The first of her race to be frankly superstitious, she consulted seers, astrologers, and necromancers, and delved for those dark powers whose commerce, discountenanced but tolerated by the Church, was of a nature she could grasp, supernatural but accessible, and whose faculty it was to conspire with man to circumvent the eternal decrees of God. Eternal? What was eternal? More than to all these remedies, she trusted to time, which comprised them all.

Although, by common consent, her disability was ignored, it was always in mind, and it needed only an untoward incident to recall the liability which the Crown had
contracted with her marriage. Her Italian dowry was still
in arrears when Pope Clement died, and his successor
annulled the grants of Papal property which Clement had
alienated. Filippo Strozzi, however, averted a fresh scandal
by a financial sacrifice, which spared her another mortification and for which she was grateful. It was a pious contribution to the good memory of the Medici, which served,
among other things, to silence the suggestion that in her
persistent sterility she was paying for the canonical sin of
her ancestors. Their usury had never been recalled while
there were any profits to be drawn from it; it was only
now that their fortunes were fading that the old superstition revived. Her superstition did not go so far, although
she continued to feel within her the flat unyielding fiat
of Nature forbidding her womb to increase.

- 3 -

But it was not only her own future that was affected; it
was that of the Valois. In 1536 the Dauphin died of
pleurisy. Hints of foul play began to circulate. A rumour
was put about that the criminals were Catherine and her
husband, but it gained no headway except among those
who were determined at all costs to discredit the Italian
woman.

For so she had come to be called—the Italian woman
—having no other ties, the isolated symbol of a land
whose connection had always allured and always deluded
the French. What was stigmatized in her was that *folie
des grandeurs* which seemed a folly because it had failed,
that misleading ultramontane dream of which she was a
present reminder, recalling the past and compromising
the future. Henri was now the Dauphin; the childlessness
of his wife became a matter of public concern, from which
it was impossible to avert attention and prejudice; and
the first murmurs of a proposal to repudiate her made
themselves heard. The mere suggestion goaded her, and
she defended herself with the genius of fear. She courted
the King and clung to him, but with a touch that never

wearied or worried or weighed. She avoided pathos; she
was all vivacity, confidence, and cajolery. She studied his
moods, she catered to his tastes, she ingratiated herself
with his friends, she won over his women. She earned her
place in the Petite Bande, the charmed circle of all the
chosen rivals for his favour, which existed only to save the
old satyr from boredom, and in which beauty, brains, and
buoyancy were indispensable gifts. Beauties she had—her
hands, her figure, her leg. She hunted, she danced. She
rode recklessly, in a side-saddle which she invented, displaying the leg; took her falls like an expert, always game.
So much spirit, such a leg, such good breeding, satisfied
her father-in-law. The murmurs were smothered.

It was two years before they were heard again. In 1538
a girl was born to Henri, by a Piedmontese peasant,
Filippa Ducci, thus disposing of the doubt raised by some
physicians whether he was not himself responsible for his
childlessness. One question was settled, but it raised the
other, and the talk of repudiation rose anew. But it made
no headway. That she preserved her position and lost no
ground was in itself progress; for her progress, like that
of a swimmer against the current, could be measured only
by her ability to remain afloat and avoid being swept
away. She could hope for no more than an indefinite
reprieve, a prolonged standstill. But is there any such
thing in nature as a standstill?

- 4 -

The child of Filippa Ducci was brought up by Diane de
Poitiers. As the putative mother was never seen, she became a myth, and her infant, who was recognized by the
father and received the name of Diane de France, passed
for the daughter of the Grande Seneschale.

Certainly the ambiguous relation between the Grande
Seneschale and the Dauphin could not remain stationary.
It began to develop when Henri became Dauphin, formed
his own set, and made of his old friends an embryonic
political party—from the day, in short, when he had a
future. His future now became a matter of serious concern.
Still puerile, shy, and mentally inert, he was a problem
upon whose development the future prospects of France

depended. The latent capacities of the man, locked in obstinate immaturity, could only be assumed. The powerful build, the physical confidence, the unsmiling manner and guarded reserve of the stripling were but the hard opaque husk of a nature green and timid that was still malleable and could be moulded by any influence that won his confidence. Who would assume that responsibility? His father could not; he was too impatient, too frivolous, too carnal, and the antagonism between them was too deep. His wife could not, for years of marriage had confirmed his indifference to her. Yet it was clearly a task for a woman. It was the Grande Seneschale who, at the suggestion of François I, undertook the task of educating the Dauphin. She succeeded easily where others had failed. Very soon the gratifying effects of her influence appeared. He unbent; if he was still grave, he was no longer melancholy. She coaxed him out of the wilderness of his inner world, and he ceased to be *sauvage* and became merely dull. She civilized him.

Their relation remained ambiguous. It began by the maternal sympathy which she showed him, as a boy, on his return from Spain, and which he repaid by an affectionate gratitude that did not fade as he grew up. He was loyal. Sentiment preceded sensuality. When he was an adolescent, she was a woman still in her prime and she was considered a beauty. The woman of forty encouraged the admiration of the adolescent but she kept it within conventional limits. When these no longer satisfied him, she allowed him some familiarities, and their relation became equivocal. Passionless she was not, but in missing the generous appetites she had acquired meaner ones, a passion for respectability and a passion for possessions. She acquired the Dauphin without compromising herself. For some time this fictitious intimacy continued. What she had once acquired she could never relinquish, however, and the day came when she risked losing him to unworthy women. Reluctantly, she made a twilight concession to her robust pupil.

By 1538 the liaison was established, and the child of Filippa Ducci was born. So consummately did Diane still preserve appearances that many still believed it the conventional relation it purported to be, and those who doubted were obliged to admit that "nothing indecent has ever been seen." Catherine had no doubts; her jealousy needed no proofs and asked no questions. She accepted the situation, she cultivated Diane, she became in the eyes of the knowing the complaisant accomplice of her rival and vied with her in preserving appearances. The advent of an accomplished and tenacious woman increased the hazards of her position; and with haunted tameness she went about her accustomed business of existing on sufferance. What she could not arrest, she could at least stabilize; and she succeeded.

The standstill was apparently achieved. It was four years before the suggestion of repudiation was raised again. It was sponsored not by Diane, who had every reason to congratulate herself on the complaisance of the Dauphine and to dread a less obliging successor, but by one of Diane's protégés, the Archbishop of Reims, Charles de Guise. This young prelate and his brother François de Guise, the Comte d'Aumale, were leaders of the Dauphin's party. They were members of that prolific and princely family of Lorraine whose junior members were accustomed to seek their fortunes at the French Court. Coming men, they naturally sought advancement in the party of the future. François, the soldier, became the Dauphin's friend. Charles became his preceptor. He was a young ecclesiastic of restless and versatile intelligence, "capable of every science, quick, keen, subtle, ready for anything, eager to see and to hear, and to know everything and everyone, always meditating something in himself, never idle." These gifts, which he failed to impart to his pupil, he applied to nursing the prospects of his family and to courting the Grande Seneschale. When he revived the suggestion to repudiate the Dauphine, it was not in the interests of Diane. He had a sister, Marie de Guise, who was of marriageable age. This time the suggestion prospered. The King listened; the Dauphin listened. They had waited eight years for an heir.

As it proved, this attack turned to the advantage of Catherine. She met it with disarming submission, hastening to the King, accepting his decision, and resigning herself to a divorce. She wept, and he melted. The crisis, on the point of materializing, subsided. It was followed by a general reaction of sympathy, a movement of apology toward the Dauphine, who was recognized finally as something more than a Medici or an Italian, as a woman in her own right. Catherine was not deceived by a passing movement of sympathy. She suspected the affection of her husband, who did nothing without the advice of Diane. She had never suspected that of her father-in-law before, but his parting words to her—"*Ma fille,* it is God's will that you should be my daughter and the wife of the Dauphin, so be it"—conveyed so much disappointment in their resignation, and such boredom with the bitter dilemma, and irritation with his own chivalry, that she understood that she could not continue to presume on his sympathy. It was not a personal but a public question.

The danger, which had lain dormant so long that it had been almost forgotten, grazed her so closely that it startled her into redoubled activity to avert its recurrence. She resorted to all the old remedies—charms, amulets, prayers, drugs—and experimented with new ones. She multiplied intercessions, she employed all her relations, she wrote to the nuns of the Murate to remember her in their prayers to a God Whom, wrapped in the inexorable jealousy which is His first attribute, she felt but could not fathom. She sought enlightenment in the Bible. It had been recommended to her by her friend, Marguerite of Navarre, sister of François I, who was overjoyed by Catherine's religious devotion and wrote to promise her that "not a year would pass before God would grant her a son." The words of the Psalms were incessantly on her lips:

> *Vers l'Eternel des oppressez le Père*
> *Je m'en yrai. . . .*

The rhythm comforted her. She took drugs so assiduously that her friends became alarmed; she ransacked the pharmacopœia at the risk of her health. The physicians teased and worried her barrenness with dogged ignorance, unwilling to admit their defeat. Nor would she. She was indomitable. If character could have overcome her constitution, she would have needed no further aid. And character was required to adopt the desperate remedy suggested by a physician otherwise so reputable as Fernel. She shrank from nothing; she was ready to go to any lengths. If strangers were willing to give of their blood, how could she hesitate, even at the risk of alienating her husband for ever? To violate her last mystery, to make him a partner in the organic mystery that makes woman, for a season, only a sick and sickening animal, was an ordeal. But it was a conspiracy to smuggle and there were no rules except to cheat the laws and cross the frontiers of nature, if necessary, in order to snatch life from a convulsion of slime. On January 19, 1544, a son was born to Catherine de' Medici.

- 5 -

Among all the congratulations which celebrated the event none was more rapturous, more lyrical, than the effusion of Marguerite of Navarre:

> *Un fils! un fils! . . . ô nom dont sur tous noms*
> *Très obligés à Dieu nous nous tenons!*
>
> *O fils heureux! joye du jeune père!*
> *Souverain bien de la contente mère!*
> *Heureuse foy qui, après longue attente,*
> *Leur a donné le fruit de leur prétente!* [1]

The happy faith to which she attributed the issue was her own. The sister of François I, whose Lutheran leanings were no secret, had long hoped that the Dauphine might also see the light. Her expectations rose when she learned that Catherine had begun to read the Bible and to sing the Psalms. These were the glimmers that foretold the dawn.

The hope to which Marguerite alluded in the hinted hosanna of her song of thanksgiving was shared by the Reformers, who speculated, then and later, on the sympathy of the Dauphine. Some colour was lent to this supposition by the religious phase through which she passed in the period preceding the birth of her son. But it was

---

[1] *A son! a son! . . . O name that of all names*
Makes us beholden to God and His claims!

O happy son! joy of the young sire!
Supreme blessing of his mother's desire!
O happy faith, after so long delay,
That vouchsafes them the fruit for which they pray!

based on nothing more substantial than her acquaintance with the Bible and her singing of the Psalms. The Psalms, translated by the Protestant poet Marot and set to music by the Protestant composer Goudimel, were then enjoying a vogue at Court, where everyone hummed them; Catherine was merely following a fashion which implied no religious bias. The Bible was a more serious matter. The Bible was a forbidden book, though the Church had not yet placed it on the Index, and this book lay on the Dauphine's table, where any chance visitor was free to open and flutter its pages. The Grande Seneschale investigated it one day and a copy appeared on her own table. The Bible was at large. It is impossible to say how far this might have gone had not the Archbishop of Reims intervened. His restless curiosity carried him frequently to the bedside of the Grande Seneschale. And when he discovered the Bible, and learned there how she had been tempted to taste of the Tree of Knowledge, he reminded her of the fault by which the human race fell. The Bible was no fit reading for women; he advised her to confine herself to her Book of Hours. She repeated the incident to the Dauphin; he repeated it to his wife; and the obnoxious object vanished from her table to make room for other novelties. Her household was investigated; it was discovered that her confessor preached a pure Evangelical doctrine; he was dismissed and replaced by a strict Sorbonnist. After the purge, Charles de Guise himself appeared on the scene. He repeated his little homily to the Dauphine and advised her to drop the Psalms. He understood and sympathized with the yearning which she relieved by singing them, but there were other books better adapted to satisfy it, and he handed her the Eclogues of Virgil.

Half feminine himself, the young Archbishop understood the nature of Catherine's religious leanings far better than Marguerite de Navarre. A less likely subject for conversion could hardly be imagined than that young woman who had never been known to express a conviction on any subject and who could hardly call her soul her own. What Madame de Navarre mistook for a dawning enlightenment was merely the fancy of a barren wife indulging those

cravings which pregnant women sometimes conceive for
forbidden fruit.

- 6 -

It was the first time that a public question had touched
the life of Catherine. She could not have trespassed on
more treacherous ground. By 1544, the Evangelical movement, which had been struggling for twenty years to
obtain a foothold in France and which, like a fire in damp
fuel, had flickered unevenly, flaring up spasmodically only
to be stamped out, had at last begun to take hold and to
become a burning issue. It preceded her arrival in France,
but it developed during her first years there. In 1534, a
year after her marriage, occurred the affair of the Placards,
which aroused Paris. The Court was then at Blois, and
when the news reached it of the riots caused by the
appearance of placards denouncing the Mass in the streets
of the capital, the scandal was intensified by a placard
posted on [the King's] door. Usually so indolent in matters
of religion, he was infuriated by this intrusion on his privacy and treated the incident as a case of lese-majesty.
To check the spread of radical literature, he published an
edict banning the art of printing, which he had fostered
in France. Although it was subsequently modified and
tempered into a censorship, he continued to smite in one
of those restless periods of reactionary zeal which alternated
with his normal lenience and neglect. The Court travelled
to Paris, where he rarely appeared, for the express purpose
of permitting the King to lead an expiatory procession
through the streets, accompanied by his family, his Court,
and his clergy, to witness an execution of heretics, and to
address a solemn profession of faith to the Sorbonne. In
the ten years that followed, periodic repression and slackness, alternating with each other, had irritated and fed
the errors to such a pitch that it was no longer safe, even
for such privileged persons as the Queen of Navarre, to
discuss them seriously at Court, although frivolously they
might afford the Court some amusement with the Psalms.
Catherine, secluded in that itinerant Court, which, wending
its way from château to château, remained always remote

from the common life of the country, was in no position to appreciate the force of a movement which was a part of her heritage.

The Lutheran heresy was a legacy from the Medici. It was involved in all the transactions between her family and the French Crown that had ended in transplanting her to France. It was a part of her marriage portion, and of that of her parents. When her mother was married, the dowry was paid by the King, out of the revenues of the French clergy, in compensation for the concessions which he obtained from Leo X in the Concordat of 1515. The Concordat was a diplomatic landmark because it defeated Gallican liberty, and Gallican liberty was the forerunner of the Reformation in France. By the Concordat of 1515 Leo X concluded a transaction with François I by which they both gained at the expense of the Gallican Church. Making some minor concessions to protect the major interests of Rome, the Pope secured these by dividing contested revenue with the King, who received the right of appointing to benefices in France, while the Curia continued to collect the annates. But above all the popular principle of election had been killed. Leo appealed to the two dominating interests of his partner, his financial requirements and his absolutism. Without the latter, the Concordat would have remained a dead letter, for it met with unanimous and prolonged resistance in France. The Concordat revolutionized the ecclesiastical constitution of the kingdom, and all the recognized spokesmen of the nation, Parlement, the Sorbonne, the clergy, united in opposing it, the preachers inveighing against it, the Sorbonne forbidding its publication, Parlement refusing to register it. The opposition provoked the King to repeated assertions of arbitrary power which subdued it only imperfectly. Active protest turned to passive resistance, and though the Concordat was registered, the last word in this conflict between the Crown and the country was not spoken until almost twenty years later. Then François I was again negotiating a Medici marriage. On the occasion of the marriage of Catherine, Clement VII extended the royal privilege of appointing to benefices to include all such monastic foundations as still retained the right to elect; and the Chancellor effaced the last vestige of Gallican safeguards by ordering all ecclesiastical bodies to turn in their original deeds attesting this right, and consigning them to the fire.

The Gallican spirit was crushed, but not without an acute contest which created a rift between the Throne and the nation. It might have been supposed, therefore, that the Reformation, rising at precisely this period, would have found the ground prepared for it and that, by reviving what were in effect Gallican issues, it would have found the same national support in France as in Germany. Yet no such result followed. In Germany it was the nobility that profited by the expropriation of Rome; in France the Crown had already reaped the equivalent advantages; and the Gallican struggle remained a purely professional ecclesiastical question, not a national issue, because the German Reformation alarmed it. By 1530, when the Reformers formulated their principle of faith in the Augsburg Confession, all that remained of what had been a living, complex social creed was a set of arbitrary, abstruse theological disputes, of no bearing on actual life. Luther had nothing more to contribute to the movement, which was substantially exhausted. It was at this stage that, impoverished at home, it spread abroad. It reached France as a professional theological question and as such was opposed and persecuted by the Sorbonne, which, with the virulence peculiar to academic trade wars, enlisted all the conservative forces of society in its attack on a movement whose earlier radical promise lent it a reputation which it no longer merited.

In France the Reformation pursued an inverse development. Beginning as a theological question, it developed only slowly into a social one. Originating among the learned, it gained a general character very gradually. Several years before Luther appeared, his Biblical inspiration had been anticipated by the Reformers of Meaux— Lefèvre d'Etaples, Roussel, Farel, Bishop Briçonnet, and the little cenacle which Marguerite of Navarre protected. But their mild intellectual radicalism made no impression and was ignored by the Sorbonne until, with the advent of Lutheranism, it turned on and dispersed them. Under the influence of his sister, the King at first sympathized with the new ideas and intervened to snatch one or two victims from the Sorbonne, but the Spanish captivity changed everything. During his absence, Duprat, the Chancellor who had quashed the Gallican question, induced the Regent, Louise of Savoy, to institute the systematic persecution of heresy in France. A mixed commission was set up, composed of two members of the Sorbonne and two members of Parlement, with quasi-inquisitorial powers—secret trials, immunity from review of correction—which broke down all guarantees of personal liberty. For this service Duprat received a Cardinal's Hat from Rome. François I returned to a *fait accompli*. He too was changed. The Spanish captivity destroyed his youthful confidence, his enterprise, his initiative, his independence; he returned to France faltering, confused, conservative. He acquiesced in the precedent established during his absence. Everything tended to make him reactionary. Of his enormous ransom the clergy had borne half, on the express understanding that heresy would be actively repressed. His designs upon Italy, defeated but undying, bound him to Rome. He was mortgaged by need, by ambition, and by habit to orthodoxy.

In the first critical years the country was solidly welded against heresy. In France the Reformation rose, not with the nation, but against it. The struggle was carried on by a small heterogeneous minority—shopkeepers, students, mechanics, artisans, priests, professional people, all from the humbler walks of life—without organization or guidance, groping, diffuse, persistent. Persecution lent them power, misrepresentation lent them importance. The opinions for which they went to the stake were little bolder than the private opinions of the King. But the Reformers were represented to him as a leaven of social agitation. It was not the nature of their opinions for which they perished, it was for having opinions at all. He persecuted without conviction, from expediency. The old axiom was dinned into his ears: the principle of authority was at stake, and that of the Church could not be questioned without affecting that of the State.

As yet the danger was purely hypothetical. But the spectacle of persecution excited commiseration as well as fanaticism; the meekness of the victims emphasized the arbitrary use of power against an inoffensive minority for the benefit of a foreign despotism, and attracted to the movement all those who were capable of questioning, or inclined or compelled to question, the existing order of things. If this sympathetic infection was slow to develop, it was because France still enjoyed an enviable state of social security. Politically compact, economically flourishing, the mighty leaven of social agitation, which favoured the rise of the Reformation in Germany, was lacking. But these conditions were beginning to change. The desultory, unsuccessful, wasteful wars of François I and Charles V, the ransom of the King, his extravagance, the increasing taxes, produced a perceptible strain. There was a revolt against the *gabelle* in Guyenne. The government accused the Lutherans of fomenting it. They were persecuted less for what they were than for what they might be—for a vague, potential pregnancy.

7

The birth of her son gave Catherine a character. "One must speak of Madame la Dauphine with all affection," wrote an Italian diplomatist on the day after the event, "for truly she is a good woman. Greater goodness and purity than hers, I believe, could not be found." And it was a singularly virginal character that was now unveiled. The conventual virtues remained intact, after ten years of marriage, embalmed by its barrenness. Her bitter experience of the world had not affected them; at most it had converted them into the conventional virtues. That was the worst that the world had done to her, but it was enough. Sterility had cloistered her and left her with a lifeless virtue. But life had come at last. Recognition, respect, sympathy, security, followed the birth of François, and under those fertile influences she expanded, her spirit quickened, and her vitality asserted itself. The organic impediment overcome, nature welled up in a late release. Thirteen months later she gave birth to a daughter, who was baptized Elisabeth.

She now had rights; the years when she existed on tolerance and dared not assert herself were over. But any hopes that the coming of children would wean her husband from Diane were soon undeceived. That tie was indissoluble; time confirmed it; it had set. The fascination which a mature woman held for a young man half her years, normal or at least understandable while he was a callow adolescent, became more and more anomalous as she passed her prime and he entered manhood. But the eccentric relation rested on a solid fact. Henri, as he matured, revealed himself a man of routine. He was deliberate, slow, and set in his ways; the lady, naturally, was also averse to change; and thus the world was afforded the curious spectacle of a passion founded on the *vis inertiae*. They were an original couple, whose liaison could be likened to nothing but the hardened affinity of two creatures of habit; but they were perfectly mated. It was a marriage, and Catherine was invited to bear children to it. For the coming of children, far from weakening the influence of Diane, increased it. She assisted in their delivery; she supervised their diet, and made herself indispensable to a new generation. Catherine accepted a partnership in which she was not consulted, for it was only by dividing that she shared either her husband or her children. The *vis inertiae* prevailed. In spite of the great improvement in her position, her maternity remained a physiological triumph, and little more. It came too late to alter a relationship upon which the deadening hand of time had set its seal. All her spirit, all her vitality were required to adapt her to a situation of which it was henceforth clear that the more it changed the more it remained the same.

Friends she had—such friends as a woman could have, whose constant concern it was to make no enemies. She was on equally good terms with everyone. She swam as easily with Madame d'Etampes as with the Grande Seneschale, though her husband's mistress and her father-in-law's favourite were often in friction. Once, when they quarrelled, the Dauphin obliged his wife to leave the Petite Bande and form her own Court, but the incident blew over, and she resumed her easy familiarity with the miscellaneous world of friends and foes of which she was a part without becoming a partner to it. The price of friendship came high, and as she would not pay it with those partialities which were expected, genuine attachments passed her by. She had no confidants—her rank and her reticence precluded them. Of interested friends, who sought her favour and her influence, she had enough to flatter her with the appearance of prestige. Affable and obliging, she was always ready to use her relations at Court or in Italy to secure a vacant benefice, to make a sinecure at home or abroad, to satisfy every sort of application; but it was influence of a private and personal nature. Of political influence she had none, since she declined to be a partisan.

The tenacity of his attachment to the dream of Milan led François I to make one more attempt to recover it, not by arms—that was visionary—but by treaty. In 1544, when the Treaty of Crépy struck a truce in his intermittent wars with the Emperor, he proposed a marriage between his youngest son, the Duc d'Orléans, and a member of the Emperor's family, with Milan as the dowry. The Duc d'Orléans resembled him and was his favourite son. Spirited, ambitious, French, he was a brilliant contrast to the Dauphin, who detested him. When the King proposed to endow the prospective bridegroom with four strategic French fiefs, Henri protested officially, in a document duly drawn and legally witnessed, against a treaty so prejudicial to his own interests and those of the country. This public criticism of his father was his first step in politics. The Duc d'Orléans died in the following year, and Milan, and the jealousies it created, vanished into the limbo of forgotten things. Bereaved of his dream, François I was a broken man; the vital spark was gone. He also missed his son. The sordid realities that remained fretted and depressed him, but having reached the age of reason—he was almost fifty—and recognizing that a man who breeds children raises critics, he resigned himself for some time to the natural law and suffered in silence. Then he made some attempts to mollify Henri, but there was no sympathy between them. Pampered, self-indulgent, lonely, the old man found filial affection only in Catherine and treated Henri as a son-in-law. Finally he made a sacrifice and gave him the privilege, which he had hitherto refused him, of attending the meetings of the Council. Henri, however, deliberately maintained an attitude of critical aloofness, attending the meetings rarely, offering no opinions, but declaring in private that he was "pleased that those who administer the government at present should have the benefit and the blame of it, since everything is going badly today, and hereafter everything would be blamed on him." The King, conscious that nothing but his death would satisfy his son, resisted strenuously, hunting incessantly, talking indefatigably, and putting off the hereafter for a year. It overtook him on March 31, 1547, at Rambouillet. There was a death-bed reconciliation at which both were genuinely moved. A passer-by chanced to look into the adjoining room some time later and noticed the heirs waiting for the end. François de Guise passed in and out, repeating at intervals: *"Il s'en va, le vieux galant!"* The Grande Seneschale stood waiting, but Henri lay prostrate on a bed. Catherine sat on the floor holding her head. It was thus that, in Italy, women were taught to mourn their dead, and François I had been a good friend to her. He was her last link with the past.

CHAPTER III

The Reign of

HENRI II

- 1 -

On his death-bed, François I recommended his ministers to his son, urging him to retain them in power. The breath had barely left his body when Henri sent a messenger to the Constable de Montmorency, who had been disgraced by his father in 1541, inviting him to return to Court, where he would be welcomed as "his father and first councillor." Filial affection Henri had, but it was entirely reserved for the man who had been his mentor and friend, and to whom he hastened to prove his fidelity by offering him a position of paternal responsibility and power in the new reign. Who was this man? A simple baron of the Ile-de-France, as his enemies called him, Anne de Montmorency had been one of that band of ambitious soldiers who followed François I to Italy, but he had lagged behind, guarding the rear and confining his military service to home defence. Glory passed him by in the years of adventure and expansion, but his reputation grew in the period of retrenchment and defeat. It assumed proportions which approached hero-worship in the imagination of the Dauphin, although the military achievements of Montmorency were mediocre. A desk-soldier who rarely took the field, he made his reputation on a series of defensive manœuvres of a cautious and unspectacular character. His one considerable exploit was the razing of Provence to starve out an invasion of the armies of Charles V: a piece of strategy which cost the country more destruction than the invasion itself. But it gave him a name for ruthless and iron determination which deeply impressed the Dauphin. As a boy, Henri judged the man by his manner, which was positive and peremptory and conveyed the impression of commanding ability. Later, he came to appreciate his true qualities. He admired his sober common sense, his home-loving habits, his prudent patriotism, his hostility to foreign adventure, qualities which he wished to adopt, as a disavowal of the spectacular follies of his father, at the outset of his reign.

Montmorency returned with the glory of disgrace. But this glory too was exaggerated. His misfortune was mediocre. It was due, not to the influence which he exercised over the Dauphin, but to a character which was incompatible with Court life. "I have only one fault to find with you," François I said, with tears in his eyes, when they parted; "you do not love those whom I love." He did not love Madame d'Etampes. After six years of retirement, his character remained intact. Quarrelsome, self-centred, despotic, he antagonized everyone. A bureaucrat and an autocrat, ambassadors found him a peculiarly trying minister, and they gave him a bad name abroad. As his enemies multiplied, the charge gained ground that he was deliberately disgusting his master with public affairs, in order to appropriate power himself. It was true that he permitted no business to be treated by the King until he had masticated it himself, that he exercised the vigilance of a martinet over every detail of the administration, that he imposed an irksome ceremonial on the diplomatic corps, ambassadors being obliged to submit their requests to him and to receive their replies, often revised, from him. His jealousy of power was patent, but it was compatible with, and even prompted by, a conscientious sense of public duty which, in time, was recognized by unbiased observers.

But, though his jealousy of the national honour was acute, in foreign affairs he was accommodating. His belligerency was reserved for domestic consumption. One of his first acts was to propose a treaty to Charles V, guaranteeing the *status quo,* and though it fell through, because of his refusal to settle the question of Piedmont and Savoy, incorporated into France by the conquests of François I, he continued to adhere unswervingly to his settled course. He was an apostle of peace. The incarnation of common sense, thrift, and conservation, he was determined to preserve France from a repetition of those fruitless and costly foreign adventures into which the romantic infatuation of François I had led it, with disastrous effects on its morale and its economy.

He had few friends—he felt himself strong enough to dispense with them—and no party. He was a party in himself. He had a large family of which he made no use. He was more devoted to his nephews, Odet de Coligny, the Cardinal de Châtillon; Gaspard de Coligny, and François d'Andelot, than to his own sons, but he was no nepotist. His first duty was to the King, whose trust in him satisfied all his affections.

The reign of Henri II, or of Anne de Montmorency, as it promised to be, began by a complete reaction against the past, and the overture announced its main themes: common sense, conservation, mediocrity, age.

This presupposed, however, that the omnipotence of Montmorency would not be contested. On his return to Court, the Guises were presented to him by the King, who made a little speech in which he dwelt on his confidence in the Constable and advised them to accept his direction.

The Guises could not be ignored. To dispute the position of Montmorency required uncommon assurance, skill, and daring. But Charles and François de Guise possessed those qualities. Their position gave them certain initial advantages. Sprung from the princely House of Lorraine, they entered the service of the French Crown on a quasi-independent and sovereign footing. They were foreigners, naturalized interlopers, whose first allegiance was to their family. They were, in short, princely adventurers who combined the assurance of an illustrious name with the insecurity of aliens whose title to favour is precarious and parasitic. Proud of their race, unsure of their place, they suffered from a psychological handicap, which they turned, however, to moral advantage. It gave them a double incentive to assert themselves. Assurance and daring they had as their birthright, and skill they acquired. The Guises had a collective ambition, every member of the family working for the other, and four other brothers were waiting for François and Charles to establish themselves. Charles managed his brother, whom he adored, like an impresario. François, the soldier, served as the professional foil to the Constable, but as his career was yet unmade and he was nearing thirty, his prospects depended on the diplomatic skill with which his impresario found, or made, opportunities for him. All the Guises had charm, and in Charles this faculty had been professionally developed. He was called the Tempter. His fascination lay in a delicate blend of worldliness and austerity. He was also known as the Saint. There was no contradiction in these impressions: he was merely a baroque saint, bland and plausible, blessed with the grace of one born to gesticulate on a pinnacle. His austerity cost him no effort, or he would not have attempted it. For a consummate facility was the secret of his superiority. A supple virtuoso, evading difficulties, avoiding defeat, never straining, never over-reaching himself, he was indomitable because he was pliant and formidable because he was fluid. Ambassadors united in eulogizing his courtesy, his tact, his ability to listen, the quick intuition with which he anticipated their thoughts but never interrupted them, and his exemplary character. His appearance, it is true, belied his ability. With his sleek and trivial features, it was easy to see why Montmorency called him a "great calf."

It was a crude mistake. Where Montmorency was masterful, Guise was masterly; the distinction, narrow but fraught with consequence, was the margin between a man who had arrived and one who meant to do so. And behind him stood his brother, a soldier of unrecognized abilities, whose youth was slipping away, and who was burning to make his mark. And behind them both was a class, or at least a claque—all those younger sons of France whom the law of primogeniture deprived of patrimony and who had no future but in war, for whom war

was both a pastime and a means of social progress, the
road to favour, fortune, and power. The Guises, who
belonged to that class, were its natural champions. The
Constable had chosen his position; he dictated theirs. They
could only conform or react. Their traditions prompted,
their progress demanded, nay, their very youth depended
on foreign adventure.

Cosimo de' Medici made an attempt to renew official
relations with the French Court. Speculating on the sweeping reaction against the reign of François I, he sent the
Bishop of Cortona to France to feel his way toward an
understanding. The Bishop began by approaching Catherine, but he found that her position was unchanged: she
assured him that it was absolutely "necessary to pass
through the door of the Constable." Following the pro-
tocol, he submitted the case to the Constable, reviewed
the dispute for precedence which had caused the rupture,
and explained that it was not the politics of his master that
were responsible for it, but the personal affront which
Cosimo de' Medici had received in seeing the ambassador
of Ferrara preferred to his own on the grounds that he
represented a prince of older and more illustrious lineage.
The arguments which had been employed then still held
good. "As for myself," Cosimo had declared, "I cannot
say, nor do I much care to, that I am born of a Duke of
Florence, not being convinced as yet which is the more
praiseworthy, to be born or to become somebody. . . ."
He had also intimated that an adverse decision reflected
on his illustrious relative. "And it has always been considered a much greater sign of the nobility and greatness
of a family to regard rather the house which their women
enter than that from which they issue." This suggestion
had more force than ever now that Catherine de' Medici
was Queen of France. The Constable referred the Bishop
to the King. The King referred him to the precedent established by his father. He had no intention of departing
from it, he said. The Bishop expostulated. He went so
far as to observe that His Majesty had done nothing, since
he came to the throne, but to upset the precedents established by his father. The King said nothing, looked at him,
and . . . smiled.

That smile was an event. Of all the changes which initiated the new reign none was more striking than that in the appearance of the King. "Cheerful, ruddy, and of an excellent colour," his manner, his very complexion, had improved. The death of his father had produced a tonic effect on him; his constitution was relieved; and he no sooner donned mourning than he shed his gloom. Grave he still was, with his long conservative face and his lame stare, but the eyes had lost their look of leaden indifference, and there was the smile. The clouds were lifting, and a new man emerged. But one misfortune passed and another appeared. Shorn of his mystery, he appeared an ordinary young man who suffered from nothing but his own mediocrity. That was his real curse. He was not aware of it; he was not self-conscious, and it could not be said that his lame stare revealed the guilty knowledge of a commonplace mind. But he suffered in the eyes of the world.

But still there was the smile. His development had begun. Though his one serious interest in life was still physical exercise, in which he excelled, and which he pursued so exclusively that many observers were tempted to write his biography as a footnote to a biped, he discharged his other duties conscientiously. Because he was so deeply imbued with responsibility, he abandoned the reins to Montmorency, while he was learning his trade. But at the same time he encouraged the Guises. As a sportsman, he enjoyed the competition of which he was at once the object and the umpire. He was confident of remaining the arbiter, although it was clear to everyone else that they were contending, not for his confidence, but for his control.

Scandal touched the life of the Grande Seneschale at last. The King made her a gift, at his accession, of the right to control, and of a percentage on the sale of, all public offices involved in the change of administration. This concession earned her 100,000 crowns and cost her her reputation. Now the murmurs of outrage, of envy, of public spirit, and of spite began.

To exploit the public revenues was more than even François I allowed his women. The sale of office, itself an abuse, was doubly venal when it lost its value. It was the abuse of an abuse. Bitter names were found for her. Before this scandal subsided, another was provoked by a grant which she obtained for her son-in-law of all estates held without absolute title and all unoccupied lands belonging *de jure* to the Crown; a scoop which not only deprived the Treasury of much-needed revenue but, by dispossessing numbers of nobles, communes, and private persons, brought her name into general odium. Some time passed, and the world learned that the King had deeded to her the château of Chenonceaux and was involved in litigation to secure her a title to it so absolute as to preclude all possibility of its recovery by after-generations.

And so scandal, the bane of her blameless life, tarnished her fair name at last, not with looseness but with avarice, the vice of age. She owed life a lust, and this was it. This lewd avarice was all that she could muster; it was her identity, she had no being apart from it, and she became a kind of abstraction of greed.

Diane turned her back on the backbiters and ignored criticism which was obviously prompted by malice and envy—no doubt because she was a success. Nevertheless, she was too conventional a woman to be insensible to criticism, and she gave the world the satisfaction of showing that she was hurt by it. Her manners, once so faultless, became haughty. She braved the world with brutal pride, offended and giving offence. Despite her high breeding, she could not escape the vulgarity of fortune or the vulgarity of the passion which it satisfied.

For scandal, once it attacked her character, spared her virtue no more than her avarice. It invaded the respectable domestic life which she led with the King. It complained of the time which he spent with her and of the way in which he spent it. Ambassadors who ate at her table sent the most prejudicial reports abroad. They called her his Nurse. They portrayed the eccentric bliss of a unique relation in the most literal and vulgar manner. "When the King has told her all the business he has transacted in the morning, whether with ambassadors or other people of consequence, he seats himself in her lap, strumming his cither, and often asks the Constable or Aumale if she is not beautiful, touching her breasts from time to time and gazing at her raptly like a man in the toils of love. And she says that she will soon be wrinkled, in which she is certainly not mistaken." She was embarrassed by these demonstrations and submitted to them with simpering surprise that she could still inspire them. She escaped to the apartments of the Queen, but only to be recalled to those punctual embraces. He never tired of love and became more and more careless of her reputation, but she was obliged to submit to public caresses, lest people say, as they did, that, one passion driving out another, avarice made her incapable of love.

As her personal reputation declined, her public influence increased. Her apartments were the political headquarters of the Court. While intrigues and manœuvres went on all about her, she reserved for herself the role of an arbiter, or the promise of it. But politics were only her secondary concern. She had no grasp of, or interest in, public affairs apart from a few prejudices against or in favour of their exponents. Her primary interest was in patronage, for herself, for her family, for her friends, and for those of her enemies whom she wished to place under obligations against a day when she might need them. Her apartments were frequented by fortune-hunters, great and small, and she had the satisfaction of seeing her protégés well set up in life.

Amid the rising influences moving to shape the new reign only the insignificant or the superior could afford to remain neutral. That double advantage Catherine enjoyed. Movement went on about her; she was becalmed. Politics died at her doorstep; her life remained purely domestic. Within her own sphere, however, she attempted to introduce a radical change. As a matter of dignity, she remonstrated with the King against his continued connection with Diane. But it was a mutiny against the immutable. There was a stormy scene, in which he appealed to her to condone a relation which he could not renounce and, having had the satisfaction at least of hearing him plead, she assented. As for her dignity, she saved it by a mental reservation. "If I received Madame," she explained long after, "it was really the King whom I welcomed, and I always let him know that it was greatly to my regret, for no woman who loved her husband ever loved his whore."

The bargain made, she broke it; there were fresh scenes and she submitted again, for the reason which underlay all her mental reservations and which she admitted freely: "I loved him so much that I was always afraid."

She was under a double disadvantage in defending her dignity. She had too much of it to risk humiliation, and she loved her husband too deeply to forfeit the respect and friendship which he showed her. She suffered from the further handicap of her origin. She could not overcome her deference for the King or her sense of the honour of being his consort. It was the last vestige of the parvenue and morally the most damaging. But it appeared only in her intimate relations with the King. In public, she was completely mistress of her dignity and performed her ceremonial and social functions with an authority as easy as it was unassuming. No one ever mentioned the misalliance. The Court could not recall a Queen, since Anne de Bretagne, so completely equal to her position.

The everlasting neutrality imposed on her by convention was clearly irksome, however, to her nature. Her habitual expression of equanimity was coloured by an underlying sadness and dissatisfaction. She had the schooled but livid look of a woman who has swallowed but cannot digest defeat. Her temperament was lively and passionate, and it had no outlet. She craved, if not self-assertion, at least self-expression, and she found it in a role which, however passive, gave her a place apart and a promise of influence in the new reign.

Much was expected of her, now that she had arrived at a position to which she had manifestly been called for the purpose of serving the interests of two countries. It was her destiny and her duty, as an Italian in France, to promote her *patria* in her adopted country. She needed no prompting. It was a duty in which she delighted. She filled the Court with the pomp and the colour of Italian luxury. She imported her gowns from Italy. She patronized Italian artists, Italian humanists, Italian culture, preserving the tradition of François I from the general reaction against his reign. But more than this was expected of her. She became the patroness of the Italian *fuorusciti,* or political exiles.

The transition was natural, since the artists, the scholars, the men of letters who formed her entourage were for the most part émigrés. Ever since the first French invasions of Italy, France had become the asylum of all the dispossessed of the peninsula, who settled there to await, or to provoke, an opportunity of returning to their homes in the wake of the next French intervention in Italy. Many were pensioned by the Crown; they formed a permanent colony, restless, intriguing, conspiring, unsettling. During the later years of François I they were dormant, but they became active and virulent again at the change of reign. The most numerous and influential group was the Florentine, whose "synagogue," as it was called, was the lodging of the poet Luigi Alamanni. Alamanni was the maître d'hôtel of the Queen. After the accession he became her adviser, spokesman, and confidential agent, and diplomats noted him as a man who should be cultivated. Alamanni was an old Republican, and his wife, a confidante of the Queen, entertained Catherine with such sinister descriptions of the tyranny of Cosimo de' Medici, that the Bishop of Cortona called upon the Queen one day and urged her not to let her mind be poisoned against his master. Nevertheless, Catherine continued to listen complaisantly to those Republicans who had been the terror of her childhood and to be outraged by the misrule of the Medici. Cosimo was so remote a connection that she hardly considered him one. If she had liberal sympathies, it was because of the Strozzi. Filippo Strozzi, the husband of her foster-mother Clarice, died in the dungeons of Cosimo de' Medici. The debt of gratitude which she felt for Filippo, who had advanced her dowry, and for Clarice, who had tended her childhood, she repaid to his sons. Of these there were four: Piero and Leone were soldiers, Roberto was the banker, and Lorenzo a churchman; they were all conspirators. The most violent was the restless, nomadic, furibund, atheistical, vain, and indomitable daredevil Piero. He was her favourite. It was from him that she acquired the convictions of an émigré.

The passions, the ambitions, the experiences, the discussions, the intrigues, of the *fuorusciti* brought into her life the fever, the movement, the agitation, of a vicarious excitement. Beyond this the connection produced no positive results. The *fuorusciti* were not a party; they were a state of mind. Nevertheless, her association with them identified the Queen in public opinion with the party of the foreigner. In reality they were alien to her. More than once her countrymen had occasion to feel how far she had outgrown her Italian habits. Even in little things, such as her taste in dress, she valued most what they esteemed least; despite her patriotic sympathy, she was a vicarious Italian. On the other hand, the French found her indifferently acclimated. They too noticed the trace of the alien in little things, eloquent of large, such as her inability, after fifteen years, to master the language, which she still spoke unidiomatically and wrote eccentrically: evidence of an indisposition, rather than of an inability, to learn. She was between two worlds, belonging to neither. But it was her manifest destiny to unite them. Though the *fuorusciti* were not yet a party, they were straining to become one and, until they did so, they had no reason for being: they led, like Catherine, a half-life which was neither real nor a dream.

One result the connection had: in Italy, at least, the Queen acquired prestige from her protection of her compatriots. The Pope, though not a *fuoruscito* himself, had the aims of one: during the summer of 1547 he was engaged in persuading Henri II to intervene in Italy and to join a league for the protection of the Papal States. The negotiations lagging, he sent the Golden Rose to Catherine, as a diplomatic compliment.

- 2 -

This situation was suddenly precipitated by the assassination, on September 10, 1547, of Pier Luigi Farnese, the son of the Pope and the despot of Parma and Piacenza. Piacenza was immediately occupied by the troops of Don Ferrante Gonzaga, the Lieutenant-Deputy of Charles V in Italy, and a *casus belli* was afforded the Pope. Henri II wrote to His Holiness, promising him the protection of the Crown. Catherine also wrote to the Pope, repeating these assurances in duplicate. A combination, or rather a confusion, of personal and political motives determined the King to take this first step in spite of the protests of the Constable: his lifelong hatred of Charles V, his desire to measure himself against the hereditary rival of France, and a family connexion which he had contracted with the Papal interests through the betrothal of his natural daughter, Diane de France, to Orazio Farnese, a grandson of the Pope. The pressure of the Farnese, the *fuorusciti*, and the Guises conspired with his own inclinations, and the push toward Italy began.

Charles de Guise hurried to Rome with full powers to negotiate. On October 22, he reached Rome. That he would produce a favourable impression there was a foregone conclusion, as he had negotiated the alliance between Diane de France and Orazio Farnese, a service for which he was promoted, at the request of Henri II, to the Cardinalate. The Hat had never been better bestowed. The new Cardinal produced from it, when the negotiations began, the most brilliant promises. His diplomacy was all prestidigitation. Whatever the Farnese proposed, and even more than they expected, immediately materialized. Cardinal Farnese suggested extending the scope of the alliance to include an expedition against Naples; within a few weeks the Cardinal produced a letter from the King endorsing the idea with enthusiasm and offering to send François de Guise to command the expedition. It seemed too good to be true: so at least thought the Pope, the oldest and shrewdest of the Farnese. Menaced by the Emperor with a new sack of Rome if he signed any papers, he began to cool precisely when the prospects were brightest. It was the turn then of the Cardinal de Guise to plead, to press, to persuade. The seduction of Charles de Guise was never so masterly. He pledged the word of his master, not merely as a king, but as a gentleman, and Henri II was one. The Pope was satisfied. A contract was drafted, by which the King undertook to maintain an army in Italy for the protection of the Papal dominions and the recovery of all States usurped from the Holy See, the expenses to be borne equally by both parties. As a matter of prudence, it was defined as a defensive alliance. Then the King began to cool. The Cardinal de Guise, still officially in charge of the negotiations, was hampered by an influence which counteracted his own and which he recognized at once. That sober, stolid, immovable influence could come only from one source; there could be no further doubt of it when he received a letter, signed by the King, inviting him to defer his return to France and, in fact, to remain in Rome. Unable to believe that the King had knowingly signed such instructions, he wrote to the Grande Seneschale to discover the truth, and his suspicions were fully confirmed. The King had, in fact, no knowledge of the letter, which had been placed before him among other papers requiring his signature by the Constable, who explained, when he was called to account, that he had acted for the good of the service. It was an explanation, not an apology. It served its purpose. The Cardinal de Guise hurried back to France in January 1548. He brought home the Hat, but there was nothing in it.

The Cardinal had still something to learn from his aged rival. Montmorency had out-manœuvred him, not merely by his personal authority with the King, but by his manipulation of an ecclesiastical question which, properly pressed, was capable of neutralizing the political understanding between France and Rome. An Œcumenical Council, the first formal attempt to deal with the issues raised by the Reformation, was in session at Bologna. The Pope repeatedly pressed for the participation of the French clergy, but the King had been in no haste to comply, alleging his reluctance to co-operate with a Council dominated by the Imperial clergy. When eventually he consented to send a delegation, the opposition took another form. The Gallican spirit, stunned but not extinguished by François I, revived under Henri II. Montmorency was its champion, as he was of every national issue. The instructions which the French delegation carried to Bologna were a protest against the Papal privileges embodied in the Concordat of 1515. Particular exception was taken to the annates. "From these prearrangements derives a great disorder in this kingdom, since the majority of benefices are filled by ignorant, unworthy, and disreputable persons who have acquired them from Rome, where nothing is considered but the purse." The Pope, anxious to avoid any discussion of the Papal privileges, was disposed to make concessions. The Council had already recognized and abolished one administrative abuse, that of pluralities, and the King was urged to enforce this reform in France. This, however, the King declined to consider. Pluralities affected the royal privileges which the King enjoyed under the terms of the Concordat. While the Pope intimated that reforms should begin at home, the King replied, in effect, that they should end there.

The French delegation reached Bologna a few days before the Cardinal de Guise arrived in Rome. The two negotiations, political and ecclesiastical, were carried on concurrently and antagonistically. The progress which the Cardinal made in the former was neutralized by the strained relations which the Gallican delegation produced in the latter. The Pope strove to dissociate the two questions and avoided the subject in his discussions with the Cardinal. Once, however, he mentioned pluralities, and in the most personal manner, by alluding to the talent for accumulation which was another of the brilliant abilities of his French friend. Guise laughingly replied that he would gladly give them up in exchange for those held by His Holiness. As the Pope took a very serious view of the question, it was not referred to again. But neither was the political alliance. The implicit connection which the Constable succeeded in establishing between the two questions, by adroit timing, was one of the most influential factors in defeating the diplomacy of Guise.

Charles de Guise was a vain man, but he was not too vain to learn. He accepted his defeat lightly and bided his time. His Italian ambitions remained intact. What they were was no secret. The Guises had pretensions to the Crown of Naples, and as the King held the same claims, based on the Anjou succession, it would have seemed a matter of elementary discretion not to recall them. Charles de Guise was so undiplomatic, however, as to propose, when he became a Prince of the Church, to assume the title of Cardinal d'Anjou. Apart from its associations with Naples, this title was reserved for members of the royal family. The French ambassador in Rome protested, and the pretender was obliged to accept the title of Cardinal de Guise until the death of his uncle, the Cardinal de Lorraine, whose title and fortune he inherited two years later.

Certainly, the first qualification for success was not to recognize defeat. Pliant, imperturbable, persevering, the Cardinal pursued his course. His Italian journey was not a failure. It was a prospecting trip and, though he had missed the goal, he had sounded the terrain and formed several valuable connections for the future—the Farnese, the Este. On his return to France, final arrangements for the marriage of his brother to Anna d'Este were concluded.

In the summer of 1548 the Court travelled to Piedmont. This journey was the object of much speculation in Italy. In Imperialist circles the most exaggerated suspicions prevailed. The Emperor himself made official inquiries. The journey had, indeed, a political object but an extremely modest one, as Cardinal d'Este explained to his brother the Duke of Ferrara. "His Majesty wishes to go directly to Turin, in order to visit this frontier, and to show not only that he holds these countries as his own by the same title as he holds France, but also that he is not disposed to abandon them so easily as some people may suppose." A demonstration, and no more, or Montmorency would not have proposed it. For the initiative came from him. As a parade of national pride, it was consistent with his views and to that extent he was prepared to cater to the war party, but no further. For once the Guises were in agreement with him, however, and they had also proposed the journey.

At Turin, the King met the Duke of Ferrara, and the marriage contract was ratified. This was a mere pretext. The journey was inspired by psychological strategy. The King had been brought to the brink of Italy. Might he not be tempted to plunge, or if not to plunge, at least to wade, to test the temperature of the deep? And indeed, although Henri was not an imaginative man and had been in Piedmont before, the proximity of the promised land—the land so positively promised by the Guises—troubled his senses. He was willing to try. He sounded the Duke of Ferrara, whose States occupied a strategic position, with a suggestion to join a League against the Emperor; but the Duke declined. Henri welcomed the emissaries whom the Pope sent to greet him and consented to resume the negotiations which had been allowed to lapse. Contact was established and the spell began to work, when he was abruptly recalled to France by the revolt of the *gabelle*.

The salt industry sustained the majority of the population of Guyenne, which was acutely sensitive to even the slightest variations in the salt-tax, as the industry at best afforded a meagre living. At the beginning of François I's reign the salt-tax had been reduced by a quarter, but under pressure of the increasing financial disorder which followed the Italian wars, it was restored to its original level. The margin of difference was enough to create thousands of paupers, and it was these elements, long-suffering but at last desperate, who began the revolt of 1548. An army of fifty thousand paupers overran the country, plundering it, and terrorizing all wealthy or well-to-do persons under the common denomination of *gabeleurs*. In Bordeaux a sympathetic revolt broke out. The upper classes favoured it, and the disorder subsided when the royal Lieutenant fled and the President of the local Parlement assumed his functions. But the former Lieutenant no sooner returned than the people rose, murdered him, filled his corpse with salt, and began a wholesale massacre of *gabeleurs*, priests, officials, and wealthy citizens. Thereupon the bourgeois and the nobility combined with the government authorities to suppress the troubles. The army of vagrants was checked and dispersed, and the leader broken on the wheel; and order was restored. The revolt had reached this stage when the King learned of it in Piedmont. Montmorency was sent to check it in Guyenne and Guise in Poitou. When Montmorency reached Bordeaux, the danger was over, the situation was under control, and the city admitted him freely. Nevertheless, he carried out savage reprisals, depriving the municipality of its franchises, burning its charters, razing the Town Hall, carrying off the church bells and artillery, replacing the Parlement by a chamber of royal commissaries, fining the city 200,000 livres, and executing the rebels with every refinement of atrocity. In striking and politic contrast to the gratuitous cruelty of the bureaucrat, François de Guise handled the revolt in Poitou with the moderation of a civilian.

An attempt was made to attribute the revolt to the spread of heresy. But the government reduced the salt-tax.

That the revolt of the *gabelle* was a symptom of a condition both grave and general was manifest in the ease and speed with which it spread, the social character it assumed, the sympathy of the upper classes until it attacked them, and the viciousness with which Montmorency repressed it. A symptom and a warning, it arrested for a time the urge toward foreign adventure.

The Guises turned their talents to other fields, consolidating and increasing the credit which they obtained from their multiplying alliances with the royal family. In December 1548, the marriage of François de Guise and Anna d'Este was celebrated in Paris. Two children danced at the wedding, the Dauphin François and the niece of the Guises, Mary Stuart. The daughter of Marie de Guise, the first of her family to reach a throne, arrived in France in the previous summer, where she assumed a position which legitimized the ambitions of her uncles and allowed them to emerge from the penumbra in which they had hitherto moved into the full radiance of a reflected glory. Henri II accorded the *reinette,* as she was called, the rank of Dauphine, taking precedence over his own daughters, in view of her projected marriage to the Dauphin and her rights as Queen of Scotland. He regarded Scotland henceforth as "the kingdom of the Dauphin." In the following year a campaign was undertaken against England, for the recovery of Boulogne, in which the credit for success went to François de Guise. The Italian adventure was for the moment forgotten. How indifferent the Court was to it was proved by the fact that the *fuorusciti* took part in the war of Boulogne: Piero and Leone Strozzi commanded the royal fleet in the waters of Scotland.

Though the Constable still retained the administration of affairs, the prestige of the Guises now equalled his own and placed him on the defensive. In the third year of the reign, his omnipotence was a thing of the past: he was the opposition. The campaign of Boulogne had been under his nominal supervision; the actual plans for the capture of the city had been drawn by his nephew, Gaspard de

Coligny; but the honour had been carried off by François de Guise. He attempted to undermine the confidence which the King placed in his rivals, but without success; apart from the loyalty to his friends which was so conspicuous a feature of the character of Henri II, the Constable had to reckon with the influence of Diane, who protected them. The old man was hard pressed: an inner council of the King, the mistress, and the Guises had been formed, from which Montmorency was excluded; and his attempts to break up this combination produced, in the summer of 1550, a scandal that rebounded and almost resulted in his own fall.

The morals of Mary Stuart, at the age of eight, were largely in the hands of her governesses. Among these was a Scotswoman who had accompanied her to France, Lady Fleming. She was pretty, and the King mentioned more than once, in his correspondence with Marie de Guise, "the good and agreeable services which she has rendered to the person of our little daughter, the Queen of Scotland," and his desire to reward her. But the opportunity did not present itself, and he did not make it. Her character was unquestioned until three months after the capture of Boulogne, when the Guises learned that Lady Fleming was receiving nocturnal attentions from the Constable. The Cardinal called a family council to discuss what was clearly a scheme of the enemy to dishonour the Dauphine and make her ineligible to marry the Dauphin by debauching her governess. Living in a reflected glory, they died in reflected dishonour. It was decided to deal with it quietly, to surprise the Constable, and to kill him. The character of the governess would suffer, but that of Mary Stuart would be saved. It would be a scandal, not a disgrace. Before the cure could be applied, it was discovered that the lover was not Montmorency, but the King. Consternation spread. The Guises, Diane, the Queen were all affected and equally furious. There was only one person capable of dealing with such a situation; it was a case for the governess. Madame de Valentinois surprised the two men, one night, emerging from the whereabouts of Lady Fleming. With all the dignity at her command, she abandoned herself to her temper, overwhelmed the King with insults, and accused him of dishonouring the Queen of

Scotland by giving her a whore for a governess. Her party
spirit, rising above her personal feelings, inspired her with
the most unmeasured abuse. Henri submitted and followed
her to Anet, the idyllic retreat which harboured their own
romance. The brunt of the scandal fell on Montmorency.
Universal reprobation was the lot of the old man who had
stooped to the role of a pander in his attempt to shift
governesses. Lady Fleming was dismissed, but she lingered
for some time, boasting that she was with child, before
returning to Scotland. Referring to this scandal many years
later, Catherine remembered how properly it had been
conducted by everyone concerned. "I had the honour of
marrying the King, and nothing in the world annoyed him
more than to know that I knew of such matters, and when
Madame de Flamin was with child, he thought it only
proper that she should be dismissed, and never showed
any temper, or spoke an angry word about it. As for
Madame de Valentinois, she, like Madame d'Etampes,
behaved in a perfectly correct manner, and when there
were any who made a noise or a scandal, he would have
been very much displeased, had I kept them near me."

The incident was closed by a political defeat of the
Constable. The Guises exacted reparations for the offence
to their honour. While the King was too much of a gentleman to sacrifice his accomplice, he was too much of a
man of honour not to satisfy the Guises. The exactions
began by widespread changes of personnel in the administration and ended by a war in Italy.

- 3 -

The Cardinal de Guise had never relinquished, he had
merely postponed, the Italian adventure. In November
1549, the Farnese Pope died. A month later Cardinal de
Guise arrived in Rome for the Conclave to press the candidacy of two members of his family who were *papabili,* his
uncle the Cardinal de Lorraine and his relative by marriage, Cardinal Ippolito d'Este. His attitude gave great
offence to the French Cardinals. This was before the Lady
Fleming scandal, and Montmorency was still strong
enough to check the pretensions of his rival. He induced
the King, who was paying for the election, to press the

French Cardinals to choose a "Spaniard" rather than a "Guisard" and, when this produced a deadlock, to sell their votes to a neutral candidate. Cardinal del Monte, who was elected, under the name of Julius III, answered the requirement, although Guise described him as "frivolous, vicious, unfit for the Tiara."

The new Pope was grateful to the French for his election, and the fact that he assumed the name of Julius III in honour of Julius II, whose steward he had been, was due merely to personal sentiment and did not imply that he meant to imitate the Francophobia of his great predecessor, as he hastened to assure the French ambassador.

Cardinal de Guise, still prejudiced and resolved to reserve judgment on the reliability of Julius III, lingered in Rome to study the situation. It was during his sojourn in Rome, in 1550, that he met one of the most remarkable men of the day, who placed in his hand an instrument as supple as steel, absolutely flexible, absolutely unbreakable. Loyola called on him to solicit his patronage. The character of this man, in its curious unconscious combination of worldliness and austerity, burning with religious zeal, but devoid of spiritual vocation, was calculated to appeal to Charles de Guise. Loyola was a medium. The soldier, disabled and disqualified for his own profession, who had hypnotized himself by mortification and discipline, by hallucination and study, by mental and physical ordeals, by indomitable determination, into the belief that he had found a substitute for it in religion, who dedicated his life to the service of what he did not understand, and who founded a Society to rationalize and propagate his sterile activity, was one of those natures destined to be the serf of an obsession. And his obsession was simple: servitude and authority—the military ideal *in excelsis*. The spiritual militia which he formed provided Rome with what was required to combat the Reformation: blind obedience, the mechanics of enthusiasm, counterfeit conviction. The systematic credulity inculcated by the Society went to the root of the *mal du siècle*. As a champion of Papal authority, it found its mission. Organizing action and sterilizing thought in a reactionary crusade, the Jesuit movement was generated by conditions which, as often as they recur, produce the same phenomenon. The necessity of defend-

ing by force an indefensible system on which the survival
of a privileged class depends was the opportunity which
called forth, in the sixteenth century, a Loyola. The
Church was on the defensive, and his success as the champion of a sick and sanctified social order was one of the
morbid symptoms of its decay.

But his success was in its infancy. It still needed foster-
ing. The Society had made its presence felt in Italy, in
Spain, in Portugal; it had begun to invade Germany; but
France, the focus of conflict, was hostile. This was the
occasion of his visit to the Cardinal, whose influence he
had been advised to invoke. He laid his case before him.
The obstacle was Gallicanism. Both Parlement and the
Sorbonne, prejudiced against any manifestation which
suggested an encroachment of ultramontane influence, refused to legalize the existence of the Society in France.
A champion was needed, a diplomat, a manager, and
Loyola invited the Cardinal to become the Protector of
the Order in France. The Cardinal listened, sympathized,
and consented to become the impresario of the Jesuits.

But the value of the Society, depending as it did on
penetration, propaganda, and education, lay in the future.
It was a matter of speculation and of promise, and in the
meantime the Gallican question became acute. Yielding
to the pressure of the Imperial party, Julius III consented
to re-establish the Œcumenical Council at Trent. The
French Government remonstrated, reminding the Pope
that he had obligated himself not to take such a step
without consulting it. A Nuncio was sent to France to
negotiate an understanding, but it was a case in which
explanations only aggravated the offence. The King disinterested himself in the Council, declaring that if reforms
were needed he had enough prelates to accomplish them
in France. The only reforms in which he was interested
were those which curtailed the rapacity of the Roman
clergy in the matter of French benefices. Relations became
strained, and the Pope, finding himself unable to mollify
Henri II, felt free to cultivate the favour of the Emperor
without further apologies. Nevertheless, the incident
would have produced nothing more than a chill if the
question of Parma had not been suddenly revived. Charles
V persuaded the Pope to cede Parma to the Empire, the

Farnese appealed to France, and Henri II would have declared war at once but for the restraining influence of Montmorency. In the meantime, the Lady Fleming scandal occurred, and the influence of the Constable weakened. Within a few months war broke out, but it was fought over the Gallican question.

Hostilities began in the spring of 1551, when the King directed the French Bishops to investigate abuses with a view to submitting them to a National Assembly of the French clergy to be convened at some indefinite future date. These instructions, which ignored the authority of the Council of Trent, created consternation in Rome. The Pope, exasperated by the alliance of the Farnese with France, stormed in the grand manner of his great predecessor, Julius II. He spoke seriously of excommunicating Henri II and depriving him of his States; he went so far as to announce this intention to the ambassador of Charles V and to add that, after deposing the contumacious sovereign, he would bestow France upon the son of the Emperor, Philip of Spain. When the echo of these words reached France, Henri II was both angry and alarmed. As he was negotiating an alliance with the Protestant princes of Germany, he was anxious lest this association be misinterpreted as a leaning toward religious heresy, and in the ecclesiastical dispute he assumed a temperate, conciliatory, and almost apologetic tone. But on the political question the King was stubborn and angry, and he took what, for a sovereign who honoured his word, was a decisive step: he signed a treaty with the Farnese, guaranteeing them the protection of France, and sent Piero Strozzi to Italy to launch the campaign. The Lieutenant-General of the Emperor mobilized his troops, and the War of Parma began.

Charles de Guise was in an embarrassing dilemma. The political conflict had finally been provoked, but once again it was inextricably involved in the religious question. As a representative of Rome, he was neutralized and was in danger of losing control of the Italian adventure unless he could dissociate it from the ecclesiastical controversy. As a consequence of this situation, he was compelled to support the pacific advice of the Constable. He persuaded the King to send Jean de Montluc, one of the ablest diplo-

mats in the service, to Rome to accommodate the ecclesiastical dispute in person with the Pope. Montluc arrived
in June. His eloquence, seconded by that of Cardinal
d'Este, who held a fortune in benefices in France, produced an impression on the Pope. Within a few days,
however, he had been recaptured by the ambassador of
the Emperor, and raged against Montluc, against France,
against the Farnese, against the *fuorusciti*, but without
ceasing to protest even more belligerently his devotion to
peace and charity. Montluc and the French Cardinals left
Rome. Julius would not accept the rupture, though he did
nothing to prevent it, and his last words to Montluc were
that he abandoned the attempt in order to give time to His
Majesty "to cool off until God inspired and enlightened
him."

Now, it was this inconsequential conduct which finally
produced a serious crisis. Slow to anger, Henri became
increasingly incensed by the menaces so casually hurled at
him by the Pope. He dismissed the Nuncio. Following the
severance of diplomatic relations, he forbade under severe
penalties the expedition of revenue for benefices to Rome.
The prospect of resuming relations was remote. The drift
to schism, academic in the schoolrooms of the Sorbonne,
suddenly materialized in a momentous meeting of the
Royal Council, following the departure of the Nuncio.
Someone proposed to test the validity of the principle by
emancipating the Gallican Church completely from its
obedience to the Pope and creating, in his stead, a French
Patriarch invested with supreme spiritual authority. The
King, somewhat taken aback by so extreme a measure,
turned to the Cardinal de Guise and asked his opinion.
Rarely has so much responsibility been laid on one man.
The circumstances were such that a decisive word would
act on the clouded situation with chemical effect, to
precipitate or to clear it. He wept. "Sire," he said, "I
appeal to Your Majesty. You must consult your own conscience, and no one else." This evasion decided the King,
who declared that the conflict with the Pope would be
confined to the temporal sphere.

France had been saved for the Jesuits by a narrow
margin. The gravity of the crisis was appreciated only
when it was past. The Pope was sobered by it. A month

later, he wrote to the King a letter of remarkable pathos. These advances were accepted, the tension subsided, and after six months of negotiation peace was concluded simultaneously on the religious and the political questions.

The War of Parma, insignificant as a military action, was of importance because of the complications it produced. The immediate object of the campaign was attained: Ottavio Farnese regained possession of Parma. This was a meagre result to show for the expense which the war involved and the political strain which had brought France to the brink of schism. But Henri II was satisfied. When the smoke of battle cleared, his personality was finally recognized. For all his mediocrity, he revealed some uncommon, superior, and costly qualities. He derived no material advantage from a war which he had undertaken purely for prestige. He allowed himself the luxury of complete disinterestedness; nor was this all. The expedition of beneficiary dues to Rome was restored, and he received as a favour what he had been so frivolous as to claim as a right.

The policy of prestige and protection was the logical outcome of a compromise between the prudence of Montmorency and the enterprise of the Guises. Eager for military glory but averse to aggression, the King elected a middle course which seemed to combine successfully the attraction of adventure and the advantage of conservatism. But the momentum of things carried him on. It was impossible, once having tasted success, not to repeat it.

- 4 -

In the first Italian war Catherine played no part. The *fuorusciti*, who had done much to foment it and who found active service in it, were no longer identified with her. They had merged with the general stream of Court politics. The Strozzi stood high in the favour of the King and of the Guises and had outgrown her. She had not outgrown her position at the beginning of the reign. Her life was still a routine of childbearing. Since the birth of the Dauphin in 1544, she had produced royal infants so regularly that her unflagging vitality inspired surprise and concern. Ambassadors speculated on the future problems of providing for so numerous a brood, and particularly the Italians. As his family grew, the King began to nurse the idea of establishing one of his sons in Italy. By 1551, three had been born to him—François, Louis, and Charles—and though the second died a year after his birth, the Queen was again about to discharge her yearly chore.

Nevertheless, though her life remained purely domestic, Catherine continued to follow the fortunes of the *fuorusciti* in general, and of the Strozzi in particular, with lively personal interest. As her children were young and sickly and were left in the care of nurses and tutors in the salubrious climate of Touraine, while the Court travelled, she saw very little of them. It was on the Strozzi that she lavished, as a young matron, the warmth of her maternal feelings. Proud of their success, she watched over it vigilantly. Her protective instincts were aroused at the least alarm; how sensitive they were she proved when disgrace overtook Leone Strozzi.

Montmorency, disliking the *fuorusciti* as political troublemakers, was antagonistic to the Strozzi, and particularly detested Leone Strozzi, who, as commander of the royal galleys, had criticized his indifference to this branch of the service. The zealous Italian, long the butt of intrigue and calumny, developed an acute sense of persecution. In the autumn of 1551, during the Parma War, believing that his life was in danger, he fled from Marseilles with two galleys and took refuge in Malta. The news reached Catherine when she was about to give birth, and the excitement quickened her labour pains. Her first impulse was to reach Montmorency before he reached the King, and to disarm his indignation by her own. She could not move, but she wrote him a letter of convulsive agitation. She understood so well what had happened—an impulse of panic, a fit of nerves, those treacherous Italian nerves—but she understood even better how the scandal would be exaggerated and represented to the King as a desertion in time of war; and she could only protect him by drowning out the clamour of his enemies with her own. "*Je suis la plus, la plus ennuyée,*" she insisted. "I wish that God had taken him out of this world at the very moment he decided to desert. . . . But one thing consoles me. I believe that he will recognize his mistake and will not linger in this world, which would be the best news I could have of him, for I am certain that he did not act in bad faith. . . ." She wrote on and on, eloquently incoherent, her wits racing with her nerves, and at last, out of the blurrings and blottings of her racing brain emerged the breathless ghost of an appeal. "I implore you, by all the favours you ever mean to do me, recommend Signor Piero to the King, for though his brother has failed, I am certain that he will die in his service, and do not hesitate to take him under your protection, I will answer for him, he will never fail. . . ." She could not sleep and found relief only when she sank into the familiar throes of birth. Six days later, she was corresponding again, this time with the King, and vehemently, and at great length: "I beg you to forgive me if I annoy you with so long a letter, and to excuse me, considering the grief I feel that a person of whom I have spoken to you so much, and who is what he is to me, should have wronged you at a time when I hoped that he would serve you so well, and the only thing that would console me would be to hear that God had made him drown. . . ." But Leone Strozzi had not killed himself; he was safe in the harbour of Malta; and her apprehensions redoubled, but with the inspiration and the courage of fear she turned them to account. *"Mon compère,"* she explained to the Constable, "the great grief I feel because of the wrong done to the King is still as bad as the first day that I learned of it, and the more I try to put it away, the greater it grows, fearing that when he considers what he has done and at what a time, in despair he will take other service, which torments me so much that I do not know how I could bear it if he did, which I do not believe, but to ease my mind I have implored the King to allow him to come and justify himself." Her intervention was not ineffectual, the scandal was checked, the credit of Piero Strozzi remained intact, and after two years, when the bitter memory had faded, his brother was permitted to return.

The boy whom she bore under such stress of spirit became her favourite, her most Italian, son. He was bap-

tized Edouard-Alexandre, but was subsequently known
as Henri Duc d'Anjou.

But the days were passing when the Queen was to be
merely a passive and accessory figure in public life. In the
winter of 1551-1552 the stimulating effects of the Italian
campaign made themselves felt in France. The King concluded an alliance with the Protestant Princes of Germany,
and in the following spring took the field to support their
struggle against Charles V by creating a vast diversion
along the eastern frontier. His allies had advised him to
occupy Metz, Toul, and Verdun; and a campaign which
promised to extend and consolidate the French frontiers
aroused general enthusiasm, recruits flocked to the colours,
and Montmorency was obliged to follow and lead the
movement. In this surge of national expansion, the Queen
was suddenly lifted into public life. During the absence
of the King, she was entrusted with the Regency.

For some time the increasing intimacy of the royal
couple had caused comment and amazement even among
diplomats who were well informed. "The King visits the
Queen and serves her with so much affection and attention
that it is astounding," noted a confidant of the Guises. The
fact was not astonishing. It implied no disloyalty to Diane;
on the contrary, it was Diane who instigated it, and who
received 5000 livres for her services to the Queen. On the
shady side of fifty, she devoted herself to consolidating
the *ménage à trois*. A little less active than she used to be,
she led the King gently back into the path of domestic
duty and lent him for longer periods to the Queen. Henri,
on his side, though he still suffered from prolonged separation, and the burden of all his letters was that he was
bored, accepted the arrangement complaisantly. A fond
father, he was attached to the mother of his children, and
there was nothing irregular in the respect and confidence
which he showed in entrusting her with the Regency.

Catherine took her position seriously and was disappointed to discover that her powers were more circum-
scribed than she had been led to expect. Bertrandi, the
Keeper of the Seals, was associated with her, and her
authority, further subdivided among other partners, was
so nominal that she remarked, after reading the docu-

ment, that "in some places I am given a great deal of authority but in others very little, and if this power had been cast in the full form in which it pleased the King to say that it would be framed, I should have been careful to use it soberly." But she accompanied her protest with a smile. For that reason, perhaps, no one took it seriously. She wrote to the Constable, pointing out the difference between the powers accorded to her and those enjoyed by the mother of François I during the latter's Regency; but she received no satisfaction from him. Finally, she refused to submit the document, as it stood, to Parlement for registration. "It would diminish rather than augment the authority which everyone believes I have," she explained, "having the honour to be what I am to the King." But what was she to the King? Something that invited a circumlocution. She herself never specified it; all her phrases circumvented the fact. The document was finally reworded so as to satisfy her dignity.

Though her powers were limited, there was nothing perfunctory in her exercise of them. The Constable placed her in charge of the Commissary, and she embraced her duties with the zeal of a recruit and the habits of a housewife. "If everyone does his part and what he promises, I shall soon be past mistress," she wrote him, "for I study nothing else all day long, and I employ most of the time of Monsieur le Garde des Sceaux and the members of the Council on this question, for fear there may be some slip, though it is difficult, when matters are so hasty and precipitate, to avoid some confusion and disorder, but I hope that, with everything well established and begun as it is, you will be satisfied; at least, you may count on me to press and push it. . . ." Her colleagues were inclined to murmur at her scrupulous attention to detail, but she tolerated no slackness and expected everyone to slave as she slaved. They found her overzealous, not realizing that for her it was a labour of love. She was on her mettle, and her sense of responsibility was unsleeping. Her forethought, her vigilance, her zeal, exhausted the Commissary and could not be contained by it. The Cardinal de Bourbon, the Governor of Paris, was not aware that mutiny was brewing in the capital until he received a letter from her. "I have been informed that there are in Paris certain preach-

ers who have nothing better to do than to talk of affairs
of State, in order to incite the people to mutiny, which
we should guard against more than fire or pest. . . . You
understand, *mon cousin,* how easy it is, under colour of
zeal and devotion, to stir the people and to foment trouble,
which it is easier to quell in the beginning than when
these speeches spread and are repeated. . . ." She recommended the arrest of the agitators, "without any noise or
scandal, putting them in a safe place, while you inform
the King." But prevention, to be effective, should go
further: another preacher, "a worthy one," should be employed to counteract the impression created by the others
and to defend the government. She supplied this preacher
with leading arguments. The Cardinal replied reassuringly.
The importance of the preachers had been much exaggerated—they were "bold and misleading but not so bitter
as you were led to suppose"—and, he added, "imprisonment would have been a bad course." Her nervousness
betrayed the novice. But her intolerance of criticism revealed something else. She had not learned it from the
Medici; she had assimilated the autocratic spirit of the
Valois, and added to it the partiality of a wife. Criticism
of Henri flung her at once into martial law.

But her heart was in her work. This was evident, indeed, to an embarrassing degree. She made a sentimental
adventure of her Regency. The business of administration,
the punctilious discharge of her exacting duties, the nag-
ging of her colleagues, the organization of routine details
—all these activities were service for Henri, and she made
of them a mute offering of love. She wooed him with
munitions, serenaded him with supplies, bombarded him
with reports, and adored him with all the resources of the
commissariat. Impassioned but practical, she put all the
poetry of which her nature was capable into efficiency. To
learn from Montmorency "of the contentment which the
King feels in me, which is all that I desire in this world,
merely to be in his good graces . . ."—that was reward
enough. Her Regency had only one meaning, one value:
"As for my powers, I am pleased since they must be published, that it should be in a form which shows that I am
in the good graces of the King." Ambitious she was, inordinately ambitious, but only to please. She never wished

to be Regent again, "not that I serve him unwillingly, but that I should not have the joy of being near him, which makes me wish that, if this need ever arise again, you may have my place and I yours, for the duration of the war, so that I may serve him as you do; I beg you, since that cannot be, do for me what I should do for you, let me be near him soon, send me news of him, tell me whether you are as close to the enemy as we fear. . . ." It was the daily burden of all her correspondence—to be near, nearer, nearest her King. Her effusions, in a woman who had been married almost twenty years, were embarrassing. She might as well never have been married at all. Years of repression had not tamed her native vivacity: a little recognition, a little encouragement, and she throbbed at thirty-four with the ardour of a young girl.

The first appearance of Catherine in public life was in the nature of a personal revelation. Her eager grasp of power, her lively sense of responsibility, her assertion of the legitimate claims of her rank, and the vigorous activity with which she justified them, amply justified the confidence which the King placed in her. The experience was too stimulating not to be repeated, and when she relinquished her functions, she continued to linger in the public eye.

The campaign was merely a military promenade. Metz, Toul, and Verdun were occupied without a blow and, after foraging in Alsace, reconnoitring Strasbourg, and watering their horses in the Rhine, the victorious armies returned with banners flying. The diversion accomplished its purpose with brilliant facility: Charles V, on the point of subduing the religious and political decentralization of the Empire, was compelled to capitulate abruptly to the Protestants and to concentrate all his forces on the recovery of Metz. With the grim siege of Metz (October 1552-January 1553) the long-dormant feud of the Habsburgs and the Valois was resumed in earnest. The siege ended in an ignominious defeat of the Emperor and the glorification of François de Guise, who defended the city with a gallantry and a generalship that made him a popular idol in France. And now the alternating current that passed from one front to the other came again into play.

If the War of Parma inspired the martial spirit that led
to Metz, the confidence fired by that victory brought the
French back into Italy.

The second Italian expedition grew out of the first. The
fuorusciti, the royal agents, and the French Cardinals who
remained in Italy combined to prepare the next advance.
In the summer of 1552 Siena revolted, expelled the Spanish garrison, and threw itself on the protection of France.
The partners who engineered the revolt, having acted
without official sanction, although with the understanding
that they would not be disavowed, took provisional measures to secure the city. Cardinal de Tournon wrote to the
King, informing him of the *fait accompli* and offering him
what was considered by himself and his colleagues "an
excellent and honourable opportunity for the King of
France to plant his influence in the centre of Italy by pro-
curing the liberation of Siena." So presented, as an extension of the policy of protection and prestige, it could not
fail to appeal to the King, and Henri, in fact, a willing subject for mind readers, accepted the protectorship of Siena
with pleasure.

But was it possible—was it even intended—to confine
this advance to a purely defensive policy? Siena lay at the
threshold of Florence, and Cardinal Farnese, on behalf of
the French group, immediately sent a message to Cosimo
de' Medici to assure him of their neighbourly sentiments.
"The King has no other aim, in this matter, than to gain
a little glory by assisting the afflicted and the liberation
of the oppressed." Cosimo de' Medici accepted these explanations coolly. He had just learned from his ambassador
in Rome that Catherine de' Medici had instigated the
enterprise of Siena with the design of extending it to
Florence.

Such was, in fact, the remarkable sequel to her Regency. The growing confidence which she derived from
public collaboration with her husband was so great that
she believed herself capable of wedding their political
aims. Serving his interests and following his lead, she
acquired the courage to form her own plans and to invite
him in turn to follow her lead. The Tuscan enterprise was
her bid for recognition and influence. Drawn to it by her
partiality for the Strozzi and, under their influence, by a

contagious sympathy for Florentine liberty, she adopted it above all, however, because it offered a glorious role for her husband. He had championed the Protestant princes of Germany. He had accepted a medal, stamped with the Phrygian bonnet of liberty, and bearing the inscription, *Pro Germaniae patriae libertate recuperanda*. Why should he not accept the same lofty mission for Florence? If others exploited his generosity for their profit, why should she not exploit it for his glory? With the courage to conceive, she had the shrewdness to achieve her vision. Alone she could do nothing, but she found powerful allies. Montmorency, at first, was opposed to the Tuscan scheme as a costly and useless adventure, but after the victory of Metz, his attitude changed. The laurels of François de Guise, the Italian ambitions of his manager, and the triumph of the war party made it likely that an Italian expedition would follow and that Guise would lead it. To prevent that eventuality, he was prepared to go to great lengths, even at the cost of consistency, of abandoning his policies, of supporting a scheme he disliked, and of befriending the Strozzi. Sacrificing both his principles and his prejudices, he adopted the enterprise, recommended Piero Strozzi for the command, and even made overtures to Leone Strozzi, inviting him to return to France. The fugitive was still resentful, but he consented to a reconciliation as a sacrifice to his patriotism.

With Montmorency to support her, the Queen felt strong enough to acknowledge the exiled children of Florence, whom she had carried under her heart so long. She worked for them, cheerfully, patiently, resourcefully. Three months after Metz, Piero Strozzi was sent on a tour of reconnaissance in Italy. On his return, in the autumn of 1553, the King appointed him his Lieutenant-General in the peninsula. Catherine now took the next step and committed herself publicly. With the permission of the King, she sold or mortgaged all her maternal inheritance in France and raised 100,000 crowns toward the expenses. Considerable as this contribution was, its greatest value was the guarantee it gave to other investors. The Florentine colony in Lyons opened its credit, and the promptness with which the bankers floated the enterprise made it popular with the Treasury.

In the winter of 1554, Piero Strozzi left for Italy, carrying confidence and enthusiasm with him. Money flowed
freely, and the reports of his progress which reached
France were glowing. The King, amenable to suggestion,
and with so much money on call, shared the general enthusiasm, and spoke of the despotism of Cosimo de'
Medici with generous indignation. Catherine was convinced that she had compromised him for his glory. When
Strozzi reached Siena, however, delays and difficulties set
in. The Cardinal of Ferrara, who had been administering
the city, resented his intrusion; there was constant friction
between the civil and military authorities; and impediments were deliberately created by the Cardinal, who was
an old friend of Cosimo de' Medici. Weeks, months,
slipped by in inaction and bickering. In France enthusiasm
cooled. Montmorency, recovering his principles, attempted
to confine the expedition to a demonstration of force without effect. The King hesitated and communicated his
indecision to Strozzi. The one person who refused to be
discouraged and who pursued unswervingly a clear and
consistent aim was Catherine. The Cardinal de Tournon
declared that "if the freedom of Florence is restored, the
Queen will have all the credit of it."

On August 2, 1554, the long suspense ended. Strozzi
met the troops of Cosimo de' Medici at Marciano and was
disastrously defeated. When the first reports reached
France, the King behaved with conspicuous gallantry. By
his orders, the news was withheld from his wife, who was
pregnant. When at last, and with the utmost precaution,
it was broken to her, the shock was less extreme than he
expected. She wept bitterly, but in rage—rage against the
cowardice of her countrymen, rage against the consideration of the King, who had spared her the truth—and she
did not quail. In the tempest of her distress she preserved
her aplomb and, womanlike, made the world ring only to
recover her balance. She took command of the situation
and steadied the morale of everyone about her. But she
was one in a thousand. Gradually she understood. The
truth was still being withheld from her: the King was preparing to treat with Cosimo de' Medici, and he was still
attempting to spare her. His generosity was the final

mortification, and she succumbed to it. Involuntarily, her own determination began to flag.

The situation passed beyond her control; the ravages of defeat could be neither checked nor concealed. When Strozzi returned to Court, he was received, but so coldly that Catherine herself advised him to retire and wait until their misadventure had been forgotten. To forget and to be forgotten—it was all that she could hope for. She did not spare herself: she was responsible for that adventure which had led nowhere . . . how could it be otherwise? . . . she had made it her own. A persistent fatality defeated all her efforts to live. She was a woman apart. It was sufficient that she should desire a thing for it to come to nothing.

- 5 -

In the autumn of 1555, the Emperor, weary and infirm, announced his intention of abdicating in favour of his son, Philip of Spain, and was disposed to negotiate for a general peace. Montmorency invited his overtures.

In France the sentiment in favour of peace began to stir. The border provinces were bruised and discoloured by the glories of war. The provinces of the interior felt the strain indirectly in the accumulating burden of taxation, inordinately swollen by the policy of foreign prestige. The war was carried on at a deficit, and the inability to meet its expenses by normal methods was an indication of the growing unsoundness of the fiscal organization of the government. In the litter of financial confusion lurked the germs of social disorder.

But Julius III died in 1555. He was succeeded by a war-maker, the Carafa Pope, Paul IV. At the time of his election, the *pourparlers* for peace between France and the Emperor had broken down. Faced by a resumption of the war, and conscious of the condition of the country, the King proposed to divert the conflict into Italy. As the threat produced no effect, he proceeded to stress it by making diplomatic overtures to the Pope. Carafa was a passionate Neapolitan, an inveterate enemy of Spain, a *fuoruscito* who had found refuge under the Tiara. When the royal agents proposed a league for the liberation of

Naples and supported it by liberal offers of money, he responded with a fervour which soon converted the conversation into a contract. When the negotiations reached this stage, the Cardinal de Lorraine, as Charles de Guise was now known, left for Italy to conclude them. On the way, he learned that the treaty had already been signed by Monsieur d'Avanson, the French ambassador in Rome, and on terms so disadvantageous that, for all practical purposes, the alliance was unilateral. The Cardinal sent an indignant complaint to the French Court, but he was advised by his brother "not to make any demonstration to Monsieur d'Avanson with respect to his mistake in hastening the treaty, as the King wishes to support him, and Madame de Valentinois is of the same mind." After appending his signature to the treaty, the Cardinal started for France, in January 1556. At Ferrara he heard the first hints of trouble when he learned that the King had not ratified the contract. He suspected the worst, and indeed the Constable had warned him. But the royal ratification arrived, and he pursued his journey without misgivings. At Blois the blow fell. He learned that the King had signed the Treaty of Vaucelles. Then the magnitude of the disaster dawned on him: he had been sent to Italy with *carte blanche* to sign a blank paper.

Profiting by the absence of the Cardinal, Montmorency had regained his ascendancy over the King, pushed his negotiations with the Emperor, and brought them to a successful conclusion in the Treaty of Vaucelles, which established a five years' truce and consecrated all the victories of the French. It was a remarkable diplomatic triumph, and a momentous one, marking, because of the peculiar circumstances which surrounded it, the apogee of French power and the dawn of its decline.

The preliminary negotiations were conducted by Coligny, the favourite nephew of the Constable, who signed the treaty on February 5, 1556, on behalf of the King. On this occasion he dealt with Charles V. A month later he returned to Brussels to receive the ratification of Philip II.

The transfer of power occurred at a critical time. For thirty years Charles V had been insolvent. The Treaty of Vaucelles provided a five years' breathing-spell in which his heir would be free to set his enormous house in order, before the resumption of the conflict. For resumed it would be: the relative position of the two countries made any lasting reconciliation impossible. The Empire was too dispersed, a vast, rambling, complex congeries of States whose vital system, extending from Spain to Italy to Germany to Flanders, encircled France, while France was too compressed and could not expand without severing a vital artery of the Empire. Philip II was equally eager for peace. He recognized its necessity and craved it constitutionally. Sedentary and unadventurous, with none of his father's love of travel and military glory, he was satisfied to preserve, without expanding, his heritage.

It was the political equinox. With a conservative sovereign rising in the Spanish and an equivalent influence in the ascendant in the French hemisphere, a balance seemed at last to have been struck. But there were many variable factors in the situation, of which the most visible was the fact that, while Philip II ruled his ministers, Henri II was governed by his.

- 6 -

The Treaty of Vaucelles, sound and opportune in its statesmanship, was compromised by the circumstances in which it was concluded and the complications to which it gave rise. Six months before, it would have been an unquestionable diplomatic triumph; six months too late, it was an equivocal one. The Cardinal de Lorraine, when he learned of it at Blois, admitted his defeat with a frankness that revealed how complete it was. "The Constable has won," he said simply. The King was in a terrible predicament, the fatal consequence of his submission to rival influences. Confident of his ability to straddle and control them, he had been carried away and torn asunder and, in the paroxysm of contention, had signed two contradictory treaties at once. The infatuation of loyalty could go no further. He now found himself in a dilemma from which he could extricate himself only by breaking his word, a solution so repugnant that he sought refuge from it in obstinate evasions, the ignominious end of his incoherent impulses.

But the scandal had already broken. The stupefaction and indignation in Rome were unbounded. When the Pope first learned of the truce, he almost fainted. For a month he seethed. He nursed a combined hatred of the Emperor who had cheated him and of Henri II who had betrayed him, and only his sacerdotal capacity prevented him from hating himself as their dupe. His moral condition was so deplorable that he refused to preach during Lent.

Cardinal Carafa, his nephew, was sent to France to endorse the truce and to undermine it. The spring and summer of 1556 were spent in this campaign. Carafa, the Guises, Madame de Valentinois, the *fuorusciti,* and the clients of the Crown in Italy combined to salvage the Neapolitan scheme. It was a measure of the desperation of the war party that they enlisted the support even of the Queen. The fatal attraction of lost causes fascinating her once more, Catherine joined the combination for motives not all of which were conscious. Those which she recognized were a revival of her old interests. Carlo Carafa, who had served in the Tuscan War under Piero Strozzi, offered her cousin an opportunity to recoup his fortunes and, in the event of success in Naples, to resume the enterprise against Florence. No more was needed to win the goodwill of the Queen, but more was offered. Had not the Pope proposed to reserve the Crown of Naples for one of her sons? Her children were growing, and the unremitting increase of her family created a political problem which was no longer remote. She was pregnant, as usual, and the King had said that, if the next addition to the family was a boy, he would put him into the Church. A foundling, a royal foundling, to be passed off on his poor relatives, the priests—such was the prospect, on one hand; on the other, the Crown of Naples, to remove one of her sons and make room for the newcomer; how could she hesitate? Her children, her husband, Strozzi, the Medici, Florence, Naples—a confusion of interests drew her into the war party. They blurred, blended, coalesced indistinctly, and she did not define them. Their vagueness was their power, their security. They were nebulous, without risks, without responsibility. Of these motives she was half-conscious, but the most powerful perhaps was undivined: the atavistic urge in her blood, the yearning for a life of her own, and the sense that she would find it only by reverting to Italy.

Cardinal Carafa, by dint of sheer persistence, by dunning the King, by hugging his heels, and by wooing the Constable, began to make an impression, perhaps not the most favourable, since it was that of a creditor, but nevertheless an effective one. The importunacy of Carafa carried the day. The King consented to renew his alliance with Paul IV. Montmorency accepted this solution, which redeemed the King's word, but attempted to invalidate it by qualifying the treaty as a purely defensive alliance, by refusing to send troops to Italy, and by disallowing the demand of the Pope for an advance of 500,000 crowns. Carafa, completely satisfied, carried the treaty to Rome, and the Pope promptly began to provoke incidents which necessitated the intervention of the French.

The provocations of the Pope prodded the Spaniards into action. On September 1, 1556, the Viceroy of Naples, the Duke of Alva, invaded the Campagna and menaced Rome. Feverish preparations filled the Holy City, feverish fears of another sack, feverish appeals to the French. Montmorency, unmoved, advised the Pope to make peace, but the Carafa deliberately exaggerated their danger. As a matter of fact, Alva was merely making a demonstration in order to talk peace, as Cardinal du Bellay discovered after a little inquiry. But his information reached France too late. The King, alarmed by the imminence of a calamity for which he felt himself personally responsible, dispatched the Duc de Guise to Italy.

The Third Italian War began under the most sinister auspices. Money, confidence, policy—everything was lacking. Guise no sooner reached Italy than he realized the nature of the difficulties which he would have to combat and the unheroic character of the adventure which circumstances had forced upon him. The original plan of the campaign called for a rapid march upon Naples, and his forces, accordingly, were lightly equipped. At the last moment he was instructed by the King to attack Parma and expel the Farnese. For this operation cannons were required and it was arranged that they should be supplied by Ercole d'Este, whose claims on the Treasury had now been honoured in full. On reaching the outskirts of Parma, Guise discovered that his father-in-law had supplied neither artillery nor munitions nor victuals, and that such supplies as he had provided were in an advanced state of disrepair and completely unfit for use. When the news reached France, the accumulated resentment of years broke in a wave of anti-Italian sentiment. "The most dishonest, lying, and unworthy race" was the least that could be said of them; "whatever they say or whatever they promise, they never perform except when it turns to their profit"; they were weathervanes "veering with every wind"; they were for sale "to the highest bidder and the fattest purse"; in short, a ruined and a ruining race, enslaved, decaying, corrupt, and contaminating, and not to be touched with impunity. Such animosity had not been known since the days when Catherine came to France, a bartered and a barren bride, the butt of Italian shortdealing. Old rancours rose about her, fugitive but haunting, in a ghostly reprise. The King was furious: the capture of Parma and the punishment of the Farnese were the only part of the campaign in which he was interested.

The enterprise represented too much of a patchwork of too many discordant ambitions not to disintegrate. Guise himself realized it, but his career was at stake; to withdraw, after so many expenses, so ignominious a beginning, and such negative results, was a humiliation to avert which he was compelled to fall in with the plans of the Pope and to precipitate the attack upon Naples without adequate preparations or supplies. When he rejoined his men in Emilia, he found them demoralized and on the verge of desertion. They had received no pay for two months. Guise persuaded his men to follow him as far as Civitella on the outskirts of the Abruzzi and to gamble on its siege. As the city proved impregnable, he attempted to provoke an engagement with Alva, who was observing him at a distance. But the one thing which could redeem him, the conflict itself, eluded him. The whole scheme— misbegotten, chimerical, unreal—resolved itself into a mist of mocking and unseizable forms. It was with frank relief that he received word from the King, in May 1557, to abandon the expedition against Naples and to retire temporarily to Tuscany or Lombardy. But it was as nothing to the relief of Alva, who admitted later that "if the French had pressed faster, they would have conquered the whole kingdom of Naples without difficulty, for it was without money or troops or fortresses or provisions for defence."

So ended the Italian dream. For it was over, in spite of some feeble efforts to salvage it. Guise sent Strozzi to France to propose several alternatives, among them the Tuscan enterprise, and the King, eager to recoup some fruit from the enormous waste of money—over a million livres a month—listened. But these schemes received no support from the Queen. She criticized them in the most eloquent possible way, by her silent abstention. She had learned her lesson at last. Italy was a delusion, and in reverting to it for life she had only been deceiving herself. The past was the past, it could not be revived, all her ties with it were severed; her family, her friends, her memories, and the country which vaguely comprised and recalled them now faded as well. She was thirty-eight; it was foolish, and it was dangerous, at her age, to live on her memories.

- 7 -

Disastrous as the Italian adventure had been, its full folly could be measured only by its consequences. The feeble resistance of the Spanish in Italy was a warning. On that far-flung front which extended from Brussels to Naples an attack in one quarter invariably provoked a counter-attack in another; and while the Spanish shirked battle in Italy, in the north they retaliated by a major offensive. In the summer of 1557 an army of sixty thousand men under the command of the Duke of Savoy invaded Picardy. The French had ample reserves of man-power. But an essential element was missing. The question of leadership was crucial. Montmorency and Alva, or Guise and the Duke of Savoy, would have been equally matched; but the teams were shifted. While Guise and Alva observed each other in Italy, it was upon the Constable that the responsibility of confronting the Duke of Savoy fell in France.

In the first days of August, the Duke of Savoy appeared

before Saint-Quentin, one of the main bulwarks of Paris. Coligny threw himself into the town before it was invested, and undertook to hold it until the Constable could relieve him.

Four days after his arrival, an attempt to reinforce him was made by his brother, Andelot, but it failed; and on the same day the enemy were swollen by the arrival of the English, whom Philip II, as titular King of England, had drawn into the war. The besiegers now numbered over sixty-four thousand, the besieged barely a twentieth part of them. Coligny held fast for seventeen days. On August 18 the Constable appeared with the full muster of France.

The battle turned on a crucial blunder. To the north of the town lay a small bridge, which the most elementary strategy commanded the Constable to take, but which he neglected. The Duke of Savoy, discovering the Constable's mistake, poured his forces across the Somme and proceeded to turn the French flank. The enemy brought up their guns; the massacre lasted from two until five in the afternoon; and when the sun sank, the Constable was in the hands of the enemy. It was another Pavia.

Four hundred of the relieving force had struggled through the marshes and reached the town; among them was Andelot. The garrison and the townsmen were demoralized. To maintain any morale required superhuman exertions, the rigour of the situation could not do it; the rigour of character was needed; between them Coligny and Andelot succeeded.

In the Spanish camp the victory, the prisoners, the ransoms created an uncontrollable excitement; the way to Paris lay open and the Duke of Savoy was impatient to press on. But Philip had appeared on the scene. He was not convinced of the wisdom of pressing on precipitately to Paris. In any case, nothing could be done until the town had been taken.

So near was Saint-Quentin to Paris that the King, who was at Compiègne, learned of the disaster at nine the next morning. He recalled the Duc de Guise from Italy; he consigned to the Cardinal all the powers of the Constable; he sent the Dauphin into Touraine; and he wrote to Catherine, who was in Paris, to raise money.

Her uses were well known; they were those of adversity. Her personal resources were exhausted, her property mortgaged, and her credit overdrawn by the Italian adventures; and she had to face a deafening confusion. Panic reigned in Paris: the inhabitants were packing for flight; placards denounced the authors of the national ruin. It was this seething public which the Queen, herself involved in the common responsibility, had to confront and outface. Her calm, and the presence of mind with which she took measures to maintain order, went far to restore confidence. Five days after the battle she addressed the Parlement. The Parlement was deliberating, sentiment was hostile, and the magistrates showed some reluctance to receive her; formal delays were placed in her way, but when she was finally admitted, she harangued the committees with such feeling, force, and effect that she was rewarded, when the session concluded, by a rousing personal ovation. Her demands for funds were unhesitatingly voted.

Meanwhile, in Saint-Quentin, the morale of the doomed garrison was flagging rapidly. Coligny, worn to the bone, nerved his captains with the grim stamina of extremity. He warned them that "if anyone heard him utter so much as a word that sounded like surrender, he begged them to toss him like a coward over the walls, and if anyone made such a suggestion to him, he promised to treat him in like manner."

Living from day to day and looking for every evening to be the last, he held out for seventeen days. On August 27, the attack was overwhelming; nevertheless, it might have been repulsed—as he subsequently insisted—but for the desertion of a demoralized company. In pursuing the fugitives he was captured by the enemy.

Looking back, he saw his brother's company still fighting; but it was the end. The town was swarming with flames. Andelot, luckier than his brother, having already suffered a Spanish captivity after the War of Parma, trusted himself to the marshes and swam to safety. Coligny's captivity was close; he was moved from fortress to fortress—Lille, Sluys, Ghent—and held incommunicado. His only resource was reading, and his reading was mainly religious. He was led to investigate the Protestant position. His brother, Andelot, during his year of captivity, had also busied himself with religion, explored the faith, and become a convert. Coligny read the same books, retraced the same steps, and reached the same conclusions. From the Reformed doctrines he took what he understood and what suited him—their tone, their general spirit. With theological problems he was not concerned. But the spirit—the disciplined independence, the proud humility, the unworldly ambition—worked in his mind with irresistible persuasion. In all the varieties of religious experience, his was one of the simplest and the most honest. He craved self-confidence and was ready to forfeit the world for it. A year after his release, he formally embraced the Reformed faith.

- 8 -

Saint-Quentin was the key to France on the Flanders front. The Duke of Savoy endeavoured in vain to obtain the sanction of Philip II to the plan of campaign which he had prepared, namely, to invade the Ile-de-France with one army and to march upon Lyons with another.

This providential delay allowed the Duc de Guise to return from Italy. The calamity of Saint-Quentin completely eclipsed his failure in the peninsula, and instead of returning under a cloud he was hailed as the national saviour. The King assembled a new army and, when the plan of campaign was discussed in the Royal Council, proposed the capture of Calais, a project which he had cherished for years but which offered difficulties so redoubtable that the Council unanimously opposed it. The Duc de Guise declined, with the prudence of an expert, to commit himself for or against it. Henri II thereupon assumed full responsibility for a scheme which everyone regarded as foolhardy and took the lead in restoring national confidence. Nothing less than a sensational antidote could revive it. The problem had been studied for four years, and the plans had been drawn by Coligny. Guise executed them brilliantly. In January 1558 Calais capitulated. The initiative of the King was amply justified by the moral effect of this victory. The country, which had lain stunned and numb ever since Saint-Quentin, responded with those unfailing powers of recuperation which needed only a sign of faith to reveal its vast reserves of vitality. The campaign which began with Calais and continued throughout the spring and summer with the capture of Dunkirk and Thionville was consistently fortunate.

The King always regarded the enterprise of Calais as his own and prided himself with quiet satisfaction on his inspiration. He had not had many in his life. The glory of realizing it raised François de Guise in his estimation to a pitch of intimate partnership by which the Guises as a family hastened to profit. With consummate generalship they followed up the fall of Calais by pressing the marriage of Mary Stuart and the Dauphin. Although this union had been settled for years, Montmorency had contrived to retard it in the hope of finding an occasion to break it. He made a final attempt from his prison in Flanders by proposing a marriage between the Dauphin and a sister of Philip II. The King immediately suspended the preparations for the formal betrothal and announced his intention of submitting the marriage to the judgment of the States-General. Besides Montmorency, Antoine de Bourbon, as the first Prince of the Blood, opposed a connection which raised the Guises so close to the throne. But all objections ceased with the capture of Calais. The ceremony took place in April 1558. In the epithalamium which Ronsard read at the celebration allusion was made to the claims of Mary Stuart to the Crown of England. The Cardinal de Lorraine hinted that an expedition would be made the following year. So little had the Guises learned, in spite of Italy, in spite of Saint-Quentin, that they still regarded France as a base for their foreign flights.

- 9 -

The King himself was compelled to account to the nation. Ever since Saint-Quentin, he had revealed a new sense of responsibility, a growing recognition of realities, and a deepening determination to assume the management of public affairs himself; at the age of thirty-eight he matured suddenly. A remarkable evidence of this was his consent to summon the States-General. The States had not met for seventy years. Throughout that period the monarchy had been developing absolute power, and a body which represented, although for purposes of consultation only, the national will had been relegated to obscurity and sedulously ignored. Henri II was as much of an absolutist as his father; and only a supreme crisis could have induced him to summon the States. Financial ruin confronted him.

The economic disintegration which had been going on for so many years was rapidly approaching a crisis. The King had entertained four armies in Italy, besides the enormous expenses involved in diplomatic intrigue, the advances made to the Pope and the Duke of Ferrara, and the army raised by Montmorency for the massacre of Saint-Quentin. Such feats could be accomplished only by exhausting every expedient and straining every resource of the country; the tension could not be prolonged; the crash was bound to follow. Already in the spring of 1557 the roads were lined by faminous figures dragging their misery into the open. In Lyons and in Picardy it was a common thing to see them collapse on the streets. The people were bled white, and as the submerged mass gave away, the whole edifice began to creak. The convocation of the States-General represented a forced effort to avert ruin.

The King met the assembly with obvious embarrassment. The Queen surveyed the proceedings from a gallery and was initiated into a political fact with which she had not hitherto been familiar—that the States-General were something more than an obsolete form and that the absolute monarchy of France rested theoretically at least, and actually in times of financial crisis, on a substructure of national sovereignty. This fact dominated the meeting and weighed heavily on the mind of the King, whose speech was a lengthy apology for his policies, particularly with regard to Italy. His arguments were familiar and were not eased by the constraint of his delivery, but he impressed his hearers by the tone of singular deference with which he addressed them. He admitted that he was at the end of his resources, having spent, besides the normal taxes, all his personal means and mortgaged or sold the whole royal domain. The Cardinal de Lorraine, in the name of the clergy, and the orators of the nobility, the magistracy, and the merchants, assured the Throne of their unqualified support. The States worked for a week over the problem of raising money. The King had asked for six millions for the month of February. They promised him seven millions for the entire year.

But a prolonged period of peace was necessary for recuperation, and to secure an acceptable peace new military successes were needed. Hence new expenses, new expedients, or rather the old ones redisguised: the confiscation of a year's revenue from the Crown lands, from all municipal bonds, from the salaries of government officials, and the multiplication and sale of new offices. This venerable abuse had reached such proportions that even those who profited by it, the magistrates, financial officials, and bureaucratic personnel who had an interest in supporting a system which they exploited, complained against its excesses. The strain was consuming the resources of the country with alarming rapidity. Fifty years of fruitless wars had exhausted its normal resistance. Suppressed bitterness was seething in all classes, the restlessness of gathering revolt. In these unsettled conditions the return of the soldiers was a risk. The government apprehended both the prospect of peace and the prolongation of war. All the preliminary conditions of civil war were present, and only the foreign war hugging the frontiers held them in check. It was a significant fact that, eight months after Saint-Quentin, Paris was still so restless, unsettled, and subject to sudden panics that, to maintain order, a member of the royal family was obliged to reside there. When the King left for the front, this duty was entrusted to Catherine, who remained either at Saint-Germain-en-Laye or in the capital itself, virtually a hostage to the nation.

- 10 -

A nation so tense and depressed, hemmed in on all sides, could hardly avoid a collapse unless some outlet were found to drain away the growing pressure and divert its exasperation. A scapegoat was needed, and in that overcharged atmosphere it materialized. It is from this period that the religious troubles date.

Four days after the battle of Saint-Quentin, the police

broke up a nest of Parisian Protestants who had been meeting for some time, unmolested, in the rue Saint-Jacques. The raid was provoked and accompanied by popular violence. The arrested comprised "an infinite number of nobles, both men and women, and others of the small people"—exactly one hundred and twenty-nine, according to the police record. A lengthy trial ensued, dragging along for months, the months when the government was preoccupied with genuine dangers, and the popular excitement gradually subsided. But in February 1558, after the capture of Calais and the floating of a new loan, the King reprimanded the magistrates for their delay and exacted a vigorous prosecution.

Hitherto Henri had left the repression of heresy to the police as a routine function of law enforcement, and it was only in the hour of national defeat, when he began to assume a more active control of public affairs, that he recognized the nature and the extent of the problem which it presented. The progress it had made during the war years came to him as a shock. It was estimated that one-third of the kingdom was "infected." He was quick to suspect a connection between the diffusion of heresy and the misery and restlessness of his people. With the ideas involved he was not concerned; of an intelligence too limited to understand what he believed, he was incapable of the independence of judgment required to discriminate between one creed and another; in his eyes, as in those of his advisers, all the disaffected were heretics, and the number was alarming. In his prejudices he was at one with the people. The sore spots which favoured the spread of infection were many. The poverty of the people, which undermined their stability and made them accessible to innovations, was the greatest. But there were others, equally difficult to control. The foreign mercenaries, who were the chief defence of the kingdom—German *Landsknechte* and Swiss infantry—were predominantly Lutheran, and they fraternized freely with the French troops. The foreign money-lenders located in Lyons, because of their claims on the Crown, exacted special privileges, which included the right to profess what religion they pleased without interference from the Inquisition or the police. This opened the door to Geneva, for it had been the masterstroke of Calvin to sanctify capitalism. Confronted with the crucial question which had ruined the Church of Rome, Calvin made a single and supreme concession to the world and invested with the divine sanction the profit system under which Luther had groaned. It was a major decision, and it recruited a solid following for his sect amid that moneyed class with whom lay the growing power of the time. If the combination of these influences conspired to hamper the King, they also exacerbated his determination to stamp out heresy wherever he could control it. Nor did he lack incitement. Rome prompted him incessantly. For years he refused to revive the Inquisition in France on the grounds that "the States of my kingdom do not wish to receive, approve, or observe the Inquisition, and it would bring troubles, divisions, and other drawbacks with it, particularly in time of war." Then, suddenly, and in the midst of war, he demanded it.

The affair of the rue Saint-Jacques soon became a *cause célèbre*. The Calvinists of Geneva, rallying to the support of their co-religionists in France, persuaded the Swiss Cantons to intercede officially in their favour. The Protestants of Paris appealed for temporary toleration of those "who create no trouble or scandal and who do not dogmatize," until the convocation of a council to discuss and settle the issues at stake. Recognizing that, as members of an international movement, they laboured under the constant suspicion of civil disaffection, they did their utmost to propitiate the King. They were only too willing to magnify his patience into open-mindedness and to believe that, chastened, he would prove reasonable. No less than he, they realized that a crisis was approaching and that it was a vital necessity to forestall it, to make a stand, and to attempt to break through his antagonism. But how was he to be reached? Through the impenetrable hedge of influence, interests, and prejudices which surrounded him, who could penetrate? The problem called for two elements: an influential sponsor at Court and, behind the lines, a supreme commander with a consummate tactical grasp of the situation. The latter was lacking. Calvin was too inflexible and unworldly for political strategy, and he was committed to a policy of non-interference in political problems. Of his disciples none had this commanding capacity. The question of leadership resolved itself into finding a skillful sponsor at Court.

This problem was passed on to the Swiss ambassadors. They were advised to write to "the Queen, to Madame Marguerite, to the King of Navarre, and to Monsieur de Nevers," urging them to intercede with the King. Of these four the only one to answer the call was the King of Navarre. Antoine de Bourbon, standing so near to the throne in his own right as first Prince of the Blood, was at the same time removed from it by his marriage to a Calvinist, Jeanne d'Albret, the Queen of Navarre. Nevertheless, as his wife was the daughter of Marguerite de Navarre, the sister of François I, he was in a position sufficiently privileged to favour the Protestant cause, and the Protestants felt themselves entitled to look to him for leadership. But this position he acquired, like his kingdom, by marriage. He was dominated by his wife. He married her sympathies and underwent her convictions. His own were unstable. In March 1558 he joined the Reformed Church of Paris. This committed him to a step in favour of the victims of the rue Saint-Jacques, and he made it, but without conviction; and as for any hope of winning the King, that was out of the question, as he informed Jean Macar, the head of the Reformed Church in Paris. "One cannot change the opinions of the King, who is decidedly opposed to the restoration of the ancient doctrine."

In the meantime, Calvin had induced the Protestant Princes of Germany to intercede. This step, natural under the circumstances, might in normal conditions have been effective, for they were in a position to bring pressure to bear. The King was dependent upon them for military and financial aid, and by closing the passage of the Rhine they could cut off the recruits he was raising in Germany and Switzerland. But at this moment foreign intercession was a political blunder. It emphasized the international solidarity of the Protestant movement, and Henri bitterly resented what he conceived to be an effort to exploit his internal difficulties in favour of a disaffected minority of his subjects. "Do they want to uncrown me?" he exclaimed one day.

The one hope which sustained the victims of the rue

Saint-Jacques lay neither in the support of the King of
Navarre nor in the agitation of their co-religionists abroad.
Despite his desperate confusion, the King realized clearly
that the progress of heresy could not be checked so long
as the war continued; and when he left for the front in
the summer of 1558 it was with the determination to fight
for peace.

- 11 -

The undisputed supremacy enjoyed by the Guises in the
absence of the Constable rapidly undermined the popularity on which they had risen. After the capture of Calais
and the marriage of Mary Stuart, the Cardinal believed
himself above criticism. The great service which François
de Guise had rendered him was recognized by Henri, but
his gratitude was taxed by the demands made on it. The
marriage of the Dauphin was a royal reward. Three of the
Guises sat in the Council; a fourth was named to the fleet; a
fifth was promised the Governorship of Piedmont. When
François de Guise applied for the post of Grand Master,
which he occupied temporarily in the absence of the Constable, the King refused. Unrebuffed, Guise applied for its
reversion when it should fall vacant. The constant repetition
of such scenes wearied the King. "The days are like years,
while I am away from you," he wrote to Montmorency,
with whom he kept up a close, clandestine correspondence. "I beg you to believe, *mon compère,* that I have
had no joy since I saw you last, nor will have until God
lets me see you again and in good health. In the meanwhile, you may believe that nothing can part us but death,
and I should consider it a good one and die happy if only
I could see a good peace and the man whom I love and
honour most in the world."

Knowing the hold the Constable had over his master,
the Spanish made their first overtures for peace to him.
The advances began in March 1558, when the old man
received a message from Brussels inviting him to set down
in writing what terms he believed would be acceptable.
Impatient though he was to return to France, Montmorency declined to compromise himself. "I am too old,"
he replied, "to let myself be induced by younger men to

undertake a matter which, if I began it without the command of the King, would make me worthy of death." The matter was dropped. Rebuffed by the Constable, the Spanish reverted to regular diplomatic channels. A conference was arranged at Péronne, in the beginning of May, between Granvelle, the Bishop of Arras, and the Cardinal de Lorraine. No agreement was reached, but the meeting had a serious outcome. As he was about to leave, one of the Spanish diplomats said to the Cardinal: "You would do well to exhort your master to make peace. When he has looked carefully into the affairs of his State, he will realize that he has more reason to reach an agreement with King Philip than King Philip has with him." "Why?" asked the Cardinal. "Because the kingdom of France will soon be divided." The Cardinal scoffed at the idea; France was the most united country in the world. One of the principal ministers of Philip II thereupon offered to show him, within twenty-four hours, a letter which had fallen into the hands of his master, in which one of the most conspicuous gentlemen at the Court of France, writing to a Protestant Prince in Germany, informed him of the divisions in the kingdom, told him to be prepared for news within a few days, and bespoke his attention for what the French Protestants would do and say. Lorraine asked for the name of the writer. "François d'Andelot," he was told. Granvelle added that Coligny "was very much of a Lutheran, never heard Mass, and led a detestable life, so that, if these seigneurs de Châtillon do not alter their conduct, it will be necessary to ruin them completely." He knew his man. The Cardinal did not ask to see the letter. So swiftly did he post back to France that the horsemen sent after him with a fresh bid for peace failed to overtake him. He arrived at an opportune moment.

During his absence the Protestants of Paris organized a manifestation which created the effect of a deliberate provocation. Rumours were current that, if the conferences of Péronne failed, a military offensive against Geneva would follow, and the manifestation was organized by the Protestants as a demonstration of their numbers—a demonstration, nothing more, for the injunction of Calvin was binding: "The ashes of the pious are always fruitful, but violent deeds are useless and sterile." But it was a demonstration in an atmosphere already overcharged. On the evening of May 13, in the Pré-aux-Clercs, a promenade outside the city, a crowd of five or six thousand men, women, and children assembled to sing psalms and march in formation. On a May evening, under the first stars, in an atmosphere charged with the heretical licence of spring, who could say that the mysterious renewal of all things was unlawful? They sang, and the bystanders stood about listening. One of the psalms, "Thy Judgment, O Lord," seemed to refer to the King. The manifestation was quiet and orderly, but the crowd was accompanied by armed men, many of them mounted, and this caused some comment. Nevertheless, the Protestants were not molested. For seven evenings they renewed their meetings, amid a growing affluence of spectators, and with increasing confidence and enthusiasm. On the fourth evening they were joined by the King of Navarre. But it was not to their numbers, their patronage, their orderly conduct, or their armed escort, that they owed their immunity; it was to the nervousness of the authorities. Paris was full of soldiers leaving for the front, and the fear of provoking a riot compelled the magistrates to be prudent. But complaints and agitation were growing. The Pré-aux-Clercs adjoined the Sorbonne and the turbulent popular quarter of students and artisans, and the demonstration took place during the celebration of Catholic saints' days. On the third evening the authorities made their first move. The gates were closed, and not only the Protestants but a great number of spectators were forced to spend the night in the fields. In the morning ten thousand people presented themselves at the gates. Parlement was pressed to act. Many of its members were sympathetic to the movement, but they were overruled, and on the sixth day, May 18, an ordinance was published forbidding the people "to sing in numbers, at unseasonable hours, and in arms." The Protestant preachers enjoined their flock to obey, but the enthusiasm of their followers could no longer be controlled. On the final evening the meeting was held in defiance of the edict; the police intervened and were routed; a riot was narrowly averted.

When the Cardinal joined the Court, the King had just

learned of these developments. He was irritated, but he had taken no steps to check them. The conjunction of circumstances lent a singular gravity to the story which Lorraine brought from Péronne of an imminent rising of the Protestants. The complicity of Andelot appeared to be borne out by the reports of the Parisian police, which named him as one of the authors of the demonstration in the Pré-aux-Clercs. The King sent for him immediately.

The scene that ensued was more trying to the accuser than to the accused. Deeply alarmed by the denunciation of Andelot, Henri resented the necessity of prosecuting the nephew of the Constable. He conducted the examination himself, and conducted it scrupulously, with a forbearance which made him extremely sensitive to rebuff; and rebuff was all that he received in return for his determination to preserve a judicial temper. Questioned as to his correspondence with Coligny, Andelot admitted that he had sent him a book of piety, and he made a suggestion which, sensible as it seemed to him, struck the King as "a very strange proposal." "I beg you, Sire, leave my conscience alone and let me serve you with my body and my worldly goods, which are wholly yours." The King listened like a man who would gladly have been hard of hearing. "So," he said at last, "the report is true." The Cardinal de Lorraine, who was present, pressed the accused to reconsider, and drew an unexpected retort. "I am very certain of my doctrine, and you know more of it than you admit, Monsieur le Cardinal. I appeal to your conscience whether you have not favoured this holy doctrine." But there was no time to press it. Infuriated by this interruption, and with the haste of a slow-thinking man who suddenly remembers the crushing retort he meant to make, Henri attempted to put in his word. Pointing to the Order of Saint Michael which Andelot wore, he cried: "I did not give you that Order to be treated thus!" Andelot attempted a reply, and the King snatched up a dish and smashed it on the floor. The flying fragments narrowly missed the Dauphin, who was sitting beside him, taking his first lessons in statecraft. Andelot was immediately placed under arrest.

The news of the arrest created a sensation. It was the first time that the King had struck one of his captains, and all his colleagues felt the blow. The military reacted as a class, with professional *esprit de corps*, and Blaise de Montluc, one of the most ardent, refused at first to accept the position of colonel of infantry of which Andelot was stripped, and only assumed it under protest and in trust. No less aroused were the *noblesse*, of whom Montmorency and his family were the leaders, and who cherished their old feudal traditions of independence and regarded themselves as vassals, not subjects, of the King. The Protestants took heart. "Many soldiers and leaders are trembling and, if they are not actually mutinous, they are menacing," wrote Macar, the head of the Paris Church, to Calvin. Andelot was a convert of consequence, and his persecution dignified a movement whose victims had hitherto been drawn from the humbler classes of society. It appeared to them encouraging that, though measures were taken to prevent a repetition of the incidents at the Pré-aux-Clercs, the demonstrators were not seriously prosecuted by the government. So many evidences of discontent, indeed, were not without effect upon the King. He was the first to regret the arrest of Andelot and to blame the Guises for his predicament. With singular obtuseness, François de Guise chose this moment to ask for the post of colonel of infantry which Andelot had vacated and which was going begging among his friends.

Of all the consequences of the arrest, none was more painful for Henri than the necessity of breaking the news of it to the Constable. He did so with every precaution. In fact, three months later, after an ambiguous recantation which disappointed the Protestants, Andelot was released. But his uncle was not appeased. Infuriated by the attack on his nephew, and burning to settle it with the Guises, the old man, caged and vindictive, was no longer unapproachable when the Spanish again proposed to conduct their negotiations for peace through him. In August 1558, the *pourparlers* began through the medium of two prisoners of war [Montmorency and the Maréchal de Saint André] who were chafing, for reasons that were only remotely patriotic, to return to their country.

The Protestants were the first to foresee their future. After the Andelot affair, the King's hatred of heretics rose to a murderous fury. "I swear that if I can order my affairs,

I shall make the streets run with blood and reap the heads of this Lutheran rabble," he said to Montluc. Of these sentiments the Protestants were fully aware. A few months before, the one hope of the Protestants lay in peace; now they dreaded it as a calamity. In August, when the negotiations began, Macar wrote to Calvin: "If the King makes peace, and he will make it on any condition, he will turn all his rage upon us; he himself makes no secret of it today."

- 12 -

The negotiations for peace transferred the war from the field to the council-table; for six months the conflict which had divided Europe for fifty years was transformed into a diplomatic struggle of tenacious intensity in which both sides, equally exhausted, spent their flagging strength in a final effort to over-reach, undermine, and outwear the resistance one of the other. For both it was a race against imminent collapse. Philip was on the verge of bankruptcy; he could no longer raise a month's pay for his army, but he speculated on the weakness of his adversary and held out for terms that were ruinous to France. Only the exorbitance of these conditions prevented Henri II from yielding to the pressure of a formidable combination of influences—his longing for Montmorency, his resentment of the Guises, his dread of the Protestants, and the internal unrest in France. Certainly, whatever held him in check, it was not the influence of the Guises.

The King eluded their influence; Madame de Valentinois deserted them; the country was exasperated. They were compelled to swim with the tide, and their only hope lay in controlling the negotiations and postponing the day of reckoning. After the preliminary conversations initiated by the prisoners, formal plenipotentiaries were appointed to continue the discussion at Cercamps, in October 1558. The Cardinal de Lorraine was appointed, along with Montmorency and the Maréchal de Saint-André. Presently the Constable obtained leave to visit the King, who was in camp at Amiens, promising his captors that he would "work wonders." Word of his approach reached the King in the morning; he announced it to no one. Late in the afternoon he remarked, merely, that he was going to hunt hares; and as he swung into the saddle, he said that he might meet the Constable. The Duc de Guise observed that it was rather late in the day for such sport, but he was left standing, in a cloud of dust. A mile from camp, Henri and the three gentlemen who accompanied him met Montmorency, alone. They were struck by the change in his appearance. He had shrunk into "a little old man," loose-jawed, weak-eyed, hesitant, and decrepit, but that shrivelled and senile figure was the Peace, and they greeted him devoutly. The King dismounted and approached him, hat in hand, hugged him to his heart, and held him for several moments in his arms. Then, passing his arm over his shoulder—lightly, as he felt it sag—he led him on a tour of the trenches. The two figures wandered away, lost to the world. For two days and nights they were closely closeted. After passing lightly over his defeat at Saint-Quentin, the Constable traced it step by step to its origin. "Your Majesty may see today which of us was right, the Guises who urged war or I who advised you to persevere in the Truce of Vaucelles and to live in peace. Your Majesty has spent and ruined a world, and obtained nothing. I ask nothing of Your Majesty, as you know, nor have I ever asked anything for myself or my family, whereas these others behave differently; they have never ceased to solicit bounties, benefices, Cardinal dignities, all the honours of land and sea, and they aspire to yet loftier destinies, to kingdoms and similar things, and this is why they have advised Your Majesty to make war." The King did not merely listen complaisantly to this charge; he agreed with it and, opening his heart at last, poured out his own long-repressed complaints against the Guises. Because that meeting turned on personal questions as much as on public ones, the promise of the Constable that he would "work wonders" was not an idle boast. When he left, he was accompanied by the King and an escort of two thousand soldiers to the limits of the trenches, and on his arrival at Cercamps he was welcomed by the enemy with ostentatious respect. He brought with him a confidence so unbounded that it was equivalent to full powers.

The Spanish seized their advantage. Of the three French plenipotentiaries, two were malleable. On the Cardinal de

Lorraine fell the whole brunt of resisting, of manœuvring, of holding out for a patriotic peace.

The great stumbling-block was the question of Piedmont and Savoy. The restitution of his States to Philibert-Emmanuel of Savoy was an obligation which Charles V had assumed ever since their annexation by the French in 1536. Philip II had renewed it, but in his war-weariness he was prepared to settle this antiquated question in accordance with his own interests rather than with those of his protégé. For the French the cession of these provinces, so long incorporated into the country and so wisely governed that they had become naturalized, represented more than a humiliation, a dismemberment of the national territory. The sacrifice of Piedmont meant the abandonment of any possibility of returning to Italy; and in previous discussions of the question the Cardinal de Lorraine had insisted on compensation in Italy—a solution unacceptable, of course, to the Spanish, whose whole object was to close the peninsula for ever to the French. Another solution was now put forward—the marriage of Philibert-Emmanuel to the sister of Henri II, Marguerite de Berry. Montmorency favoured it, and it was welcomed by the King, who could be induced to surrender Savoy but not Piedmont. The discussion had reached this pass—a negotiable impasse—when the conference suspended its sessions for a week. The plenipotentiaries left for Paris. The presence of the Constable was urgently required there. It was another wonder-working visit; when Montmorency left Paris, the King could not conceal his elation. He considered the peace settled and already spoke of the sports and the feasts with which he was planning to celebrate the nuptials of his sister and the Duke of Savoy. The tailors were called into conference. These rejoicings were premature: no sooner did the Spanish catch wind of them than their demands rose. Besides Piedmont and Savoy, a host of latent claims were resurrected. The King was bitterly disappointed, but he ordered the negotiations to be broken off. He pledged his word to Guise and the Queen that he would not restore Piedmont. The inclusion of the Queen was remarked.

In the night a courier brought letters from the Constable

for the King and Madame de Valentinois. The favourite was now a firm ally of the Constable, and their alliance was about to be sealed by a family marriage. The King rose early, went hunting, and on his return paid his accustomed visit to her. Immediately afterwards, he summoned the Council and made an announcement which left everyone dumb with amazement. "After having better considered my situation," he said—and his manner had never been so commanding—"I have decided to make peace with King Philip by any means; therefore I consent to restore all my conquests in Luxembourg, in Montferrat, in Corsica, in Piedmont—with the exception of three, four, or five fortresses—and in Tuscany. But I mean to keep Calais." He concluded brusquely: "I have convoked you to inform you of my will and for no other reason." The Council was stupefied. A voice ventured to protest; he silenced it sharply. Never before had he manifested such imperious assurance. A courier was immediately dispatched to countermand his instructions of the previous evening, bearing a letter to the Constable written jointly, in alternating phrases, by the interlinked hands of Henri and Diane.

The Guises were stunned. But they retained their presence of mind. If the King was so easily reconquered and could be induced overnight to break his word, it might not be too late for another reversal. But who could make the attempt? With that untamed assurance which lurked under her habitual meekness, and of which only her familiars had fleeting glimpses, Catherine hurried to the King, cornered him, sank on her knees, and wrestling with his will from the knees up, "The Constable," she cried, "has done nothing but harm." "He has done nothing but good," Henri replied, bracing his knees, for she weighed. "All the harm has been done by those who advised me to break the Truce of Vaucelles." And, swinging on his heel, he left her.

The spectacle of the Queen, suddenly emerging from her marginal existence, pushing into the vortex of State affairs, and reaching for the bone of contention, was a startling reminder of her capacities for self-assertion. Who could say that they were extinct? Piedmont—who would have thought that it meant so much to her? To be sure, it closed the peninsula; and her protest was perhaps the last posthumous throb of her pangs for her country. Or perhaps the reverse: the dawn of a new life and her determination as a Frenchwoman to resist the dismemberment of France. Or perhaps she had merely been prompted by the Guises. A more personal version occurred to her intimates: it was not impossible that she had seized this opportunity to pit her influence against that of the ageing Diane. That evening Catherine was reading in her room when Madame de Valentinois entered and inquired "what she was reading that was so beautiful." It was not a question that required an answer, and the reply came as a complete shock. "I am reading," said the Queen, "the chronicles of France, and I find that from time to time, at every period, the affairs of Kings have been governed by strumpets." And she rose and left the room.

The question of Piedmont was settled.

Madame de Valentinois was fifty-nine, but a letter from the Constable begging her to induce the King to "accept the peace as it was offered" could still change the face of France. For the Guises nothing remained but to await the return of Montmorency and their dismissal. François de Guise anticipated it. When the King asked him what he thought of the decision, "I had rather lose my head than say that it is honourable or advantageous to Your Majesty," he replied. Perversely, he applied again for the reversion of the post of Grand Master and, when it was refused, tendered his resignation from the royal service. The King could not accept a resignation which was equivalent to a vote of censure. He was uneasy; the sacrifices he was making for peace were excessive; and his self-confidence was shaken.

The Cardinal de Lorraine, less impulsive than his brother, clung tenaciously to the few reservations which the King had made. Of one he was sure. "I shall lose my crown rather than return Calais," Henri had said. It was his conquest. On the problem of Piedmont his conscience was beginning to work, and in his dread of public opinion he insisted on retaining three or four strategic strongholds there. These were promising obstacles, and the Cardinal developed them for all they were worth. A master of dickering, he used all his skill to prolong the discussions, but at this juncture an untoward event occurred before which he threw up his hands. Mary Tudor died—of grief, it was said, over the loss of Calais—and the conference suspended its session as a sign of respect to the royal widower. Philip had already obtained all that he required. Calais no longer concerned him, now that he was no longer King of England, and Piedmont and the three or four fortresses he left to the Duke of Savoy to settle.

Philibert-Emmanuel, forced to shift for himself, proposed an arrangement to the Constable. He declined the offer of the Duke of Savoy, but he thanked him and assured him of his gratuitous support. A gentleman's agreement was reached, and when Montmorency left for France it was with the understanding that he was free, on the payment of a ransom of 200,000 crowns.

His homecoming was a triumphal progress. But the crowning glory only the King could bestow—that of a supreme intimacy. Only he could afford to waive ceremony. The delicate surprise which he arranged was to make no preparation at all. He was playing tennis, under the watchful eye of the Queen, when the Constable appeared. Flinging down his racket, he embraced him three times, and held him hard, listening to the beat of the old heart. Before this demonstration, the Queen retired rapidly Everyone else gave way, and every impediment faded at the approach of the viceroy; for such he was without question. The Cardinal de Lorraine sent him the Seal, resigned all his powers, and paid him the tribute of showing his pique. With his brother, he declined to attend the meetings of the Council and, when the King demurred, replied that he had no wish to "pass for the lackey of the Constable."

Montmorency was not the man to forgo his triumph, and he left nothing undone to irritate his rivals. Feeble in body, the vigour of his temper was unimpaired—brutal, arrogant, annoying. He flaunted his friendship with Madame de Valentinois, supping with her nightly, covering her with attentions, and barking out endearments as if he were reviewing a battalion. In the administration he was aggressive undoing whatever the Guises had done, naming Andelot to the government of Picardy with orders to break and reorganize all the measures taken by Guise, for the mere satisfaction of humiliating him.

The Guises were sustained in their extremity by that mania of grandeur which baffled the very reality that defeated it. Their faith in their star was never more buoyant than when it was under eclipse, and so long as they could dream, they were invulnerable; the danger lay in a lasting disillusionment. The effect upon François was painfully visible. Too morose to be stoical but too proud to scowl, he wore, unawares, a guarded air of hangdog gravity. The "great calf," as Montmorency had once called him, was now full-grown, wiry and tough, and he absorbed shocks easily.

They were saved by a marriage, which had long been held in reserve, between the young Duke Charles of Lorraine to Claude, the second daughter of the King. Henri was eager to propitiate them, the Constable raised no objection, and the ceremony was celebrated, with great pomp, at Notre Dame, on January 22, 1559.

- 13 -

In the first days of February 1559, the formal negotiations for peace were resumed at Cateau-Cambrésis. The period of royal mourning was over. Philip had spent it in lamenting his late consort and in courting her half-sister Elizabeth, but the new Queen of England was cold to his advances; and, convinced that his hopes of recovering the English Crown by marriage were vain, he made no attempt to support the English claims to Calais. Thus the last obstacle to the conclusion of a general peace was removed. By a separate treaty between France and England the question was adjusted. France was to retain Calais for eight years and, at the end of that period, if it was not restored, to pay an indemnity of 500,000 crowns for it. This treaty was signed on April 2. On the following day the Franco-Spanish Peace was proclaimed, with an effect that resounded throughout Europe.

Suddenly, the majestic structure of French imperialism, laboriously built up by fifty years of war, crumbled. By a stroke of the pen the conquests of two reigns were abandoned. The futile conclusion of that long and lame epic of national pride was that France forfeited close upon two hundred possessions—a fortune in foreign prestige, her life-savings in glory. Corsica reverted to Genoa; Montferrat to Mantua; Valenza to Spain; Siena and Montalcino to Florence; Savoy, Piedmont, Bresse, Bugey, Valromey, to the Duke of Savoy. Philibert-Emmanuel recovered his patrimony intact, with the exception of five garrisons, title to which was to be adjudicated by arbitration within three years. The verdict upon that peace—"the Prisoners' Peace" as it was commonly called—was wellnigh unanimous. France was stripped to the bone, reduced to her natural boundaries. But to an obstinate minority this was a blessing in disguise. The position of the country was not weaker but stronger, more compact, organic, and commensurate with its resources. The loss of its extrinsic possessions relieved it of ruinous obligations and entangling alliances, and the retreat to its natural frontiers—in which Calais and the three bishoprics, Metz, Toul, and Verdun, were now incorporated—meant a gain in independence and integrity. The validity of this view was impaired, however, by the circumstances which dictated that retreat. If the country had been at peace with itself, it could only have gained by coming to terms with the world; as it was, it was forced back by an overwhelming pressure on its own inner troubles; and it was for this reason, and not for the humiliation of national pride, that the peace of 1559 was a calamity.

By the Treaty of Cateau-Cambrésis, the long struggle for the hegemony of Europe ended in the abdication of France and the undisputed supremacy of Spain. Master of an empire whose preponderance was overwhelming, Philip was in a position to dominate the Continent and to dictate to his neighbour, and this fact was to have as prolonged and overpowering an effect on the internal history of that country as it had had on its external development. Outwardly despoiled, inwardly weakened, France was in a position to write under dictation the pathological history of a nation humiliated, turning on itself, groping for a scapegoat, and wreaking its defeat on a disaffected minority. The conditions were ripe, and the impulsion was given by Spain.

The Catholic King was in as desperate a situation as his neighbour. The negotiations for peace had been a race against ruin. On the eve of Saint-Quentin he was facing bankruptcy. The year 1557 was one of widespread depression, of financial panics, of universal collapse: the creakings of the economic machine announced one of those periodic breakdowns in which the entire Continent was involved. Two years later Europe was still wallowing in the trough and rocking in the long aftermath of the crisis. The panic of 1557-1559 produced a political crisis. Philip was cornered. A disturbance in the centre of the vast imperial system which he governed and by which he was ruled affected every nerve and artery of it. The Low Countries were groaning under the weight of an empire of which they were the support. The burden bore too heavily on the most productive member and the most exploited not to breed a spirit of rebellion. The excesses committed by the unpaid Spanish troops in the Netherlands quickened it, and the first sullen murmurs of revolt began to be heard, and though peace averted an immediate outburst, it came too late to quench them. The malady had progressed too far. Victor and vanquished were in the same situation. Both monarchs were threatened by domestic uprisings, and both reacted to that menace alike. What began as a financial panic became a political alarm and ended in a religious nightmare. Through that seething revolutionary ferment, formless as yet and latent and obscure, but steadily swelling, both discerned clearly the lurking influence, the leavening agent, of heresy. They were obsessed by a common fear. For years the Church had instilled into every sovereign mind the belief that heresy was synonymous with subversion and that, the bonds of religion once broken, every other rebellion must follow. In the brain of Philip, an autocrat, a bigot, and a bookworm, this prophylactic belief had lodged with the tenacity of mania. Henri, little inferior in bigotry, was no less susceptible to suggestion; and the dictation of the victor became a reflex in the mind of the vanquished.

The Treaty of Cateau-Cambrésis contained a significant clause: "The two princes, moved by the same zeal and sincere determination, have agreed to procure and to employ all their powers in behalf of the convocation and

celebration of a holy universal Council, so necessary for
the reformation of the Christian Church and its return to
true union and concord." Specifically, this meant the
abandonment by Henri of his opposition to the Council
of Trent; and practically it implied far more than the mild
diplomatic formula revealed. In private discussions, suggestions were advanced by both sides for a concerted
attempt to stamp out heresy. A plan was proposed by the
Cardinal de Lorraine to launch an attack upon Geneva;
but this was abandoned as impractical and impolitic at
the moment. What was feasible was a resolute effort on
the part of both sovereigns to repress an infection with
which, because of the propinquity of their dominions,
neither could deal effectively single-handed. On his return
to Paris, the Cardinal addressed Parlement and explained
the motive which had moved his master to make peace:
"The opinion of the King has been to make peace at any
price and on no matter what terms, in order to be free
to devote himself to the extermination and banishment
of the heresy of Calvin." What Parlement heard was a
policy; what it recorded was a psychological law—the
law by which a nation, profoundly humiliated, finds a
morbid relief in religious persecution. The Calvinists had
long foreseen their fate: peace was upon them. On all
sides, from Paris to Brussels, the mounting tide of revolutionary unrest was reaching a point where it could no
longer be dammed; it could only be diverted—a leaking
cataract—onto the doomed sect.

- 14 -

The preponderant influence of Philip II reached no less
deeply into the domestic life of the King. The Treaty of
Cateau-Cambrésis included a matrimonial alliance as well.
Rebuffed by the English Elizabeth, Philip turned to the
French and chose as his bride Elisabeth de Valois, the
eldest daughter of Henri II. Henri was delighted. Of all
the sacrifices which the Peace entailed, and he regarded
them all as meritorious acts of personal abnegation, the
surrender of his daughter was the most appealing to his
pride. That the marriage might some day serve Spain as
a lien on the French Crown was a possibility too remote

to be seriously considered. Henri was forty, in the full vigour of manhood, with many years of life before him, and surrounded by a prolific family. The advantages of the marriage, on the contrary, were all with France: over it hovered, on whirring wings, the dove of perpetual peace. The Spanish renamed their Queen *Isabella de la Paz*. Preparations for the ceremony were made on the most lavish and elaborate scale. Henri was disappointed to learn that the bridegroom would not be present. This, Philip explained, was contrary to custom. "Custom," he wrote, after mature consideration, "demanded that the Kings of Spain should not go to fetch their wives, but that their wives should be brought to them, in their own country and their own house." It was decided, therefore, that the marriage should take place by proxy in Paris, Philip to be represented by the Duke of Alva. Henri concealed his chagrin.

In celebration of the Peace, he cancelled the past, forgot all his grudges, forgave all his enemies. The Farnese, who had betrayed him so brazenly, recovered his favour and their benefices in France. The Duke of Ferrara, who had fleeced him so scandalously, found the welcome of a prodigal. Cosimo de' Medici, who hesitated to send an ambassador to France, was encouraged to do so. Henri's foes, in fact, fared better than his friends, for it was easier to forgive than to give. He would gladly have rewarded everyone by a distribution of honours and offices, but he had reigned thirteen years. His generosity, however, was not exhausted. He offered Philip the hand of his youngest daughter, Margot, for Don Carlos. To the Pope he gave his word to persecute the heretics—a word which the Nuncio passed around like a collection and which netted him the pledges of Madame de Valentinois, the Guises, and the Queen. What Henri could give, he gave with lavish freedom. Never had he appeared so carefree, so happy; everyone remarked on his benevolence, his optimism; he was like a man reborn; and indeed a new life was beginning, purged of all the errors of the old, and from which the Spanish clouds which had oppressed it ever since his childhood were lifting and revealing the radiant vista of universal peace ahead.

Preparations were pressed for the double marriage which

was to solemnize the Peace. The marriage of his daughter was to be followed by that of his sister, and the latter was regarded as the more important politically of the two—as in fact, "the key of universal concord and peace." The loss of Savoy and Piedmont, by closing the peninsula to France, liquidated those Italian adventures which had been for fifty years the bone of dissension with Spain. The marriage marked a return to realities, the end of dissipation and dreams, the dawn of maturity. It was a middle-aged event, and as such it carried some shocks. Philibert-Emmanuel was trying. His manner, when he came to Paris, was undiplomatic. Blunt, overbearing, beggarly, unaccustomed to Court life and contemptuous of it, he made no concessions, dressed and acted as if he were in camp, and made it abundantly clear how he had come by his nickname of *Tête-de-Fer*. He showed no enthusiasm for his bride, who was middle-aged and impatient to belong to him. Henri, however, repaired her undiplomatic errors of the heart: he wooed her soldier, tamed him, and won his friendship; and Philibert-Emmanuel, if he was not reconciled to the marriage, consented to behave as if he were a party to it.

An excellent example was set by the Queen. Bitterly as she had opposed the surrender of Piedmont, she accepted her defeat with a good grace and welcomed Philibert-Emmanuel with the friendliest overtures. Catherine knew when she was vanquished. For her the marriage was a personal crisis. Piedmont was lost, Italy was lost, the past was lost, and after her prolonged, clinging, and futile efforts to retain them, she yielded abruptly with the ready good sense of a woman of forty. Forty: it was a fact, and a hard one. For her too a new life was beginning—the second half of her allotted span, and if the first had been ineffectual, what could the next be but a blank? In the normal course of things she could look forward only to a natural decline; and the end and the beginning would be one—a life of illustrious nonentity. Piedmont had been her last stand, the final effort to play a political part, and her failure brought home the sharp realization that the one role which remained to her, the only one which life had allotted to her, was that of a *mère de famille*.

But even that role was slipping from her: the marriage

of Elisabeth was a startling reminder that already it belonged to the past. It was the third wedding within twelve months. Unawares, the years had stolen over her and her children were deserting her when she needed them most. The normal fate of mothers was abnormally difficult in her case, because the common glory of womanhood had been for her an acquired achievement. The mere fact that she had borne and raised children was a triumph, but how fugitive that achievement now seemed! Now, for the last time, she gathered her whole brood about her, and surveyed her complete accomplishment in life.

Of ten children, three had died, three no longer belonged to her, and all in varying degrees eluded her influence. The eldest might have been a changeling. The Dauphin François—the boy whom she conceived in defiance of nature—bore the marks of his forced birth. Physically feeble, he was mentally indolent, incapable of study or sustained effort of any sort. In appearance he favoured his mother at first, but gradually the look of his father emerged in the chubby little face and mastered it. The pulse of his father, as it beat more strongly in him, reduced itself to a single instinct—the family passion for the chase —which he pursued in spasmodic and exhausting gusts. He worshipped his father with an exclusive affection which Catherine was the last to begrudge him. If she felt any jealousy, it was only when another woman took possession of him. Mary Stuart absorbed him completely, fondling him as a playmate and enervating him as a wife, for she was herself a greensick, unhealthy girl, and she drew him so wholly into the sphere of the Guises that Catherine became an outsider. He was fifteen, and marriage, though it had not made a man of him, finally severed their intimacy; but her first-born had never belonged to her.

The two daughters who followed, Elisabeth and Claude —thirteen and twelve respectively—had also been frail at birth and had suffered a variety of illnesses throughout their childhood. As children they were vivacious and charming and became intelligent by virtue of sustaining each other rather than by mimicking their teachers. As they developed, they too began to show the traits of their father in a reserve which was certainly not relaxed by the

severe discipline to which they were submitted by their
mother. Like all the children, they stood in awe of her;
and what timid affection might lurk under their docile
demeanour she was not to know until she parted with
them; and it was too late then to claim it.

Louis, her fourth child, was only a memory. He died a
year after his birth.

In the four children who remained her influence was
happier. The dreadful heritage of infirmity was on the
wane, and the youngest were almost healthy. Charles,
however—her fifth child—was an exception. At the age
of nine he was already a nervous case, subject to uncontrollable fits of temper that abruptly belied his normal
docility and natural goodness. He was immoderately
addicted to violent exercises for which he was unfitted,
losing his breath after the least exertion, and straining
for a strength which constantly failed him. But in one
respect he was a promising contrast to his elder brother.
He had a quick and capable mind. Yet here too he was
capricious and unaccountable. Like François, he studied
unwillingly and only to please his mother, who was determined to develop an intelligence unfortunately so rare in
her brood. But for serious studies he had no aptitude; his
fancies were vagrant, he had a liking for poetry and a
gift for it. Perhaps it was the budding poet that baffled
his mother; perhaps it was his nerves; but in the bosom
of her family she created the impression that she disliked
Charles.

All her affection was reserved for the next-born. He was
the most robust of her boys, and the only one who was
completely unblemished. Edouard-Alexandre, or Henri,
as he was afterwards called, deserved the peculiar predi-
lection which she showed even in changing his name. This
was a matter in which she indulged one of her minor
superstitions, believing that among the many unfathomable influences which governed human life names might
also have a bearing not understood—but what forces
could ever be understood? At all events, she took her
precautions: her offspring needed them. Charles had begun
life as Charles-Maximilien; in his case she merely dropped
the suffix, but for Edouard-Alexandre, nothing was too
much and she bestowed on him the most cherished of all

names. Yet he resembled his father far less than he did
her. In him the Medici began to emerge and to blend
with the best features of the Valois. He had her beautiful
hands and complexion; he was exquisitely shaped; his
features were regular; and his nature was composed. He
was not fond of strenuous sport, though he was physically
fit; he was mentally able-bodied; he was born civilized—
an Italian birthright. The partiality which Catherine
showed him was rewarded by a complete devotion and
docility, but also by the self-sufficiency of a child who
soon understood that he was a unique, a privileged being.

Something of this generous endowment fell to Marguerite, her youngest daughter; but it was differently
rewarded. Sympathetic, impulsive, and warm-hearted, extremely pretty, precociously clever, she had too many
wanton gifts of body, mind, and heart not to inspire
a stern mother with misgivings for the future, and Catherine was exceptionally severe with her. What was so
endearing in the boy—beauty, charm, facile feeling, brilliant promise—was a danger in the girl; and the discipline
which Catherine imposed on her had the chilling effect of
discrimination and jealousy. The motives which prompted
it were naturally as mysterious to the child as they were
obscure to the mother, and both suffered from this misunderstanding. The little prejudice and estrangement
which resulted became fixed. Of her two most favoured
children Catherine sacrificed the real rarity. But there
could not be two of a kind—that was the first principle
of perfection—and her pride in Henri blinded her to the
capacities for affection of his sister. *La p'tite Margot,* as
the blindest could see, was made for love, but she had her
pride, too. Rebuffed by her mother, she turned to her
brothers and, when they failed her, snuggled up to anyone who would have her. She was put to play with two
cousins—Henri de Navarre and Henri de Guise—and
when she was asked why she preferred the former, she
replied that what she disliked in the little Guise was his
pride. She recognized and avoided it instinctively. Long
familiarity with its effects on her mother gave her a
precocious discernment, and the little princess never
allowed her pride to interfere with her happiness. In time
she came to understand that the pride of her mother, so

long mortified, had become her vulnerable point, her
besetting weakness; and it was characteristic that, when
she saw through her, it was with no loss of sympathy or
respect. She had much to put up with in the chastening
years of her childhood: not only a drastic discipline, but
frequent outbursts of temper, scoldings, and beatings,
when her mother, as she afterwards wrote, *"jetait feu et
disait tout ce qu'une colère outrée et démesurée peut jeter
dehors."* But neither these dragonings nor the more galling
experience of unbecoming costumes and tight headdresses,
which made her look plain and brattish—a most misleading impression—could alter her disposition. She responded,
like a kitten, to the lightest caress, and a word of praise
from her mother filled her with bliss. Then the plump
little person swung proudly on her hips and the bland
little face beamed with arch gaiety. A hint of encouragement, and her clinging affection revived. But fear and
love—the sentiments demanded by the Deity—were difficult for Margot to reconcile in her relations with anyone
less than the Supreme Being; and the only result was that
of the most tender of her children Catherine made the
most frivolous.

If there could not be two of a kind, much less could
there be three: mediocrity was the lot and indifference
the portion of the last of her sons. Ercole was distinguished
only by his good health, and even this could not save him
from a serious setback which he received early in life.
A violent attack of smallpox, though he survived it, dis-
figured his good looks, threatened the sight of one eye, and
left him not only abnormally sensitive to his appearance
but suspicious of slights, neglect, or derision; he was
spared none of these by his brothers and sisters, and from
his mother he received so little consolation that he could
only repay her indifference with his own. Named after
the Duke of Ferrara, he subsequently assumed the alias
of François, without sensibly improving his position: he
cut so negligible a figure that he was commonly referred
to by his title, Alençon.

Two twins, Victoire and Jeanne, were mere names. They
died, one at birth, the other six weeks after.

Such was her achievement: the reckless increase,
throughout a decade, of intimate strangers who called her

mother. She had been a good one, to the best of her ability, and if in return she had reaped duty rather than devotion, it was not due entirely to her stern discipline. That discipline had been aggravated by the fact that she was an unloved wife. It was her radical weakness that she shared not only her husband but her children with an interloper. Diane presided over their birth, their education, their illness, their daily lives, and they were always aware of an alien influence supplementing her own. If it was not a weaning influence, it was worse: it weakened her natural authority by supporting it. Diane made her not merely a nominal wife but a nominal mother. Even the pet names which Catherine bestowed on her children—the little names which she and the King invented together—were divulged and became common property. There could be no privacy where there was always a third person present; the third person made everything formal. It was the penalty of the compromise to which she submitted in her domestic life that her relations with her children became as impersonal as those of a step-mother. The severity which she visited upon them was a futile attempt to rivet her hold on them; and the result was to make their relations more and more formal. The habit hardened as they grew older, and it was only when she lost them that she felt that they belonged to her. She possessed them, as she possessed everything, in the past, the embalming past, the everlasting past, the last refuge of the defeated; secret, secure, and safekeeping.

At the moment of parting, there was, however, a fleeting illusion of intimacy. The child whom she was losing was always the one whom she loved most: it had been François, it had been Claude, and now it was Elisabeth. But Elisabeth was indeed her favourite daughter—a serious, docile girl on whom she relied, the only one to whom she opened her heart and of whom she made a confidante. In time they might have become friends, but for this marriage. The marriage represented a sensible sacrifice on her part to the cause of peace, but she faced it cheerfully. Her one disappointment seemed to be that she would not see the bridegroom and, though that was obviously impossible, she nursed an ambition to meet Philip which persisted for years. She was pleased to learn that he had hung a portrait of Elisabeth in his bedchamber; she was easily pleased, having found it the best way to please others. She went to great expense to shine at the wedding, ordering three hundred lengths of gold and silver cloth from Italy for her gowns; spending money was always a relief to her, and the cheapest way to cheat care.

But the marriage had its compensations. A match had recently been proposed between a daughter of Cosimo de' Medici and a son of the Duke of Ferrara, and Anna de Guise, when she heard of it, was outraged. "My heart," she protested, "cannot bear to have such a girl for my elder sister and for my allies tradespeople who are not worthy to call themselves our servants." The old prejudice was undying; it cropped up again and again; and time, which cures everything but feminine malice, could not obliterate it. While there was a woman left to nurse it, it was a foregone conclusion that Catherine would suffer from a bias which women were as prone to magnify as time was to mitigate it. It was a mathematical certainty that the whole could be no greater than its meanest part. But now, by the marriage of Elisabeth to the master of the world, the stigma was at last to be brilliantly obliterated. Whatever she lost by it, she gained the greatest of gifts—an honourable oblivion. She could afford, after June 22, 1559, to retire and to be effaced, forgotten, and perpetuated in her progeny.

- 15 -

The Peace, which reconciled so many losers to their destinies, reconciled even the Guises to theirs. But they rallied to it only because it was a Catholic Peace and the religious crusade proposed by Philip offered them a new outlet for their energies and a sacred cause on which to rebuild their career. The abrupt check which they suffered by the triumph of the peace party was followed by something like a religious conversion. Not that their orthodoxy had ever been open to doubt, but it had lain dormant. The Cardinal de Lorraine was known to entertain liberal opinions in private, to read the Lutheran writers, and to favour the Confession of Augsburg. The Pope complained of his laxity in the prosecution of heretics, particularly of

Andelot. The effect of these proddings, combined with the promptings of an ambition which, dammed and stagnant, filled the mind of Charles de Guise with rankling fever, was evident in the zeal with which, at the conferences of Cateau-Cambrésis, he seconded the Catholic crusade and the vigour with which, on his return, he launched the reaction and capitalized it. When he appeared before Parlement to announce the initiation of a campaign against heresy, it was as the champion of a movement of which he realized the enormous political backing and which it would have been culpable negligence to allow another to lead. And if anything further was needed to rouse him, it was the reception which he received from Parlement.

That reception was rousing precisely because it was so lukewarm as to confirm the rumours long current that Parlement was itself deeply infected. For years the Jesuits had drilled this suspicion into his ears. Though they had overcome the hostility of the Sorbonne, they still found themselves balked by the stubborn anti-Roman spirit of the other great stronghold of Gallicanism, and their existence in France was jeopardized by the refusal of Parlement, in spite of the pressure of the Crown, to register their letters of naturalization. Again and again they had complained to their Protector that the laxity of the magistrates was responsible for the spread of heresy and would defeat any vigorous prosecution of it. The facts now spoke for themselves. Coming so close on the Andelot affair, which revealed the infiltration of heresy among the upper classes, the contamination of the great organ of the professional middle class was an alarming symptom that a movement which had begun among the people was rapidly gaining the whole body of society. According to the statistics which the Cardinal supplied to the Spaniards at Cateau-Cambrésis, two-thirds of the kingdom was infected. A year before, the ratio had been one-third. The subversion of States induced by a change in religion was common talk in Paris. "All Paris and even all France is full of Lutherans; unless the King acts promptly, his kingdom will be worse than Germany"—"If the King does not form a good army to chastise this accursed sect, he risks losing his crown"—such opinions were everywhere, large generalizations which had become small talk, and the danger of such talk was obvious: it domesticated the idea of revolution and made it familiar: what so readily passed for a fact was always apt to become one. No responsible minister could ignore it; and Charles de Guise was all the more responsible for not being in office. To save the Crown, which his chimerical policies had brought to the brink of ruin, was an act of reparation that he was sincerely determined to accomplish.

On June 2, 1559, the long-impending campaign against the heretics was launched by the King in letters-patent to his officials, announcing a purge and warning them against any laxity in its execution. This left the Protestants no choice but rebellion or flight. That it was no idle menace was proved within a week. The situation in Parlement could not be ignored: a majority had long opposed the edicts of persecution, and the criminal court consistently evaded or tempered their execution. The Cardinal de Lorraine obtained the names of the ringleaders and persuaded the King to preside at an investigation. On June 10, the King attended in force the *mercuriale,* or Wednesday session, of Parlement. The event was of major significance. The Wednesday sessions were devoted to private discussions among the members of public and professional questions, and in invading their privacy the King was violating the *esprit de corps* and a recognized right of the Parlement.

It was an act of arbitrary authority exercised over a body which was accustomed to regard itself as, not the acolyte, but the counsellor of the Crown, and which, by its sympathetic attitude toward heresy, lent a legal colour to a movement which affected a growing majority of the nation and which the King had prejudged and declared to be subversive. The result of a clash could only be to pave the way for civil war and to legitimize it. The magistrates themselves had no doubt that the King had come to cow them. The proceedings opened with a vehement harangue by the Cardinal de Lorraine, after which the assembly was invited to continue its discussions frankly and fearlessly. Five of the leading liberals accepted this challenge to declare themselves, and Henri listened with growing indignation to a series of speeches which were,

in effect, an attack on the policies of the Crown. The
climax came when Louis Dufaur, dwelling on the disorder
of the country and tracing it to the abuses of the Church,
invited the King not to provoke the retort which King
Ahab drew from the prophet of old: "It is thou that
troublest Israel." The next speaker, Anne du Bourg, continued the arraignment and denounced the corruption of
the Court, carrying the personal allusion yet further and
reflecting on the superstitious practices of the Queen and
the immorality of Madame de Valentinois in a vigorous
diatribe against "the various superstitions, astrology, sor-
cery, and magic, not to mention the blasphemies, adul-
teries, and horrible debaucheries and perjuries, crimes
which are committed with impunity in the face of Heaven,
while the blasphemers strain every nerve to invent the
most atrocious tortures for the destruction of human be-
ings whose only crime is to demand a salutary reform."
The temerity of the speakers left their hearers breathless,
and it was noted that even the Cardinal de Lorraine made
no attempt to reply. The only possible retort was made
by the King. Rising stiffly, he consulted the clerics who
accompanied him and ordered the arrest of the speakers.
Four days later he charged the magistrates to deal with
the accused with the utmost rigour of the law. The resistance of Parlement was broken; a muffled *coup d'état* had
been accomplished. But du Bourg, against whom the King
was particularly bitter, vowing to see him burn, employed
all the resources of a vast legal skill to defend himself
from a fate which he knew to be sealed but to which he
was determined to lend the notoriety of a test case.

In this charge Henri was actuated by his besetting
obsession: the confusion of heresy and sedition was becoming a mania with him. An ironic comment was supplied
on this *idée fixe* by an event which occurred two weeks
before the famous *mercuriale* of June 10. On May 25,
the Synod of the Protestant Church of Paris met in a
house in the faubourg Saint-Jacques to organize a movement which for sixty years had been unsystematic and
helpless. This meeting was of no less significance than
the *mercuriale* and might have caused the authorities some
legitimate concern. The constitution which it laid down
was that of an ecclesiastical republic. Republican forms,

popular control, principles of self-determination, a democratic spirit, were the features of a brotherhood which
the pressure of events was steadily transforming into a
party. What was to prevent its members from attempting,
in self-defence, to translate the form and the spirit of a
religious republic into its political counterpart? What indeed save the will of its founder? But this ecclesiastical
republic was ruled by an autocrat; and Calvin had laid
down as the first of his principles the duty of submission
to the will of God and the right of the authorities to
persecute. The peace which Henri was risking so much
to preserve was foreordained from the beginning by the
father of predestination. But Henri, more than most
rulers, was destined to wander always in a world of seeming, a prey to appearances, apprehensions, and prejudices.

- 16 -

So, in abrupt alternations of splendour and gloom, the
month of June passed. On the fifteenth, Alva arrived,
accompanied by the Prince of Orange and Count Egmont,
to celebrate the marriage by proxy. Jousts, banquets,
concerts, plays, succeeded one another, and in the intervals
there were attempts to talk business. The King approached
Alva with a proposal to attack Geneva, but it was received
with a reserve as chilling as the face which Alva brought
to the marriage. With the Prince of Orange, Henri fared
no better. Assuming that he was in the confidence of his
master, Henri unwittingly revealed to him the plans of
Philip against the Flemish heretics—information which
the Prince passed on to his countrymen and which fore-
armed them. Amid these diplomatic accompaniments—
dismal arpeggios to the wedding march—the marriage of
Elisabeth was celebrated on June 22. On June 28, the
marriage contract of Marguerite de France and the Duke
of Savoy was signed. On the same day began a three-day
tournament which brought to a close the long antiphony
of splendour and gloom, of mating and manslaughter,
which marked that month of June.

The lists had been set up in the rue Saint-Antoine, adjoining the Palais des Tournelles and near enough to the
dungeons of the Châtelet for du Bourg and his fellow-

prisoners to hear the music, the shouts, and the din which accompanied the jousts. It was their last reprieve. "A truce seems to have been accorded to us until the tenth of July, the day of the marriage of Savoy," wrote Macar, the head of the Protestant Church, to Calvin. "Then the King will turn on us in full force; he has a long list of names drawn from all classes of society. He will not attack us all at once, but, breaking us one by one, will gradually purge France of what he calls the Lutheran sect." But the hautboy and clarion carried no sinister undertone, the shock of arms and wheel of horses no premonition of slaughter, for the spectators in the rue Saint-Antoine. On the first two days of the tournament the King distinguished himself by his prowess and skill. He was in peerless form and when, on the third, he failed to unseat Montgomery, the Captain of his Scottish Guard, who was his antagonist, he was so piqued as a sportsman that he insisted on interrupting the schedule and running an additional course. Montgomery was reluctant, but his master would take no denial. Twice they circled the lists, met, and missed one another; in the third encounter they splintered their lances; but Montgomery, in passing, failed to drop his in time, and the jagged point pierced the King's visor and entered his eye. He reeled, clutched the pommel of his saddle, and sagged. There was a shriek from the Queen, the tribunes rose in an uproar, and the grooms, running forward, caught him as he was about to fall. The visor was raised, and his face oozed. As Henri pitched forward, the Dauphin, his wife, and Catherine fainted. Henri was carried into the Tournelles. The dismal honour of this duty brought the Constable and the Guises together; the Constable seized one arm, the Cardinal and his brother the other, and over the drooping body they found themselves marching in step at last. As they reached the stairs, the King revived and insisted on regaining his feet. He dragged himself up, groped for the bed, climbed into it as if it were a saddle, and pitched forward again. But this brief rally deceived no one. He was no sooner on his back than he smuggled his arms from the sheets, folded them on his chest, and began to pray. The physicians expected a fatal issue at any moment. Nevertheless, his constitution was mighty, like his courage. He had the strength, as well as the will, to endure without flinching the extraction of five splinters from his temple and eye, and only once did the surgeons rip an agonized cry from him.

About his bed there now gathered, in a jealously shifting vigil, all those whose lives hung on the rise and fall of his breast. The first night was watched by the Queen, the Cardinal de Lorraine, and the Duke of Savoy; at three in the morning they were relieved by the Duc de Guise and one of his relatives. On the next day, however, Montmorency asserted his rights and took his place among them.

On the third day the King showed signs of improvement. He was conscious, murmured, took nourishment, slept a great deal, and appeared to be holding his own. He asked for Montgomery and, on being told that he had fled Paris, he absolved him from all blame. "He must be brought back at all costs," he said, closing his eye and speaking with firmness. "What has he to fear? I know that this accident happened not through his fault but by an unlucky chance." As the day wore on, however, his sufferings increased. The physicians, quailing before the agony they inflicted, neglected to cleanse the wound, and dancing pains made the patient cry out, again and again, in spite of himself. At this turn the watchers lost their heads. The Guises spoke of impeaching the Constable, on the pretext that he had neglected to fasten the King's visor. But the Constable was beyond their reach. Leaving the sickroom, he roamed through the palace like a lost soul, mumbling to himself, dogging the physicians, and insisting that they explain the wound to him on a corpse he had procured for the purpose, as if he expected to discover a cure himself. He recalled the premonitions of disaster which had overtaken the Queen, the warning she had received from her astrologer—a warning which he impressed on the King, but which the King dismissed with a commonplace on death, the lot of all men.

On the fourth and fifth days Henri continued to gain. Vesalius, the physician of Philip II, arrived from Brussels and was confident that he could save the patient. In Brussels the news of the accident had caused consternation, and the possibility of the King's death was regarded as a fatal blow to the Catholic cause. The same anxiety was expressed by the Nuncio in France. The Protestants awaited the outcome no less tensely. "The judgments of God," wrote Calvin to a correspondent in Paris, "are a profound abyss which are sometimes illuminated by a light more brilliant than that of the sun. The terrible tempest of persecution which has upset this whole kingdom, sparing neither hamlet nor town, will perhaps be allayed by this blow of Providence." But it was a forlorn hope. As the King revived, his piety quickened. He dictated a letter for the Pope in which, with both the solemnity of a testament and the confidence of recovery, he renewed his pledge to "punish, chastise, and extirpate those who imitate these new doctrines, sparing none, of no matter what quality or dignity; so that I shall purge my kingdom if it is humanly possible." What could death teach a man who had learned so little of life? It was the final triumph of his unimaginative mind that he managed to make of death itself a poor, impotent, unimpressive, everyday matter. Heroes and philosophers have done no more, and martyrs much less. As if this were all that he had been spared for, he began to sink rapidly. Oblivion lapped up his faculties, only pain kept him alive, and an acute disintegration. An abscess formed in his brain, obliterating its besetting obsession. As hope for the sovereign waned, anxiety centred on his heir. The Dauphin, who had fainted twice when he visited his father, was confined to his bed, and his mother had transferred her vigil to him. Ruin brooded over the King; the end was approaching, no one was ready; the State was at a standstill, confused, disorganized; and a sickening sense of danger and disorder emanated from the royal bedchamber.

As if in response to this pressure, the labouring body quickened again. On the eighth day the King roused himself and, in an interval of twilight lucidity, called for the Dauphin and dictated to him a letter for the French ambassador in Brussels, imploring Philip to protect his country and his son after his death. He authorized in advance all the pretensions of Spain which he had spent his life in combating. After willing this trust, he relapsed, and was shaken by long fitful spasms of agony. Long fitful spasms of agony also swept over his heir. The wretched lad, as often as he realized the truth, threshed about helplessly, beating his head against the walls and crying: "My God, how can I live if my father dies?" Impressionable and undeveloped, he was suddenly forced by this crisis into manhood. The next morning the King sent for him again to bestow his supreme benediction. Groping for his hand, he felt him slowly with impalpable fingers. "My son," he said, deep in his bandages, "you are about to lose your father but not his blessing. I pray God that he make you happier than I have been." In that moment of supreme intimacy Henri spoke as man to man, and the bandages seemed to break from his heart, and the cere-cloth to slip from his soul, in an unconscious confession that revealed at last his lifelong secret. No, he had never been happy. Despite his goodness, his correctness, his high sense of duty, his conscientious discharge of it according to his lights, he had missed the one compensation of mediocrity. From his long incurious exploration of life he brought back, like the most far-seeking, only the miserable and baffling mystery of being.

During that night the marriage of Marguerite de France and the Duke of Savoy was quietly performed in the apartments of the new Queen of Spain. Catherine did not attend it, being confined to her bed, on the verge of collapse. But she still guarded the bedchamber of the King. "Madame la Seneschale," it was noted, "has not entered it since the day of the wound, for fear of being expelled by the Queen."

On July 10 the long strain ended. In the morning an emissary arrived from Brussels with a message which he delivered to the Royal Council. Philip II pledged himself to protect the Dauphin if any trouble menaced the Crown. Everyone breathed easier. A few hours later Henri II expired.

CHAPTER IV

The Reign of

FRANÇOIS II

- 1 -

The heritage left by Henri II was chaotic and clouded, but within a few minutes of his passing the substantial shapes of the new reign began to emerge. The gates of the Tournelles opened, and the waiting crowd saw a group advancing whose composition precisely defined the redistribution of power. The heir to the throne, his wife, his mother, his brothers and sisters, appeared, shepherded by the Cardinal de Lorraine and the Duc de Guise, who carried the youngest of the royal children in their arms. The Constable was conspicuous by his absence. It was an elopement for power. The coaches drew up and, as the party entered them, it was noticed that Catherine insisted on yielding the place of honour to the new Queen. The whips cracked and the coaches lumbered away to the Louvre.

A drive from the Tournelles to the Louvre—no one believed that the transition would be accomplished so

easily. The rumours of revolution, the unrest in the country, the factions at Court—all promised trouble, and
nothing was more calculated to precipitate it than the
step which the Guises had taken. The new King, who
had been half out of his mind during his father's illness,
was obviously incapable of acting on his own initiative:
what had occurred was less an elopement than an abduction. The presence of Catherine, and her mournful pas-
sivity, merely sanctioned the arrangements which the
Guises had already made. François II was fifteen, he had
attained his legal majority, but he was in effect a minor;
his youth, his inexperience, and the feebleness of his
faculties called for a Regency; and it was this function
which his uncles were, in fact, exercising. That they
recognized the weakness of their title was evident in the
formal partnership which they had established with Catherine: they were bolstering their claims with hers. The
situation, however, was by no means clear. The claims
of a Queen-Mother to the Regency were themselves open
to dispute. This right belonged, by tradition, to the
Bourbons as the Princes of the Blood. The Bourbons were
absent from Paris. The King of Navarre, the first Prince
of the Blood, was at Nérac.

Throughout the first day the Constable remained at the
Tournelles, guarding his master's body. On the next day
he came to the Louvre, with a large escort, to take the
King's orders for the funeral and to offer him his services
and those of his family. The King received him nervously,
informed him that he had entrusted the whole conduct
of affairs to the Guises, and added a few remarks on his
age, his fatigue, and his need of rest. The old man digested
them calmly, betraying their effect only in the brevity of
his reply. After supper he visited the Queen-Mother and
offered her the only thing of which no calamity could
ever bereave her—a little judicious advice. It was more
than she could bear. Exhausted with grief and fatigue,
she broke down, sobbed, and dismissed him with a promise that he would not be deprived of his estates or his
prerogatives. Satisfied that his advice was valued, he left
her, deeply sensible of the service he had rendered her
and too preoccupied by it to express any gratitude for
that which she offered him. For a few days longer he

lingered in Paris. When he finally decided to leave, it was
with an escort of such impressive proportions that it
resembled a private army.

The other storm-centre remained quiet. The Bourbons
were propitiated. A friendly message was sent by the
Guises to the King of Navarre, assuring him that when he
came to Court they would meet him in person, as a sign
of respect. His younger brother, the Prince de Condé,
was promised the government of Picardy and invited,
with his cousin the Prince de la Roche-sur-Yon, to join the
Council. For the moment the dreaded disputes were
averted: all was conciliation, submission, and order. For
this unlooked-for result the influence of the Queen-Mother
was largely responsible. Unfortunate, friendless, self-effac-
ing, the widow with her children was a figure to inspire
sympathy and command respect; and the Guises were the
first to appreciate the pathos of her situation and to exploit
it. The semblance of power satisfied her, it was all that
she expected or had ever enjoyed, and in conceding it
the Guises gained much and risked little. She was too
inexperienced, too unambitious, and too stunned to claim
more.

Above all, she was too stunned. Visitors found her sunk
in settled apathy. When she spoke, it was in a tone so
low that they had to strain to catch it. They could only
fathom her silence and divine by sympathy or supply by
rote what she was unable to communicate. But what no
words could impart, her flesh did: it was cold and sickening to the touch, with the clamminess peculiar to mourning women, and to hold her limp hand was to feel her numb
heart and to weigh, as it were palpably, the mortal insipid-
ity of her dazed eyes and her blank heavy face. "The
Queen is so wept out," as one of her friends expressed it,
"that she brings tears to our eyes." But it was wasted
sympathy. Her barren finality defeated them, and they
worked on her feelings without reviving her.

So much insensibility worried her friends. A breakdown
would have been a relief. Had her spirit been tense, it
must have snapped; but it merely collapsed, and the
compliance of those on whom she leaned cushioned it. "I
believe," Mary Stuart noted, "that if the King her son were
not so obedient that he does nothing but what she desires,

she would soon die, which would be the greatest misfortune that could happen to this poor country and to all
of us." This was a remarkable tribute from the younger
woman; but the misery of the older one subdued all her
critics. It tamed even the one satisfaction which everyone
expected her to take from her ruin.

Madame de Valentinois was dismissed from Court and
forced to relinquish the Crown jewels, but she was not
further molested. She retained all her properties, with the
single exception of Chenonceaux, which Catherine acquired in exchange for her own château of Chaumont.
Nothing was more eloquent of [Catherine's] grief than this
half-hearted revenge. The woman who had cheated her
of love had swindled her also of hate. Everything wears
out, even hatred, bitterness, jealousy: for years she had
waited, and she had waited too long: the day of reckoning had come, and she was herself too crushed by it to
care.

As the days passed and lengthened into weeks, the
situation settled and cleared. The expected troubles failed
to materialize. The only revolution which the world saw
was a revolution of the palace.

- 2 -

But the test was yet to come. The situation which confronted the Guises on their arrival in power was a
withering comment on the vanity of ambition. Henri II
had died just in time to elude the consequences of thirteen
years of prodigality, disorder, and corruption. The mere
enumeration of the liabilities of the government occupied
the first two weeks of the new reign, and their solution
compromised it at the start. No minister who accepted
these responsibilities could hope to escape with his reputation unscathed. Montmorency, in resigning power to his
rivals without a struggle, performed the shrewdest act of
his political life. It was the deadliest service he could
render them. It required an inordinate courage or an
inordinate blindness to claim so crushing a heritage, and
whichever motive impelled the Guises, one thing was
clear: the realization of their ambition was its retribution,
and they were fated to know the common tragedy of

those for whom the fulfilment, and not the frustration, of desire spells their doom.

Between them they divided the State, François de Guise assuming the War Office, and the Cardinal de Lorraine the direction of internal affairs and the finances. Both were controlled by the financial situation. It required the abandonment of all military activity, and François de Guise, in entering the War Office, found himself to all intents and purposes retired. The burden of power fell upon his brother, and he in turn was governed by a financial breakdown which called for heroic measures. After negotiating with the bankers and reducing the interest from 16 to 8.3 percent, he undertook a sweeping and drastic plan of retrenchments, which included the suppression of a credit of one hundred thousand livres for the postal service, the reduction of the army, the suspension of pensions to the great lords, of salaries to the magistrates, of accounts to the Court traders, and the revocation of all gratuitous grants made from the royal domain during the preceding reigns. For these drastic measures, affecting as they did so many interests, he paid with his popularity, and for a man who had spent his life in courting goodwill, it was a stiff price; but he paid it proudly. He was sustained by a conscious sense of duty, a lofty pride, and a contempt for misunderstanding as serene as his brother's scorn for physical pain. Yet he suffered. A conscious sense of rectitude was small compensation for his friendliness and it had a chilling effect on a nature not overly warm or innately genial. For his superiority he paid with his humanity, and it was a sacrifice he could ill afford. The role was heroic, but he lacked the stature for it; where a great nature would have been stimulated by tragic stress, an ordinary one could only be withered and hardened by it. The martyr as statesman, the saint as financier, made a dangerous combination.

In this difficult situation the Guises conducted themselves with exemplary caution. Though the financial condition of the Crown forbade the thought of any further foreign adventure, there was one enterprise to which the Crown was already committed and which could not be abandoned. This was the support of Marie de Guise, as Regent of Scotland, against the Protestant insurgents in a kingdom which the marriage of Mary Stuart had united to France. The preparations which were made for this purpose—mercenaries recruited in Germany, ships outfitted in the Channel—were viewed with misgivings in England and interpreted as the preliminaries to an attack upon England itself. Under these circumstances, a peculiar weight attached to the question of whether or not the claims of Mary Stuart to the English Crown should be included in the style assumed by the new sovereigns. The English ambassador was instructed to withhold his credentials until the question was settled. It was finally resolved by a compromise, the questionable claims being eliminated from the public documents and armorial bearings of François II and confined to those of his consort.

The prospect of friction with a foreign power was manna to the malcontents and it was about this question that the first forms of domestic danger gathered. When the policy was debated in Council, the Prince de Condé advised adjourning its decisions until the arrival of his brother, the King of Navarre. He reassured the British ambassador, and informed all his colleagues, that the decisions of the government were not binding, the government itself being merely provisional. At the same time he wrote to the King of Navarre to hasten his arrival at Court. These hints, obviously meant for the Guises but not uttered to their face—a method characteristic of Condé—were the first intimation that the Bourbon opposition was raising its head. The Guises wisely declined to take it seriously. The character of the King of Navarre, frivolous, fickle, and futile, made it difficult to take his pretensions seriously, and it was clear that he was a mere figurehead for Condé. The timidity of Antoine de Bourbon was intelligent. He was in a false situation. Had the Regency been offered to him, he would no doubt have accepted it, but he was not prepared to fight for it. The only cause for which he was prepared to fight or to scheme was the recovery of Spanish Navarre. This was understood by his enemies far better than by his friends. His friends, blinded by their own interests, insisted on pushing him forward on a course which he lacked the spirit either to pursue or to renounce. Of these friends the most persistent, because the most persecuted and most in need of protection, were the Protestants. Their spokesman, Jean de Morel, an ardent young pastor from the Parisian Church, had a fruitless but significant interview with the pretender. Following the instructions he had received from Calvin, he urged Antoine de Bourbon to convoke the States-General, to press his claims to the Regency, and to secure an amnesty for his co-religionists: this was the full extent of his commission. But, realizing that the only condition on which the pretender would give support was that of receiving it, he went a step further and hinted at the vast backing which Calvin might furnish if his proposals were accepted. At this Navarre manifested the first sign of interest and he pressed him to specify the nature of it. Morel, hoping to confine his offer to moral support, evaded the question and merely assured him that he might trust Calvin, whose pledges were not lightly given and were never broken. But Navarre was not to be put off, and the pastor, pressed to declare himself, alluded to a confederation of the Calvinists and the Lutheran princes which Calvin was about to negotiate. Antoine de Bourbon bit, but promptly relinquished the bait. "The Germans," he said, "are great makers of promises, but when the time comes to keep them, they find a hundred thousand excuses to evade them." On reflection—and reflection invariably drained him of ideas—he decided to do nothing for the moment, adjourned the discussion until his arrival in Paris, and dismissed the pastor with impressive recommendations of secrecy. This conversation—a feeler thrown out by two helpless champions—was significant as the first intimation that the Protestant movement, forced to choose between martyrdom and resistance, might, under the protection of a legitimist cause, be converted into an active opponent of the government.

But the legitimist cause, in view of its leader, was a weak one. Antoine de Bourbon joined the Court at Saint-Germain, in the middle of August. The delay in his arrival and the conferences at Vendôme justified the Guises in welcoming him coolly. On the following day, the King of Navarre took his seat at the Council. A scene was expected, for it had been rumoured that he would demand the dismissal of the Guises and the tutelage of the sovereign until the age of eighteen; but none was forthcoming. At supper he was the first to agree when François II alluded to the heretics and animated the table-talk with his determination to allow no innovations in the kingdom. For a week he remained at Saint-Germain, the most docile of courtiers. Even the Cardinal was surprised. The man who had blown in from Navarre, a would-be burr, was pure thistledown. They touched him to the quick. When, at the suggestion of the Queen-Mother, the Guises offered him an opportunity to meet Philip II and broach the question of Spanish Navarre by accompanying Elisabeth de Valois to Spain, he accepted with alacrity; and the crisis was over.

The defection of Antoine de Bourbon was regarded by all his friends as a betrayal. To a mere conspirator the submission of Navarre might not seem irreparable; but to Morel it was fatal, for it deprived the Protestants of their one legal means of defence, and Calvin expressly forbade any other. Morel, on the spot, face to face with the realities of the situation, chafed at such inhuman restrictions and addressed an anguished appeal to his master: "Really, excellent father," he pleaded, "if the King of Navarre is so cowardly and so senseless as to fail in his duty to us and to himself, are there no other means of delivering the Church from its present sufferings? I know that those which you regard as the primary ones are prayers to God and all the offices of piety. But of methods less sublime than these, except for that which concerns Navarre, you propose none. Though you are the most perspicacious of all of us, and though for my part I am not so presumptuous as to pretend to discover what you cannot discern for yourself, I shall permit myself nevertheless to propose one idea, for I am extremely eager to know whether you approve of it. In France the law is that if the King dies, leaving minor children, the Orders of the Kingdom should be assembled, that it should be they who decide on the tutors and governors to be given to the said minors, and that others should be proposed for the affairs of the kingdom according as they are more or less nearly related by blood to the King, and that they should govern everything until the majority of the said children. According to law, it is legitimate, therefore, to convoke the States-General. But does this prerogative belong only to the man whom we have mentioned? Is it not permissible for anyone to call them, even the most insignificant of this kingdom, when the great do not stir and, frozen by fear, dare not speak plainly? If these demands are not satisfied, is it not in accord with justice that all of us together should claim by arms what a small faction and foreign tyrants have appropriated?" The issue which he raised was a far-reaching one: it was nothing less than that of popular sovereignty, and it had some basis not only in the constitution of the Calvinist Church but in the instructions of the Reformer himself. The convocation of the States-General appeared to him the only means of saving both his cause and the country by restoring to the nation a portion of authority. His fiery disciple, however, developed his idea far beyond the bounds he had set for it, and his reply was categorical. As a lawyer, he was bound by the letter of the law, and if the first Prince of the Blood failed to help them, no one else had the legal right to do so. As a Christian, he was bound by the spirit of the law, and "to conquer by force is unlawful." His judgment of Antoine de Bourbon was severe—"a being who trusts neither God nor man"— but it authorized no evasion of principles. The lawgiver left the French Protestants in a tragic dilemma. Necessity forced them to choose between the law of Christ and the law of nature, and the future of the movement depended on the decision. For a moment it had appeared possible to reconcile these alternatives and, by rallying to the Bourbons, to defend themselves without becoming rebels; but the defection of Antoine de Bourbon had revived and intensified their problem. On the one hand, if they elected to defend themselves, they committed themselves to political action and all its consequences. On the other, if they submitted to persecution, the prospect was one of unrelieved blackness.

- 3 -

The plight of the Protestants was indeed desperate. The policy of persecution launched by Henri II was continued with unabated rigour by the new government. It was the sole exception to the rule of moderation and caution which the Cardinal de Lorraine had imposed on himself. He sincerely deplored his ungrateful duty, but he was a martyr to it. Coming to power at a moment of grave national crisis, when the country was in imminent danger of upheaval and disorder, he took the obvious measures to avert the troubles which menaced the government on all sides; and his methods varied with their nature. The mighty—the Montmorencys and the Bourbons—he handled with moderation and caution; the heretics with ruthless severity. The mighty were easy to handle, for they were governed by their interests; the menace of the heretics lay in their ideas, and they represented the deeper danger to the government. They were subversive in principle, if not in practice; or, what amounted to the same thing for a conservative minister, they passed for such. Yet here the Cardinal was guilty of a radical insincerity. He was too emancipated a mind and too familiar with Protestant doctrines to believe the cant prejudice which had been foisted upon them; personally, he had no animus whatsoever against heresy. But in his public capacity he was overpowered by the pressure of public opinion, by popular restlessness, by the promptings of Spain and Rome, by his pledges to the Pope and Philip II, by political precedents, by his professional obligations—a combination of forces too powerful to ignore. To withstand them would have required character of a heroic order; and morally, he was an ordinary man. That was not his fault; but it was his error as a practical statesman that he dealt with the Protestants by the same obvious measures as the most routine functionary. Minds far less superior than his already recognized that persecution defeated its own ends, that every victim made new proselytes, and that repression, far from extirpating, was merely exasperating the sect and tending to convert it into the seditious movement which it was charged with being and which the policy of the government was inviting it to become. The patience of the persecuted was wearing thin. Victims were rescued from the pyre; and President Minard, the leader of the persecuting wing in Parlement, was assassinated by a Scotsman suspected of heresy. This was a warning symptom, but its only result was to intensify the severity of the authorities, and in retaliation Anne du Bourg was condemned to die.

Under this fresh wave of terror, the Protestants, wavering between submission and resistance, found themselves in a desperate extremity. Forsaken by Antoine de Bourbon, they cast about for another protector. They appealed to the Queen-Mother. Already, a few days after the death of her husband, an attempt had been made to enlist her sympathy. A letter had been addressed to her by the community of Parisian Protestants, reminding her that they "hoped much of her gentleness and benignity" and that "they had prayed particularly to God that it would please Him so to strengthen her in His spirit that she might serve as a second Esther"; they recalled the days of her sterility and the consolation she had found in chanting their psalms. The assumption underlying this appeal was that she was well disposed toward them and that, if she had not hitherto manifested her sympathy, it was only through prudence, ignorance, or fear; but these considerations could no longer avail, now that she was at the head of the government. With a singular shrewdness or a singular ingenuousness they credited her with a power which she possessed only in name; but the suggestion worked. The appeal was calculated to stir more than one responsive chord in the desolate widow—her humanity, the memory of her sterility, and her possible power. She acknowledged it with a graciousness which encouraged Morel. To three highly placed Protestants, Coligny, the Princesse de Condé, and Madame de Roye, she promised to induce the King to temper the persecution, on condition that the heretics observed discretion, lived "secretly and without scandal," and abstained from assemblies. Nevertheless, the persecution continued. Bitterly disappointed, the Protestants addressed another letter to her, in which they reproached her for "constantly dissimulating" and warned her that "as God had begun to chastise the late King Henri, she would do well to think that His arm was still raised to complete His vengeance upon her and her children." It was her first taste of radical manners, and naturally she was irritated. The bitter letter roused her from her apathy and, when she finished it, she remarked sharply: "Humph! they threaten me. . . . But they are not yet where they think." The tactlessness of her petitioners left a lasting impression upon her; and for several weeks the arrogance inherent in any dogmatic belief summed up her understanding of the Protestant faith. Madame de Roye endeavoured to correct this impression and placed their case before her in more diplomatic terms. Catherine listened impatiently, but she finally relented so far as to say that "she understood nothing of this doctrine and what had moved her to favour them before was rather compassion and pity than any desire to be informed or instructed whether their doctrine were true or false: for, when she reflected that these poor people were so cruelly massacred, burned, and tormented, not for thieving, larceny, or brigandage, but simply for maintaining their opinions, and that because of them they went to death as to a marriage, she was moved to believe that there was something in it which surpassed natural reason." In short, her sentiments were those of a motherly lady, with a taste for welfare work, who regarded the martyrs as a worthy object of charity. She was shocked by their sufferings, but their sufferings alone entitled them to her sympathy.

The atrocity of the persecution pleaded their cause more effectively than they did. After a raid on a suspected house in the Pré-aux-Clercs, provoked by the authorities and carried out by a mob, she ordered an investigation of the circumstances. The official explanation failing to satisfy her, the Cardinal placed before her a Protestant pamphlet seized on the premises, in which she was accused of equivocal relations with him, and in which her husband's death was described as a judgment of God. She was shocked and wounded. To confirm her in these feelings, he plied her with sensational tales of their secret abominations and produced, in proof, two young apprentices who gave her a circumstantial account of a scene at which a numerous assembly of heretics were described as partaking of pig on Maundy Thursday and plunging, like Gadarene swine, into an obscene orgy. She was "astounded and outraged." Her women, however, were even more amazed at her credulity and protested in private, only to meet, however, with the scandalized severity of a respectable matron. If she were certain that any of them belonged to the sect, she said, she would send them to death, no matter what favour or friendship she might feel for them.

When her agitation had subsided and the Gadarene swine and the obscene orgy had been digested, they persuaded her, however, to recall the apprentices, who were notorious spies and tools of the government, and whom they promised to expose. Flattering, petting, and feeding them with sweetmeats—for they were mere children—the ladies, by pretending to know their tricks, induced them to recount and to boast of their childish feats as false witnesses; but the result was not what they expected. Catherine listened and, for the first time since the death of her husband, began to heave with laughter. It was the only satisfaction which they drew from her; and it was a forcible reminder that she was both incurably maternal and incurably Italian: children were children, and tricks were tricks, under any circumstances. What their poor little ruse failed to accomplish, Madame de Roye then attempted to do. She vouched for the virtue of the Protestants and endeavoured to combat the prejudices which had been instilled into the Queen-Mother's mind. Those scandalous tales, however, were not easily forgotten by a respectable matron, and she was reluctant to disbelieve them. "But," she objected, "I hear many people say that there is nothing more dissolute than these sort of people." Madame de Roye, a "heroine" of the cause, replied that it was easy to traduce them, "since no one dares to defend us and if she knew us and our cause she would judge us differently." To this the response was all that could be desired. Catherine was open-minded; indeed her mind was so open to every impression that she retained none of them long. She consented to meet an authorized pastor. Madame de Roye lost no time in writing to the Synod in Paris, and she took the occasion to relieve the elders of one of their cherished delusions: "It is not true, as has hitherto been believed, that the Queen has read pious books or listened to learned and truly Christian men." After some hesitation, the elders consented to enlighten the Queen-Mother. La Roche-Chandieu was appointed for this purpose. A secret meeting was arranged at a village in Champagne, on the occasion of the journey of the Court to Reims for the coronation. The pastor kept the appointment, but Catherine failed to appear.

- 4 -

The protection of the Queen-Mother was a delusion. There remained one other possible patron—the Prince de Condé. But the assistance which he was prepared to offer them was compromising: it was indistinguishable from self-help—the same condition upon which God was prepared to help them. When his brother faltered, he determined to advance his claims himself; but, without legal rights of his own, he was forced to graft this design upon some public cause, and, a Protestant himself, it was only natural that he should cast a sympathetic eye on the plight of his co-religionists and exploit it for whatever it might yield.

Under other conditions, Condé might have made a successful demagogue. Shrewd enough to exploit a public cause for his personal ends, he was one of those unconsciously and attractively unscrupulous characters to whom everything is forgiven. Out of the national grievances, which contained the material of civil war, he fashioned for his own ends a conspiracy, the object of which was to oust the Guises from power, to try them before the States-General, and to secure the Regency for the Bourbons. But the role which he assumed in this plot was that of a sponsor, a mute chief, reserving its rewards to himself and leaving its risks and its organization to a subordinate.

The agent to whom this task was entrusted was Jean du Barry, the Sieur de La Renaudie. He was an adventurer of good family, of whom circumstances had made an outcast and a rolling stone. Drifting into the entourage first of the King of Navarre and then of the Prince de Condé, he attached himself to the legitimist cause and volunteered for the hazardous service which Condé required. It was a role which called for a man of supreme disinterestedness or a desperate gambler; and the former being difficult to discover, Condé contented himself with the latter.

To this man fell the task of organizing the conspiracy and coordinating, single-handed, the varied causes of discontent on which it was to be built. He had many connections: he was in contact with the Court, with the military, with the provincial nobility, with the religionists; but he laboured under a heavy handicap. His work was far-reaching and required numbers and time. The classic precept of a successful conspiracy—speed, secrecy, and few partners—was violated by the very nature of the scheme. In scope and substance it had the proportions of a national revolt, in execution those of a private plot, and the consequences of this discrepancy jeopardized it at the start. But La Renaudie addressed himself to these difficulties with unthinking aplomb. In September he appeared in Geneva to enlist the support of Calvin. It was not to be expected that the lawgiver who had rejected the appeals of his own disciples would countenance the factious proposals of an adventurer. Calvin would have nothing to say to him of his venture. To the question whether, "if one of the Princes of the Blood were induced to embrace it, even though he might not be the first in degree, it might not be permissible," the reply was a categorical negative. From Geneva, La Renaudie passed to Paris, where the religious persecution, then at its height, proselytized for him. The autumn of 1559 marked the peak of a wave of terror. Heretic-hunting became, for the government, a method of distracting attention from its financial stringency, and spoil for the unemployed. The growing excesses of the rabble were such that the Governor placed the city under a virtual state of martial law, and the Guises took precautions against a popular outbreak by concentrating arms in strategic depots throughout the densely populated quarters. The prisons were full, and the accused, deprived of all legal safeguards, were summarily sentenced as examples. And such examples bore fruit. Even the orthodox magistrates resented the lawlessness which they were constrained to administer and, whipped to their work, evaded it. Rescues became more and more frequent. Amid this unrest La Renaudie found himself in his element, but to hatch it required money. The pursuit of it carried him across the Channel. Queen Elizabeth was willing to invest liberally in an enterprise which promised to occupy the Guises at home and paralyse their intervention in Scotland, and the secret funds which he received from her enabled him to return to France, to tour the provinces, and to recruit soldiers of all sorts—unemployed veterans, stranded gentlemen, foreign mercenaries—many of whom engaged themselves blindly to a cause of whose object they remained in ignorance, satisfied to ask no questions as long as they received a living wage—16 or 18 cents a day for mounted men, 10 cents for infantrymen. Others were partly initiated into its purpose, and its purpose varied according to the support which it invited.

What characterized this support was that it was composed of individuals and their immediate followers, not of coherent groups or classes. This was peculiarly true of the nobility, the class on which Condé counted and to which his apologists appealed. None of the higher aristocracy or of the no less influential new nobility—the financial nobility of titled and parvenu bourgeois—participated; and of the minor gentry, to whom La Renaudie himself belonged, he succeeded in recruiting only a scattering among his personal friends. The reason for this was not far to seek. The Court aristocracy, provided with places, was unapproachable; the provincial nobility was organized, in a last vestige of feudal life, about the most powerful family of the district. These families, which protected and controlled a clientele of less favoured gentry, were either in the pay of the Guises or sufficiently well provided to be immune to temptation. The most conspicuous, and the one whose influence would have been decisive, was that of the Montmorencys, controlling in their own right over six hundred fiefs and a clientele so numerous that its appearance in state or in force was the equivalent of a private army. But the Constable viewed the conspiracy at first with neutrality and later with hostility. La Renaudie laboured under the same difficulty in his other sources of support. Disavowed by Calvin, he was able to muster only a dissident fraction and not the Protestant movement as a whole. As for the "fleeced financiers," they were the most conservative element in the State, and at Lyons he made little headway. These were serious flaws in a movement aiming at national support; nevertheless, by planting a nest at every strategic point, he hoped, in the event of success, to sweep the country with him.

It is always difficult, in a country in which the latent conditions of revolution prevail, to gauge the precise pressure at which it will rise. The preliminary survey covered a wide area and consumed six months, and the delay allowed many to reconsider and to cool, so that he soon found himself in the position of a man riding a circuit and constantly compelled to retrace his steps. In January 1560 he returned to Switzerland to rally the refugees. On February 1 he was in Nantes, where, under cover of an affluence of pleaders crowding the town for the sessions of the local courts—it was the legal season—he was able to assemble, with their brief-cases, a semblance of conspiratorial States-General, which he described as "representing the body of all the Estates of France in this so extreme necessity and urgent business," and whose pledges he obtained on the express understanding that the enterprise would attempt nothing "against the Majesty of the King, the Princes of the Blood, nor the legitimate constitution of the realm." The plan of action was then determined. A concerted movement was to be made upon Blois, where the Court was expected, on March 10. The Guises were to be seized and, in case of resistance, killed. In the event of success, and only then, Condé was to declare himself and present to the King a petition for the convocation of the States-General. The person of the sovereign was sacred.

The sovereign, in those six months, had shot up into a strenuous stripling. A few days after his accession, he had begun to seek relief from the long agony of his father's passing in the violent exercise which, for a Valois, was the only antidote for the vicissitudes of living. The first half-year of his reign was a prolonged hunting-party broken only by brief snatches of business and a hurried coronation at Reims. Six months of this life had produced their effects. He had grown rapidly and was in figure enough of a man to embarrass those who regarded him as a minor. He was a star witness, and a major exhibit, for the claims of the Guises. Mentally, however, he was still immature and sexually he was backward. It was believed that his union with Mary Stuart, herself constantly ailing, would be fruitless. This was disturbing, but there were yet more immediate causes of concern for his family. The immoderate exercise to which he was addicted taxed his constitution, and he was subject to sinking spells against which he kicked, like a winded colt, in vain. It was clear that his forced growth was consuming his vitality, but there was no checking him. He fell gravely ill. He complained of an abscess in his ear, and the throbbing pain which racked him was like the knock of a loose, rattling, run-down and over-driven machine. Catherine called a consultation of physicians at Fontainebleau. They advised her to take him to Blois for the winter—the most salubrious climate in the kingdom—and in the spring to treat him with aromatic baths. To the Guises they confided the truth. The King had not long to live—at most two or three years—and they advised them to look to their enemies.

The truth from which the physicians guarded her reached her, however, through other channels. On her way south, she paused at Chaumont for a last visit before ceding it to Madame de Valentinois in exchange for Chenonceaux. Here she held a séance with her astrologer, Cosimo Ruggieri. The habits of superstition which she contracted at the time of her sterility had grown on her and become confirmed by a forecast of her husband's death. The sense of her impotence against destiny predisposed her to supernatural searchings. At her request Cosimo Ruggieri consulted the occult world on the destinies of her sons and produced, in a darkened chamber, a shadowy vision in which three of them succeeded each other as kings, only to be superseded at last by an alien phantom.

It was at Blois, early in February, that the Court received its first warning of the conspiracy. The King had resumed his hunting, and it was in the course of an expedition in the vicinity that his uncles received a letter from a German prince, giving them an intimation of what was afoot, a month before the date set for its execution. It was remarkable—a little too remarkable—that they should be informed from abroad of what was occurring under their noses at home, and the Duc de Guise made light of the warning. The hunting continued. A few days later, however, at their next halt, he was met by his secretary, coming post-haste from Paris with a story and a witness to back it, which gave him pause. The witness was a Protestant magistrate in whose house La Renaudie had lodged and who denounced what he had learned of the plot.

What he knew, or what he chose to reveal, was not enough to enlighten the Duke, but it was sufficient to convince him of the reality and the imminence of the danger. Blois being an open and pregnable place, the Court removed to the fortified town of Amboise, on February 21, and awaited developments. As yet the Guises were in the dark as to the extent and the origin of the conspiracy. Their first impression was that it was fomented by Queen Elizabeth, so far were they from believing that it could be either spontaneous or home-grown. This impression was confirmed by Coligny, who arrived at Amboise from Normandy, where he was mustering a fleet for the Scottish wars and who, when he was informed of the plot, promptly and indignantly expressed the same suspicions. Once more the two estranged soldiers saw eye to eye; but it needed a national emergency to make them do so; and no sooner did Coligny agree with him than François de Guise mistrusted his own judgment. The days when they had been inseparable were as far-gone as their youth. Nor was their understanding improved by what followed. Invited by Catherine to express his opinion on the cause of the conspiracy, Coligny drew her attention to its obvious basis in "the great discontent of all the subjects of the King . . . not only on the grounds of religion, but also in political affairs," and pointed out that there was "extreme resentment that the affairs of the kingdom should be controlled by people who were regarded as foreigners, while the princes were held at a distance, and all those who had well served the public interests." Coming from so disinterested a critic, this charge could not be imputed to personal motives, and he was the first to subscribe an appeal to the Constable to send troops for the defence of Amboise. The messenger who carried it returned from Paris with three prisoners, from whom, as they had been arrested for complicity with the English agents, the Guises hoped to extract some clues. They were put to the torture, but they revealed nothing.

If La Renaudie had planned to keep his victims in suspense and anxiety, he could not have done better. The ten days which the Court spent at Amboise—from the twenty-first of February to the first of March—were days of deepening confusion and tightening tension. On March 2, as nothing had happened, Catherine and Mary Stuart decided to spend a few days in Tours. On the morrow, however, the phantom danger for which they were weary of waiting revived. Two couriers arrived, one from the Duke of Savoy, the other from Granvelle in Brussels, bearing specific and consistent accounts of the plot: it would explode within four days—on March 6—and its object was to kill the King, the two Queens, the royal children, the Cardinal de Lorraine, and the Duc de Guise. The conspirators had allies in Germany and Geneva and accomplices among the Knights of the Order, the highest dignitaries in the country, and their leader was "a great Prince." His identity was unknown, but the information was sufficiently precise to state that the King of Navarre was not a party to the plot. The tension of the previous ten days was as nothing to the nightmare of the four that followed. A state of suppressed panic prevailed, suppressed only by the sang-froid of the Duc de Guise and the prompt precautions he took. Yet they were singularly feeble ones. Paralyzed by uncertainty and by pride, he had done nothing since he learned of the plot beyond retreating to a small fortified town, setting sentinels, and sending for aid to his old rival, the Constable. There was little more that he could do without mustering a large body of troops, creating a commotion, and exposing the insecurity of the government. But with every hour swelling the size of the unseen enemy, these measures seemed meagre to the trapped Court and the besieged government, and the Duke finally sent for reinforcements and dispatched the governors and lieutenants residing at Court to their posts. The fatal day of the sixth dawned and the cup of bitterness overflowed: it passed without so much as a stir on the horizon. The strain had been too great not to be followed by a relaxation; but instead of a clean crisis and a definite relief, the disappointing escape left behind it a sediment of unsettled doubts and nervous exhaustion. On the seventh the Duc de Nemours sallied out with a few soldiers to explore the country and question the patrols, and on the eighth normal life was resumed with a session of the Council.

This session was marked by an important move—the

formulation of an amnesty in favour of the heretics. Politically, it was important as a first tentative step toward a policy of toleration and, personally, as the first political initiative of the Queen-Mother. For it was from her, after a consultation with Coligny and the Chancellor, Olivier, that the suggestion came. In an interview with the King on the previous evening she secured his assent, and the Council accepted her decision. A sharp distinction was drawn between two classes of heretics: the amnesty specifically applied to those who "lived peaceably" and excluded, among the fomenters of disorder, the preachers —the propagandists who carried the seed of infection. These reservations indicated clearly the purpose of the edict and narrowed its scope so much as to neutralize its effect as anything but an emergency measure. Nevertheless, the edict was a significant measure. It suspended, if it did not reverse, the time-honoured policy of the Crown, and it established a precedent. The mere fact that a distinction had been admitted between conscientious and seditious heretics, and that the profession of heresy *per se* was regarded as less culpable than an attempt on the State, was sufficient to alarm the ultra-Catholics, as appeared after the publication of the edict. It was an implicit recognition of the Protestants and their civil rights: these were conceded by the King in an article which allowed them to present collective requests to the Crown, in other words, to negotiate with him. In view of the fact that they had hitherto been treated as at once pernicious and non-existent and had been outlawed throughout two reigns as enemies of society, this clause contained a minor revolution. However provisional, the amnesty marked the first political check of the Guises. In this measure, wrung from the government by fear, the conspiracy had already achieved a success.

The ides of March had come but they had not gone. On the following day the King resumed his hunting, while his mother and wife, accompanied by the Court, went to Chenonceaux, where they remained for three days to recover from their experience. Four days later, the patrols began to bring in the first detachments of prisoners— stray groups of a dozen or twenty men, picked up in the neighbouring forests, obviously lost and bewildered, who surrendered not only without resistance but with relief. The information they furnished was vague and confused, but it afforded some clues and led to betrayals and denunciations. Meagre though these revelations were, they had a moral value: they were contagious, and a captain of the Royal Guard, who had been suborned by La Renaudie, succumbed, sought out the Queen-Mother, and disclosed the plan and date of the enterprise, the points of concentration of the troops, and the complicity of Condé. The testimony of the prisoners rounded up during the next four days confirmed this confession in full, and it was impossible to doubt that the danger was overwhelming and imminent. The nightmare revived. A concerted attack was to be launched on Amboise; accomplices in the château were to hold the passage to the King's chamber; the Guises were to be overpowered or killed; the date was the sixteenth; and behind all this lurked . . . Condé. On the fifteenth Condé arrived at Court, to take up his post; he was coldly received but not apprehended; he was allowed to play his part through to the end. He had the satisfaction, at least, of seeing the consternation of the Guises at first hand.

Two days before the date of the attack, on the evening of March 14, the Comte de Sancerre, who was patrolling Tours, fell afoul of a band of armed men, led by the Baron de Castelnau, whom he attempted to arrest but who outnumbered and escaped him. They were traced to the château of Noizay, within a few leagues of Amboise. There, on the following morning, the Duc de Nemours, who had been sent out to reconnoitre, picked up two captains, who were walking in the meadows. The gates of the château being closed to him, he returned to Amboise for reinforcements. When he reappeared with these in the afternoon, he was admitted and treated with Castelnau, who disclaimed any treasonable intentions, insisted that his sole object was to present a request to the King, and who surrendered on the understanding that he would secure an audience and that his life would be spared. A search of the château disclosed a hoard of munitions. The party reached Amboise at nine that night. Castelnau and his companions were questioned in the presence of the Cardinal de Lorraine, his brother, and the members of

the Council, and the result of their disclosures convinced
the Guises that they held the principal lieutenants of La
Renaudie and that all that remained was to disperse the
leaderless and disorganized bands who were roaming the
environs and drifting every day into the royal patrols.
This impression was confirmed on the morrow. The appointed day of March 16 passed as uneventfully as that
of March 6. The haul continued but only of small game.
Toward noon the royal beaters reported a concentration
of five or six hundred men in a wood within a mile of
Amboise. Troops were dispatched to the spot. At their
approach, the rebels dispersed in headlong flight, flinging
down their arms, and vanished into the forest. Fifty-six
prisoners were brought in and questioned by the Duc de
Guise in the courtyard of the château. They too spoke of
a request to be presented to the King and declared that
in their province, Poitou, ten thousand gentlemen were
preparing to follow them. They were for the most part
poor artisans, shuffling and jostling each other like sheep.
The King addressed them from a window, distributed
money, and sent them home. These scenes were repeated
throughout the day. Stupefied groups of ten, twenty, thirty,
men trudged in, under guard, cheap captives, as docile
as children, who mumbled vaguely something about the
Bible, the Bible, and an appeal to the King. The King,
the Duc de Guise, and the Chancellor took turns in addressing them, paying them, and sending them away under
pain of death. The Guises could afford to be lenient: the
back of the nightmare had been broken, and the stagger-
ing nag that had devoured their sleep was now feeding
out of their hand. But they reckoned without Condé.

On the night of the sixteenth they slept, and the Court
and Amboise slept, in security. In the faint light of dawn,
only the boatmen at work on the Loire, quietly grazing
the limpid waters, were astir, and they were the first to
descry, as the glow spread, a company of two hundred
horsemen with fluttering white scarves bearing down on
Amboise by the road from Blois. It was a picked band
levied by Condé in Orléans. From this quarter no attack
had been expected, as all the information gathered from
the prisoners pointed to a movement of troops from the
south. From subsequent indications this surprise seems

to have been a last rally of Condé's friends, improvised when the failure of the main movement was clear, to save him from its consequences. Conceived at such short notice, its secret was kept, and when the alarm was given and the Court tumbled out onto the ramparts, the assailants had already swept through the faubourg and attacked the town gate. Two hours of utter confusion followed, while the Duc de Guise worked to arm and to mount everyone within reach; at last he was able to muster a troop, to sally out by a side gate, to attack the enemy on the flank, and to rout them. They made good their escape. The countryside was scoured again, and successfully, for vagrants, but these told a new tale. Examined as to their leader, they replied that they received orders from the Prince de Condé. The Duc de Guise gave strict orders to prevent these revelations from transpiring.

With Condé he was still on his guard: too great game to be prematurely startled. The delations, damning enough for an ordinary enemy, were too weak to impeach a Prince of the Blood, without the support of written testimony which could be produced at a trial, and the Duke was on the trail of proof. Maligny, the Prince's equerry, whom he suspected, and who had been for several days in the town, had disappeared in the heat of the fight. While Maligny was hunted, Condé was watched; but, so far from betraying himself, the Prince baffled proof by taking an active part in the defense of the town. A precipitate move might ruin everything.

But if he was cautious with Condé, Guise retaliated on his subordinates. Up to the seventeenth no blood had been shed; now the executions began. Letters-patent were issued by the King appointing his uncle Lieutenant-General of the Kingdom and conferring on him full authority to punish the rebels, letters which recalled as a precedent the terrible repression of the revolt of the *gabelle* in 1548 by Montmorency. What this portended was illustrated by the bludgeoning vengeance which now began at Amboise. Batches of rebels were tied in sacks and drowned in the Loire. These were meanly born. Others, according to their class, were hanged or beheaded, and their carcasses suspended from the ramparts. Thirty-one perished on the first afternoon, but the pace was accelerated on the next day and continued with increasing intensity as the situation became more settled. On the eighteenth La Renaudie was surprised in a forest and killed. His body was brought in and spread bat-wise on a bridge, with a placard identifying him as the author of the conspiracy tucked, like a bib, under the loose head.

La Renaudie was accounted for; there remained Condé. He carried his head high. Proofs of his complicity accumulated, but they were not written ones. Twenty of the first victims had acknowledged him as their leader, but their mouths were shut. Condé continued to appear at the Council, to go and come at his pleasure, and to be treated as if he were above suspicion. So much forbearance baffled observers. The Cardinal, when he heard of the machinations of Condé at Orléans, flung his biretta on the ground, stamped on it, and gave vent to feelings that were ungovernable. The King was no less indignant. He was a man now, he felt the promptings of virility, the right to punish and the power to kill; and he could not understand why, all danger being over, he should still be restrained from the satisfaction of his legitimate impulses. But his mother checked him.

Catherine was herself in a quandary. The attack on the town by Condé's men completely altered the character of the conspiracy and warranted the extreme penalties provided for an act of armed rebellion. She herself urged the King to punish the rebels pitilessly, and she could not complain if his orders were executed rigorously. But she made exceptions. She intervened on behalf of individual prisoners and found her wishes disregarded. When one whose life had been promised her by the Cardinal was dispatched by his orders, she expressed her displeasure, but without avail. She became uneasy. The initiative which she had shown a week before had reverted to the Guises, and the influence she had won then was once more overruled. It was not to her influence that they had yielded in accepting the amnesty but to that of fear. It was the old story all over again. Cowed by adversity, they were overbearing in triumph, and they had learned so little from a revolt provoked by their prepotence that they were resuming, recklessly, incorrigibly, their old courses. Where was this to end? The revolt, it was true, had been quelled, but it had come within an inch of success, and it had been too terrible an experience to risk another. To temper rigour with mercy was the obvious course of wisdom—obvious, that is, to a woman. And in a timid woman it was only a step from forethought to presentiment. What if, as the physicians feared and Cosimo Ruggieri believed, it were true that the King had not long to live? Condé was the only possible counterpoise to the Guises; the Constable was equally intractable; but Condé—Condé might be manageable.

If François de Guise, for his own ulterior motives, also watched over Condé, he did not spare him the ordeal of witnessing the deaths which his followers died many times over for him. The Prince bore the ordeal without flinching, and he even put a point of bravado into his coolness, remarking one day to the courtiers crowding about him in the window that it was a pity to see so many gentlemen die who had served France well and whose death exposed the King to the designs of the foreigner. After ten days the atmosphere of Amboise became unbreathable, and for the sake of the health of the King it was decided to move to Chenonceaux. The final performances were planned on an impressive scale. On March 29, Castelnau and his captains perished. As he had surrendered on the solemn word of Nemours that his life would be spared, he protested stubbornly up to the last moment. He appealed to Catherine and to Coligny, who was his cousin, and they persuaded the King to commute his sentence to a term in the galleys, but the dictatorial powers granted to Guise by the King were invoked by the Cardinal, who declared that Castelnau should die and that there was no man living who could prevent it. Nevertheless, in view of the word given by Nemours, some legal colour had to be given to its violation; this was provided by the usage that no pledge was binding when given to heretics. Castelnau confessed his heresy freely, and finally lost his head so far as to appeal to the Duc de Guise, who cut him short with the curt remark that he did not know how to discuss, what he did know was how to lop off heads. The debate ended in the headsman's lap. On the following morning the Chancellor, who had fallen ill in the effort to reconcile legal guarantees with

dictatorial liberties, expired. A natural death passed unnoticed on that day; for the thirtieth was the day of the
last, and the crowning, spectacle. It was a command
performance at which not only the Court but the inhabitants of the outlying country within a radius of miles
were compelled to appear. Tiers of seats were erected
about the courtyard of the château, in which the spectators
took their places not so much to see as to be seen: a
vacancy was incriminating, and no one was excused. Beside the scaffold, the Duc de Guise, on horseback, commanded both the public and the platform. The King was
accounted for in a window, with his mother, his wife,
and his two little brothers, and his sister, while the Cardinal, hovering behind them, moralized on the scene.
Fifty-six victims took their turns at the block, and as the
long, monotonous hours of the afternoon dragged along,
the effect became oppressive, and the examples they provided, with their courage, their piety, their psalm-singing,
called for constant exegesis on the part of the Cardinal.
Anna de Guise became hysterical and would have disgraced the man on horseback, had not the Queen-Mother
prompted her sharply to maintain her self-command. As it
was, her behaviour did not escape his eye, and the correction which both he and his family administered to her
that night was broad and brutal.

With these mass executions the stage was now cleared
for Condé. On the following morning one of his equerries,
suspected of having arranged the flight of Maligny, was
placed under arrest, and when the Prince protested to
the King, François II took the situation into his own hands
and enumerated the charges which incriminated Condé
himself. Condé requested permission to reply formally and
in public, and this he did, three days later, at Chenonceaux, before the King, the Court, the Council, and the
Knights of the Order, by inviting his accusers to declare
themselves and offering to waive the privileges of his rank
and meet them on the field of honour. No one took up
the challenge, and the Duc de Guise turned to the King.
"Sire," he said, "in all that concerned the service of the
late King, your father, I have always seen the Prince
conduct himself with great courage; given his past conduct and his rank, I cannot believe that the suspicions

of which he complains are warranted." The Cardinal, it was remarked, sitting with downcast eyes and an expression of extreme sadness, shaded his face with his hand, "without making the least sign of assent to what was said." The intervention of his brother closed the incident and retrieved the rash initiative of the King. But Guise, in defending Condé, was not merely making a prearranged move to preserve appearances. A new element had entered into his calculations, and one which threatened to upset them. The bloody purge of Amboise slaked his resentment and restored his normal generosity. Condé was a cousin and an old comrade in arms, and he was reluctant to press the charges against him. To these considerations was added another, even more compelling. He shrank from impeaching the Prince, above all, because of his rank. The caste-system was so essential a part of his being and his respect for it so commanding an emotion that, pitiless toward his peers and his inferiors, he could not overcome his instinctive sense of deference toward his superiors. When the critical moment came, when the last decisive step was to be taken, and he faced the responsibility of spilling forbidden blood, he quailed. All the proofs, all the promptings, which supported and impelled him, were powerless against the repugnance which welled up within him, unreasoning and obstinate. Scruples so irrational were a mystery to his brother, who could account for them as little as the Duke could explain them, and they saddened him. It was like a secret estrangement. The understanding between them had always been too sympathetic to make any explanation possible, when they disagreed. He shared the prejudices of his brother but not his convictions, and it was an enormous difference. Though he submitted, like an impresario baffled by an unaccountable case of temperament, it was with a reluctance which was visible to everyone. To hesitate was to risk everything; and the sequel confirmed his misgivings.

Two weeks later, at Tours, another incident occurred. The apartments of the Prince were broken open during his absence, and his papers ransacked by a gentleman belonging to the household of the Queen-Mother. When he protested, the perquisition was imputed to robbers. But his patience was exhausted. Slipping out of Court on a pretext, he made his way south by cautious stages and, eluding his pursuers, reached Navarre in safety.

- 5 -

The abortive outbreak at Amboise was not the end, but the beginning of a rebellion. What began as a personal scheme, which espoused public disorders only to exploit them—"a debauch of ambitions," Calvin called it—ended by engendering a genuine national upheaval. The conspiracy miscarried, but it succeeded in startling the government, in exposing its weakness, and in driving it to extremes which provoked a vast sympathetic reaction. How much their violence had aggravated their position, the Guises were compelled to realize when they found themselves the objects of fanatical hatred, all the more baffling for being nameless, headless, immaterial, and implacable. The Duke was beside himself, more incensed than he had ever been at Amboise, and his correspondence was a constant injunction to his lieutenants to arrest *ces paillards séditieux*—a feat of which he recognized the difficulty by the estimation he set upon it: "It would be so fine and useful a capture that it could not be sufficiently esteemed." For, while the authors were unseizable, their productions were everywhere, finding their way even into the royal apartments; the Queen-Mother could not appear in public without having them smuggled into her hand. What galled the Guises even more deeply than personal detraction was the denunciation of their government as a dictatorship. They were the first to deny, because they were the last to recognize, that the innocent pursuit of their legitimate ambitions had led them into a position which could be described as either illegitimate or despotic. Their conscience was clear, and so was their record. The aftermath of Amboise changed the whole character of their situation. They were suddenly confronted by an overwhelming antagonism for which they could not account, and which staggered them. Their disintegration began . . . with their bewilderment. A direct and self-conscious ambition is obviously less dangerous than a befuddled and aggrieved one.

Beset and baffled by an unaccountable storm of censure,

their first impulse was to seek cover. They confounded their cause with that of the Crown, and the official accounts of the tumult of Amboise described it as an attempt on the lives of the King and his family as well as themselves. To lend greater credit to this version, it was presented to Parlement, for public promulgation, by the Constable. At the request of the King, Montmorency consented to perform this service, but he managed to defeat its effect by the most perfidious parliamentary methods. In extenuation of the executions at Amboise, he dwelt at unnecessary length on the hatred of the conspirators for Messieurs de Guise, and concluded that, if a private person was in duty bound to defend his domestics, all the more was a monarch under obligation to protect his dependents—a galling comparison which was not lost either on his hearers or on the Guises. The Constable, in fact, made his position perfectly plain. If the Guises hoped to use his prestige to bolster their own, they were singularly ingenuous: old feuds were not so easily forgotten. His services were rendered, not to them, but to the Crown. Nevertheless, the Guises continued to court him; their insecurity was such that they could neglect no ally; they even made advances to the King of Navarre. These moves, however, were mere stopgaps: every day made it clearer that something more than party alliances was needed to disarm public feeling. What it demanded, with damning unanimity, was their dismissal. This raised a dilemma which far surpassed their own fortune. To ignore that demand was, inasmuch as the King was merely their mouthpiece, to admit that their government was a dictatorship; to yield to it was to recognize a sovereignty distinct from, and superior to, that of the Crown. They shrank from the former alternative, and the latter was unthinkable. So completely had they confounded their interests with those of the Crown that, in either case, they compromised it.

The only escape from this dilemma was to elude it. In their isolation and confusion they were reduced to consulting and collaborating with the Queen-Mother; and the woman who had chaperoned their assumption of power served to shield them from its consequences. There was

no abrupt transfer of power, merely the gradual manifestation of a new influence.

That influence was limited, in the first place, by her
inexperience. Apart from her Regencies under Henri II,
she had taken no part in public life. But she had over her
colleagues one inestimable advantage: she knew her ignorance and was willing and able to learn. When Coligny
returned to Normandy, she entrusted him with a mission
to investigate and report to her on the troubles there, and
his reply, which ascribed them to the violence of religious
persecution, was shown by her to the Guises. She attempted
to renew her contacts with the Protestants, inviting the
congregation of Tours to send her the pastor, La Roche-
Chandieu. The congregation replied that they cherished
their pastors and that, inasmuch as her past actions gave
little evidence of her goodwill toward them, what she
wished to learn could be as well communicated by letter.
Their prudence pleased her; she encouraged them to
correspond with her and, ignoring their mistrust, promised
"to show by effects that she did not disdain their advice."
She was careful, however, to recommend that "they keep
secret whatever they might determine to send her, for
she wished to avail herself of it in such a manner that
it would be thought the overtures she would make came
only from her own reflection and industry, and not from
other hands, or else in thinking to aid them she would
ruin everything." What greater guarantee of her good
faith could she give them than her own caution?

For, in addition to her ignorance, she was singularly
hampered in her search for information by the close
surveillance which the Guises exercised over her. Morbidly
susceptible to mistrust, they were quick to resent any
initiative on her part, to suspect her investigations, to
control her sources of information, and to dread the influences which might insinuate themselves among them.
She could assist them only in spite of themselves, with the
furtiveness of a physician forced to humour a moody
patient; having lost confidence in themselves, the least
indication of distrust in others was fatal. Too proud to
admit their weakness, but uneasily aware of it, they
coveted the cure and were insanely jealous of the hand

that administered it. Mary Stuart spied on her with a vigilance which she could evade only by subterfuge. The reply of the Protestants was delivered to her by the son of her furrier. She was occupied in mastering the contents of this memorandum when Mary Stuart entered the room and surprised her before she could pocket it. Her behaviour on this occasion was that of a culprit caught in flagrant commerce with the enemy: she surrendered the letter and disavowed the bearer, who was placed under arrest. When, later, he was examined in her presence by the Guises, she reproached him for abusing herself and her son and insisted, against all his denials, that "it was she who was attacked in the person of the Sieurs de Guise, uncles and ministers of the King." What greater guarantee could she give them of her good faith?

Catherine could not afford to compromise herself; she could accomplish her purpose only by a strict appearance not only of neutrality, but of orthodoxy. It was her purpose, not to dissociate herself from the Guises, whom she needed in her apprenticeship, but to dominate them; and this object could be accomplished only by bringing to bear on them a constant pressure of public opinion and impressing them with their insecurity. It was essential that her channels of information should not be tainted, that her sources should be as many and as overpowering as possible, and that she should on no account commit herself. Shortly after this incident, she sent for Louis Régnier de la Planche, a gentleman high in the confidence of the Montmorencys, to sound him on their opinions, and she invited the Cardinal to listen to the interview behind the arras. La Planche was reluctant to talk, but by an artful mixture of involved menaces and vague cajolery she induced him to enlighten her. He explained to her that the troubles were at once religious and political, and that there were two distinct kinds of Huguenots, as they were beginning to be called, the one confessional, whom the fury of persecution and the persuasions of La Renaudie had combined to stir up, the other professional, whose interests were political, and who were irritated by the appropriation of the government by foreigners and the exclusion of the Princes of the Blood. The former would be easily appeased, he believed, by the convocation of a

Council; the latter could hardly be satisfied "except by granting the Princes of the Blood their place and gradually dissolving the Guise party by an assembly of the Estates." The pretensions of the Guises to rank as princes themselves excited his verve; the sovereign himself could not create princes without the help of the Queen. He concluded by advising her, "if she wished to avoid a very dangerous agitation, to confine the Guises within their limits or, at the very least, to give them a bit and a counterpoise of native Frenchmen, and to keep them all under control." It was now her turn to explain: in employing the Guises, she said, she had merely followed the traces of her late husband, and she led him on, with the remark that the conspiracy of Amboise had been directed against the King, to declare that "those who occupied the place of the Princes of the Blood, knowing that these could not be ousted, according to their ancient privileges, except for the crime of lese-majesty, had forged this accusation, substituting the person of the King for their own." At this point, she dismissed him for dinner, and the Cardinal extricated himself from the tapestry. Catherine confronted him, blinking mildly—the same familiar widow with her bloodless face, her reddish hair, and her colourless eyes, but with something quizzical and searching in her noncommittal stare that drove him back under the arras. After dinner the session was resumed, under the same conditions. The morning had been spent in scorching the Cardinal; the afternoon was devoted to consoling him. She began by observing that "she could not persuade herself that this quarrel had been caused by the honours claimed by the Guise"; she even indulged in a little imperceptible persiflage on the subject, suggesting that it might be easily settled, since it was no more than a matter of precedence, by allowing the first place to the Bourbons and the second to the Guises, so that one Bourbon would always be followed by one Guise, the first by the first, the second by the second, the third by the third, and so on; then, wearying of her little game of mental solitaire, she became serious. She quizzed him on the conspiracy and begged him to aid her in apprehending the principal rebels. He declined sharply, declaring that he was neither a police captain nor a spy. She arrested him. But as he was Montmorency's man, and as he cleared himself of complicity in the conspiracy, he was released and lived to compile a precious, if prejudiced, account of the reign.

The explanations of La Planche analyzed the situation in a manner which all her other sources of information confirmed. There were two sources of unrest, the one religious, the other political, which were confused and which it was essential to separate. The religious malcontents could be appeased by a suspension of persecution and the convocation of a Church Council, and it was of the utmost importance to appease them, in order to dissociate them from the political malcontents whom it appeared impossible to satisfy with anything less than the dismissal of the Guises. That demand she had no more intention of conceding than the Guises themselves. She needed them; she was too inexperienced to face the situation alone. To dismiss them would have entailed, moreover, a domestic struggle to which she felt herself unequal, though she had both formal authority and the backing of the country to support her. And, finally, imbued as she was with the monarchical tradition, she understood that to yield to the clamour of public opinion would have been damaging to the prestige of the Crown. Far from sacrificing them to the hue and cry of their enemies, she associated herself with them in order to guide and control them. She had learned by their experience. In spite of of their good intentions, their laudable attempts to restore a ruined country, their methods, like their temperament, were too drastic and violent; they lacked authority and measure; and it was for her to supply the moderation which her experience of life had made second nature.

She would hardly have succeeded, however, had not the Guises been already more than half converted by the force of circumstances. It was her peculiar strength that she made herself a medium for public opinion; in spite of their affected superiority, they were acutely sensitive to it. They lacked the stature of impenitent dictators; however much they might brave criticism, at heart they could never steel themselves against it. In the case of the Cardinal, this factor was of decisive importance. He yielded to her promptings the more readily that they were those of his temperament. The whole bent of his nature was conciliatory; the rigour of his public conduct not only belied, it violated, his natural inclinations and aptitudes. In a conversation with the English ambassador on the religious question, shortly before the outbreak of the tumult of Amboise, he amazed the latter by opinions so emancipated and so liberal that he seemed "more than half a Lutheran himself." This versatility, which was notorious, was the nexus of his mind and the tragedy of his character. He could never reconcile his convictions and his interests. His official principles and his private opinions were at variance; of such are the most violent persecutors made. Not only his religious zeal, but also his financial reforms were forced measures, the consequences of which embittered him. No sooner was he convinced that concessions were necessary than he made them with a facility which betrayed his relief.

The collaboration of Catherine and the Cardinal initiated a cautious change in the policies of the government. The royal acts resulting from the aftermath of Amboise were marked by two closely related courses: while the claims of the political malcontents were ignored or evaded, an increasing measure of tolerance was granted to the religious dissidents. The Edict of Amboise, published in March, had suspended the persecution for opinion and offered an amnesty to the non-political Protestants. Two months later, in May, appeared the Edict of Romorantin, which supplemented it. The prosecution of heresy was transferred from the secular magistracy to the jurisdiction of the bishops, and as the bishops had no means of effective action except through the civil courts, this amounted to a permanent stay of persecution. The other measure claimed by the Protestants—the convocation of a Council—had already been anticipated by the Cardinal, who had issued in March, in the thick of the tumult of Amboise, royal letters announcing the intention of the Crown to procure either a universal or a national Council for the open discussion of the religious differences agitating the kingdom. But these concessions were too belated to be satisfactory. The distinction between political and non-political Protestants, on which their spokesmen had always insisted and upon which the government now laid such stress, was itself theoretical. The Edict of Romorantin granted virtual freedom of conscience to the Protestants, but individually, not collectively: freedom of assembly and public worship were forbidden, and the preachers—the propagandists— were still menaced with the extreme penalty. The purpose of the government was to appease and to disintegrate, and naturally the Protestants were dissatisfied. The very meaning of the word *religio* is "binding together"; and in being denied organization they felt that they were denied everything—a revelation of what religion meant to them, not moral force nor mystical communion with God but a social movement for the propagation of certain beliefs. Those beliefs might be religious, but the fact that an organization existed to spread them constituted a public danger in the eyes of the government. In the first place, the concessions which it had already made, meagre and grudging though they were, were a source of embarrassment with foreign powers. The edicts, and the promise of a Council, excited a prompt and alarmed reaction in Rome and Madrid. In the second place, it was no less disturbing at home. It was notable that, ever since Amboise, the Protestants were popularly known, no longer as Lutherans or Calvinists, but as Huguenots. They were no longer foreign elements: the familiar nickname naturalized them. The point at which a struggling movement earns a popular nickname is always indicative of its ripening strength and suggests the degree to which it has penetrated the general consciousness. The origin of the name no one could explain any more than the mysterious swiftness with which it sprang up in the popular mind; some ascribed it to a corruption of the Swiss word for confederates, *Eidgenossen*, others to their neediness which could only be compared to the value of an old coin of the days of Hugh Capet, others to more fanciful sources, but all these derivations showed a range of conceptions not religious but social. The fact that the movement was illegal and that it was organized served to attract, to rally, and to focus other forms of disaffection about it and to infect and to adulterate it. How far this infusion had advanced was evident in the conspiracy of Amboise; and it was accelerated in the months that followed. Troubles broke out, in the name of religion, all over the country. As the ferment increased, the government realized that, not only were its religious concessions too meagre, but that the political opposition had not disarmed.

To avoid the demand for the convocation of the States-General and the prerogative of the Bourbons, the government resorted to a final manœuvre. An Assembly of Notables was announced to take place in August, at Fontainebleau, for the purpose of "finding a remedy for the recent evil and appeasing the troubles." An exceptional pomp and publicity accompanied this announcement in order to impress public opinion and to convey the suggestion that the Notables—who were merely the members of the Council and the Knights of the Order and whom the King could consult every day—were assembled for an extraordinary occasion and that their deliberations would have a representative character. The Assembly, in other words, was to be the equivalent of the States-General; and in the address which he composed for its opening the new Chancellor, Michel de l'Hospital, said as much: "It has pleased the King to call this Assembly, legitimately composed of all the Estates of the Realm, with the exception of the Third Estate, which is in no wise needed since the only aim of the King is the relief, peace, and repose of the said Third Estate." The careful omission of the Third Estate was sufficient to make the assembly notable. Words could not have expressed more plainly where the real danger lay and the determination of the government to cover itself by a constitutional sham and the confederacy of the ruling classes.

The demand for the States-General being thus circumvented, the claims of the Bourbons were met by an adroit move. Pressing invitations were addressed to the King of Navarre and to Condé to appear. The invitations with which the Guises seconded those of the King were remarkably cordial. They had nothing to fear. Knowing the character of the Bourbons, they were confident that they would not come or, if they did, that they would not venture to raise the question of the King's majority in his presence, since they had not ventured to so so under far more favourable circumstances in the first days of the reign. The invitations of the Queen-Mother were equally cordial, but for a contrary reason. She sincerely desired, and expected, the Bourbons to appear, and when it became clear from their evasions and delays that they had no intention of doing so, she conceived for them a lasting grudge. The idea of the Assembly had, as she took care to point out, originated with her; and she expected much from it, nothing less, in fact, than a union of princes which would stabilize the State and pacify the country. How this was to be brought about was not clear, perhaps, even to herself; but her confidence sprang less from the head than from the heart. She had been remarkably invigorated by a few weeks of public activity. The apathetic widow for whom the world had ended with the death of her husband revived rapidly under the responsibility of protecting his heritage.

The Bourbons eluded the snare, however. Up to the last moment they promised to attend, and at the last moment the King of Navarre wrote, announcing his departure and begging the King not to wait for his arrival. In spite of its fictitious character, the Assembly of Fontainebleau produced some surprises. The opening session took place on August 21, in the apartments of the Queen-Mother, and was attended by fifty-four dignitaries, conspicuous among whom was Montmorency, who came to Fontainebleau with eight hundred followers and his three nephews, and to whom the most marked deference was shown by everyone, beginning with the Guises. After a harangue by the new Chancellor, L'Hospital, in which the Assembly was urged to seek for the general causes of the national troubles, the Duc de Guise rendered account of his administration of military affairs and the Cardinal of the finances. The deficit was estimated at two and a half million livres, a statement which spoke for itself, and upon which no one proposed to comment. The first session progressed no further. On the next day the subject was abruptly changed. As the King was about to call a scheduled speaker, Coligny rose, approached him, and handed him a request, to which the King at once gave precedence, passing it to his secretary to be read aloud. The request formulated an appeal, in the name of the faithful of France, to the Crown to permit them the use of temples for the purposes of lawful assembly and the celebration of their cult. At the conclusion of the reading, Coligny implored the King "to take what he had done in good part, in view of the proofs and the evidence that he had of his fidelity." He added that the Queen-Mother had expressly commanded him to inquire into the complaints of the sect in Normandy. The King replied that he had never heard anything but the best reports of his services and that he accepted this one in good part. This was the first surprise of the Assembly. The temerity of a request, on the part of the Protestants, not merely for liberty of conscience or private reunion, but for public assembly, which implied the equality of cults under the guarantee of the State, left many of the audience aghast. Even more startling was the complaisance with which it was heard by the King and the complete absence of protest from his ministers. To seasoned observers this could mean only one thing: it was prearranged, and the majority of the Assembly, assuming that Coligny had presented the request with the secret authorization of the King and his advisers, showed no surprise. The boldness of this move was purely technical. It was designed to impress the foreign powers opposed to the convocation of a Church Council—the Pope and Philip II—and by its audacity to overshadow the equally contrived attacks upon Rome which followed, and to make them appear relatively inoffensive. The next two speakers, in fact, both of them liberal ecclesiastics, favoured by the Queen-Mother, enlarged on the necessity of reforming the Church, "beginning with the Popes who have done nothing but amuse themselves with wars and foster enmity and disunion among Princes."

On the third day the debate broadened and became, at moments, bitter. Coligny, after reverting to the request which he had presented and declaring that, though it was anonymous, fifty thousand persons were prepared to sign it, criticized the Guises for secluding the King from the country, taking exception particularly to the new and enlarged mounted guard which surrounded him and which gave the impression that he mistrusted his subjects. This "dangerous and disaffecting" impression, he insisted, was in fact prevalent, and the only means of dissipating it was to convoke the States-General. To these strictures the Guises replied. The Duke was curt: the sovereign was in no need of advice; if he were, his mother would give it, not his subjects; as for the guard, it had been increased to protect him against armed attempts on his life. The question of the States-General he left to His Majesty to decide. The Cardinal then explained himself. His tone was less cutting, but on one point it was equally peremptory: the request presented by the Admiral might be signed by fifty thousand petitioners; the King could oppose a million to them. The demand of the Protestants for public assembly was inadmissible: to grant it "would be to approve their idolatry, which the King could not do without being perpetually damned." The perturbers of the public peace, in his opinion, must be rigorously punished, particularly when they had recourse to arms; but, these reservations made, "he believed that, as for those who, without arms, and for fear of being damned, attend services, chant psalms, and abstain from going to Mass, inasmuch as penalties had so far served no purpose, the King should forbid their punishment by justice." For his own part, he was greatly distressed that they had been persecuted. Persuasion, not violence, was the proper method to win these misguided souls; if his life or death could serve, he was ready for any sacrifice; meanwhile, the Bishops should labour to reclaim them on the evangelical principle: *Corripe fratrem tuum inter te et ipsum*.[1] The Bishops should also determine, within two months, whether to wait for a General Council or to proceed to a National one. Finally, in order to dispel the calumnies levelled against the King and his ministers, he declared himself in favour of summoning the States-General.

This conclusion, coming from a man who had always opposed the convocation of the States-General as *a curb on the King*, was an astounding concession. A force had asserted itself which upset every calculation and overcame every resistance. When the Assembly concluded its sessions, two days later, the King announced that a National Council would be called, unless the Pope agreed to a General one, and that on December 16, at Meaux—the birthplace of the French Reformation—the States-General would assemble. If the former decision was expected, the latter was unforeseen. What had happened to make the

---

[1] Correct thy brother in secret.

Assembly take the very step it had been convoked to evade? The clue to the enigma was simple: it was contained in the statement made at the opening session and avoided at the last one—a deficit of two and a half million livres. The financial crisis had superseded the political one, and imposed itself upon it. From the moment that it was stated, nothing else mattered; the Crown was compelled to reckon with the nation at large and the Third Estate in particular. A force which overruled everything —religious creeds, political compromises, personal interests—an irresistible force which they recognized with dim unseeing eyes, bore them all helplessly on, notables and nonentities, towards its own predetermined ends.

- 6 -

It was at this juncture that the Bourbons were again heard from, and in the usual way. On the closing day of the Assembly, Jacques de la Sague, a courier of the Prince de Condé, was arrested and brought to Fontainebleau, in consequence of a denunciation received by the Duc de Guise. The papers found on him indicated the existence of a new conspiracy, which was on the point of breaking. Examined under torture, La Sague incriminated, besides Condé and the King of Navarre, a number of great names—Blaise de Montluc, La Rochefoucauld, Rohan, Gramont, Bouchavanes, Tende, the Vidame de Chartres, Madame de Roye. These revelations created a new crisis, but the alarm they inspired was not unmingled with relief that, instead of incurable problems, it was merely incurable conspiracies that threatened the government. The Guises found themselves once more in command of the situation. On the following morning, the Vidame de Chartres, the only one of the accused within reach, was arrested and placed in the Bastille; and prompt measures were taken to meet what investigation revealed as a *reprise*, on a larger scale, of the conspiracy of Amboise.

In one respect the new plot differed from the old. Where the conspiracy of Amboise had been engineered by an agitator, the present disturbance was spontaneous, and the impulse came not from above but from below. The place of La Renaudie was taken by Maligny—a brother of the equerry who escaped from Amboise—who met Condé on his flight from Court and accompanied him to Navarre to induce both Antoine de Bourbon and his brother to renew the attempt. Retracing the steps of his precursor, Maligny left Nérac for Geneva to enlist the support of Calvin in "stimulating the King of Navarre." On learning that Antoine de Bourbon was reluctant to commit himself, Calvin disapproved of the idea, but his disapproval did not prevent Maligny from recruiting troops in Geneva, and the enthusiasm of his disciples was such that Calvin felt it necessary to make some concessions in order to prevent a schism. Torn between his sympathy and his scruples, he yielded to a request of the King of Navarre and sent his leading disciple, Théodore de Bèze, to Nérac. When Bèze reached Nérac, the King of Navarre was wavering in the dilemma raised by the convocation to the Assembly of Fontainebleau. Bèze did his utmost to dissuade him from accepting the summons, and his presence served to "stimulate" not only the King but the surrounding provinces, thickly populated with Protestants who, encouraged by the recent concessions of the government, were already anticipating their next success and publicly assembling for worship. The entire left bank of the Rhône—Provence, Languedoc, Guyenne, Périgord, Poitou, Limoges—was seething with incipient civil war, while in Dauphiné it had already broken out under the leadership of two survivors of the conspiracy of Amboise, who were preparing to attack the Papal State of Avignon, and against whom the government was raising a force of 4500 men. These varied incitements finally roused the King of Navarre to the point, if not of committing himself, at least of countenancing what his partisans were prepared to do in his behalf. As the original impulse came from below, so did the final plan. Its object, in the words of an historian of the party, was "to seize the city of Lyons, in order to give courage to the Princes of the Blood, and to convoke there all those who wished the state of the kingdom to be restored and to bring the usurpers to reason" . . . in other words, an armed enterprise, covered by and serving as the basis for a spontaneous and partisan States-General. The generalship behind this plan was far more effective than that which underlay the conspiracy of Amboise. Instead of a petition to the King and a plot against his ministers, here was a movement acting independently of the Crown and aiming to impose its will on it by an appeal to the country, constitutional in form, supported by organized force, and sanctioned by the patronage of the first Prince of the Blood. The entire plan was executed, with consummate secrecy and dispatch, taking shape in June and becoming active by the end of August. The date was set for the fifth of September, and the preparations were completed, when they were suddenly countermanded by a message from the King of Navarre.

The unforeseen turn taken by the Assembly of Fontainebleau, ending in the announcement that the States-General would be duly convoked, scuttled the legal structure of the plan. It had progressed too far to be abandoned, but not to be modified and adapted to the changed situation; and the plan which the King of Navarre substituted for it was to accept the summons of the Crown and to proceed with his brother to the meeting of the States-General, but in such force as to guarantee them against any hostile move on the part of the government. Accordingly, it was arranged that, while the bulk of his followers were to remain inactive, awaiting further developments, a certain number of his sympathizers would join him in small groups at each stage of his journey north, swelling his escort and making an imposing display. Maligny was instructed to meet him, with the troops introduced into Lyons, at Limoges. The change was made, however, too late. On the night of September 4, Maligny's troops were discovered and attacked by the royal garrison and, after a hot fight, routed and dispersed, Maligny himself escaping.

The report of this outbreak, coming ten days after the capture of La Sague, confirmed his revelations, and determined the government to treat the Bourbons as rebels. Up to that moment there had been, not doubt, but reluctance to provoke an irreparable rupture. The most rigorous precautions had been taken. The Duc de Guise had placed the country on a war footing. The King had sent a thundering message to Antoine de Bourbon, commanding him to bring him his brother and warning him that "if he refuses to obey, I am capable of teaching him that I am

King." But he allowed the Cardinal de Bourbon to leave for Guyenne in order to meet his brothers and induce them to submit peacefully. He even sent a message to Antoine, assuring him that he did not suspect him personally, but that he expected Condé to appear, to clear himself, and to ask pardon. The thundering message was his own, the accommodating one that of his mother. This tractable disposition lasted until the outbreak at Lyons. Then his patience was exhausted. The Court learned that the arrest of Condé had been decided.

Officially the change was manifest, however, only in an intensification of the measures already taken. While the concentration of troops continued along the route which the Bourbons were following, friendly messages were sent to Antoine de Bourbon by the Queen-Mother to induce him to advance. The grudge which she had conceived against the Bourbons for spoiling her plan of a union of princes had deepened with the discovery of the conspiracy. The pacification of the country, the security of the throne, her most cherished schemes, her most vital interests, were jeopardized by those inveterate troublemakers.

"What do they want? What do they demand?" she complained to her confidants. "If they see that affairs are going badly, why do they not come and prove it, so that measures may be taken, instead of provoking so many troubles by their absence?" Intractable characters always antagonized her; and when intractability turned to treason, she was not far from being vindictive. Mary Stuart later admitted to a confidant that the worst enemy of the Prince de Condé at this moment was the Queen-Mother. In him she recognized the real menace, persistent, irresponsible, furtive; without him the Bourbon agitation would have subsided. Antoine de Bourbon caused her far less concern, because he was pliable; and all her efforts were bent to detaching him from his brother and cajoling him into bringing Condé to Court. Her letters, as bland as those with which she bade him to Fontainebleau, betrayed no change in her sentiments except in an intensification of amiability which would have warned a wiser man. "You cannot arrive soon enough to please me," she wrote.

While Catherine cajoled, the Guises brought force to bear. The Duke launched a campaign of merciless repression in all the suspected or disaffected districts, crushing or anticipating local revolts before they could coalesce into a general movement, and rapidly isolating the Bourbons in order to reduce them. The two principal danger zones on either side of the Rhône were brutally pacified. Despite these energetic measures, the Court was uneasy. The frontiers were stripped of their garrisons, Saint-Quentin was evacuated, and the King, in informing foreign courts of these unprecedented movements, dwelt on his deplorable situation, compelled as he was to march "against his own subjects." The feeling that the country was honeycombed with disaffection and that there was complicity with the rebels in all classes obsessed him, and gave rise to some incidents of a pathetically puerile character. Eighteen new members of the coveted Order of Saint-Michel were created, all of them clients of the Guises, the Constable, or the Queen-Mother, at the express desire of the King, who wished, it was explained, to bind to his religion and his person those who were about to combat the rebels. This did not prevent Madame de Crussol, a friend of the Queen-Mother, from remarking that, if the King had named two more, they would have been known as the *vins nouveaux*, the vintage that year being notoriously bitter; while the Court at large remarked on the cheapening of a distinction which made the collar of the Order "a yoke *à toutes bêtes*." Several days later the King convoked the Knights of the Order and the members of the Council in the apartments of his mother in order to announce his decision of taking the field and to ask them, individually, to renew their oaths of allegiance. Catherine attempted a comment, but her feelings overpowered her. The extraordinary scene was solemnly performed. The Duc de Guise set an example, followed by Montmorency; one by one, amid a silence of constraint and embarrassment, everyone recited the formula. The Cardinal de Bourbon pledged the good behaviour of his brother with tears in his eyes. "If they behave well, I shall treat them as my kin; if not, I shall punish them," said the King firmly. His masterful manner impressed everyone. He spoke without prompting, and it was difficult to maintain the fiction that he was a minor, particularly when he turned to Catherine and in the same sharp tone of command said: "You also, my mother, shall take part in this war." For a moment the audience half expected him to invite her to rise and take the oath of fealty herself.

Between the coaxings of the Queen-Mother and the military demonstrations of the Duc de Guise, Antoine de Bourbon found himself circumvented. He announced his arrival at Orléans, with Condé, for the middle of October. They travelled slowly, malingering to the last. What reception awaited them was not clear. The message brought by the Cardinal de Bourbon assured Antoine de Bourbon that he was not under suspicion and that Condé would be given an opportunity to explain himself. But since then time had passed, and the delay in obeying the summons of the King aggravated their situation. Warnings reached them not to appear at Court, if they valued their lives, except at the head of an army. The Princesse de Condé sent one desperate appeal after another to her husband not to walk open-eyed into the net. But it was too late to retreat. They were in the net already. Their only hope lay in disarming the anger of the King by complete submission and, dismissing their followers, they took the road to Orléans with so small an escort that the King of Navarre could point to it as a proof of his unquestioning loyalty. He hoped, in view of the friendly asssurances he had received from the Queen-Mother, that she would spare him any unnecessary indignities. But he was soon undeceived. At a town in Poitou, one of her officers produced an order, signed by her, forbidding the admittance of the Princes of the Blood to any fortified place. He was outraged and wrote to her promptly in protest. She replied imperturbably: "I am amazed. I assure you that no one has been authorized either by the King or myself to address you in such language. . . . I trust, my brother, that this will not prevent you from pursuing your journey and joining us as soon as I desire, and you will find nothing at variance with what I have written you before: in this I am certain that you believe me." The officer, confronted with this denial, signed a statement reading: "I, the undersigned, certify to the King of Navarre that what

I told him in the name of the Queen-Mother is true. Nor do I believe that the Queen-Mother will deny it, since I received my instructions from her own lips, as I shall remind her whenever it pleases her to do me the honour of hearing me."

The followers of the Bourbons made much of the "perfidy" of the Queen-Mother, accusing her of deliberately luring them to their doom, and the subterfuges which she used to entice them to Court undoubtedly justified the charge of duplicity. But it did not follow that her intentions were sinister. As her subsequent conduct proved, she had not yet abandoned the hope of realizing her original policy of a union of princes, which she believed indispensable to the pacification of the country and the stability of the State. It was a forlorn hope, but she clung to it blindly. She still believed that, if she could secure the persons of the princes without bloodshed and separate them from their followers, the agitation which they inspired would subside, and that, once Antoine de Bourbon was in her power, she could induce him by persuasion or force or a combination of both to collaborate with her. Her ultimate aim, which she never relinquished, was to prove to the country that the King was not the subject, but the arbiter, of factions and parties. For obvious reasons, however, she could not avow it. While she co-operated with the Guises, she was nursing an aim which was not theirs. Extreme measures were both impolitic and repugnant to Catherine; and it was not to punish the King of Navarre, but to subdue him that she exerted her equivocal blandishments.

The ruses to which she resorted in her eagerness to reassure Antoine de Bourbon were not always skillful; in one case she over-reached herself. In her first message to him she attributed the arrest of La Sague to Montmorency. When the Constable learned of this accusation, his indignation knew no bounds, and he complained bitterly that "if it had been anyone else but the King and the Queen-Mother who wrote such things, I should have used the language befitting a man of honour when he is charged with a thing of which he has never thought." A violent scene ensued between himself and Catherine. All the pent-up bitterness in his heart broke out: he complained of the neglect to which he had been condemned since the death of her husband, and he reproached her for "wishing to govern the country, inexperienced as she was, and for surrounding herself and her son with ministers who were incapable and detested by everyone." These home truths were too galling to pass without a retort; but the only retort she could find in her confusion and anger was to laugh, and to invite her old crony to laugh with her, at the trick she had played on him. On the following day, he left Court.

But, after all, it was not the art of the Queen-Mother which decided Antoine de Bourbon to submit; it was the concentration of Spanish troops on the frontiers of Navarre. This move was the result of a joint manœuvre on the part of Catherine and the Cardinal. In the first alarm caused by the revelations of La Sague, they had written to Philip II, appealing for aid. He furnished it promptly, but it was aid dearly purchased. In promising his assistance, he took occasion to protest against the religious policy which the government had pursued since March, and to recommend a return to the orthodox methods of repression and force. "It might well encourage many other people to be insatiable." He expressed his "strong desire that the National Council, which so exercises the Pope, should not take place." The same recommendations came from Rome. "Sire," the French ambassador wrote to François II, "our Holy Father expressly charges me to exhort you to punish all those spirits who are studious of innovation, without exception, and says that the only medicine for this malady is fire and sword." The government was in a difficult position; and that it had the courage and the skill to ignore this pressure and maintain its independence was no mean triumph. The honour and the brunt of it belonged to the Cardinal de Lorraine. The moderate policy initiated in March so obviously corresponded to the necessities of the situation, and was dictated by it, that he had now become its foremost champion. From the moment that he made it his own, he defended it with an energy as formidable as that with which he had formerly opposed it. To both Philip and the Pope he offered an inescapable alternative: either a National or an Œcumenical Council. The latter filled Philip and his ministers with dismay. The French ambassador in Madrid described them as being "half beside themselves with fright" lest, under cover of the Council, the negotiations of the French Crown with the Emperor and the German Protestants should lead to "some scheme which might menace the Low Countries." In these quarters the diplomacy of the Cardinal met with a steady underhand opposition which exasperated him. The old hatred of Spain rose in his breast. With the Pope he was at the end of his patience. He persevered and, powerful with the power that comes only from complete identification with a principle, succeeded in imposing it. The Pope promised to reopen the Council of Trent. The Cardinal found himself the most unpopular man in Europe.

Meanwhile, at home, the complications arising out of the Bourbon conspiracy were equally disturbing. The agitation which it created jeopardized the progress which the government had made in pacifying the country during the past six months. The religious question was reopened by the repression of the rebels. Many of the partisans of the Bourbons were Protestants; the presence of Bèze at Nérac was known; the connivance of Calvin was suspected; and the King had, in fact, instructed his ambassador at Berne to investigate the source of the attempt upon Lyons and to denounce the complicity of Geneva to the Cantons. The Duc de Guise wrote to the Duke of Savoy, urging him to attack Geneva and stamp out once and for all the focus of infection; the same recommendation came from Rome. The temptation to revert to the old policy of repression was one which the government resisted with difficulty. The Protestants themselves expected a new wave of persecution and were surprised when they found that the repression was confined to dispersing their illegal assemblies, and that no one was sent to death for heresy as such. The underlying gains made by the Edicts of Toleration were preserved beneath the surface agitation. But, obviously, it became more difficult than ever to distinguish between the religious and the political Protestant. He was convinced that not only the authority of the State but that of the clergy was in danger. Fear and violence dominated him and he found himself involved, by the force of circumstances, in a radical contradiction. While, abroad, he defended vigorously a policy of conciliation, at home he slipped back into the rut of reaction; and if his efforts to promote a Council antagonized foreign powers, his determination to suppress dissension incensed the country.

All these factors singularly aggravated the situation of the Bourbons. In the two months which elapsed between the discovery of the conspiracy and their appearance at Court, the irritation and anxiety of the government accumulated. If any doubt of the reception awaiting them still existed, it was dispelled at every stage of their journey. As they approached their destination, they were under constant surveillance and the outposts they passed closed in silently behind them. The countryside teemed with troops; the approaches to Orléans presented the appearance of occupied territory; and the town itself was crammed with soldiers. It was in this atmosphere of tension that the Princes entered the city, on October 30. They proceeded directly to the Hôtel Groslot, where the King was awaiting them. The scene which ensued had been too long awaited not to be recorded in detail by those who witnessed it. Antoine de Bourbon was admitted alone. In a room adjoining the cabinet of the Queen-Mother, the King, his mother, his wife, the Cardinals de Lorraine and de Tournon, the Duc de Guise, and the Maréchaux de Brissac and de Saint-André confronted him. He advanced and bowed once, and again, and yet again, before the silence was broken. The King saluted him stiffly, touching his hat, and said: "Did I not send you an order to come with the Prince your brother and place him in my hands?" "Yes, Sire, and I have done so." "You may be certain that if you had not done so, I should have inflicted the same punishment on you as he is about to receive." Antoine attempted a protest, but the King cut him short with a brusque command not to leave Court without express permission. Condé was then introduced. The same formal salutations were executed. Condé bowed repeatedly, murmured something unintelligible, and embraced the King's knees. The King sketched a nervous salute; then, for greater privacy or because the light was failing, he turned abruptly and led him into the adjoining cabinet. The bystanders heard his high rattling voice reproaching

Condé and enumerating all the charges against him. A few moments later the King came out, called the officers of the guard, and ordered them to place the Prince under arrest. Through the open door the curious caught a fleeting glimpse of the finale. Catherine was weeping. The King of Navarre and the Cardinal de Bourbon were pleading. The Guises stood erect and motionless. Then Condé passed out and, so far as the outside world was concerned, all was over.

After so much expectation the scene was a little flat and perfunctory. But one feature of it was worthy of note. The King conducted it. With impeccable correctness, the bystanders, whatever their sentiments or their interests, abstained from participating in any manner which might detract from its official character. It was as if they wished to accentuate the fact that the King was exercising his regal functions. He in turn assumed full responsibility for them. Other arrests followed, among them that of Madame de Roye, the mother-in-law of Condé. As she was a niece of Montmorency, this was a blunder which neither Catherine nor the Guises would have countenanced, and Catherine in fact was the first to disclaim it. To those who implored her to intercede she replied that she had been unable to resist the "formal command" of the King, her son. The King, her son: two words which held her spellbound. For several days after the arrest of Condé, her attitude of dismay was so marked that even the King of Navarre was moved by it. The attitude of the Guises was one of no less compunction. It was all sedulous neutrality and melancholy resignation. A tacit conspiracy seemed to exist in the official family of the sovereign to refute in the most unmistakable manner the contention of the Bourbons that the King was in tutelage. But one person was not impressed by it. At last, after a year of mute responsibility, Condé found in his extremity the courage to state the issue explicitly. Examined by a commission of magistrates, he steadily refused to submit to questioning on the ground that he was answerable to no jurisdiction but that of his peers, sitting in Parlement, all chambers assembled. The authority of the Privy Council he repudiated, "inasmuch as the King in his minority does nothing by himself." The Council overruled his repeated appeals and objections and summoned him to answer on pain of lese-majesty. Nevertheless, the formal preliminaries to his trial lagged and after four weeks were suspended. During that period a combination of influences had been at work to save him.

The King, whose emancipation was so carefully emphasized, was a prey, if not to divided counsels, to conflicting impulses. Left to himself, he faltered. Nothing more clearly revealed his sense of responsibility, or his neurotic temper, than the irresolution which beset him after the arrest of Condé. He allowed him legal counsel; and where the law entered, delay followed. The examining magistrates accepted the legal impediments raised by Condé and his lawyers with a facility which laid them open to the suspicion of temporizing; and the examining magistrates, du Moutier and L'Hospital, were the confidants and creatures of Catherine.

It was at this moment that Catherine wrote a remarkable letter to the Constable. They had parted, some weeks before, in bitterness; but that was completely forgotten in the maternal solicitude which led her to write: "*Mon compère,* the King my son sends you the Marquis de Villars to inform you of his affairs and of all that has happened since I wrote you, and I regret that we must so often return to our irksome affairs, for everyone is weary of them. I wish that your health would permit you to join us, for I firmly believe that in that case we should be more judicious and, if we were not, that you would help to take the King out of tutelage, for you have always wished your masters to be obeyed everywhere. I shall not weary you with a long letter. . . ." She had said enough. The appeal of a woman in distress did not admit of long-windedness, and least of all when it was addressed to an unwelcome rescuer.

But, after all, a more potent ally than Montmorency was to curb the Guises. Five days later—on November 17— the King fell ill. For ten days the abscess in his ear had been running more freely than usual, but as this condition was chronic, and as he had been exercising violently, the physicians laid the attack to a cold in the head. The Duc de Guise took command of the situation. He closed the sickroom to all but the immediate members of the official family, and took prompt precautions to prevent alarming reports from leaking out. It was noted by the Spanish ambassador that Catherine and the King of Navarre promenaded long and often together in the wooden hall erected for the forthcoming sessions of the States-General. A cold in the head hardly accounted for these meetings in an out-of-the-way quarter. "Everyone speaks in an undertone," another ambassador said, "and the courtiers comment as their passions prompt them on what may occur, even on the possibility of the accession of the King of Navarre." The latter, ever since the arrest of his brother, had been treated with a mixture of vigilant courtesy and wary slights which had completely disheartened him. But now his spirit stirred. At a meeting of the Privy Council he made for the first time a heated protest in behalf of his brother, recalling the services of his family and expressing his amazement that a grandson of François I should show himself so "thirsty for the blood of the Bourbons." Catherine checked him, assuring him that Condé would enjoy every legal safeguard and that the King would merely confirm the verdict of the judges; whereupon he subsided, wept, and apologized for his outburst.

On November 26, the Privy Council met to reconsider the appeal of Condé for a trial by his peers. It was again rejected, but from this moment the proceedings were allowed to languish. His fate hung on that of the King. On the following day François II rallied and was able to receive visitors and sign some official papers, but a relapse followed. For the next three days the patient continued to sink, and on December 1 the Cardinal de Lorraine offered him confession.

The physical crisis now produced a political one. So soon as she felt that her son was lost, Catherine announced that she would assume the Regency. On her own authority she forbade the couriers to leave Orléans without her permission and dictated a letter to the lieutenants of the King in the provinces, informing them of her decision and commanding them to anticipate any manifestation. The Guises, with everything to lose, the Bourbons with everything to gain, were paralyzed by uncertainty. The one person who was not caught unawares was the

woman who in every situation had always been eliminated. She had digested her destiny, and it was her turn
now to deal.

But it was one thing to announce her decision and another to realize it. It would not have been like Catherine
to take so determined a step without muffling the shock of
it. No formal announcement was made, it was merely
intimated to a few friends, and relayed to the right ears,
and while it permeated the Court, she took her precautions. But every precaution, at a moment so tense, was a
provocation. That her claim would be disputed was a foregone conclusion, and the first move was bound to provoke
a conflict of which no one could foresee the outcome. The
rival ambitions of the Guises, and of the Bourbons, were
equally fatal to hers; and every day brought the outbreak
nearer. With every day that the King lay dying, power
was slipping from the Guises; with every day the Bourbons felt their power approaching. The Bourbons were
backed by the States-General; and the States were to
assemble in ten days. Beyond the factions loomed another
force, even more formidable, the nation: a combination of
factors too overwhelming to challenge. Her one chance
was to anticipate and disarm them; and to this manœuvre
she devoted the last five days of her son's life. She was
never more maternal.

Her anxiety was no longer for her dying son, but for
the coming one. She dared not fail him. She mustered
allies wherever she could find them—Philip II, the Duke
of Savoy, the Constable—but before their help could
reach her, she had to master her rivals alone. In the infinite resourcefulness with which, alone and unaided, she
dealt with them, she discovered the might which maternal
passion lends to the meekest creatures; and it lasted for
life.

Between the Guises and the Bourbons she manœuvred
swiftly and noiselessly. The weakness of Antoine de Bourbon offered her an advantage of which she availed herself
at once. In the few remaining days while he and his
brother remained at the mercy of their enemies, she
harped on his helplessness and played on a nature whose
feelings were as facile as hers had once been. He was
nervous. His followers were convinced that the Guises

had designs on his life and that Condé was already
doomed. She posed as his protector. On December 2 he
was summoned to her cabinet. In the corridor one of her
ladies warned him, in a whisper, to accept whatever she
proposed; his life was in danger. As he entered he found
himself in the presence, not only of the spinner of his
days, but of the Guises and several members of the Council. The clipped words and measured voice with which she
addressed him were well calculated to work on his nerves.
She informed him that in view of the imminent end of the
King it was necessary to consult on the measures to be
taken, and invited him to listen while a secretary read
aloud certain extracts from the Chronicles, establishing the
right of the mother of a minor sovereign to the Regency.
She cited examples. Then, passing from precedents to
facts, she rehearsed the accusations under which he and
his brother laboured and reminded him that, in view of
their recent conduct, he was no longer qualified to assume
sole charge of the government. Whatever rights he possessed had been forfeited. She added that neither she nor
the Guises had prompted or were responsible for the acts
of the King. She requested him, in consequence, to renounce formally his claims to the Regency and to content
himself with the title and prerogatives of Lieutenant-
General of the Kingdom. The whole speech was an elementary exercise in bluff, but her fingering was skillful. A
man with any self-possession would have seen through it;
Antoine de Bourbon was aware only of his own weakness.
Her very lack of emphasis defeated him, dampening his
spirit and foiling the spontaneity which might have served
him in lieu of a collected reply. He attempted a heated
one, heard himself flounder, and lost heart. Suggestible
and emotional, he was both agitated and half-hearted, and
all his efforts to flare up collapsed. He denied all the
charges brought against him: he was not ambitious, he
wished to submit his conduct to judges. He knew his rights
to the Regency, but he was ready to waive them. His one
desire was to leave a Court where he saw himself
"mocked, despised, and disliked." He appealed to the
Guises to bear him out. When he finished, he found himself, he hardly knew how, in the arms of his enemies. The
Duc de Guise embraced him; he embraced the Duke. The

Duke swore that in all that he had done he had only obeyed the commands of the King; he assured the Duke that he could not have done otherwise without betraying his honour. Catherine congratulated him on this reconciliation and promised that he would not regret it; and with the quick decency of a man who feels himself naked in public, he disappeared, shorn.

The Guises had lent themselves to this transaction deliberately. With them Catherine had dealt adroitly. She induced them to rally to her by the simple and subtler method of dissociating herself from them. She consulted no one but herself and the venerable Cardinal de Tournon. The shock of this discovery cut them to the quick. Too proud to beg power or to await their dismissal, they gave out that they would retire, the Duke to his estates, the Cardinal to his diocese. But this did not suit Catherine. She wanted the impossible—her own freedom of action and their support. Her aim, and she had never relinquished it, was to found her Regency on the formal consent of all her competitors. She pursued it with a cool head and an unerring sense of character. At the proper moment she consulted them, but in their interests, not in her own; she pointed out the danger of aggravating the situation if she retained them in power: it would be wiser if they confined themselves to their functions and left the conduct of public affairs to the King of Navarre, the Cardinal de Tournon, the Constable, *and other men of experience*. They were helpless. After a year and a half of power, they were not unwilling to relinquish its burdens to her. Time would tell. The future would vindicate them; for the present they resigned themselves to her protection, accepted a reconciliation with the Bourbons, and seconded her in circumventing the King of Navarre.

The ease with which he had been fleeced dawned on Antoine de Bourbon when he came to his senses. Alone, he recovered his presence of mind. As he re-enacted the scene, all the right replies occurred to him, all his dazed feelings revived, and the supreme opportunity he had missed stung him to furious reflection. Three days later he reopened the question. In a heated scene with Catherine he attempted to wrest from her the right to the Seal, the symbol and instrument of sovereign power, allowing her merely the custody of her son. But it was not a governess who confronted him, it was a guardian. Beaten out of every argument, she was still a match for him. The unyielding denial of the woman prevailed over the mere self-assertion of the man, and the dispute ended by his signing a paper resigning the Seal to her "except in case of her prevention or illness." That night François II died. When word was brought to her, she was sleeping, inert with exhaustion. Early the next morning, however, she was on her feet, with another son by her side, waiting for the homage of the world.

CHAPTER V

The Reign of

CHARLES IX

- 1 -

Catherine had reached her goal so gradually, so imperceptibly, that not only the means by which she had glided to
the fore but her achievement itself seemed as insubstan-
tial as a dream. To prolong and materialize it, before it
could fade and dissolve as everything always dissolved
when she grasped it, was the first impulse of her superstition and of her practical sense. She rose early and prepared for her first formal functions as if they had the
mysterious virtue of a formula to evoke and substantiate
what was still ghostly and impalpable. The secure sleep
of exhaustion and sorrow into which she sank while her
son died was dispelled, long before dawn, by the haunting knowledge of how precarious was the power she had
improvised on a basis of understanding and deals and concessions.

The first day of the new reign, December 6, 1560, was
a day of quiet confirmation, of cautious adjustment, of

diplomatic spellbinding. The city was still sleeping when the Duc de Guise and the gentlemen who had spent the night watching the body of François II made their way to the lodgings in which the Queen-Mother resided with her children. There they found Catherine, the King of Navarre, Mary Stuart, the little king, and his brother Alexandre waiting in the wintry half-light. Charles IX stood beside his mother in the patient attitude of a child already aware that he was both protected and protecting. He was a boy of ten, physically frail, with weak features and the look, docile and alert, of a friendly puppy. Despite his dutiful attitude, his attention wandered from his watchful mother to his brother, whom he adored and whose vivacity he observed with disapproval and envy. The Duc de Guise and the courtiers tendered him their service in a formal monotone.

In the afternoon the Privy Council met to organize the new government. Catherine opened the session with a few words, pronounced in the low monotone in which she was accustomed to dictate to her secretaries, listening profoundly to her own voice. "Since it has pleased God," she began, "to deprive me of my elder son, I do not mean to abandon myself to despair, but to submit to the Divine Will and to assist and serve the King, my second son, in the feeble measure of my experience." Suddenly she heard herself speaking as if she were in the confessional, not in the Council, and saw the councillors listening like unwilling eavesdroppers; her voice created a void about her; and as she scanned those familiar faces—the Cardinal de Lorraine, the King of Navarre, the Duc de Guise, the Cardinal de Tournon, the Maréchaux de Brissac and de Saint-André, and the Chancellor—she realized how remote they became as soon as she dwelt on herself. Tuning herself to their indifference, she continued coolly: "I have decided, therefore, to keep him beside me and to govern the State, as a devoted mother must do. Since I have assumed this duty, I wish all correspondence to be addressed in the first place to me; I shall open it in your presence and, in particular, in that of the King of Navarre, who will occupy the first place in the Council as the nearest relative of the King, without whose knowledge nothing should be done; you will then deliberate among yourselves, so that whatever is considered advisable may be done. Such is my will. If any of you wish to speak, let him do so." The King of Navarre declared himself satisfied. He suggested merely that, in case of her illness, all correspondence should be delivered to him. Then, for the first time, the lifeless deliberation of her voice quickened, and a caustic note crept into it. "My brother," she replied, "all that I can say is that I shall never be too ill to supervise whatever affects the service of the King my son. I shall ask you, therefore, to withdraw your request. The case you foresee will never arise." He acquiesced quickly and too politely. "So be it; I yield once more to the wish of Your Majesty; I beg her to believe that, whenever her interest may be in question, I shall prefer it to my own, and my present conduct, I am certain, will testify to my sincerity." She thanked him, and the Council proceeded to business.

During her first day of power she eased herself into place. On the next day she was sufficiently composed to write to her daughter in Spain. It was not her habit to refer to herself—one of the reasons, no doubt, why she won so little sympathy from the world as well as her children—but the need of opening her heart to someone overcame, for once, her maternal reserve. "*Madame ma fille,*" she began correctly, "the bearer will tell you many things, which dispenses me from writing a long letter; all I shall say is that you need not trouble your mind about anything, and may rest certain that I shall govern myself in such a manner that God and the world will have cause to be pleased with me, since my principal aim is to honour God in everything and to preserve my authority, not for myself, but for the conservation of this kingdom and the welfare of all your brothers, whom I love as springing from the same source whence you all came." Then, becoming more familiar, she added: "So, *ma fille m'amie,* commend yourself to God, for you have seen me as happy as you are now, never knowing any sorrow but that I was not loved as much as I wished to be by the King your father, who honoured me more than I deserved, but I loved him so much that I was always in fear, as you know; and God has taken him from me and, not content with that, has deprived me of your brother whom you know

how I loved, and has left me with three little children and
a divided kingdom, where there is not one man whom I
can trust, who is not governed by private passion of his
own. So, *m'amie,* think of me and take me as an example,
not to trust so much to the love your husband feels for
you, and to the honour and the ease you enjoy, as to
neglect to pray to Him who can continue your blessing,
or, if He please, can place you in my position; I had
rather die than see you in it, for fear you could not bear
so many ordeals as I have had and still have, which, without His aid, I am sure I could not endure." A glimpse,
but only a glimpse, she gave her daughter of the dismay
with which she assumed the responsibilities of a position
of which she could no longer doubt the supremacy; her
profound sense of isolation confirmed it. But she did not
falter. Her lifelong loneliness supported her, and her very
friendliness nerved her for her solitary task. It was her
destiny. She was marked apart from the beginning to scale
the heights, as she had already plumbed the depths, of
destitution. But what she could not tell the daughter whom
she commended so devoutly to God was that there was no
help but self-help: Elisabeth was too young, they were
still mother and daughter, she could not open her heart
completely. But the fact confronted her daily, and daily
she faced it with her unblinking oblique stare.

On the same day the Council decided to proceed, in
spite of the change of reign, with the meeting of the
States-General. The question was hotly debated. But, in
reality, the discussion was academic; the occasion for calling the States remained unaltered; the financial question
dominated every other consideration. Catherine, certainly,
did not underestimate the risk of consulting the country
at a period so unsettled politically and so crucial. If the
States refused her the credits to govern, they could undermine her Regency and offer the Bourbons an opportunity
to reopen their claims. But, since the meeting could not
be shirked, the safest course was to face it immediately,
while she was in an exceptional position to impress the
deputies, with the union of princes on the one hand; on
the other, the army assembled by the Duc de Guise.

During the few remaining days before the opening of
the States, which had been set for December 13, Catherine

prepared for the final test of power. She took every precaution to anticipate the outcome. She announced the
constitution of her Regency, "with the aid of the King of
Navarre," to foreign Courts, to the diplomatic corps, to
the officials of the kingdom. While the Chancellor prepared the accounts to be submitted to the States, she
announced sweeping economies in the royal household.
"The kingdom must be cleared of debts," she said. Her
atavistic instincts were sound, but with the bank three
generations behind her, the last daughter of the Medici
could muster no more than a royal gesture: the horses
and the dogs and the falcons of the late King were
sacrificed, and his private chapel was disbanded. Above
all she relied on the union of princes as her trump policy.
The reconciliation of Antoine de Bourbon and the Guises
was the result of an emergency, too provisional as yet to
be secure. The King of Navarre, it was true, courted his
late enemies assiduously, but it was a question how long
Antoine de Bourbon would consent to be friendly since he
expected to succeed the Duc de Guise as Lieutenant-
General of the Kingdom. Nor was he the only contender.
The Constable, who reached Orléans with an escort of
four hundred followers on the day after the death of
François II, showed an inclination to give orders and
provoked some incidents. To check them, Catherine announced that the Duc de Guise still retained command of
the army. The King of Navarre made no objections. The
Constable was surly, but she relied on his inveterate loyalty
to the Crown. Her supreme consideration for the moment
was to change nothing, to avoid friction, and to preserve
the union of princes until she had cleared the States-
General.

Within a week the situation at Court was sufficiently
settled for a highly placed observer to analyze it with
confidence and to establish the hierarchy of influence:
"The Queen-Mother is the most powerful of all. Then
comes the King of Navarre, who would have more influence if he were able-minded. Third, the Cardinal de
Tournon, who either will not or cannot assert himself on
account of his ill health. The Duc de Guise might yet do
much, but he waits deliberately to be called. The Cardinal
de Lorraine speaks of leaving the Court and retiring to

his estates, or pretends that he intends to do so. The Maréchal de Saint-André is highly influential, the Maréchal de Brissac less so; the Constable de Montmorency counts for little. . . . In conclusion, the Queen-Mother does everything; she is properly the sovereign." Her impalpable power had been coaxed into being, subject only to one unknown factor. On the morrow the States-General met. The unbidden partner was imponderable. It was the nation.

- 2 -

The States-General had not met for seventy-six years. In that period, which had seen the consolidation of the monarchy, there had been two assemblies which purported to represent the country, one in 1506, under Louis XII, the other in 1558, under Henry II, but neither was regular. The first was composed only of the Third Estate; the second, although regularly constituted of the three Orders, was appointed by the sovereign. The States-General of 1560, on the other hand, was imposed on the Crown by the country, which reasserted the original charter of an institution exercising, if not popular sovereignty, something akin to it—the right of consultation and a measure of co-administration with the Crown. Though the constitutional function of the States was confined to the presentation of grievances and the voting of funds, these powers were sufficient to lend it an effective control over the government and to make it a genuine organ of the national will. Hence the reluctance of the Crown to convoke a body whose prerogatives were incompatible with those of an absolute monarchy; and in fact, throughout the reigns of Louis XII, François I, and Henri II, the sovereign had deliberately ignored the States. Only a national emergency could overcome this bias. The financial crisis of 1558 was such an emergency, and the present convocation was the sequel to it. But in two years conditions had changed. The weakness of the monarchy, battling against bankruptcy, offered the States a supreme opportunity to reassert their constitutional claims, nor was it likely that the opportunity would be lost. The government was informed, in fact, that an energetic minority was preparing to raise an issue which, long latent in the institution itself, threatened to involve the States and the Crown in a fundamental conflict. This was nothing less than the embryonic claim of a constitutional monarchy.

The most vigorous advocates of this thesis were the Protestants. Calvin had been drilling it into the Huguenot deputies. "It is more than necessary to insist on the establishment of a Council, which can only be done by the States. Now, the States having received no commission for this purpose, it will be necessary to re-elect them for a short term, and in the meanwhile, and purely provisionally, to establish a temporary government. In this there may well arise disputes and conflicts. . . . But we must insist on the principle, namely, that those to whom the right belongs cannot be deprived of it without good and sufficient cause." Calvin hoped to protect his movement by curbing the arbitrary power of the Crown; but the issue which he raised surpassed the occasion for it and was potentially of a general and revolutionary character. The King of Navarre was a figurehead, moved by forces which, in supporting, over-reached him, and the political propaganda of Calvin was a clear case of propulsion from below, of mass feeling pressing upward, of obscure forces forming to control their leaders.

As the deputies assembled in Orléans, the Queen-Mother questioned a number of them, but though their replies revealed widespread discontent, they disclosed nothing of a nature to alarm her. Whatever opposition might be brewing in the States, she felt confident of disarming it. The speech from the Throne, which the Chancellor composed for the opening session, was carefully designed to conciliate all parties. In this man she had found an invaluable collaborator. Michel de l'Hospital was a character after her own heart, moderate, prudent, unbiased, unpartisan. Though he had begun life as a creature of the Guises, and owed his position to them, she had weaned him away from his patrons without difficulty; his temperament made him cleave to her. He had been called to the Chancellorship in the troubled days succeeding the tumult of Amboise; they immediately gravitated toward each other. "I arrived at Court," he wrote later, "much troubled by a great rumour of war. . . . I had to deal with persons as bold as they were powerful, who preferred

to settle matters by violence rather than by counsel and
reason, as the Queen-Mother can testify, who at that time
was reduced to a condition such that she was almost
excluded from the administration of the kingdom; she
complained of this to me frequently, and I could suggest
nothing but the authority of Her Majesty, with which, if
she employed it skilfully, she could readily defeat and
reduce the ambition and cupidity of her adversaries." He
felt himself responsible for arousing her; she let him understand that he owed his elevation to her. Out of this
happy misunderstanding grew a lasting attachment and
a genuine understanding. Their common aims, their tem-
peraments, their mentality, drew them together. She felt
a penetrating sympathy for men whom she could always
persuade; and among his other merits, Michel de l'Hospital
was a practised courtier. Sympathetic, subservient, he
reflected her, and in a manner which magnified her mental
stature. His practical experience, his legal training, his vast
erudition, and his classical eloquence lent weight and dignity to her groping ideas and clothed her plain common
sense in a polished and impressive form. As a spokesman,
he was indispensable to her; and to him she entrusted the
trying task of interpreting her policies to the States—
trying, because she had not made up her mind what policy
to pursue beyond following the old adage, *when in doubt,
do nothing*. The speech which he prepared was a com-
summate evasion and an elaborate confession of this fact.
Conciliatory in substance, liberal in tone, but carefully
qualified and guarded, it was couched in a form so smooth
as to be swallowed without question—a speech to be
heard and forgotten.

Traffic was still Catherine's notion of statecraft. The
nation was an entity as shadowy to her as the quarters
knocked together to house it. It was something to be
mastered, disposed of, and dismissed; at one moment, a
risk; at another, a refuge; and now, after seven days of
security, an encumbrance. She was still wandering in a
land of shadows.

The opening session was devoted to the address of the
Chancellor, who delivered it in so low a voice that only
those sitting close to him heard it. The deputies listened
patiently, knowing that it would be printed. The Chan-

cellor spoke for an hour; at intervals he raised his voice, to underline salient passages; but in these snatches what he conveyed was as cryptic as what he suppressed. It was comprehensible that he should impute the merit of convoking the States to the Queen-Mother, but it was straining credulity to extol the reconciliation of the princes. He drew a glowing picture of the harmony and peace prevailing among them; for eighteen months the deputies had heard nothing but the feuds of the princes, and the magical change, or the optical illusion, produced by the great orator only deepened the unreality of the scene, particularly as it carried fiction so far as to whitewash the grinning sepulchres of the past reign. When he concluded the political portion of his speech, he had made it clear that the Queen-Mother was determined to bury the past, that she would countenance no claims or complaints based either on the present or past constitution of the government, that the decisions of the Crown were above question, and that all political debate was to be ruled out beforehand. The deputies, more than ever, were made to feel themselves unbidden guests; since the government had settled its difficulties without them, the only question which remained to consider was why it had summoned them.

The Chancellor then passed to the religious situation. The policy which he announced, less as a fact than as a feeler, was so cautious as to be equivocal. There were passages which echoed the old reactionary thesis. "It is folly to expect friendship, peace, and calm among persons of different faiths. We must not be so prompt to adopt and follow a new religion, each according to his fancy. We must remember the maxim of our forefathers: one faith, one law, one king!" But the traditional commonplaces were tempered by a reasonable tone which was in itself an innovation and which defeated their value as a bid for conservative support. They were followed by passages in which Catholic persecution was rebuked as firmly as Protestant presumption. "The knife is of no avail against the spirit, save to lose both body and soul. We should seek by every means to win back the erring and not to imitate those who, when a man or a laden beast lies in the ditch, instead of helping, belabour and kick them out. Gentleness will accomplish more than rigour. Let us put by these devilish inventions—watchwords of faction and sedition —these names of Lutheran, Huguenot, and Papist, and hold to our one name of Christians." Through a careful counterpoint of checks and cautions, the underlying theme began gradually to emerge, the first faint strains of an unheard-of harmony, the muffled prelude to tolerance. But the theme was still timid and tentative. It was tolerance inspired by expediency. It was a means to an end, and the end was to place the Crown, on the religious issue, above creed, as, in the political question, it stood above faction. But to an audience permeated by religious partisanship such impartiality was unintelligible, and the impression it created was one of evasion. In the interpreter of the Crown the deputies heard only the mouthpiece of a woman. His survey of the religious situation brought him back to the *status quo*. The Edicts of Amboise and Romorantin were to be maintained: the preachers, the propagandists, the fomenters of disorder, were to be rigorously punished; the law-abiding Protestants were to be protected, but purely provisionally, pending the outcome of a Church Council. The whole problem not only remained unsettled; it was indefinitely adjourned; and the States were left to consider a question which the government had raised only to beg it. Under those circumstances, what advice could they offer which the Crown would consent to accept? And in that case, for what purpose had they been convoked?

To that question at least the Chancellor offered a plain answer. His statement of the financial situation was frank, and it explained the eagerness with which, up to that point, he had avoided contentious subjects. The public debt had reached a total of forty-three million livres, almost four times the normal revenue of the kingdom. With all its normal resources mortgaged, it was reduced to a point at which it functioned for the sole benefit of the international financiers. The independence of the sovereign was at stake; for his independence derived, in the economic structure of the State, from his possession of personal property. In the commonwealth he was merely *primus inter pares;* and it was through the accumulation of Crown lands that the pre-eminence which the monarch had obtained over his feudal vassals and rivals was substantially maintained. It was the condition of his political supremacy that he should be economically self-supporting, and his only legitimate and permanent resources were the revenue which he derived from the royal domain. The taxes were in the nature of a supplementary contribution. The sovereign was expected to assure the normal functioning of the monarchical State from his personal resources, and he had done so successfully as long as land remained the basis of wealth, that is, throughout the feudal period when society was normally regulated by a subsistence economy. But the growth of Capitalism transformed the whole structure of society. The rising cost of living, which resulted from an economy of competition and profit, affected the monarchy in common with all the institutions of the old order. While its resources depreciated, its expenses increased. The sovereign lived on expedients—on the one hand, on loans from the bankers, on the other, on subsidies from the country. The former had ruined, the latter threatened the throne. Constant recourse to "exceptional" means—to forced or voluntary loans, *aides*, or *tailles*—during ten years of fruitless warfare had exhausted the patience of the nation and created a demand that the States control the expenses of the Crown. The day of reckoning had come; the financial crisis had raised the issue of national partnership inherent in the States themselves and fatal to the pretensions of an absolute and irresponsible monarchy. A beggared government confronted the States, intent on obtaining their financial assistance without sacrificing the independence of the Throne. The deputies could no longer doubt for what purpose they had been called.

All that had gone before was mere by-play. The financial question dominated and explained everything. With a courage that contrasted with his previous caution, the Chancellor attacked it boldly. He appealed to the States for a subsidy to repurchase the patrimony of the Crown and restore the independence of the monarchy. Politically, this was a cool proposal, and economically an impudent one. To touch those vested interests was a hazardous proposal, and the Chancellor did not venture to make it officially. What he wished was that it should come spontaneously from the States, and after inviting them to repurchase, either immediately or within six years, the domains, *aides,* and *gabelles* alienated by the Crown, he confined himself to a hint that the subsidy might be raised by selling the property of the Church. On this the session closed, and a week's recess was declared to allow the deputies time to prepare their replies.

The deputies had not foreseen that their consultation with the government was to be merely a formality for picking their pockets. It took them several days to digest this fact; but when they had done so, the troubles foreseen by the Cardinal de Tournon began. The Clergy alone, led by the Cardinal de Lorraine, voted an address to the Queen-Mother, recognizing her Regency. The Nobility voted to repudiate her government. The deputies of forty districts, representing a majority of the Order, declared that they were not bound to recognize a regency constituted without consulting them. Though they denied that they intended to "lay down the law to the King," the sequel made it clear that that was exactly what they were doing; they invoked their privileges, which required that, in the minority of a sovereign, "this government be confirmed and authorized by the States"; and they demanded that they be returned to their electors to obtain a new mandate on this question, on penalty of provoking fresh troubles if this right were ignored. This demand was communicated to the Third Estate, where it obtained some support; it was then presented to the King of Navarre. This was a serious departure. The principle of the monarchy was challenged. To the unqualified power of the Crown the Nobility opposed the restrictive rights of the nation, and the mere fact that they regarded their authority as deriving from a mandate of their electors posed the principle of popular sovereignty. The deputies demanded, moreover, that the States be assembled whenever new taxes were to be levied or whenever the kingdom was in the hands of a minor sovereign: exceptional occasions, but likely under present conditions to become as chronic as the exceptional means by which the King lived. Here was the constitutional thesis raising its head.

Catherine was on the verge of a crisis more serious than any she had faced since the days when she had been threatened with divorce. Then it was the sovereign who proposed to repudiate her; now it was the nation. The crisis surpassed her personal interests, however, and demanded uncommon resources. She was face to face at last with the nation, and she resorted to her usual methods—bargaining and intrigue. She suspended the sessions of the States until the question of her Regency had been settled; and she insisted on settling it out of court. She reduced a public issue to the proportions of a private deal and delegated several of her confidants to meet the recalcitrant deputies and to reason with them. The most hostile proved to be also the most ignorant—hard-headed country squires, fresh from the provinces, unaccommodating, unworldly, uneducated; it was impossible to argue with them. Examined on their views, they repeated the constitutional thesis like a lesson learned by rote. They admitted that it had been instilled into them, and not by their electors. They revealed a vague understanding of it and a complete inability to defend it intelligently. But they clung to it, and it was clear that they expected their manifestation to be supported by someone in authority. This was precisely what Catherine suspected, and where a pitfall had opened beneath her feet she now felt a foothold of firm ground: the old familiar realities. The leaders of the opposition represented five provinces in which the influence either of the Montmorencys or the Bourbons was paramount. With this information to guide her, she saw her way. To subdue the opposition, she had only to suborn its patrons. The Montmorencys she propitiated by transferring the command of the army to the Constable and showing a measure of favour to his nephews. The Bourbons she bought off by a supreme concession. She released Condé. On December 19 he left Orléans for his estates in Picardy, pending his public vindication. Both these moves were made during a temporary absence of the Guises on a pilgrimage.

So far as such resources could serve her, they were successful. The Constable and the King of Navarre visited the deputies and loyally used their influence in silencing them. But it appeared that their influence was limited. Some unaccountable force seemed to be at work, some spirit which eluded every calculation. An obstinate minority still resisted—twenty-eight instead of forty, but those twenty-eight were animated by a conviction which they could not explain but in which they believed with a blind faith that made them unyielding. Conviction was an obstacle which the usual resources failed to dissolve. Catherine tried to over-ride it. Summoning the leader of the bloc to her cabinet, she informed him that the deputies who protested against the constitution of the government would be obliged to sign the remonstrance with their own names. Curiously, this failed to deter them, and a few days later the papers were presented to her. Her reply was remarkable. She published an edict announcing her Regency. The deputies retorted by a public demonstration. Assembling before the royal residence, they demanded a hearing of the Council; after a long wait, a secretary came out and requested them to leave their petition in writing, but they insisted; there was a violent wrangle; they forced their way in, and repeated before the Council their official protest against a government constituted without the consent of the States. A secretary registered their remarks and filed them, and the demonstrators withdrew. For several days the agitation continued; then it slowly subsided. To make their protest effective, they needed support; and the Third Estate, where they might have found it, was dazed by the public debts and eager to speed the closing of the States without voting a subsidy. The factor which fired the revolt stifled it. The firmness of the Queen-Mother, the abstention of Antoine de Bourbon, the desertion of the Third Estate, and their own unenlightenment, finally subdued the irreconcilable deputies, and under protest they subscribed the address of the official orator of the Nobility, accepting the Regency.

Strategically, the opposition succumbed to a fact it had not foreseen: the adhesion of Antoine de Bourbon to a government which foiled him of his rights. Politically, however, its collapse was due to an inner weakness. The constitutional thesis suffered from its identification with the cause of the Bourbon princes; it could develop only by sacrificing its aristocratic sponsors, spreading through all classes, and becoming genuinely independent and representative. This was the next step in its evolution, and it was a long one; but already the way was being paved by

Protestant preachers in the provinces who were disseminating doctrines of social equality. Futile though it proved, this flare of revolt was none the less significant; it was the green flicker of a force which had been smothered but not extinguished.

The political opposition having been disposed of, the religious question remained to be negotiated. It dominated the session of January 1, when the States reassembled, and its repercussions lasted for a month. If the political agitation convinced Catherine of the risks involved in consulting the country, on the religious problem she found it a refuge. A majority of the deputies approved her policy. The orator of the Third Estate opened the session with a ringing censure of the ignorance, avarice, and luxury of the Clergy; the orator of the Nobility followed with a speech denouncing their activity in secular politics and recommending the concession of public worship to the Protestants. Stung by these attacks, Dr. Quintin of the Sorbonne, who spoke for the Clergy, filled the great wooden hall with the sound and fury of a theological fanaticism which had not been heard, in its pristine purity, since the days of François I. The violence of his fulminations deafened his hearers—and bored them. The resonant doctor ended, like all those who fail to digest their ideas, by eating his words. In the course of his tirade he had recommended that anyone presenting a petition on behalf of the heretics should himself be declared a heretic. This was taken by the assembly as an allusion to Coligny; the Admiral, who was present, understood it as such and complained of it to Catherine. She sent for the Doctor and demanded an apology. He furnished it readily, explaining that he had merely read a memorandum which had been entrusted to him. He was a Doctor of Canon Law, but he had discovered that he was morally isolated; the old certitudes had left him in the lurch. To the rhythm of *Tempus fugit*, he beat a retreat.

The anti-clerical sentiment in the States convinced Catherine that the nation was with her. Her only real danger lay in interfering with its will; she was not likely to forget it and her greatest difficulty lay in averting foreign interference. In January a special envoy from Philip II reached Orléans with instructions which differed only in their tone from those of Dr. Quintin. "Respecting the affairs of religion," the Spanish memorandum read, "you are to speak to Queen Catherine very clearly and frankly, exhorting her on our part to the greatest care and vigilance: she must never permit the innovations which have sprung up in her kingdom to make further progress; and she must not favour in any manner whatsoever or admit to her intimacy any of those who are not as firm in their faith as they should be." From a crowned canonist these admonitions could not be ignored. She counted on the support of Spain in establishing her government; and to secure support without submitting to dictation was a problem which taxed her skill. She was fond enough to believe that she could reason with Philip, and she sent him, through her ambassador in Spain, an apology of her religious policy shrewdly adapted to his understanding—as she conceived it. "As for the fact of religion"—and she stressed the word *fact*—"the examples which we have seen for several years have taught us that to cure an evil of such long standing one remedy alone will not suffice, but that, as new accidents occur, we must vary our medicaments until we find the one which will procure a complete cure. For twenty or thirty years now we have tried to cauterize it, thinking to tear out this infection by the roots, and we have learned by experience that violence only serves to increase and multiply it, since, by the harsh penalties which have been constantly enforced in this kingdom, an infinite number of poor people have been confirmed in this belief, until it has been said by many men of good judgment that, to abolish these new opinions, nothing is more pernicious than the public death of those who hold them, for it has been proved that this fortifies them. Matters have reached such a pass that we have seen what never yet happened here, that is, a manifest sedition for this cause alone, which God has done us the grace to appease and reduce to such calm that we have no longer anything to fear. It is true that, the King my son being a minor and the ashes of this fire still so hot that the least spark will set them flaming higher than ever, I have been advised by all the Princes of the Blood and the other princes and lords of the Council to consider the season in which we live, and in which we are sometimes obliged to dissimulate many things which in other times we should not endure, and for this reason to pursue a course of gentleness in this question, and to endeavour by honest remonstrances, exhortations, and sermons to subdue those who still err in matters of faith, and to punish severely those who create scandals and seditions, so that the severity of one course and the gentleness of the other may preserve us from the troubles from which we are only just beginning to emerge. All this I shall be happy to have you explain to the King my son [Philip], so that he may not conceive a worse opinion of my actions until he has sifted them, as he should; for he must consider that the situation is not the same here as in Spain: there the evil is only beginning, and to purge it and prevent it from spreading, rigour is needful, but here it is so ingrown that it is difficult and even impossible to uproot it, and there is no cure but a Council, the one remedy for the union of Christendom and the healing of all our woes. In the meanwhile, you may assure the King my good son that I shall hold a firm hand, as I should, in support of religion and the Catholic faith, without allowing any innovations whatsoever, and shall be careful to contain everything in peace and tranquillity until the Council; hoping that there by the grace of God so good a decision will be reached that we shall no longer suffer from these afflictions among which we have so long been living." The reasons of expediency which she advanced were, undoubtedly, the only ones which Philip could be expected to understand; what she herself did not appreciate, however, because her own mind was devoid of it, was his bigotry. Her very phrases betrayed her—"medicaments," "cured," "afflictions," "healing"; her whole approach to the question as a malady to be medicated instead of a crime to be crushed revealed a rational instinct, a sympathetic intelligence, utterly alien and profoundly antipathetic to his mind. Her temperate spirit needed a passport to cross the Pyrenees. It was challenged even at home.

The arrival in Orléans of the Spanish envoy stimulated the ultra-Catholic party into furious activity. The Papal Nuncio, always difficult, now became insufferable; he expected her to burn all the Protestants in Orléans, beginning with the Huguenot deputies. The Duc de Guise took fire. Returning from his pilgrimage to find the Constable in command of the army and the army itself disbanded, he suffered an attack of acute piety. As Grand Master he was responsible for the royal household, and in the royal household what did he find? Psalm-singing in the precincts of the Court. He protested to Catherine and threatened to use the flat of a halberd on those who allowed themselves such liberties. She remained unmoved; and her phlegmatic calm goaded him to a nervous paroxysm. He became sick—for two days—overwhelmed with grief—"half out of his mind"—the bulletins read. When he recovered, it was from the depths of discouragement, disillusioned and world-weary. When the States met to choose a common orator, his brother was nominated by the Clergy and rejected by the Third Estate; as for the Nobility, their hostility was such that neither he nor the Cardinal ventured to propose themselves.

The Catholic agitation did not disturb her unduly. It was *extra muros*, and the bulwark which she had found in the States steadied and strengthened her. From the nation she derived a support which enabled her to ignore foreign pressure, and the understanding between them increased her self-confidence. Not only did she retract none of her liberal tendencies; she accentuated them, writing to the Parlements to suspend judicial proceedings and to release all prisoners of religion, including those arrested for bearing arms and participating in public assemblies. These advances won her a measure of tolerance from Calvin. "Hope grows in us daily, because the hardness of the Queen is yielding," he wrote in reviewing these events. "Though the hypocrisy of the Queen makes her suspect to right-minded people, for she has too often deceived us with her clever caresses, it seems as though the concessions which she accords us under the dictates of necessity may have some serious results. If she keeps her promises, our Church will progress rapidly far and wide." And Calvin's distrust of her was at least as deep as Philip's.

The *rapprochement* which the religious question effected between the Regent and the country was a tentative understanding, which might have developed in time, had it not been for her besetting handicap. On the financial question the government met with a flat rebuff from the

States. Instead of a subsidy, the three Orders voted a unanimous recommendation that the Crown furnish its own endowment by reducing its expenses. In vain did the Regent comply, scrupulously working for a fortnight with the Chancellor, lopping, pruning, suppressing superfluous offices, diminishing her domestic staff, liquidating the Department of Venery, scraping a third from the pensions and a quarter from salaries. In vain did she stint, ignoring complaints, with an unsparing determination that was an earnest of her goodwill, and that led a friendly observer to remark that "the greatest of subsidies is the drastic economy which the Court imposes on itself in all things." At the closing session the Chancellor was able to report that the King had already realized economies amounting to 2,300,000 livres, "no mean sum," as he remarked. But the only impression which this great effort made on the States was that, if the Crown could do so much, there was no reason why it should not do more. The irreconcilable deputies of the opposition, reviving from their recent defeat, proposed that all the former favourites of Henri II should be compelled to restore to the Treasury the gifts they had drawn from it. This impolitic because impractical motion—for the interests which it attacked were too deeply entrenched to be uprooted—was an emotional extravagance which produced a serious consequence. The Duc de Guise, the Constable de Montmorency, and the Maréchal de Saint-André—the three most conspicuous monopolists of the past—drew together in defence of their common interests.

When, on January 31, 1561, the deputies filed out of the hall for the last time, leaving Catherine with the title but without the credits to govern, she found herself stranded. She was once more alone, not merely isolated but deserted. Everything was as before and yet . . . something had happened. She had met the nation. The dreaded encounter was over. She had been disowned, supported, and finally rebuffed by it. But if nothing had been accomplished, much had been initiated. The Crown and the country, after a long period of estrangement, had met, appraised their mutual powers, and parted; and their relations were destined to continue. Because the financial question remained unsettled, Catherine was compelled to recall the States for the following May, at Pontoise. She announced, however, that they would occupy themselves neither with politics nor religion, but solely with settling the debts of the King.

- 3 -

From Orléans with its painful memories Catherine retired to Fontainebleau. There, enjoying for a few weeks a respite from official responsibilities, she took her bearings and began to compute coolly what she had achieved. The King of Navarre, the Duc de Guise, and the Constable accompanied her, prolonging their reconciliation as if they felt that, in the first difficult days of her debut, she was entitled to a housewarming. The union of princes, born of one emergency, had weathered another; it had carried her through the States; but how long, in the nature of things, would it last? Already, from Orléans, she had written to the Bishop of Limoges, her ambassador in Spain: "Considering how difficult it is that this farce should be performed with so many characters without someone looking black, and that the diversity of men's minds, moved by so many passions, of which this world is full, is much to be feared, especially since so sudden and unforeseen a change cannot, I fear, be accepted at once by everyone, and above all by those who lately held the first place here . . ."—considering these common truths, she thought it well to explain her position. "The position which the King of Navarre holds here is beneath mine and under my authority, and I have done nothing for him or for the other Princes of the Blood who have been called to the Council except by force and necessity, but I have so won him that I dispose of him and do with him what I please." It was not the Bourbons she dreaded, but the Guises. "As you say, there are some people who would like to have it thought that nothing can prosper without them," and she suspected them of prejudicing Philip II against her because of the forced favour she showed to the King of Navarre. Of the legitimate pretender she was sure; of the illegitimate she lived in constant apprehension, and it was with something like panic that she caught wind of a scheme to marry Mary Stuart to Don Carlos, the heir to the Spanish throne. She redoubled her dispatches to Spain, composing them in pairs, one to the ambassador, one to her daughter, and harping with both hands on the danger to the country and to herself of such a match. "I am doing and I shall do everything to prevent it. What amazed me most," she admitted, with remarkable surprise, "is that the author and promoter of this matter has never mentioned it to me, not even remotely." The conduct of the Cardinal de Lorraine shocked her. "I have tried to draw him out, but he has never admitted the least likelihood of it, and now that he knows that the fact is winded and disclosed, he proceeds very coldly, dragging it out, perhaps to put us off our guard, and speaking merely of taking the character from Court and sending her after a time to her own country"—a consummation devoutly to be desired. Mary Stuart, as a wife or a widow, brought her nothing but trouble. She was a magnet for it; it was her fatal attraction; and Catherine longed to see the last of the woman who had come between her and her son and now threatened to alienate her son-in-law. The allegiance of the Guises, she felt, was escaping her. Finding that she had no intention of recalling them, they visibly disinterested themselves in public affairs. The Duke remained at Court, unoccupied and moody. But the Cardinal had retired to his diocese in Reims, and out of sight he was more than ever on her mind. What he might be doing in a diocese passed her imagination.

But it was not her habit to borrow trouble. She had come to Fontainebleau to forget it. For a few halcyon weeks she found relief and a breathing-spell in the pure air, the spacious seclusion, the unmortgaged majesty, of a landscape where every vista was focused on a palace and every avenue held the profane world at a distance. The *genius loci* worked a spell on the senses which everyone felt. In that sedative atmosphere tempers relaxed and friction was forgotten. The semblance of union was about her; she asked no more. The illusion was valuable; with every day that it lasted, she gained time, and time was her best ally. Time to heal, to repair, to consolidate—time to form a film of habit—with time she could accomplish anything.

She had come to Fontainebleau to recuperate, but she

was not idle. Daily she worked over the finances with the Chancellor, presided at the Council, and conducted affairs "with an absolute mastery." Her health was poor; she suffered from vertigo, a chronic complaint which the strain of the past two months had aggravated, but she had promised the King of Navarre that she would never be too ill to attend to business; and she kept her word.

For, indeed, the health of her children had now become a public debt, for which she was responsible to France. The liabilities under which they laboured were heavy. One had already succumbed to them. Charles, though he had a better start in life, was frail and over-excitable. At Fontainebleau, with his governor Monsieur de Cypierre and his brother, he spent his days hunting, shooting, and improvising sham battles, and despite his peaked face and his thin legs he began to belie his lagging vitality. Charles was sound, and she would not coddle him, though she watched over him jealously. He slept in her room, she supervised every detail of his life, no alien influence ever came between them, except when he found freedom in the sport of kings, which was already making a king of him. His high spirits and his promising ways impressed everyone; the word spread, and even the creditors of the Crown began to take heart.

With the same tireless vigilance she watched over her daughter in Spain. For the health of Elisabeth she was also responsible to France; Elisabeth was her link with Philip II, and the influence which she could bring to bear on him was of diplomatic value to the two countries. Catherine carefully guided her daughter through the first difficulties of her married life. The most fundamental was her health. Before she left France, a word of warning had been dropped by her mother, who since then had found it necessary to allude once more to the organic disability under which her daughter laboured. "Remember," she wrote, "what I told you before you left, for you know how much it would concern you if they were to learn what you have; if your husband knew it, you may be sure that he would never see you again." The discretion of Elisabeth left something to be desired; she favoured, among her ladies, those of her own age, and was apt to neglect her elders, and this, as Catherine pointed out, was imprudent since one of her elders, Madame de Clermont, was in possession of her secret. She expected the impossible: responsibility and cheerfulness, circumspection and gaiety, and while she urged her cheerless wisdom on Elisabeth, it was because "I desire nothing more in this world than to see you happy and gay and contented all your life long. . . ." It never occurred to her that the experience she supplied might be withering. She had acquired it at the same age and had succeeded, in spite of it, in preserving her vital spirits. Why should Elisabeth do less?

Why indeed? Of all her children, Elisabeth was the one who resembled her most. She was the most warped. When the Queen of Spain was reported to be pregnant, Catherine received the news with sad incredulity. "I fear that nothing will come of it," she confided to the Bishop of Limoges; but on the chance of cheating fate she poured out the benefits of her experience. Above all, no pampering, no self-indulgence, no lying in bed. She begged the Bishop to remind the invalid that "she has seen me pregnant, when I was so sick that I could not walk, and much older than she is; and with all that, I forced myself to lean on two women, so as not to let myself be coddled in bed. I know only too well that for the least pain she will refuse to stir, and this will only end by harming her."

Sentiment and policy blended in her solicitude for Elisabeth, but sentiment eclipsed every other consideration as the infirmities of the Queen of Spain grew more pronounced. Her pregnancy proved a delusion, and a few months later she was taken with smallpox. The news reached Catherine while François II was dying, and for a moment her self-control forsook her. Her letters to Spain were a weary moan. "After so many losses and misfortunes as I have had in the last year and a half, I am always dreading others and, above all, the loss of one who is now the dearest thing that remains to me." Her foreboding was abject.

But Elisabeth recovered. Catherine regained her sane view of things. Sentiment was weakening, and she spared her daughter any display of it; she had an example to set, and she set it stoically. As soon as the invalid was con-

valescent, she enlisted her aid in defeating the intrigues
to marry Mary Stuart in Spain, prompting her daughter
to propose the hand of the little Princess Margot for Don
Carlos, or the hand of an old Princess of Portugal, anything to block the interloper in Spain; and in the prosecution of these schemes, though they came to nothing,
Elisabeth showed a healthy alacrity which cheered her
mother. Catherine rapidly recovered her moral aplomb.
Reviewing her situation and weighing all the handicaps
under which she had assumed power, she felt that she had
accomplished much; and she said so.

- 4 -

It was rash. The condition of confidence was, as experience
had taught her, to dissimulate it. The vigorous activity of
the Queen-Mother, her sanguine vitality, her serene self-
possession, her expansive good humour, betrayed too
clearly her assurance that her period of insecurity was
over and that she had a firm grasp of power. In the third
week of February, Antoine de Bourbon became unruly,
made a violent scene in the Council, and demanded the
vindication of Condé. His tone was so aggressive that
Catherine was shocked by it, and sharp words passed
between them. But she attached no importance to his
outburst. She ended the day by dictating an order for
twenty new swans to stock the lake, and gave no further
thought to Condé. A week later Antoine de Bourbon
returned to the attack. This time he demanded the Seal
for himself, and the Lieutenant-Generalship, and the dismissal of the Duc de Guise from Court. He offered her an
ultimatum. He proposed to exercise an authority in the
government at least equal to that enjoyed in the past by
the Guises and the Constable, and if his demands were not
met, he threatened to resign from the Council and to
carry his claim to the Regency before Parlement. This
scene occurred in private, and Catherine was patient. It
was not Antoine de Bourbon who troubled her, it was
Condé. Invariably, when one brother asserted himself, the
other was at the bottom of it; and it was clear that Condé,
who had been waiting two months for his vindication,

would have to be satisfied. The union of princes would collapse unless he were included in it, but it would also collapse if he were.

She began by submitting her dilemma to Guise. "I implore Your Majesty," he exclaimed, "not to command me to leave Court. I could not obey such an order; being, thanks to God and Your Majesty, Grand Master and Grand Chamberlain, I propose to exercise my office and to serve the King my master where I should." "I am so far from suggesting it," she assured him, "that I command you to remain." She consulted the Cardinal de Tournon, her adviser *in extremis,* and together they sought a solution.

Although Guise refused to leave Court, he was induced to make a conciliatory declaration to the members of the Council. The members of the Council, impressed by this speech, begged him to repeat it to the King of Navarre. "I shall never do so," he replied. "It is not in my nature to stoop to such cowardice. It is enough that I have spoken before you. I have taken you and God as my witnesses that I am neither quarrelsome nor seditious. The rest does not concern me. Do as you wish."

Grand seigneur to the last, the declaration of the Duc de Guise was of no help to Catherine, particularly as the members of the Council were all men and abjectly moved by it: the Cardinal de Tournon, the Duc de Montpensier, and the Maréchal de Saint-André declared that if Guise left Court they would follow, and even the Chancellor said that, in that event, he would be compelled to resign. Her whole structure of government was compromised unless she could mollify the King of Navarre. But Antoine de Bourbon, obdurate with the obstinacy of a weak man and the perversity of one in the wrong, announced his departure for the twenty-eighth, and on the twenty-eighth his baggage and escort were drawn up in the courtyard. Montmorency joined him; his baggage and escort were also drawn up in the courtyard. Catherine, in a fury of indecision, kept to her room, watching the exodus from her window. As the Constable climbed into the saddle, the Cardinal de Tournon brought him a command from the King to return to the palace. The old man dismounted, followed him, and found the King waiting for him alone. The lad implored his *compère* not to forsake him. To such an appeal the veteran loyalty of Montmorency responded: he agreed to remain. Antoine de Bourbon dismounted and instructed his servants to unpack. He was not prepared to risk isolation.

This crisis compelled Catherine to take a step which she had deferred because of its difficulty. The necessity of satisfying Condé could no longer be avoided; the security of her Regency depended upon it. Of his guilt she was convinced, and she had not abandoned hope of proving it; whenever the trail of the Malignys was reported, she spurred the pursuit, but the Malignys continued to escape; and since the incriminating evidence was lacking, she was compelled to exonerate the incurable conspirator.

Guise was accommodating. He agreed to a reconciliation which should be binding on himself and his followers. She was relieved, and a little irritated, by his generosity; men forget and forgive so lightly. When Condé arrived at Fontainebleau, he went directly to his brother's apartments and sent her a message that he would abstain from presenting his respects to her and the King if the Duc de Guise were present. She was waiting to receive him in state, surrounded by the members of the Council. A hurried consultation took place; the Constable consented to serve as a peacemaker, but he had to make several trips to and fro before a compromise was arranged. It was finally settled that Condé would appear but would not address the Duc de Guise. The latter shrugged; he could dispense with courtesies, he said; all that he demanded was that his adversary should not look at him. On this basis an understanding was reached. It was considered advisable to transfer the scene to a spacious gallery, and everyone hastened to his post. The Queen-Mother took up her station with her children in the centre of the hall, while a crowd of curious courtiers assembled to observe the strange spectacle. It passed off successfully: Condé appeared and went through his motions; neither he nor Guise saw each other; but the feat required such concentration that it created an intolerable tension, and someone suddenly broke it by crying that the roof was falling. Bedlam broke out; Catherine snatched up her children and fled; and the witnesses dispersed in confusion.

Several days later, the Council acquitted Condé, on his solemn oath that he had never conspired against the late King. The personal reconciliation with Guise which she then endeavoured to bring about was more difficult. Both were in a belligerent temper. Condé made no attempt to deny that, though he had not conspired against the Crown, he had planned to overthrow the Guises; and Guise announced to anyone who would listen that, "whenever the Prince wishes, I shall take him by his little finger and we shall go wherever he pleases to explain ourselves." The utmost she could manage was a chance meeting, at which they exchanged a stiff nod; and she was deeply relieved when Condé left Court six days after his arrival. But he left in the same irreconcilable spirit in which he came, completely unchastened. Unsatisfied by his acquittal by the Council, which he regarded as a favour, he announced his determination to obtain the legal vindication which was his due from Parlement, and rode off, menacing the Guises and their accomplices. The Council was uneasy, but Catherine minimized the importance of these incidents in her correspondence with Spain. "I have done so well that my brother, the King of Navarre, and Messieurs de Guise are reconciled and have pledged friendship," she wrote. "It only remains to do as much with Monsieur le Prince, who has shown himself a little more difficult; nevertheless, I hope he will allow himself to be brought to reason. . . ." She had an inexhaustible supply of optimism . . . for foreign consumption.

- 5 -

The importance which Catherine attached to Court politics was amply justified by the conduct of Condé after he left Fontainebleau. He proceeded directly to Paris, and his arrival in the capital coincided with an incident of exceptional gravity.

In preparation for the next meeting of the States-General, preliminary assemblies were being held throughout the provinces to designate the new deputies. The function of these assemblies, as of the States themselves, had been expressly limited by the government to discussing the settlement of the King's debts; the discussion of political questions was forbidden; and a censorship was enforced, prohibiting the publication of information dealing with the States-General of Orléans. The Assembly of the Prévôté of Paris was the first body to challenge these restrictions. At the opening session, on March 15, when the President announced that the purpose of the meeting was to settle the debts of the King—"Of what King?" a voice cried. "Of King Charles, the minor son of the late King Henri," he proceeded. "But who governs him?" four or five voices shouted. The President named the members of the Council. The opposition rose, disavowed the acts of the States of Orléans, and declared that no subsidy would be voted unless the government were entrusted to the King of Navarre. The opposition was numerous and noisy and gained control of the Chamber. This agitation was the tail-end of the storm of Orléans, two months late; but in one important respect it differed from that explosion. Instead of a spontaneous popular movement, it was a partisan agitation, promoted by the Comte de la Rochefoucauld and instigated by Condé; and the names of the authors were communicated to Catherine at the same time as the news of the scandal itself. The most disturbing feature of the information was that the manifestation of Paris had been organized as an example to the rest of the country; and though she promptly took her precautions, writing to the governors of the provinces to warn them, her agitation was so intense that she neglected the most elementary of precautions. She made no attempt to conceal her dismay. "They have deprived me of my authority, leaving me the mere charge of rearing my children," she wrote to the Governor of Brittany. "You can understand, my cousin, what shame and dishonour it is to find myself deprived of what was granted me, something to which all the Princes consented and which I believe has been rightly conceded to me, and I am determined before I endure it to accept poverty rather than that they should take my life with my honour. . . ." She sent for the King of Navarre and ask him point-blank if he were responsible for what had happened. She thought it *extremely strange*, she said, "that after having granted me authority and all the States having approved it at Orléans, there should be some madmen who wish to deprive me of it." He replied coolly that "he was very well pleased by what he saw"; it would teach her to recognize his rights and the service he was doing her by sacrificing them. "I know very well what you are doing for me, but to be obliged to you for something which I believe to be due me and which would deprive me of my honour, I cannot admit," she replied. Her voice broke. The dispute continued. It continued intermittently for three or four days, each worrying the other without result; and with every encounter his spirit rose. Reopening all the questions so recently and so ill closed, he demanded the Lieutenant-Generalship and exacted the dismissal of Guise. She protested, she appealed, she pleaded; but he merely pointed to Paris. Her agitation increased when she learned that Condé was raising troops, distributing arms, and appearing in public with hundreds of horsemen. She appealed to Guise, but his patience was exhausted. "No one," he said, "is strong enough to drive me away. Before I go, forty thousand men will fall at my feet." The Spanish ambassador, anxious to prevent the high military command from passing to the King of Navarre, placed his influence at her disposal, visiting her every other day, offering to do anything she desired, to say anything she suggested, to repeat his demonstrations wherever she wished, and, if need be, to support her by a direct appeal to his master; but she was not so hard-pressed as to accept such assistance. She had recourse to the Constable and to her intimate friend Madame de Montpensier, who negotiated with Antoine de Bourbon. Peace was patched up, but at a hard price. To save the principle of her government, she parted with the integrity of her power; to preserve the union of princes, she sacrificed everything else. Antoine de Bourbon obtained the command of the army and the control of the Chancery, and she consented to share with him the use of the Seal, the symbol of sovereignty. With the exception of the dismissal of the Duc de Guise, she submitted to every demand; and the first Prince of the Blood became, in effect, her partner in authority. While she sought to convey the impression, both abroad and at home, that she had outwitted Antoine de Bourbon, granting him merely a nominal authority and retaining the substance of power herself, her defeat was recognized by every observer, friendly,

inimical, or neutral, who had seen her at close quarters
and noted her agitation during the crisis and after it. "The
Queen," as one of them said, "has at last shown that she
is only a woman." The world showed her no quarter; she
had committed the cardinal sin in a ruler, she had allowed
herself to be intimidated. The attitude of the princes, of
the diplomats, of the Court, underwent that slight but
significant change which spells discredit; she ignored her
defeat, but it rankled and she was never more of a woman
than in the obliquity of feeling which followed her mental
evasions. It was not against the Bourbons that she was
most bitter, it was against the Guises. All their past errors
returned to plague her, and it was she who paid their
penalty; and the loyalty, or at least the correctness, with
which they had behaved since her accession only added
to their offences the supreme one of being irreproachable.
Her patience was tried, and her bitterness overflowed
when François de Guise finally took a step which placed
for ever beyond dispute his conscious rectitude.

- 6 -

The religious situation was simmering. The amnesty announced by the government at Orléans produced a vast
unrest throughout the country, scandalizing the Catholics
and emboldening the Protestants. The latter, wherever
their numbers warranted it, assembled publicly and occupied "temples," despite the warnings of Calvin. "To
occupy temples and to rejoice overmuch," he wrote to the
Church of Paris, "has never been our counsel, as you know,
unless it is done by permission. Where it has been done
without authority, it has been in contempt of us. If they
continue, we leave events in the hands of God. We fear that
this heat will be cooled suddenly by some hard storm." But
the lawgiver had lost touch with, and control over, his
followers in the spring of 1561. The preservation of
public order became daily more difficult. The officers of
the Crown, struggling with their task, received nothing
from the Regent but instructions designed to facilitate it.
They were advised to use discretion, to conform to local
conditions, to muffle trouble, to wink at infractions of the
law where strict enforcement would breed disorder. "I

shall be very well pleased, as you learned before our departure, and I have not changed my mind since," she wrote to the Governor of Brittany, "if they will live in such a manner as not to scandalize their neighbours, and, when they assemble, if they do so in such small numbers and so peaceably that there will be no noise or necessity of preventing them." She expected the Protestants to co-operate with her and "to accommodate themselves to the times in which we live, when everything must be conducted on both sides with reason and great gentleness and moderation, without precipitating anything." She commanded the Procuror-General of Paris not to "investigate too curiously those who keep to their houses nor inquire too closely into what is done there." But she understood the inexorable nature of a revolutionary movement as little as Calvin. Protestants and Catholics alike made free with the royal authority. The magistrates interpreted the law according to their convictions, the Parlements revised the royal edicts and corrected them, and though she protested, she was powerless to check a condition which was the inevitable consequence of her caution. In applying to the country the same personal expedients with which she managed the princes, she magnified on a national scale the impression of her weakness, her compliance, and her vulnerability. One month after the assembly at Orléans the whole country was in a ferment of unrest.

Nor was the danger merely domestic. As usual when a nation is in the throes of social change, the habit of imputing internal disorder to alien influence was too convenient not to be employed by impotent authority. Catherine protested formally to the Senate of Geneva against the subversive activities of the Calvinist preachers in France, "in which we see well enough what is the bent of their spirit and intention, and if these are the fruits of a pure and simple religion, such as they claim to profess," she left the world to judge. She exaggerated the influence of the Calvinist preachers because the foreign influences which were really dangerous she dared not denounce. The English ambassador was working on Antoine de Bourbon to swing France into the Protestant orbit; and a corresponding pressure by the Catholic powers to return to the old policy of repression was brought to bear upon

Catherine herself. Philip II, finding that his representations produced no effect, went over her head. The envoy whom he sent to France to inspire her carried letters of like tenor for the leaders of the Catholic party at Court.

To such solicitations no one was more susceptible than François de Guise. His religious zeal, quickening with his political decline, became his ruling passion. Never was the saving grace of religion better bestowed. Sustained by an ideal which sublimated his sense of duty and sanctioned the irresponsible exercise of his passions, by an evolution as simple as his mental processes, he became a militant champion of the Catholic cause—the last cause left to command.

Somewhat similar was the experience of the Constable, for whom too the new reign had brought nothing but delusions. His conscience was also alarmed. As the claims of the Bourbons were legitimate, and jealousy of power was an inadmissible motive, they were both driven to embrace a disinterested cause, the last refuge of disappointed politicians. The Constable, always a zealous, now became an active Catholic. But his conversion to the Guises was the triumph of a third person. The Maréchal de Saint-André, who had amassed a scandalous fortune under Henri II, was the apostle. No one had benefited more from the confiscation of Protestant property, and no one had persecuted heresy more zealously. His talents attracted the attention of Philip II, whose confidential agent he became.

The political miracle which Saint-André accomplished was prepared by his diplomacy and precipitated by the manifestation of the Prévôté of Paris, which had a Protestant colour that he recognized. The one scruple which prevented Montmorency from declaring himself was his attachment to Coligny, with whom he was reluctant to break; but Saint-André succeeded in persuading him that the Admiral was personally responsible for the attack on their fortunes, and the scruple vanished.

The manifestation of the Prévôté of Paris was, in fact, of crucial importance. During those four strenuous days when, as a result of it, Catherine was struggling to save her Regency from the Bourbons, a far more formidable event was taking place in the basements of Fontainebleau.

There every morning, at dawn, in a little chapel of the
basse-cour, the Duc de Guise, the Constable, and the
Maréchal de Saint-André met, with a few other Catholic
leaders, to hear the sermons of a humble Jacobin friar.
The significance of these meetings escaped Catherine.
Obsessed by the Bourbons, when the Constable and the
Duc de Guise announced their reconciliation, she discerned
nothing more than a gesture of support for which she was
grateful. Support it was, but not a gesture. On the same
day, in a letter to one of her confidants, the Duchesse de
Guise announced the birth of the Catholic opposition.
"Monsieur de Guise and the Constable have pledged
themselves to be eternally united, and they have sworn it
before the Queen. With them will be united the Cardinal
de Tournon and the two Marshals. Together, they will
undoubtedly be the stronger and curb the Queen. Monsieur de Montpensier will lend them at all times his entire
aid for the defence of religion." Two weeks later the
movement came out of the basement. On Easter Monday,
the Constable received the Duc de Guise and the Maréchal
de Saint-André at his table, to celebrate the formation
of the coalition known as the Triumvirate. Immediately
afterwards both he and the Duc de Guise left Fontainebleau, after informing the Regent that they would not
return. Then, at last, the full extent of the disaster dawned
upon Catherine. At the very moment when she had capitulated to the Bourbons, she found herself abandoned by
those for whom she had made a sacrifice that was irreparable, humiliating, and . . . useless.

- 7 -

As the only injury which they had not yet done was to
poison the mind of Philip II against her, she hastened to
prevent it. The long letters which she wrote as an antidote to Elisabeth were an aching indictment of "those
who wished to take me from your father, and later to turn
the King your brother from me." Memory and resentment
flooded the pages with a long leaking complaint: "I must
tell you the truth. All this trouble has been caused by the
hatred which this whole kingdom feels for the Cardinal de
Lorraine and the Duc de Guise, supposing that I wished

to return them to the government, which I denied, for I am under no obligation: you know how they treated me in the time of the late King your brother; and even now, when they have no support but me, you know how they work against me in the marriage of your sister. I decided, therefore, that I would preserve them from harm, but that I would look to the security of your brothers and myself, and no longer mingle their quarrels with mine, knowing that they would have appointed themselves, if they could have, and would have left me out, as they always do whenever it is a matter of their greatness and profit; for they have nothing else in their hearts. . . . They are hated for the folly with which they have offended everyone, giving out that I was not a good Christian, to make everyone suspect me and to force me to trust no one but them; telling me that everyone is my enemy and that, without them, I could not retain my authority, and now that they see that I allow the King of Navarre to be the Lieutenant-General of the King under me, and that I have discovered just the contrary of what they told me, and that I was hated only for favouring them, they are amazed. Therefore, *ma fille m'amie*, do not let your husband the King believe an untruth. I do not mean to change my life or my religion in anything; I am what I am in order to preserve your brothers and their kingdom." She returned to the subject again and again, with a rage which nothing but repetition could appease. "God be praised, I am at peace," she announced hotly, "both in the matter of religion and the preservation of my authority. And since I am at peace, I hope that neither of you will believe the lies that are sent you from here. . . . You may be sure that those who used to be kings and who have so embroiled our affairs that this is the only reason why I cannot do what I wish to do at once, will overlook nothing to malign my behaviour and actions, for fear their faults and great ambitions will be discovered, foreigners as they are in this kingdom, for they are so hated that as long as they were associated with me, I was never able to obtain the complete obedience which I have now that they have retired until the coronation of the King my son. *Madame ma fille*, if your husband the King mentions it, you may tell him the truth, for I state everything just as it is, and

I am angry that they strengthen themselves with him now; when they had the power and were like kings themselves, they did nothing but malign his actions. . . . Do not believe what they send you from here, I beg you, they are so furious at no longer governing that they wish to make me hated by everyone whom they know that I wish to keep on good terms with my son, thinking that, if war broke out, I should have to put myself in their hands and employ them; but I give you my word of honour that I will never do so, for they have been ungrateful and have ruined this kingdom. Instead of concluding that all is going to ruin because the Cardinal is no longer here, I assure you that this gives me a chance to put everything to rights again. Therefore, do not worry and answer sensibly, as I am sure you will do, but so as to close the question, assuring them that I have all the authority which you could wish me to have and that I am a Christian, observing the same form of life both for myself and my children as did the King your father and grandfather, and that I have no intention of changing it; and assure the King your husband of it."

Gradually the violence of her feelings subsided, and indignation gave way to relief. With the departure of Guise, Antoine de Bourbon became once more the most docile of men. To humour him, she set her diplomacy in motion, and begged Philip II to promise the poor man whom he refused to recognize as a sovereign in his own right some compensation for the loss of Spanish Navarre: Sardinia, for instance, or some such small possession of no military importance to the Spanish Crown but of inestimable diplomatic value to her. Whatever the effect of these suggestions on Philip II, the impression on Antoine de Bourbon was all that could be desired. He seconded her diplomacy by the most complete submission to her wishes, waiving the sovereign prerogatives which he had wrested from her and leaving her the full administration of affairs. In effect, she governed alone.

Yet the uncontested supremacy, which Catherine enjoyed with the retirement of Guise, gave her no rest. Her authority, supreme at Fontainebleau, had no real hold on the country. The country was agitated, throughout the whole month of April, by disturbances culminating in a re-

April

ligious riot in Paris. This rising unrest, serious enough in
itself, was rendered doubly so by the fact that it occurred
at a time when she had lost contact with the Catholic
leaders. A coalition was forming which, if not opposed to
the Crown, was independent of it, and over which she
had no control, and she would not have been a states-
woman, she would not have been a woman, if she had not
determined to investigate its activities in person. The opportunity was offered by a visit to the Duc de Guise at
Nanteuil, on her way to Reims for the coronation of the
King.

The Duc de Guise received her with a hospitality so
strained that the least misstep was likely to lead to an
unpleasantness. And, in fact, the incidents began on the
day after her arrival. She had given orders for the doors
to be closed to a gallery in which she was holding a conference. The Duc de Nemours, an intimate of the household, an ex-member of the Council, and an old friend of
François de Guise, took exception to his exclusion, forced
his way in, and demanded an explanation, first of the
King, then of Antoine de Bourbon, and upon being satisfied that neither had given the order, followed Catherine
to her room and made a scandalous scene. Jacques de
Nemours-Savoie was an ex-friend of hers. There was a
secret between them. He had once offered to disfigure
Madame de Valentinois for her sake. Such services are
most valuable when they are not performed, and he reminded her of it. He had been good enough to share her
secrets once, but she closed her door to him now. Tres-
passing to and fro, he complained of her ingratitude; it
was not the first time he had felt it. She might favour the
Protestant party, if she wished, but he would return to the
service of his cousin, the Duke of Savoy. She explained
that her orders had been misunderstood. The guard would
be punished. "No," he exclaimed, "it is not right that he
should suffer for the errors of others." And he added: "A
day will come when Your Majesty will need good men and
will have difficulty in finding them. I hope at least that
your son the King will learn the truth later." She listened
to him critically. On the next day he left Nanteuil. The
Duc de Guise did not let the matter rest. Far more incensed by the slight to his old friend than by the insult

to her, he made no effort to conceal his resentment and reminded her that Nemours was the one man in France to whom she was most indebted for his past services. She let that pass. But she came to the point. She broached the question which brought her to Nanteuil. Was it true, she asked him, as she had heard, that he had formed a league for the support of religion? He did not deny it; on the contrary, he declared that he would submit to the judgment of Parlement to be punished if he had erred in doing what he had done. Then she put a leading question: "What would you do if the King my son were to change his religion?" The reply was as prompt as it was plain. "The Cardinal de Tournon, the Constable de Montmorency, the Maréchaux de Saint-André and de Brissac, my entire family, our many friends and myself, are all resolved, if that should happen, to oppose it, and we should undoubtedly be the stronger in defence of a faith preserved by all the kings from the first who embraced Christianity. Therefore, Madame, consider well what you do, you may meet with some surprises." He had never been wanting in candour; of all his aristocratic qualities, it was the one she most disliked and, murmuring a vague reassurance, she brought the conversation to a close.

She knew, she had always known, what to expect; there was no escape for her; the Guises were part of her destiny; they would be with her for life. She had boasted that their retirement gave her the opportunity to "set everything to rights," but their absence was more troubling than their presence, and she recognized that her security depended on inducing them to return to Court. She forced herself to propitiate them; she wrote an apologetic letter to the Duc de Nemours; she manifested her Catholic zeal; but she produced no impression. Both Guise and Montmorency, who joined him at Nanteuil, ignored her advances and evaded her invitations. She would have failed, had not another influence supported her. Though the Pope congratulated the Catholic leaders on their firm stand, he disapproved of their absence from Court, where their presence was needed to oppose Protestant influence, and the Nuncio urged the Cardinal de Lorraine to resume his place in the Council.

The political situation in the sixth month of her Regency cast a gloom over the coronation of the King. She had counted on the great ceremony to visualize the divine right of majesty and eclipse factional differences in a solemn apotheosis of the Crown. Through the glamour of the occasion, however, the shabby realities showed. At Reims the princes assembled about her—the Montmorencys, the Guises, the Châtillons, the Bourbons—in a perfunctory truce. But their attitude made it plain that in manifesting their loyalty to the Crown they distinguished between the principle and the person who represented it. Apart from her functions, she had no weight, and when she forsook her official capacity, she was constantly reminded how readily they dissociated her from it. Her son Alexandre having expressed a desire to figure in the first rank of the Peers, she requested Montmorency, whose right this was, to waive his prerogative as a personal favour to her. He replied brutally that she might deprive him of this dignity by force but not by persuasion, and if she persisted, he would appeal to Parlement. The coronation, which took place on May 15, was an unimpressive and apathetic performance. The necessity of economy curtailed the splendour of the occasion, and the impression of regal authority which it was designed to inculcate was impaired by the youth and frailty of the King. When the heavy crown was placed on his head, he wept. The Cardinal de Lorraine, who performed the ceremony, prolonged the ordeal by a lengthy address in which, ignoring the anointed tears of the ninth Charles, he elaborated the maxim that "anyone who advised him to change his religion would at the same time tear the Crown from his head." The ceremony over, the Catholic leaders hastened to disperse, the Duc de Guise returning to Nanteuil and the Constable to Chantilly. Catherine did not allow them to elude her. One by one, she followed them up. She spent a day with the Cardinal in Reims, and another with the Constable at Chantilly, on her way to Paris. The bantering tone in which she announced her visit to Montmorency was not without a bitter undertone. "Lansac tells me that you have asked whether the King my son and I will remain more than one night at Chantilly. I shall give you a day if you wish, but I must see you; I am sure that if I promised more, you would drive us from your door." It was fair warning that she would take no rebuff. After the Constable, it was the turn of François de Guise. His persistent evasion of the invitations which both she and the King of Navarre addressed to him to return to Court compelled her to resort to extremities: she sent him word that his presence was required in Paris to defend "the honour of God." He rose to it heroically. "Since it is a matter of the honour of God," he announced, "I go, and whatever befalls, I shall die, for I could not die better." When he arrived, he discovered that his presence was required to lead a parade. But his dedicated spirit did not desert him. On June 5, followed by Charles IX and the King of Navarre, he led the procession of the Fête-Dieu through the crowded streets of the capital. Catholic Paris gave him a tremendous ovation, and the acclamations of the multitude consecrated and crowned his cause. The procession was repeated by popular request, with the Cardinal de Lorraine bearing the Host. To all outward appearances the Guises had triumphed, and that was sufficient for Catherine. They were with her again, and they served her purpose—a political parade.

- 8 -

After her tour of investigation she could no longer doubt that the formidable menace of the Catholic coalition, combined with the rising agitation in the country, would breed civil war, unless she intervened promptly to check it. The time for temporizing was past; she was obliged to take an initiative. But what initiative could she take, short of committing herself to either party, that would not ruin her policy of national union and provoke the very disorders which she was determined to avoid? Her inclination was to arbitrate. For the religious question, she had always insisted, there was but one cure—a Council. Her faith in reason was implicit: to raise the issues above passion and prejudice, to place them on a plane of judgment and sanity, to submit them to the searching white light of reason; the solution, so simple that it was bold, seemed unavoidable. But to such an experiment how enormous were the obstacles—the intolerance of both sides, the vital interests involved, the partisan passions, the political complications—which had grown with time into an inextricable complex; how could the white light of reason penetrate a problem to which reason was as alien as it was fatal? At the first touch of intelligence the religious problem would evaporate and reveal what underlay it—the blind, blundering, inexorable logic of life. But the magnitude of the difficulty did not deter Catherine; she failed to grasp it. The only difficulties which she foresaw were diplomatic ones.

These were formidable enough. At the States-General of Orléans she had pledged herself to procure the convocation of a Council, either Œcumenical or National. Theoretically, a Council was the basis, therefore, and the apology of her religious policy, the measures of toleration extended to the Protestants being merely provisional, a *modus vivendi* in view of an eventual settlement. This arrangement might have been indefinitely prolonged, had not the religious agitation developed so rapidly that the solution could no longer be adjourned. The only question was what form the Council should take. Under pressure, the Pope had announced the reopening of the Council of Trent, but this was merely a political manœuvre, as everyone knew, to prevent the convocation of a National Council; and in any case to reopen the old Council instead of convening a new one was to reaffirm all the verdicts of the past and to close instead of reopening the discussion. Moreover, as the Protestants were not to be represented, the possibility of a genuine consultation—of a "free and honest Council"—was eliminated beforehand. On the other hand, to convoke a new Council involved the old ague of Conciliar or Papal supremacy; and the religious problem resolved itself for Rome into a single issue, the principle of Papal supremacy, which, being arbitrary, would not bear discussion. Catherine complained repeatedly of the Curial tactics. "Our Holy Father," she wrote, "leads many people to think that he desires the Council in form but not in fact." But this was not the only impediment. The Pope, even had he been able or willing to yield, had to account to and to accommodate Philip II, who was unalterably opposed to a Council of any kind, whether Œcumenical or National, and refused to accept the summons even to the sonorous simulacrum of the Council of

Trent. Under these conditions, the Œcumenical Council was of no value to France, and Catherine had no choice but to risk a National Council. Ever since the formation of the Catholic coalition, she had been secretly negotiating with Geneva to induce Théodore de Bèze and the Protestant pastors to co-operate. In June the first intimation of her design leaked out abroad. The expected outcry followed. The Pope, protesting that the kingdom of France "was going to complete perdition," sent a Legate, to witness and ritualize the end; "it is an Extreme Unction," he explained to the Spanish ambassador. Philip II promptly accepted the Œcumenical Council and announced that the Spanish prelates would leave without delay, reaching Trent in the first days of August.

It was in preparation for this situation that Catherine had used all her resources to recall the Catholic leaders to Court. She needed them as a guarantee against foreign interference. Their presence was a blind, and their fanaticism a foil, to mislead public opinion and to mask her negotiation of the National Council. The skill with which she made them her unconscious accomplices revealed her remarkable gifts as a strategist. As she could no longer deceive them by words, it was necessary to outwit them by acts. The diplomacy she displayed in pursuit of this plan involved her official acts in a seeming confusion which successfully baffled all her interpreters.

Certainly that confusion was the product of clear thinking. Studying her approach to the religious problem and organizing her attack on it, she decided to dissociate the political from the religious problem, treating each separately, the latter in the National Council, the former in an Assembly especially selected for the purpose. By these tactics she hoped to remove the doctrinal problem from the jurisdiction of the Council of Trent and the political problem from that of the States-General, and to control both herself. The civil problem—that is, the measures necessary to settle the political status of heresy, the only aspect of the question which was of vital concern to the Catholic coalition—she entrusted to an Assembly of Parlement sitting with the members of the Royal Council and the leaders of the coalition. As the Parlement was notoriously reactionary, and she promised to abide by its deci-

July 30.

sion, this seemed to offer an unquestionable guaranty to the Triumvirate. The Assembly met and deliberated for twenty-three days, and the result was what might have been expected: the verdict was overwhelmingly in favour of cancelling the concessions already made to the heretics and reverting to the old methods of repression. Paris hailed the victory with clamorous enthusiasm. The government had pledged itself to embody the verdict in an inviolable edict. After three weeks of reflection, Catherine and the Chancellor produced the Edict of July, which they concocted between them, a masterpiece of calculated incoherence, deliberately designed to be inapplicable. A final clause was added by way of epilogue, stating that the Edict of July was a provisional measure dependent on the outcome of the National Council, which, as it happened, met on the day that the edict was published (July 30). The Protestants had been forewarned. Assured that they would not be molested, they took full advantage of official connivance. In one place, where the Protestants protested against its publication, the Royal Governor was instructed to reassure them. "Since it is to be feared that the publication will produce the contrary effect from what we wish, it is not advisable to proceed. Give yourself no trouble about exacting a strict observation of the edict," Catherine herself wrote. Among the Catholics the first transports of joy were succeeded by perplexity; officials who read the edict literally and attempted to apply it wrestled with its mysteries, and some accused the Queen of *naïveté*.

Under cover of this manœuvre she pursued her scandalous negotiations with Geneva. In these she had the assistance of three men who for various motives made themselves her accomplices. The King of Navarre vouched for his Catholic zeal to the Assembly of Parlement and cooperated with her in winning the confidence of the Calvinists. But his gratuitous character would have carried little weight in Geneva had it not been supported by the influence of Coligny. The Admiral was beginning to be recognized as the foremost lay leader of the Reformation in France. He alone displayed the consistency and courage of a disinterested conviction, combined with political instinct and caution—qualities which recommended him to Catherine as much as to Calvin. The guarantee which she needed in Geneva was that of integrity. Between them now began a close collaboration. He vouched for her good faith to his co-religionists and assisted her in selecting the Calvinist delegates. She wished the sect to be well represented, and as it was necessary to encourage those who dreaded the personal or the intellectual risks of the encounter, to repress the enthusiasm of others, and to cool the native preachers who, accustomed to the crude polemics of the provinces, were positive that they could sweep everything before them at Court, his experience relieved her of much anxiety. She accepted all his suggestions with one exception. She drew the line at Calvin. "As for you, Sir," Coligny informed him indirectly, through the minister Le Maçon, "we see no means of bringing you here without grave dangers, seeing the rage which all the enemies of the Evangel have conceived against you and the commotions which your mere name would excite in this country if you were known to be here. We know also that the Queen would not have the heart to see you, and she said frankly that she would not undertake to assure your safety as she does that of the others, and the bishops could not bring themselves to look upon you or to listen to you. Such, Sir, is the esteem in which you are held by these venerable prelates." Catherine was herself a venerable prelate in this respect. The official excuse thinly veiled her personal sentiments. The Protestant pontiff alarmed her far more than the Catholic Pope, and she accepted with relief the substitution of his lieutenant, Théodore de Bèze, who had the supreme merit in her eyes of being a man of the world. One addition she made to the list on her own responsibility: that of Peter Martyr, whose heterodoxy inspired her with confidence; he was an Italian.

But her most valuable collaborator was the Cardinal de Lorraine, whose co-operation served to silence the Catholic coalition and to coax out the French clergy. She converted him to the Council by representing it as his own idea, and so it was: he had proposed it once, as a bargaining measure to induce the Pope to call an Œcumenical Council, and was readily induced to adopt it for his own satisfaction. He had a weakness for Councils, being a brilliant speaker and a born parliamentarian. The most eloquent, learned, and subtle orator of his day, he longed to measure himself, in theological debate, with the doctors of the Reformation; and indeed he offered, for her private delectation, to give a private exhibition of his powers, rehearsing all the main questions of dogma and engaging to accept whatever could be proved by Scripture to be true. He was a latitudinarian, expert, self-confident, unprejudiced. The Cardinal de Tournon detested him—another reason that decided him. Tournon had usurped her confidence ever since the beginning of the reign, was an irreconcilable reactionary, blindly opposed to the Council, but old and inarticulate, at least until he discovered the complicity of the Queen-Mother and Lorraine, when he wrote to Rome, eloquently stigmatizing the Council in Italian superlatives.

Lorraine was her most valuable collaborator also because he was mentally congenial to her. Coligny, with his plain honesty, she saw through at a glance. He lacked that reticence which nourishes the communion of two minds, that pregnant reserve which suggests more than is spoken, or than there is, which Lorraine possessed, and to which as a woman she was intensely susceptible. She luxuriated in the chiaroscuro of his mind.

Vanity, ambition, conviction—whatever the motive, Catherine manipulated it, in each of her collaborators, to her purpose. Her grasp of character was her one solid hold on the situation and it served her well as far as intrigue or diplomacy could go, allowing her to elude the preliminary difficulties and to pave the way for the Council. But beyond that point lay an uncharted void where the deep threatened to engulf her, and other capacities were required. She had now to deal, no longer with men whom she could manipulate, but with ideas, of which men were merely the pawns.

- 9 -

On July 31, in the Dominican Convent of Poissy, an unfrequented retreat within easy reach of Paris but far from its fanatical crowds, the National Council opened, and the maddening experiment of rationalizing the religious conflict began. On one inconceivable condition such an experiment might have succeeded: if the basis of religious belief had been honestly explored, if the infinite fallibility of the human intellect had been recognized, and the reconciling conclusion reached, then, and then only, the confounding truth might have dawned and the folly and crime of persecution for opinion been exposed. An impossible hypothesis, but not because the human mind was not ripe for it in 1561. Was it not Montaigne who wrote that "it is setting a high value on one's opinions to burn men because of them"? Montaigne was exceptional only because he was candid. Every man who is honest with himself is an agnostic at heart; there has never been a time when men have not known better than their acquired beliefs; but it has been the labour of ages to develop their natural enlightenment. The Colloquy of Poissy could have accomplished its historic mission only if its members could have been hypnotized to testify to the truth, if they had been inspired to avow the void that every man born of man bears within him from birth.

But no radical solution could be reached where no fundamental question could be considered. The only basic religious beliefs which came within the scope of the Council were dogmas, and dogmas are by definition immutable. The dogmas themselves were inflexible, and the forces behind them intractable. How was this dilemma to be solved? Religion by its very nature is incapable of accommodation. Founded on the unquestioning faith of its followers in a set of immutable principles upon which eternal salvation depends, it cannot compromise without confounding its claims. Nor was this dilemma merely theoretical; it was above all practical. Who could expect a living, growing, expanding organism like the Reformed Church to return to the fold any more than that the offspring should re-enter the womb? Or how could the Mother Church reassimilate the deserters who had once known independence and outgrown her? The logic of life was likewise immutable.

The inherent difficulties of the problem dawned upon Catherine only when she was in the thick of them. Her mind was fundamentally incapable of distinguishing religious from political questions and she discovered too late that the venture on which she had launched had swept her far beyond her depth. A shrewd and not unsympathetic observer wrote: "It seems to me that the Queen does not understand what is meant by this word *dogma*, and I fear that she confounds, as if they were one and the same thing, dogmas, rites, and abuses; hence arise all manner of misunderstandings in discussion and perhaps also in opinion." Though the dilemma was insoluble, she continued to seek a solution, trusting to some chance inspiration, some unforeseen turn of debate, some unimaginable expedient, to provide the compromise which neither she nor anyone else could conceive. Where men were so certain of what they did not know, she had the wisdom at least of not thinking at all.

Out of one hundred and thirteen prelates who had been called, some fifty made their appearance at Poissy at the opening session. They came reluctantly, with no clear idea of the nature of the conference, uneasy as to its propriety, suspicious of its purpose, critical of its conduct. To this little knot of persons the Chancellor outlined the object of the "Assembly" or "Colloquy" or "National Council"— the very designation of it teemed with difficulties—in terms of studied vagueness, minimizing its importance, guaranteeing its orthodoxy, and explaining without committing himself. But he failed to reassure the Assembly. The Cardinal de Tournon rose and demanded a copy of his explanations in writing. The Chancellor explained that it was impossible to reduce them to writing; he had improvised them; only a few hours before he had been obliged to revise all his ideas. The Cardinal insisted. The Chancellor, a practised hand at parliamentary tactics, resorted to sarcasm. "Surely," he said, "there are men of learning and good memory in this Assembly who will be able to remember what was said." But the Cardinal would not be balked. He remembered enough of the speech to say that the explanations furnished by the Chancellor did not correspond to the expectation of the Assembly. The Chancellor was compelled, at a sign from Catherine, to satisfy him. It was clear that there was a disaffected and stubborn spirit in the Assembly which could not be ignored. And, in fact, on the next day the Cardinal de Tournon took control of the situation. The Assembly voted that all questions pertaining to faith or doctrine were debarred from discussion, and that its deliberations would be confined to morals and abuses. Thus, the National Council was spared the dilemma of dogma.

Catherine returned to Saint-Germain, leaving the Council to work out its salvation and giving strict orders that the prelates were not to leave Poissy until their labours had been accomplished. Another assembly demanded her attention. The States-General were in session at Pontoise to settle the King's debts. The Nobility and the Third Estate were recalcitrant, but the Clergy offered to redeem the royal patrimony by the payment of an annual subsidy of two million livres for eight years. This timely service, which rescued the Crown from bankruptcy, constituted an obligation which could not be ignored. While the clergy at Poissy eliminated dogma and discipline, the clergy at Pontoise settled morals and abuses for two million pounds. Nevertheless, Catherine still expected some results of the Council at Poissy. Solvency made her sanguine. More versed in chrematistics than in theology, she supposed that she could manage the religious question as she had the financial one, by sheer perseverance. Her self-confidence returned.

The Calvinists arrived three weeks late. When the heretics whom she had conjured up actually appeared at Saint-Germain, Catherine became uneasy. She dreaded their radical manners, and she sent them word, privately, that when they appeared before the Council, they should be careful not to offend the susceptibilities or the dignity of the prelates and other notable persons before whom they would appear, particularly as women and children would be present in the persons of herself and her son. What was her relief, then, when she met Théodore de Bèze and found in the Calvinist leader, not a cantankerous iconoclast, but a genial and accomplished man of the world! Her whole opinion of the Reformation rose. Like most right-thinking people she judged the revolutionary movement not by its doctrines but by those who professed them. Of the doctrines she knew nothing; but she was a judge of manners, and she suspected some radical connection between breaches of form and of faith. Heresy was a subversive movement that undermined all social laws. But her prejudice melted when she met Bèze. She did not send for him. When he arrived at Saint-Germain, he was welcomed by Coligny, the King of Navarre, and Condé, but otherwise ignored. Two days later, after supper, he was summoned to the château. On entering the apartments of the King of Navarre he was startled—and disconcerted—to find himself in the presence of Charles IX, Catherine, the Cardinal de Lorraine, Condé, and some ladies of consequence. A little apologetically, he explained the reason for his intrusion. Catherine replied "very humanely," put him at his ease, and presented him to the Cardinal de Lorraine. Her ability to adapt herself to everyone she met was one of her great charms and, placing herself on his level at once, she launched him on a theological chat with the Cardinal. The Cardinal displayed his wide reading in both Calvinist and Lutheran literature, discussed their ideas with moderation, and made some concessions, luring him on toward the subject of the Eucharist. But Bèze remained on the defensive, to the disappointment of Catherine, who hoped in this manner to gain a few esoteric notions for herself. The conversation ended cordially, the Cardinal inviting his opponent to confer with him frequently. "You will find that I am not so black as I am painted," he said. A lady laughed, but not at Bèze. Lorraine retired to explain to the Nuncio that he had been "forced" to meet the Reformer and that he had overcome him easily. Catherine was agreeably disappointed in Bèze. Although she had not been able to manage the trial bout, his prudence raised him in her esteem; she felt that she could trust him in the Council. She prolonged the preliminaries; there she was in her element; she excelled in preparations and shrank from conclusions, which she could not control. If only the whole vexing question could have been transacted in private, if the clash of creeds could have been tempered by personal contacts, if theological controversy could have been reduced to a conversational tone, the Eucharist solved after supper, the Sacraments dropped in a corner, how easy it would have been!

Bèze was confident of the outcome. "Things are wondrously shaken," he wrote to Calvin. He shook Saint-Germain with a *succès de scandale:* he preached every day in the apartments of the Admiral or of the Prince de

Condé; half the Court attended his sermons; heretical books passed from hand to hand; and the Catholic leaders were beside themselves. Chantonay, the Spanish ambassador, warned the Queen-Mother that he would be obliged to report to Madrid what he saw; she invited him to do so. The Nuncio complained, but she out-talked him. Montmorency ran a fever, taking to his bed and leaving it to relieve his temper. He disowned his son, he disowned his nephews. Saint-André, after making a scene in the Council, was requested to retire to his estates. The Duc de Guise returned to Court, after accompanying Mary Stuart on her exit from France, on the day that Bèze arrived at Saint-Germain. It was expected that he would refuse to remain under the same roof as the Reformer, but he lingered in disgust, as a matter of duty, at the request of the Nuncio, cursing the Council—*une couillonnerie*, he called it. The atmosphere was not favourable to private talks and personal understandings; and when, in spite of it, Bèze proposed that Calvin be invited to the Colloquy, Catherine was shocked. She saw that she had overestimated his judgment. She let the Council take its course.

The Council took its course, deliberate, dismal, dilatory, to its foreordained end. Five weeks after the formal opening, the interned Catholic prelates at Poissy were confronted by the Calvinist ministers. Bèze addressed the Assembly, outlining the doctrinal differences which distinguished his creed from that of the Catholics, in a long Profession of Faith which made a favourable impression by its moderation and its style. Even his enemies admitted that he was "an eloquent speaker," that he had composed "a very beautiful speech," that his language was "learned and well linked," and that "his fine French idiom" touched their hearts. But the spell was abruptly broken by a banal figure of speech. Touching on the burning question of the Real Presence in the Eucharist, Bèze had the misfortune to illustrate the Calvinist position by declaring that "the body of Jesus Christ is as far removed from the bread as are the heavens from the earth." The words were no sooner out of his mouth than they rebounded, and not with the flatness of a banality, but with the bombination of a blasphemy. A wave of dismay passed through the Assembly; Coligny passed his hand over his eyes; then the murmurs rose, a mounting expostulation of protest, voice vaulting over voice in defence of the venerable dogma of sacramental cannibalism. The Cardinal de Tournon appealed to the Queen, who allowed Bèze to finish and then announced a week's recess.

The scandal had its advantages. It called for a rebuttal and thus, despite the refusal of the Assembly to discuss dogma, a basic article of faith slipped into the public domain. The choice of a champion lay between the Cardinal de Tournon and the Cardinal de Lorraine. The latter was elected. Far more intent upon displaying his form than his faith, he delivered an address that was remarkable for its learning, its eloquence, its moderation, and the subtlety of its dialectics, but that left everything in suspense. Bèze asked permission to reply. Then the Cardinal de Tournon intervened. Fatigued by the effort of following his colleague, he was able, nevertheless, to supply the one element missing in the orthodox defence, that of finality. There could be no question, he declared, of entering into a discussion of the dogmas already expounded: the debate was closed. The Bishops supported him; and Catherine was obliged to suspend the sessions.

The basic, the insurmountable obstacle, had been laid bare. No discussion was possible on the fundamentals of faith. The failure of the ambitious experiment could no longer be denied, but Catherine refused to admit it. In the *compte rendu* of the Council which she sent to foreign Courts, she explained its failure very simply: it was a success. The purpose for which she had convoked the prelates, it appeared, had been merely to discredit the Calvinists. "There was no better nor more fruitful means of causing these ministers to be abandoned and of withdrawing their adherents from them than by contriving to confound their doctrine and revealing and exposing the errors contained in it." Unfortunately for the impression which she wished to convey, her conduct completely belied it. While the prelates at Poissy were preparing to depart, she detained the Calvinist ministers at Saint-Germain and, in a series of private conferences with the Cardinal de Lorraine and a group of liberal Catholics, continued to seek a working solution. She had the invincible quality of never knowing when she was vanquished, because she had the inveterate defect of not understanding why she had failed.

In ever-dwindling committees, first of twelve, then of five theologians, carefully selected for their conciliatory views, repeated efforts were made to find a formula of agreement. As a basis for it, the Cardinal de Lorraine proposed the Confession of Augsburg, but the Lutheran programme was as alien to the Calvinists as the Catholic, and the proposal embarrassed Bèze, driving him into transparent shifts and evasions. The intolerance of one revolutionary school for another, the doctrinaire jealousies, the parochial spirit of the emancipators of mankind, made the prospect of final reconciliation yet more remote. The conferences came to a standstill. At this point the Jesuit General Lainez, who had come to France in the train of the Papal Legate, intervened. He protested against the conferences, which he attended as an unofficial observer. On one occasion, he rebuked Catherine for presumption, reminding her that it was prohibited to treat with heretics or even to listen to them, that it was not for any temporal power to meddle in the Faith, that princes had received no authority and no lights to deal with such questions. Tears swam in her eyes, but she said nothing. The Cardinal de Lorraine was also troubled. His supple and protean spirit was stiffened by contact with the true spokesmen of the Catholic principle; blind and unquestioning obedience was the only real issue at stake. In a revolutionary world there was no place for compromise, no room for reason, no choice but partisanship, and he recognized the futility of his liberal leanings. The intervention of Lainez dealt the final blow to the conferences. A feeble effort was made to continue them; then they quietly collapsed. The Cardinal read the anathema on the Calvinists and declared the National Council closed.

- 10 -

The failure of the Colloquy of Poissy was not merely negative. The penalty of failure—civil war—drew steadily nearer. The menaces of the Catholic leaders had risen in muffled accompaniment to the Colloquy, and if they were not yet a reality, they were already more than talk. On their behalf, the Nuncio sent an agent to Rome with a proposal to form an alliance between the Triumvirate, the Holy See, and Philip II: a suggestion which was forwarded unofficially, but with the approval of the Pope, to Madrid. The measures recommended were that Philip II and the Pope should make a concerted demonstration, semi military, semi-diplomatic. "Your Majesty would advance troops from Flanders and Spain on the frontiers of France, without for the moment undertaking any further expense. At the same time the Queen-Mother and the King of France would be made to understand the peril that threatens the kingdom, and it would be impressed on them that Your Majesty wishes with all his power to prevent the French King and his States from being governed by heretics, and that you are determined to exterminate them and to drive them out of this country by arms. . . . Such an enterprise is, for Your Majesty, a duty, as well as a pious, just, honest, easy, and glorious Work." In this form, as a gesture, Philip II accepted the suggestion. No more was necessary, because of the internal unrest in France. The Nuncio declared that "it would be a mistake to doubt the possibility of a great rising of the people, since there are so many over-wrought spirits in this kingdom, and in many provinces the Catholics can no longer contain themselves and are rushing to arms without being prompted by any foreign prince." A crisis was clearly at hand, and one which made the affairs of France an international concern, for "the loss of this kingdom will soon involve that of the other States of Christendom, despite all the diligence of princes, and, above all, of Flanders and Spain, because of the commerce which keeps them in continual relations with France." The supreme struggle for the preservation of the Spanish Empire and the slipping hold of the Catholic Church upon Europe was destined to take place in France; and the calamity became more inevitable the longer it was deferred. But Philip was determined to defer it, because of the uncertainty of the outcome, his solicitude for peace, and his habitual procrastination. He made the gesture.

Acting on the representations made to him, Philip II addressed a series of sharp remonstrances to his mother-in-law. He was scandalized by the Colloquy, alarmed by the progress of heresy in France, shocked by the favour she showed to its spokesmen, and he hinted at the possibility of bringing pressure to bear. These representations coincided with the departure from Court of the Catholic leaders, immediately after the Colloquy. On the day before their exit an incident occurred which indicated to what lengths they were willing to go, and of which Catherine learned from her son Alexandre. Like all her children, he had been trained to conceal nothing from her, and the story he told was circumstantial. Finding himself in a room with Monsieur de Nemours, Monsieur de Guise, and his son, Monsieur de Joinville, he was accosted by Monsieur de Nemours with an abrupt question: "Monsieur, are you a Huguenot or a Papist?" To which he replied that he was of the same religion as his mother. He thought the question very personal, but Monsieur de Nemours was accustomed to take liberties. Monsieur de Nemours then led him aside, sat with him on a coffer, and began to talk politics. "Monsieur," he said, "I see that the kingdom of France is lost, ruined by these Huguenots, and that the King and yourself are not safe, since the King of Navarre and the Prince de Condé wish to become kings and will put you and the King to death. Therefore, Monsieur, if you wish to avoid this danger, you must take thought and, if you wish, Monsieur de Guise and myself will help you and rescue you and send you to Lorraine or to Savoy." To this Alexandre replied that he did not wish to leave the King, or his mother, which was true as well as correct. But Monsieur de Nemours insisted and insisted so much that, not knowing what else to say, he became very uncomfortable and kept silence. Monsieur de Nemours left him at last, warning him not to repeat what had been said. Then Monsieur de Guise, who had been warming his back by the fire and talking to his son, came up to him, and the young Guise said: "Monseigneur, I hear that the Queen means to send you and Monsieur your brother into Lorraine, to a very beautiful château, to take the air, so make up your mind, if you wish to travel with us, we shall treat you well." Between boys of an age there should have been no constraint, but Alexandre was more embarrassed than ever. He replied in a low voice: "I do not think the Queen my mother wishes me to leave the King." He would not look at the Guise lad, but the Guise lad insisted: "If you wish to come to Lorraine and attend to what Monsieur de Nemours told you, you will do well." The tempted stole a glance at the tempter, but preserved a safe silence, which the little Guise mistook for consent. For, on the next morning, there was young Guise again, and not with a proposal, but with a plan. "You will be carried off at midnight," he told him, "and passed out of a window near the gate of the park, and then you will be placed in a coach, and you will be in Lorraine before anyone knows that you are gone." Such was the story which Alexandre told his mother. She was highly alarmed but, beating about blindly for safety, she could think of nothing better to do than to write to Philip and ask his advice.

But buried injuries breed. Coming so close on this incident, the menace of Spanish intervention produced an effect. She was suggestible, and the gesture sufficed. Throughout the following weeks the reports of her ambassadors abroad spoke of the prevailing impression in foreign capitals that there would soon be war in France. She was so far impressed that she began to reckon her resources. She estimated that the subsidy promised by the clergy for the repurchase of the Crown lands would provide her with a means of "raising twenty million livres by remortgaging the domains and the *aides*, in order to meet the expense of a long war, when it is necessary." She prepared for the worst and gained confidence from her familiarity with danger. The gesture engineered by the Catholic powers produced, in fact, an effect that was completely unexpected.

The Protestants, at this period, enjoyed a psychological advantage. After the departure of the Catholic leaders, Catherine showed them a favour, at first personal and then political. The Protestants were represented by their most illustrious leaders—Coligny, Condé, Andelot, the Cardinal de Châtillon, Antoine de Bourbon, and Théodore de Bèze. The latter remained at Saint-Germain at the express request of the Queen, and became, in effect, the political ambassador of Geneva at the French Court. The deference and understanding which he showed her were his diplomatic credentials, and he proved himself an adroit diplomat. Sympathetic and subservient, he sounded the most responsive chord in Catherine's heart. He won her confidence from the day when he described her as "our Autocrat." The word, the life-giving word, for which she thirsted, sank deep in her heart, and she refused to part with him. Although Calvin and the Senate of Geneva recalled him insistently, he arranged for a leave of three or four months. She was duly grateful; overcoming her distaste for the name of Calvin, she inquired politely about his health and his domestic habits and actually listened to the replies. A thrill of expectation ran through the churches. What might not follow? The cult enjoyed an extraordinary licence at Court. The Papal Legate complained that the sound of sermons and psalms besieged him, above, before, and both sides of his lodgings; and one day, in the immediate vicinity of the château, Bèze administered communion to seven hundred souls. Nor was this all. The missionary held out, in his correspondence with Calvin, yet higher prospects. He was too prudent to promise, but he did affirm—"I affirm," he wrote, "that this Queen, our Queen, is better disposed toward us than ever she has been before. You should know that her three sons show an admirable disposition and such as, for their age, we should wish. . . . Would to God that I could reveal to you, under the seal of secrecy, what I hear every day from the most reliable witnesses of these children." The King, indeed, made little secret of his sympathies: if he still went to Mass, it was merely to please his mother. As for Alexandre, the attempt to abduct him had made him a convinced Calvinist. He persecuted his little sister Margot incessantly, shouting at her to convert her, flinging her *Hours* into the fire, pulling her pigtails, forcing prayer-books and psalms into her hands, and, when she cried, sneering at her "childishness and folly" and threatening her with a whipping from her mother. The Gospel made great progress.

But far more remarkable than the religious licence which the Protestant party enjoyed at Court was its political prestige. For now there began, between their leaders and the Queen-Mother, a close and prolonged collaboration. Catherine insisted on retaining Bèze because she needed his credit in order to govern. Such was the amazing result of her ill-fated experiment. The Colloquy had

excited the Protestant masses, and their increasing aggres-
siveness threatened at any moment to provoke Catholic
reprisals and to kindle the civil war. The menace of Spanish intervention made it imperative to check this excitement, and Catherine had determined to placate the Catholic powers by a demonstration for which she needed the
connivance and the co-operation of the Protestant leaders.

The fruits of this collaboration appeared with the publication of a decree directing the Protestants to restore
all churches, chapels, and religious edifices which they
had appropriated. Coligny and Bèze sponsored it, and
thanks to their influence, a measure which might otherwise have produced serious disturbances was accepted
without complaint and enforced without protest. Catherine was able to boast abroad that by this act she had
deprived the "dissidents" of shelter against the "incom-
modity of the coming winter." In return for their assistance, she had promised Coligny and Bèze to provide in
every township a locality in which their co-religionists
might assemble freely up to the number of five hundred
and to guarantee them police protection; and she kept her
word. No sooner had the decree appeared than private
instructions, in the form of *lettres de cachet*, were sent to
all the officers of the kingdom, embodying this arrangement. Catherine was studying the possibility of providing
a legal status for the Protestants, based on the official
recognition of their cult and its transfer to the suburbs of
the cities. To pave the way for this measure, she announced the convocation at Saint-Germain of an Assembly, composed of delegates from the various Parlements
of the kingdom, for the purpose of "advising her on the
police problem and the means of checking the troubles
deriving from religion." It was the same manœuvre which
she had employed, five months before, in preparation for
the pseudo-reactionary Edict of July; but this time the
delegates were chosen from among the most moderate and
conciliatory groups, and two months before they met she
was already drafting with Bèze the resolution which they
were to present to her.

This initiative, remarkable as a departure from her
makeshifts and evasions, was yet more remarkable because
of the risks under which it was undertaken. The seething

impatience of the Protestants, the rising exasperation of the Catholics were generating the war temper. Massacres of Protestants occurred, throughout the month of November, in Amiens, in Cahors, in Carcassonne, in the vicinity of Toulouse. In Paris the violence of the Catholic preachers became more and more factious and inflammatory. Because of the fanaticism of the capital, the Protestants had been forbidden to assemble except secretly and in small numbers, but Bèze admitted his inability to muzzle them: "For two hundred persons who should assemble there come six thousand." The expectation of a clash was so general that the clergy had begun to take a secret census of the strength of the heretics. The Bishop of Paris and the Constable de Montmorency conducted, in every parish, a house-to-house investigation. The Maréchal de Saint-André took the same measures in Lyons. From these statistics the Nuncio estimated that for every hundred Catholics there were no more than three or four heretics. The Catholic leaders remained quiet, talking war but avoiding it, while they exhausted every diplomatic means of intimidating the government. A concerted attempt was made to detach the King of Navarre from the Protestant cause. The Cardinal de Tournon, the Legate, the Nuncio, the Spanish ambassador, the Constable, and the Maréchal de Saint-André put their heads together; the Vatican promised to support his claims with Philip II; and his conversion transpired through the aggressive attitude of the Catholic leaders. They declared themselves ready to oppose to the death the proposed plan of the Queen-Mother to "place heresy on the same footing as the traditional Church."

Catherine was uneasy but obstinate. Warned by her ambassador in Spain of the solicitations which Philip received from France, she dictated a sharp protest to her son-in-law. The patient, the obsequious tone of the past vanished, and the word which had so long been waiting to be spoken—the word of independence, of dignity, of resentment—was uttered at last. She authorized Coligny to take a census of the Protestant forces. Bèze disapproved of this step, but he was overruled, and Calvin himself endorsed it: "When the Queen sees what help had been prepared, perhaps she will have more courage. For my part, I shall urge our followers, as I have hitherto done, not to let slip such an opportunity." Coligny sent a circular to the churches, inviting them to read the appeal from their pulpits and to enumerate the strength which they could muster in case of aggression. Many of the churches, suspecting a snare, refused to reply; but after a careful computation of the returns, the Admiral was able to inform the Queen that some 2150 churches had signed the pledge and that they "offered full service to the King of their property and persons at their own expense." Perhaps the most remarkable evidence of the spirit she derived from her associates was the fact that, in her determination to resist coercion, she was willing to rely on a minority to secure her independence.

With a skillful variation of prudence and boldness she convoyed her undertaking through the lurking and manifold perils of the situation. The Assembly which was to charter it met at Saint-Germain in the first weeks of the new year (January 3-16, 1562). The Chancellor enlarged on the growing strength of Protestantism which threatened, if it were felled, to crush in its fall those who attempted its overthrow; and submitted to the delegates as the programme of their deliberations the following hypothesis: freedom for the Protestants to assemble, hear sermons, and celebrate their cult; prohibition for them to occupy churches. That the purpose of the Assembly was "to bring forth an Interim" was well known, and its meetings took place amid intense excitement on the part of the Catholics. The Sorbonne sent deputies to the King, warning him that he would lose Paris, that the recognition of two religions would overthrown the State, that the consequence would be to create two kings in France, agitating, in short, all the taboos, which were now in danger of being tested and exposed, of orthodoxy at its last gasp. But every fallacy can be substantiated by force: Saint-André talked wildly of Spanish intervention and strenuously advocated a return to the system of repression. The Constable, in a violent altercation with Coligny, publicly disowned his nephew; the greatest sin of which he felt himself guilty, he declared, was to have advanced him in the past. Despite the sound and fury surrounding it, the Assembly pursued its deliberations and discharged its function. The majority pronounced in favour of toleration. In fact, when the final count was taken, out of forty-eight delegates twenty-seven went beyond the prescribed limits and favoured the concession of "temples" to the Protestants. Catherine gained a great deal of credit among the Catholics by opposing this excess, which she had inspired; her speech carried conviction. Its echoes reached the Vatican. The Nuncio vouched for it. "No orator," he said, "has ever been heard to express himself with more eloquence or more success. Her Majesty herself declared that at that moment it seemed to her as if God had placed the words in her mouth." Her prearrangements were not merely profane. On January 17 the government published the Edict of January or, as it was henceforth known, the Edict of Toleration.

The first avowed pledge of toleration in France was a measure too crammed with political explosives not to be carefully padded, or it would not have been the signed handiwork of Catherine de' Medici. The preamble was an elaborate apology rehearsing her customary excuses, the danger and futility of repression, the necessity of establishing a *modus vivendi*, "in order to keep our subjects at peace until such time as God will do us the grace to be able to reunite them in one fold." The epilogue repeated her habitual formula, namely, that the decisions embodied in the edict were a purely provisional measure, biding the determination of a General Council. Between these two waddings lay, buried in official verbiage, the inflammable matter. This was contained in two articles: the first prohibiting the Protestants to assemble within city limits, publicly or privately, by day or night; the second authorizing them, on the other hand, to meet by day, outside the city limits, to celebrate their services. The second article was a revolution in itself. It established the cult, under certain restrictions, but even these were modified by the Chancellor in reply to an interpellation by the Huguenot deputies. "Domestic prayers in each family in the city are not forbidden, nor consistories, nor propositions," he explained. The churches were sanctioned in the very restrictions imposed upon them, the limitations in form conveying a licence in fact: "We forbid the ministers and leaders of the new religion to make any synod or consistory, except by leave. . . . But if they consider it necessary to constitute among themselves certain regulations for the exercise of their religion, let them show these to our officers, who will authorize them." The officers were to be present at Protestant services, and "the ministers shall report to our officers to swear in their hands the observance of these articles." The Edict of January was ostensibly no more than an administrative measure; in reality it was a political concordat which conferred official recognition and a legal status on the Protestant cause.

Catherine had faithfully carried out her promises to Bèze and his colleagues. The question now was whether they could carry out their promises to her. The revolutionary impatience of the Protestant masses represented a formidable danger of which Bèze had continually complained. To the extremists of the party the edict was a disappointment. The restrictions which it involved were galling checks to the inbred revolutionary temper for which half-measures were more fatal than outright repression. A preliminary campaign had been launched by the pastors, explaining the purport of the edict, before it appeared. The credit of Bèze was of inestimable value to the government. Thanks to his precautions, his appeals, and his prestige, the edict was accepted and observed, grudgingly in places, in others with gratitude. The combustible elements in the measure were not exploded by the Protestants.

A measure which legalized a rival religion could only be accepted as a challenge by the Catholics and seemed destined to produce an open rupture with the government. But nothing of the sort occurred; the French Catholics were far more intransigent than their foreign allies. Tension there was, but no rupture with Rome. The Pope protested feebly and, as it seemed, merely *pro forma*. The explanation of this remarkable complaisance lay in one of those small diplomatic facts which so often account for what would otherwise be historic mysteries. The Council of Trent had just reopened its sessions, and the Pope, in order to obtain the participation of the Gallican Church, was careful not to irritate the Regent. The edict, moreover, was expressly stated to be a provisional measure, bidding the outcome of a General Council, and that formula, which had hitherto been used to defer every final decision *sine die*, was now a definite commitment; the General Council was a fact, or would be one so soon as the French prelates arrived in Trent, and in due time the edict would be superseded. The ease with which she mollified Rome so encouraged Catherine that she began to believe nothing impossible. Confidently and indefatigably she assembled once more a little conference of Catholic and Protestant theologians at Saint-Germain to draw up a programme and to reach an understanding on the thorny questions to be discussed at Trent: the question of images, of baptism, of the Eucharist, of the Sacrifice of the Mass, of the cult of saints, of the ecclesiastical vocation, of religious instruction, of the communion in both kinds, of prayers in the vulgar tongue. She made herself conversant with all of them and had decided opinions on those which she conceived to be the least vital. But she soon discovered that there was no such thing as a least vital dogma. She did not lose heart, however; on the contrary, she grew bolder: she began to negotiate with Rome for the admission of the heretical ministers to the Council of Trent. *Feliciter audax:* to this overweening proposal the Pope made no objection and even carried complaisance so far as to suggest that it might be accepted, provided the Protestants pledged themselves, after expounding their doctrine, to accept the sentence of the High Court of Christendom. The diplomatic indulgence of Rome necessarily affected the reaction of Spain to the edict. Philip II acquiesced, and the successful challenge of his opponent was a sudden astounding revelation that all his menaces had been merely a whispering campaign of political bluff.

Never had Catherine's diplomacy been happier. At the outset of the second year of her reign, she found herself on good terms with Rome, with Spain, and with Geneva, not only in spite of the provocative Edict of January, but because of it. Firmness and decision had proved fruitful, both at home and abroad.

- 11 -

Yet the Edict of January, which satisfied Geneva and did not antagonize Rome, defied the omens. An act which legalized the co-existence of two religions in one State was an anomaly that questioned the organic structure of society, a half-measure that undermined the whole order, and it could not pass unchallenged, because it unsettled without balancing the social basis. The Reformation was as uncompromising as Rome: its promoters were moderate only where, and as long as, they were in a minority; once recognized, they were as intolerant as their opponents, because they believed in the same fundamental contention as the Catholics. Tolerance in the sense in which Catherine understood it, as the civil co-existence of two creeds, presupposed the existence of a purely secular order; and this was what lent such momentous importance to the compromise which she established. Her purpose was legitimate: it was to strike a balance between two irreconcilable factions in order to preserve the supreme authority of the State, in other words, to subordinate the religious to the civil issue; but this was a more radical challenge to the accepted order than even the religious feud, and she herself hardly understood its full import. A helpless woman, struggling to preserve the heritage of her children, had become an agent of history. Circumstances transformed her into a pathfinder, for it was clear that the compromise she had initiated existed nowhere in Europe save as the result of exhaustion; it was a truce, an arrested development; and in France, on which the international feud of faith was now focused for the supreme trial, it could not be established without a commotion which threatened to shake the State to its foundations.

The French Catholics rose to the challenge of the edict with a bitterness that rebuked the complaisance of Rome and the inaction of Spain. Paris was stunned by it, and after the first shock had passed, a reaction of outraged resistance set in. Placards appeared, calling for the extermination of heresy; the pulpits resounded with denunciations of the government; Catherine and her advisers were likened to Jezebel and the prophets of Baal; the Catholic leaders were excoriated for their failure to strike. The sound and fury of fanaticism might evaporate, but a mutinous temper was brewing. Copies of the edict, printed in Paris for circulation in the provinces, were seized and sequestered by order of Parlement. The Provost of the Merchants came to Saint-Germain and called upon Catherine for explanations, which she had the simplicity to give him. When she pointed out what they both knew, that the heretics were forbidden to assemble in Paris but that she had been compelled to assign them a meeting-place in the suburbs, and he still continued to protest, she lost patience and exclaimed: "Would you have the rain fall on their backs?" "Madame," he replied, "if it does not rain upon them, it will pour upon you and your children." And they stared at each other in amazement, two blank faces, nonplussed and appalled. The deputations, on the same errand, baffled at Saint-Germain, reversed their direction and addressed their appeals, their protests, and their perpetual motion to themselves, to each other, and to Parlement. Parlement refused to register the edict. A long struggle ensued with the government. Pressure, persuasion, negotiation, everything proved unavailing; the deadlock lasted five weeks. Finally, Catherine had the sense to lose patience and assert her authority. She took horse, galloped ten miles to Paris, and swept in among the assembled magistrates, still travelling at the gait of her nag; she demanded obedience in an imperious speech which shook their resistance, if not their convictions; and she made an impression. The Protestants, already complaining of infringements of the edict, assembled 25,000 persons in a demonstration, managed by Condé. The government moved troops into the capital to preserve order; rumours spread, confirmed by the Governor, that five or six thousand men were marching on Paris; panic stirred; and to quiet the city Parlement surrendered, conditionally, and registered the edict under protest, explicitly stating that it did so "as a provisional measure, awaiting the majority of the King."

Meanwhile, at Saint-Germain, the pressure of opposition was swelling. When the Catholic leaders had left Court after the conclusion of the Colloquy, Catherine had said nothing. The edict brought them back, humming. Montmorency and Saint-André re-appeared at the first rumour of its preparation. The King of Navarre was in a position to bring the same pressure to bear in favour of the Catholic faction which he had previously exerted in behalf of the Protestants, and with the zeal of a convert he was will-

ing to go to any lengths to satisfy Philip II. Accompanied
by Montmorency, he closeted himself with Catherine,
revived his claims to the Regency, and demanded the dismissal of the Admiral and his brothers, Andelot and the
Cardinal de Châtillon. Catherine refused, and in her annoyance with Montmorency invited him to leave Court.
He left on the next day. Antoine de Bourbon returned to
the attack, alone, but with no better success. He was followed by Chantonay, the Spanish ambassador, who served
an ultimatum upon her: she could choose between retiring
the Châtillons and a rupture with Spain. She showed him
the door. But Coligny, to avert a crisis, insisted on retiring.
He averted a crisis, but he shook her confidence. In their
recent association she had come to depend upon him. What
she needed was a man to stand by and steady her, to
guard her against her own weakness, to prevent her from
bowing to the storm. Without him, she would be exposed
to the most haunting of dangers—to herself. But he would
not see, and she could not tell him. The disinterestedness
of Coligny was, from a worldly point of view, his defect;
he derived his self-confidence only from duty; and having
secured the edict, he considered his work done and his
presence at Court an impediment which he was bound to
remove. Before he left, however, Catherine conveyed
something of her dilemma to him, and they came to an
understanding at which Bèze hinted discreetly in his
reports to Geneva: "The Admiral and his brother have
been forced by the fury of that madman, the King of
Navarre, to leave, but they left only after taking a decision which, I hope, will turn to our advantage. For my
part, I should have greatly preferred that they should have
remained here with invincible firmness to the end. But
those who knew better than I do the secrets of this Court
have judged otherwise. What I do know is that they left,
assured of the friendship of the King and the Queen."
And he added: "With their departure it will be possible
to expel those who least expect it."

Such, in fact, was the first result of the departure of
Coligny. The King of Navarre, her restless sleeping partner
in the State, she could not remove, but at the other leaders
of the Catholic faction she struck swiftly and unsparingly.
Saint-André she sent to his government of Lyons, in spite

of the complaints of the King of Navarre. The next blow
fell on the Cardinal de Tournon, who was commanded to
retire to his diocese. He kept to his rooms. The blows
which she aimed at the leaders of the Catholic faction, too
feeble to be effective, merely quickened its cohesion, and
she soon perceived that the opposition could not be
quenched unless she traced it to its root and paralysed it at
its source, in Spain. She must meet Philip II; she must
explain to him what she was constantly repeating in her
letters, that "religion is a cover which serves merely to
mask ill will," and persuade him "to examine well the intention of those who employ that cloak and yet have
nothing less than religion in their hearts." She wrote to
the Bishop of Limoges to arrange the meeting and "to
make it sooner today than tomorrow" and to inform her
at once and to agree to any place agreeable to Philip and
to plan the appointment with secrecy and dispatch, because she was "desperate" and saw "no better remedy to
break *their* evil designs than that *we* should meet."

Such an effort required energy, however, and as she was
fatigued by the combined opposition of Paris and the
Court, she resolved to recuperate for a few weeks at
Fontainebleau, where it was her custom to meet the
spring. She left Saint-Germain on the day on which Parlement finally published the edict in Paris. On her way she
paused at her château of Montceaux-en-Brie; and there
she learned of the Massacre of Vassy.

Since the Colloquy the Guises had disappeared from
the public scene. They had taken no part in the political
agitation preceding the edict and, despite the appeals of
their partisans to return, they persisted in maintaining a
conspicuous retirement on their estates in Lorraine. Their
rare letters spoke only of birds, dogs, domestic pleasures.
Nevertheless, they were not idle. The private life of a
grand seigneur was limited. Birds, dogs, domestic pleasures—besides these, there was little to pass the time but
talk, and their intellectual recreations turned inevitably on
public topics and above all on the religious question. Antoinette de Bourbon, the mother of the Guises, had pronounced views on the subject. At Vassy in Champagne, a
village which originally lay within the jurisdiction of the

House of Lorraine, there had sprung up a little community of Protestants whose rapid growth scandalized her. A complaint was sent to the Royal Council, requesting that a commission be issued to the Duc de Guise to deal with the delinquents. The Council, finding that no crime had been committed, disallowed the request, and there the question rested. The little community continued to grow; it soon numbered a thousand, but nothing could be done; no crime had been committed.

On March 1, François de Guise left Joinville for his estates at Nanteuil, accompanied by his family and an escort of two hundred armed men. The way lay through Vassy. The sound of a tolling bell attracted his attention, and upon being told that the Protestants were assembling for service, he ordered his company forward. "We must have a look at these people," he said. Then he remembered that it was Sunday and, changing his mind, decided to go to Mass instead. The Protestants worshipped in a neighbouring grange, and as their psalm-singing drowned Guise's devotions, he sent his servants to admonish them. A dispute arose, a scuffle, and he appeared on the scene. Stones were thrown at him. His escort charged the barn. Thirty Protestants were killed, one hundred and thirty were wounded. The slaughter lasted an hour. As it was late, and he had a long journey before him, Guise did not linger. Having restored order, he sent for the Justice of the Peace and rebuked him for permitting the Protestants to assemble. The magistrate mentioned the Edict of January. "The sword will soon cut the knot of the edict," Guise replied and pushed on. He was a man of quick reflexes.

In Paris the news created an electric tension. The Governor conferred with the Reformed ministers, urging them to suspend their meetings for a few days, in the interest of public safety, but they refused to make any concessions and demanded the strict application of the edict as a test case. Having little confidence in the inflexibility of the law, however, they began to cast about elsewhere for protection. Condé was in Paris; he summoned the Huguenot gentry within reach of the capital to confer with him. A warning was sent to the provincial churches. Bèze insisted that the first step should be to "seek justice through the ordinary channels," as the validity of the edict was the paramount issue. Condé humoured him and continued to take precautions. "We have sent a good number of representative persons from this Church with Monsieur de Bèze to Court," his instructions read, "to demand justice of the Queen and to inform her that otherwise we shall all be compelled to take arms to protect our lives against the violence of these brigands. . . . We beg you, therefore, to be prepared not only to defend your church, but also to aid those who will be the first to be attacked."

At Montceaux, Bèze and his colleagues were received by Catherine in the presence of Charles IX and the King of Navarre. She was "gracious." She put him at his ease at once, assuring him that she had forbidden the Duc de Guise to come to Paris and that an investigation would be made. "Good information will be taken and everything will be arranged, provided you contain yourselves," she said. Her manner was perfect. The King of Navarre broke into the conversation, blaming the Protestants for assembling in arms for their services. Bèze replied and demanded justice against the Duc de Guise. Flying into a fury, Antoine de Bourbon declared that anyone who touched his "brother" touched him. His brother was Guise. Finally, Bèze turned to Charles IX and, ignoring everyone else, said: "It is for the Church that I represent to bear blows and not to give them. That is true. But it may please you, Sire, to remember that this is an anvil which has worn out many hammers."

The collaboration of Catherine and Bèze had now reached a crucial point. An investigation was begun, and she promised in subsequent interviews to see full justice done, to preserve the King from the influence of the Catholics, and to maintain the edict at all costs. Her goodwill might be a feeble guarantee, but it was the only political asset of the party. It was expressly contingent, however, on the condition that they contain themselves. When Bèze returned from Montceaux, he found that the situation had outgrown his control and that his counsels were ignored. The law-abiding policy upon which Calvin had always insisted—the policy which had won the confidence of the Queen-Mother and which had made possible the progress of the movement—was not discarded but it was seriously strained; and that was sufficient to alter the whole situation. The military preparations of Condé in Paris provided Guise with a pretext to ignore the commands of the government.

For Guise was himself in a dilemma. His quick reflexes were followed by reflection, and hence by confusion. When, twelve days out from Vassy, he reached Nanteuil, he was still drifting, undecided on his course. That the government held him accountable for the violation of the edict he was informed by an imperative message from Catherine, forbidding him to approach Paris and summoning him to Court to explain himself. For three days he lingered at Nanteuil, a prey to scruples at last. On the third day, Montmorency and Saint-André joined him with two thousand men and an argument which was decisive: Condé was in Paris, the Catholic capital looked to him for protection. On March 16, the Triumvirs marched into Paris amid triumphal ovations in which a lesser man might well have recognized the call of destiny. Like most unimaginative men, Guise felt the full force of his act only when he committed it. Proud, impulsive, passionate, but not lawless, on the contrary, to his eternal misfortune, a creature of custom, he was a tissue of traditions, whose tenacity he felt as soon as he transgressed them. His loyalty to the Crown could not be violated without spraining his self-confidence. At the crucial moment qualms overcame him, and from that moment he was lost. Finding himself in a false situation from which he could neither advance nor retreat, he made a supreme effort to arrest or control it and began to equivocate with the facts. Condé chose the moment of the triumphal entry of the Triumvirs into Paris to lead a Protestant procession to church. The procession passed through the Catholic multitude, but not a hand was raised save those of the leaders—in salute. Later, Guise sent a message to the Prince begging him to preserve peace. Montmorency did as much. Meanwhile, the factions were arming, but a paralyzing sense of responsibility curbed both parties. For ten days Guise manœuvred to evade his moral liability.

But it was too late. The occupation of Paris created a three-cornered contest between the factions and the Crown, a siege of wills that was stubborn and static, and that bred the unnerving strain of strenuous inaction. Catherine, accustomed to such ordeals, was the first to assert herself. She sent orders to both factions to evacuate the capital. Condé replied that he would leave Paris when the Duc de Guise had withdrawn. The Triumvirs made their submission conditional on that of Condé, but their reply offered an exit from the deadlock. Guise saw his opportunity and seized it. If the government could be induced to sanction his coup, then obviously his misstep would be retrieved and his liability obliterated: that way redemption lay, and escape. By a supple twist, the entire strategy, the whole ambition, of the lawbreaker were now bent on legalizing his transgression. The King of Navarre was invited to come to Paris and judge the situation for himself. With the Lieutenant-General—the representative of the law, the partner of the Regent—converted, the King and the Queen-Mother would be compelled to follow.

It was easy, too easy. There are no easy solutions for saviours who retreat. The King of Navarre came, saw, and was conquered. His desertion, which lent the Triumvirs the formal approval of the Lieutenant-General of the Kingdom, her equal in right, left her no power to enforce her authority on the Catholic leaders. Letters and emissaries arrived daily at Montceaux, urging her to join them. She replied that religion and authority had too many defenders in Paris to require her presence and she moved to Fontainebleau. There she received a peremptory letter from the King of Navarre recommending her to proceed no further, to cease the "dissimulation and connivance which had favoured the increase of their enemies," and to declare herself openly by appearing in the capital where, she was promised, "nothing would be treated to her disadvantage." It was both a bid and an ultimatum. She refused to move.

Yet, as between two evils, she inclined toward the lesser. She made advances to Condé, pleading with him to evacuate the capital and come to Fontainebleau. She appealed to his loyalty to set an example which the Catholics would be compelled to follow or assume the responsibility of rebellion. He parried her appeals and remained in Paris and . . . filed her letters. She mistrusted Condé, and the absence of Coligny, in whose honesty she had implicit confidence, was a serious handicap. He sent her a message offering her a refuge in Orléans, but she refused to consider so compromising a solution, and he at least understood her. He sent word to Condé that he was coming to Paris and that "they would all take the lead in pulling toward Fontainebleau." But by then it was too late: the Prince, in the meanwhile, made a move which played directly into the hands of the Triumvirate.

Suddenly the deadlock broke. Condé yielded—not to the entreaties of Catherine but to the risks of his position. He had mustered three hundred gentlemen, four hundred students, and some bourgeois volunteers to oppose to the three thousand trained troops of the Triumvirate and the fanatical population of Paris; the odds, in the words of his apologists, were those of "a tiny fly against a great elephant." Under such circumstances, it was suicide to provoke a conflict which could only turn into a massacre in the capital. He evacuated Paris, but it was not the road to Fontainebleau which he took. He marched to Meaux and, setting up his headquarters there, broadcast his mobilization orders and continued to recruit forces among the volunteers flocking in from the provinces.

Meaux, the birthplace of the French Reformation, was now to behold its final transformation into an organized and armed insurrection under the leadership of Louis de Condé. The protection of princes, essential to its progress, adulterated its development; and this was never more clear than when Condé assumed control of its destiny. A far more sincere Protestant than Antoine de Bourbon, he did not speculate in religion to promote his ambition, but he did something almost as fatal: he identified his interests with those of the Cause.

The march to Meaux was a declaration of war. All the manœuvres of Guise were abruptly foiled, and the fatal course of events could no longer be arrested. Guise acted with lightning-like dispatch. The King of Navarre and the Constable were sent to Fontainebleau with a thousand men to escort the royal family, willingly or unwillingly, to Paris.

When the King of Navarre, the Constable, and their escort reached Fontainebleau, Catherine begged for a few days' delay. That night she led the King of Navarre into her study, and attempted to change his mind. She was desperate, and she exerted something more deadly than her tenacious inertia and her maddening volubility. She stung. Such a scene he had never endured even with his wife, and here he lacked his domestic privileges; he could not silence her; she exposed his frivolity, his fickleness, his irresponsibility; she revealed him to himself, she touched the quick of his unnecessary and culpable being, and he never forgave her. She won him over, but it was a costly victory.

Antoine de Bourbon relapsed into responsibility. He saved Catherine, but he ruined Guise. Losing by this sudden desertion all that he had gained by his desperate jockeying for position, Guise was exposed to the accumulated charges growing out of the Massacre of Vassy, the march on Paris, and the march on Fontainebleau. The logic of Vassy worked itself out. He had no choice but disgrace or dictatorship. Hurrying to Fontainebleau, he recaptured the King of Navarre, and as the latter was also suffering from acute moral exposure, and was equally anxious to retrieve himself, the original plan was resumed. The Lieutenant-General, accompanied by the Triumvirs, was escorted into the Queen's study. Some hours later a note was sent to the Nuncio to be transmitted to Rome: "The Catholic lords, speaking to the Queen, offered to pledge themselves in writing or in any other manner she pleased, to maintain and increase her authority. But they gave her to understand that she must raise the mask and cease all practice of conciliation since matters had come to such a pass that nothing could follow but the total ruin of one party or the other. Pursuing their argument, they ended by declaring to Her Majesty that, if she refused to act on their advice and if the King her son thought of changing his religion, they would not hesitate to change their King. Convinced by these assurances and recognizing that hitherto she had been mistaken, the Regent firmly resolved to join them completely for the extermination of the heretics." When all was over, Antoine de Bourbon spoke. The King was to be conducted to Paris for his safety. She might follow, he added, a few days later, if she wished.

When the day of departure came, the King of Navarre supervised the preparations, and had to threaten to thrash the domestics who refused to dismantle the King's bed-chamber, "for fear of the Queen." The last stick of furniture was finally carried out. Charles IX was lifted, sobbing bitterly, into a litter. Catherine was handed into another. Up to that moment she maintained her composure. Antoine de Bourbon, lording it over lackeys, she could endure; he was but the lackey of Guise; but his master demoralized her. Guise remarked that "a benefit is a benefit whether bestowed by affection or force." Her mouth worked, and she wept. He stripped her even of the power to pretend.

The abduction of the royal family was promptly capital-ized by Condé, who proclaimed himself the protector of the sovereign and his party the legitimate defender of the monarchy. Removing to Orléans, where he was joined by Coligny, Andelot, Rohan, La Rochefoucauld and other leaders of the Huguenot aristocracy, he issued a great manifesto explaining the reasons which compelled him to undertake "the defence of the authority of the King, of the government of the Queen, and of the repose of the realm." The Civil War had begun.

- 12 -

The significant feature of the first phase of the Civil War was the respect for legality which inspired both factions. The clash was actually precipitated by their contention for the sanction of the Crown. Nor was this mere lip-service. So strong still was the inbred loyalty of the lead-ers, so unanimous their zeal for legitimacy, and it was so evident that war must weaken and demoralize it, that they had already slipped over the brink when, dismayed and deterred, they clung to the crumbling ledge and drew back. The Civil War began by a prolonged negotiation for peace.

It was this saving sense of responsibility which allowed Catherine to maintain the appearance, and to recover a measure, of freedom. The Triumvirs, anxious to show that she had joined them without coercion, permitted her, on the day after her arrival in Paris, to send agents to Orléans to treat with Condé. To justify his refusal to disarm, he published excerpts from the confidential let-ters which she had addressed to him in Paris, appealing for his protection. The passages which he selected were susceptible of more than one interpretation and distinctly implied that she authorized him to arm. The correspondence was published not only in France but abroad. It was a crucial blunder. Questioned by the Catholic leaders, Catherine denounced Condé as "a madman," "a slanderer," "a man with a grudge." She complained of his spite. She protested confidentially to everyone, except to Condé himself, because, as she explained later, "I did not wish to make him despair of my goodwill." But he had forfeited it for ever. His indiscretion at a critical moment injured his cause. He compromised and antagonized her, and the result was to reconcile her to her captivity and to accommodate her to her captors.

While the negotiations continued, the conflict broke out in the provinces. Tours, Blois, Le Mans, Angers, Rouen, and Lyons fell into the hands of the Huguenots; and the Triumvirs, fearful of losing their tactical advantage, pressed her to break off. She persisted; but Condé naturally refused, while his party was gaining ground, to abate his original conditions.

The negotiations were protracted for more than two months. She returned to Montceaux, in order that "everyone may know that we are not prisoners." Physical freedom she enjoyed, but it was more difficult to demonstrate her moral liberty. Both sides, in the meanwhile, completed their mobilization, and by the beginning of June, when the fighting season began, Condé issued from Orléans to meet the advancing armies of the Triumvirate. She transferred her residence to the battlefield. A series of interviews with Condé followed, each as inconclusive as the last. In one, which took place in a grange, she arrived limping from a fall which had injured her knee. She was the first victim of the war. For two hours she pleaded that the edict was impossible, that the people abhorred it, but she made no impression. "Ah, *mon cousin*, you will drive me mad," she exclaimed, stamping the floor with her stick, "you will ruin me." "What, Madame!" one of his gentlemen said. "Is this what you tell us, now that you are so free and that we are mistaken, as it seems, in calling you captive? If you have full power, as you say, who can drive you mad?" She stopped, completely disconcerted. His flippancy offended her. The face of Condé, with its mildly vulpine expression, too debonair to be vindictive, but so knowing in its good humour, was a provocation. She persevered. Another conference was called, but this time she was careful to prearrange the result. She sent him an elaborate plan by which he might throw dust in the eyes of the Catholics and assist her in securing more favourable terms for his party. Since he was reluctant to war against his own nation, he might make some "fine offers and beautiful effects": he might propose, for example, to emigrate with his friends. She would then show her surprise at so much generosity, and as a matter of *noblesse oblige* would be obliged to reciprocate and meet his demands. Condé was not guileless but he loved a fine attitude. He accepted the suggestion with alacrity. At their next meeting he performed his part and declared before witnesses that, to spare his country the horrors of civil war, he was prepared, if necessary, to go into exile. "When do you leave?" she inquired. It suddenly dawned on him that she was taking him at his word—before witnesses. He was too startled to reply. If the false situation in which her capitulation to the Catholics placed her had hitherto made her conduct equivocal, it now made it ridiculous. It was impossible to treat seriously a public character who indulged in such dodges. Condé returned to camp laughing bitterly but deliberately, his companions deploring their fate with facetious dismay, chaffing each other on the occupations with which they would earn bread in foreign lands. Gaiety, not indignation, was their response to her confidence game. But in the morning the farce became serious. The staff met to consider whether Condé was bound by his word. In speculating on their patriotism and making a fine attitude of a genuine sentiment, Catherine had offended a feeling the force of which she misjudged and which could not be abused with impunity. The proposal to emigrate was submitted to the camp, and the reply was unanimous, and lyric: the soil of France had borne, the soil of France would bury them. The conduct of Catherine found an apologist in Coligny. "I do not believe," he said to Condé, "that in accepting your offer the Queen acted with any bad intention; on the contrary,

I believe that in her desire to save the State from disaster she seeks any and every expedient, and that those who took up arms circumvent her in order to circumvent you."

Her conduct was a purely academic question; the real question was not how to treat her, but whether to treat with her at all. Andelot brought out his own peace proposal, a profound one—to engage the enemy without delay. "We shall never be friends," he observed sensibly, "until we have scrimmaged a little." This solution was unanimously accepted, the negotiations were broken off, and hostilities began.

When war finally broke and engulfed her, she was still unreconciled to it. Throughout the negotiations with Condé her tenacity, her duplicity, her subterfuges, were dictated by a haunting fear which tormented her. "I see," she wrote to the Bishop of Limoges, "all the great men and good captains and the leaders of the nobility armed against one another, and so embittered and inflamed that we can expect only the approaching ruin and loss of one or the other party or perhaps both; the outcome will be to open the door to all the foreigners who wish to invade this kingdom; it will be stripped and deprived of its defenders. The victor will be able to dictate the law to this country and I do not know whether he will dictate it to the son or to the mother. When I think of the appetites which such an opportunity may excite, you can appreciate my anxiety, Monsieur de Limoges. I see the Prince de Condé very strong and with a large following, and I must fear that, if the victory falls to him and the leaders of our army suffer, my son the Catholic King may undertake to avenge them and, on the pretext of aiding me to defend the realm, introduce all his forces into it, to protect and become the tutor, as it were, of my son, which would be the crowning calamity and the total ruin and destruction of this State, which has been envied so long and by so many people that we may well believe that he would not miss such an opportunity, and no alliance and no friendship will ever reassure me. . . ." To counteract the incubus, she explained: "I have sent for six thousand Swiss and six thousand *Landsknechte*, who will soon be here, together with two thousand German cavalry. . . . The Catholic King will be informed, and by this means you may avert the blow and cool his appetite to enter this turmoil with a large force—something I mean to avoid by all means, and, I beg you, use all your five senses, for I dread like death to see so cruel a calamity befall my son and myself, knowing the counsels, plots, and schemes of those who have caused us all these troubles, from which more danger threatens than I can tell you; but having found this bearer, I wished to send you this letter in any case."

Philip II had pledged the government the service of three thousand Flemish troops and nine thousand *Landsknechte*. Having solicited them herself, she was unable to dispense with their assistance; but she speculated on building up a superiority of force so overpowering that the conflict would be brief and decisive.

The danger of foreign complications developed in another direction. The initial successes of the war went to the Catholics. Accordingly, in the first days of July, Andelot was sent to Germany to recruit mercenaries, while an emissary left for London to negotiate with Queen Elizabeth. This move had long been anticipated in London, and Elizabeth, acting on the advice of her ambassador in France, had merely been waiting until the French Protestants were compelled to make advances to take advantage of their necessity to recover Calais. As this was the only condition on which she consented to assist Condé, and the patriotic scruples of the French were at first insuperable, the negotiations turned on it for three months. Finally, a formula was found which left the question of Calais in suspense, although Elizabeth renounced none of her claims to it—a diplomatic formula open to compromising constructions—in return for which she advanced 140,000 crowns and six thousand men for the defence of Rouen and Dieppe and obtained the surrender of Havre as an English base for the duration of the war. In accepting terms which involved a violation of French territory, the Huguenots assumed a great liability.

When Catherine first caught wind of the negotiations, she attempted to check them by diplomatic pressure. Philip II was induced to caution Elizabeth, but his representations were disregarded. Jealous of the integrity of

France, Catherine felt the threat to Calais acutely and
the transaction prejudiced the Protestants in her eyes.
The Catholics and the country were incensed by it. Six
months had now elapsed, during which the Catholics had
recovered Poitiers and Bourges and reduced the centre
of France. When the English landed at Havre in October,
the Triumvirs suspended the investment of Orléans and
concentrated all their forces on the siege of Rouen.
Catherine lent them the moral support of her presence,
surveying the operations from advanced outposts and exposing herself to stray fire with an indifference to danger
on which she prided herself. When Montmorency and
Guise remonstrated with her, she laughed. "Why should
I spare myself, when I have as much courage as you?"
The value which men placed on physical courage amused
her. The soldiers paid her the compliment of naming their
big guns after her.

The King of Navarre also distinguished himself at the
siege of Rouen by his indifference to death. Nevertheless,
a stray bullet struck him. Stunned but undiscouraged, he
lingered for six weeks. He was not blessed, however, with
a charmed life. Blood-poisoning set in, and he died on
the day that the city fell.

The first conspicuous casualty of the war was followed
by others which, snapping her fetters link by link, released Catherine from her political captivity. After the
fall of Rouen, Condé took the field, menaced Paris, and
met the enemy at Dreux (December 19, 1562). Saint-
André was killed, the Constable was captured by the
Protestants, and Condé by the Catholics, and the engagement ended in a draw. The fortunes of battle, elim-
inating all the leading commanders on both sides, with
the exception of Guise and Coligny, radically simplified
the situation. The long-standing feud between Guise and
Condé was settled. On the night after his capture the
Prince slept in the same bed with Guise, the past was
forgotten, and the reconciliation which Catherine had so
long sought to accomplish by diplomacy was spontaneously achieved—by force.

In the reshuffling of roles which followed the battle of
Dreux, Coligny and Guise emerged as the final antagonists. Catherine wished to conclude peace on the out-

come of the battle, that is, on a draw—the only solution consistent with the independence of the Crown—but the partisan passion of the two surviving commanders was uncompromising. Her strongest argument in favour of peace was that it was necessary to expel the foreigner from France. Guise insisted that this could best be accomplished by pressing the war to a decisive conclusion. Throughout the winter at the beginning of 1563, siege was laid to Orléans. Catherine continued a desultory negotiation for peace through Condé, but as Condé was still under the influence of Coligny and demanded the recognition of the edict, no progress was made. The decisive victory which Guise promised her was deferred from month to month, and new exertions were demanded. In February Guise joined the camp at Orléans to supervise the siege in person. Coligny, to avert a mutiny of his unpaid mercenaries, had been compelled to leave the town and lead them to Dieppe to collect the English subsidy, leaving Andelot, who was sick with fever, in command of a depleted, discouraged, and disease-ridden garrison. On the day after his arrival, Guise captured a bastion, three days later, another, and he sent Catherine a bulletin to encourage her. A general assault had been set for February 19, but it was never delivered. On the day before, Guise was assassinated. By this providential accident the last obstacle was removed, and a month later she signed the Peace of Amboise March 19, 1563) which brought the civil war to a close by restoring, with some modifications, the Edict of January.

- 13 -

The outcome caused Catherine a grim satisfaction. Force had served merely to demonstrate its futility and to justify her policy. The war had served her logically, and accidentally as well. The Triumvirate was shattered. The three prepotent figures of the past, Guise, Saint-André, and Antoine de Bourbon, were eliminated, the Constable was impotent alone, the Protestants were pacified, Condé was subdued, and she had recovered her freedom of action. She looked forward with something like confidence to a protracted period of peace, recuperation, and stability.

Yet a civil war had been fought, and the experience left a lasting impression on her policy. She never recovered her moral freedom; her initiative was checked and her courage cooled. The change was manifest in the modifications which she introduced into the edict. The basic principle—the legal recognition of two faiths—remained intact, but the public exercise of the cult was restricted in two important respects. It was granted to the aristocracy on their estates and to the lower classes in only one town in each bailiwick, while in Paris it was completely forbidden. The result was to make full religious rights a class privilege and to divide the aristocracy from the masses. For the latter, the designation of a single town in each district necessitated a long journey for those who lived at a distance and was calculated to hamper their zeal and to act as a deterrent to assembly. The aim of these restrictions was immediately discerned by the ministers, who protested and demanded a return to the edict in its original integrity. But Catherine had learned her lesson. The civil war, in impairing the integrity of the Crown and the country, had convinced her of the impossibility of maintaining a balance between the warring creeds. She was disillusioned and shaken. The change in the edict measured exactly the change in her attitude: it was the difference, narrow and enormous, between tolerance and toleration. The one was a visionary good, the other a necessary evil. Though she did not revert to the policy of repression, she set herself to achieve the same end by dividing and compressing the Protestant movement, in the hope that, if the embers were scattered, the fire would eventually cool and die out. What she did not realize was that such a policy might produce even more serious complications. Religion, she insisted, was a cloak for secular interests, and those of the upper classes she understood and could manipulate; but she was too far removed from those of the masses to foresee that in cooling the faith of the people she was likely to kindle the unrest for which it was an outlet. Religion, even an illegal religion, because it was unworldly, offered a guarantee of social security, and to deprive the masses of their drug might quicken their real complaints.

Coligny had an intuition of the truth. Knowing his intransigent views, Catherine had persuaded Condé to accept the modifications, or as the Protestants called them, the mutilations of the edict in the absence of the Admiral, who learned of them on his way to Court. Recognizing that the class distinctions established by the edict were destined to undermine the solidarity of the movement and to lead to its gradual disintegration, he exposed the ulterior motive of the articles so cogently that "most of those who had accorded this peace wished that it could be remade." Condé himself felt compelled to explain and apologize and ended by assuring him, confidentially, that "he would soon be in the place of his brother, the King of Navarre, and that then, in concert with the Queen, as he had been promised, they would obtain all that they desired." Coligny, unsatisfied, insisted on pressing the issue in a series of private conferences with Condé and Catherine. He succeeded in estranging Catherine. The Admiral's impersonal passion of principle alarmed her. Condé she could manage, Coligny eluded her. She suspected his loyalty and she satisfied her suspicion disloyally by failing to come to his defence when, as a result of the assassination of Guise, the Admiral became the object of a dishonourable accusation which demanded, in elementary decency, a prompt and searching investigation.

The assassin, Poltrot de Méré, was an embittered Protestant employed by Coligny as a spy. Sent into the lines before Orléans, he was engaged by Guise as a counter-spy and ordered into the city just before the general assault. On the previous evening he found an opportunity to accomplish his mission. Stationing himself behind a hedge, as Guise was riding through a lane with two or three companions, he shot him and escaped, but after riding for several hours in the dark he lost his way and wandered into the Catholic lines, where he was arrested. Questioned and put to the torture, he incriminated Coligny, retracted the charge, repeated it again, substantiated it in agony, and embroidered it in excruciating confusion. One of these variations affected the Queen-Mother.

Catherine had been deeply affected by the crime. She was as shocked as she was relieved by it. But she was personally touched only when she learned that Poltrot in one of his frenzied confessions had warned her to beware of the Admiral, who "hates her infinitely," and that he had implicated a man who was arrested at Blois on the suspicion of planning to assassinate her and her children.

To clear himself of the charges of Poltrot, Coligny issued a sworn statement explaining the facts of the case, in which he carried his scrupulous accuracy so far as to make certain admissions which were the most convincing proof of his honesty but which could readily be turned against him by his enemies. He begged Catherine to defer the trial of Poltrot until he could confront him in person. "I fear," he explained, "that the members of the Court of Parlement may wish to execute him, in order to leave this calumny and imposture upon me." While he was on his way to Court, Poltrot was executed.

The accuser perished, the accusation remained. Intolerable to the Admiral, it was even more so to the Guises, who moved heaven and earth to bring him to justice. But Catherine evaded the complaints of both parties. To bring the Admiral to justice was the last thing she desired; he was compromised, and that was enough; there would always be time to clear his character, and in the meanwhile his good name was at her discretion. The Guises were indemnified. The remains of the Catholic hero, royally exposed at Notre Dame, received a final ovation from the people of Paris on the same day that his assassin was dismembered in the Place de Grève. Poltrot perished in a lingering agony, but a longer ordeal was reserved for the Admiral. The law, which had acted with such vindictive swiftness in the case of the assassin, resumed in his case its customary deliberation. The result was more cruel. He was persecuted by provocations and threats, and his friends feared for his life whenever he appeared at Court. To do nothing in such a situation was dangerous, but Catherine continued to procrastinate for six months; she would investigate when the country was pacified. The pacification of the country required the expulsion of the English from Havre, which occupied the summer of 1563. It required the proclamation of the majority of the King, who was thirteen and still lacked a year of legal manhood but who assumed henceforth official responsibility for her acts (September 1563). By then it imperatively required the pacification of a private quarrel which had assumed such menacing proportions in six months that it had become a public question. The spirit of Guises, more formidable in death than in life, had at all costs to be laid. Throughout the summer the Guises assembled their partisans, and in September the entire clan, clad in accusing black—the mother, the widow, the son, and the brothers of the murdered man—met the King at Melun and renewed their petition to prosecute the case. The King acceded, but as the Guises insisted on prosecuting the case in Parlement, and Coligny refused the jurisdiction of a court notoriously swayed by religious prejudice, he reserved judgment to himself. He studied it for three months, and produced a solution. He adjourned it for three years. The leaders of both parties accepted it, and the question was apparently closed. But, in reality, it no longer rested with the leaders. Their personal feud had become involved in and identified with public questions.

The Protestants, rallying about Coligny, made his cause their own, because they were themselves in need of protection. The Catholics, on the other hand, made a political and religious issue of the memory of their martyr. But Catherine was confident that the question had been solved by evading it. The leaders had agreed to a truce, and the leaders she could always control. Coligny was compromised, and her hold over him was generally recognized. "The Admiral is entangled in the accusation of the death of Monsieur de Guise: a rein by which the Queen checks him with threats of the vengeance of the relatives of the deceased." And the Guises were checked by the loss of their hero. For who could replace François de Guise? Who could succeed the man of destiny? That question was answered when, in January 1564, the entire family retired to their estates at Joinville to await the return of the Cardinal de Lorraine from the Council of Trent.

- 14 -

The Cardinal had been absent from France for fifteen months and behind his homecoming lay the latest and not the least ambitious of his foreign adventures. In September 1562, in the thick of the civil war, he led the French delegation to Trent on a mission which was a test of his mettle. Determined to find a pacific solution for the conflict, Catherine attempted a heroic remedy. She undertook to secure from the General Council of Trent what she had failed to obtain from the National Council of Poissy, namely, a series of concessions and reforms calculated to appease the Protestants. Monsieur de Lansac, who represented the French Government at Trent, no sooner broached the project than he fell into bad odour with the Pope, but she observed sensibly that "it is no wonder, when you wish to reform someone, if he complains; people usually do." To hold the Pope to his promise she enlisted the support of the Emperor with the object of forming a moderate bloc in the Council, composed of the two great Powers whose internal problems made a policy of conciliation of vital concern to each of them. A common plan of action was concerted, and the guiding principle which she adopted showed that she had profited by her experience at Poissy. Questions of dogma were to be avoided and questions of reform were to be pressed, though not so vigorously as to allow the Pope a pretext for closing the Council. But in the final reckoning it was clear that the fate of her venture depended less on the backing which she could muster than on the leadership which she could provide for it. It was a heroic measure, and it required for its successful execution a heroic character. Charles de Guise undertook it.

Clearly, he was the man for it. His commanding position, his diplomatic skill, and his liberal tendencies offered a more favourable average than any other prelate in France could furnish. Fully appreciating the resistance which he would encounter, he prepared for it carefully. The secret of his strategy was to use the Gallican question to bring pressure to bear on the Council to satisfy the complaints of the Protestants. The combination of the two movements, so closely related to each other, might be expected to create an impression. The Gallican question had been long dormant, but the schism which it almost produced in 1551 had not been forgotten; the progress which Protestantism had made since then was irrepressible; the double menace offered him a formidable engine of power. The only difficulty was that he was himself a firm Romanist, but this he solved by reserving the Gallican issue as a last resource.

The Pope mustered all the available bishops in Italy, packed them into the Council, and sent directions to Trent that the Cardinal be received with the most conspicuous attentions, including those of a Papal spy. The Cardinal was welcomed with the honours befitting his station and the dismay which his approach inspired. Great was the anxiety with which the Council awaited his opening address, and great was its relief when, instead of innovations, it heard only the familiar strains of custom. But this was merely a beginning. In due time he produced his instructions. They had a distinctly heterodox tone. His Majesty recommended that, in general, in order to win back so many provinces lost to the Church, every possible allowance be made to the Protestants on such points as the marriage of priests, images, indulgences, the invocation of saints, permission to retain ecclesiastical property which they had usurped, etc. The Council reserved judgment and the suspense rose. The Pope, however, did not reserve judgment. Through his Legates, he sent a surprising reply to the programme of the Cardinal, which he criticized not, indeed, because it was too bold, but because it was too mild. The time was past when the heretics could be reconciled by a few formal concessions or superficial reforms; at the stage which the struggle had reached, the Council could do nothing to settle the schism but to declare itself Protestant. The Cardinal completely mistook the nature of the problem. It was a revolution, not a reform, and though every grievance were to be redressed and every abuse corrected, the revolution would continue none the less inexorably. The root of it lay, not in this abuse nor in that doctrine, but in the spirit of independence and freethinking which was agitating society and transforming the mind of man. The original issue had long since been outgrown; what the Protestants wanted was freedom; reforms and concessions could no longer arrest the progress of a disorder equally fatal to ecclesiastical and secular society. They were mere palliatives applied to a remorseless organic malady; half-meas-

ures were futile; and the only real issue confronting the
Council was what it had always been—the question of
authority. So frank a statement of the position of Rome
challenged the Cardinal to state plainly where he stood,
on pain, if he evaded it, of accomplishing nothing. If it
were true, he had no choice but to recognize it and return home; but in that case what became of his mission?

In reply, he attacked the abuse of authority. Dwelling
eloquently on the wretched conditions of France—turmoil
and feuds, murder and pillage, anarchy and chaos—"to
whom must we attribute these evils?" he concluded. "To
heresy, no doubt, but not to heresy alone." The inference
was clear, but dignity forbade him to develop it himself;
his subordinate, the French ambassador, Monsieur du
Ferrier, took up the indictment where he dropped it.
"And if reformation does not come from you, in vain
would it be were all the princes to come to the aid of
France. As for those who may perish, even though they
be ruined by their own iniquities, you, and you alone,
will be held responsible for their blood."

Recriminations and menaces merely transformed the
argument, however, into a spectacular alteration; at bottom the argument of Rome remained unanswerable. And
so the contest settled down into an unyielding siege. As
the weeks wore on, the Cardinal was slowly dragged
down into that morass of aimless ruminations which constituted the daily routine of the Council. One after another, as each burning question arose, it was deposited in
committee, passed from hand to hand, dropped, and the
performance repeated with another. These discussions,
which were the traditional and legitimate function of a
General Council, although purely technical, were at the
present juncture highly inopportune. The principles of
the faith, resting on a body of obscure and inconsistent
traditions, could not be discussed without revealing the
variable interpretations and codified fallibility upon which
the Church founded its authority; the mere act of inves-
tigating it exposed the transcendental vacuity at the heart
of the sacred organism; and the spectacle was so damaging and gave such aid and comfort to the enemy that
the Fathers by common consent combined to maintain the
principle of all inorganic life, and do nothing.

To move that inert mass, or even to make an impression upon it, required uncommon purpose; and the struggle disclosed the mettle of which Charles de Guise was made. The Cardinal became fretful and impatient. There was no liberty, he complained in the Council, or rather there were two Councils, one sitting at Trent, the other at Rome, and nothing could be accomplished in Trent until the Holy Ghost, as Monsieur de Lansac said, had been brought by courier from Rome.

Occasionally, the Cardinal roused himself, chafing against the inertia of his colleagues like a draught in a vacuum. The news of the battle of Dreux led to a crisis. The Council celebrated with a solemn Mass of thanksgiving what the French delegation described as a decisive Catholic victory. It was time for a test, and the Cardinal, suddenly resuming the offensive, produced thirty-four demands for reform which alarmed the Legates, and were promptly transmitted to Rome. The Pope protested that the French were in open rebellion: they proposed to abolish the Datary, the Rota, and the entire authority of the Holy See; and he adjourned the discussion. The Cardinal could do nothing but pray for patience and the power he needed—staying-power. The momentum of his first move carried him on. For the sake of the world, it was time to take the extreme step and apply the pressure which he held in reserve. He intimated that, if he could obtain action in no other way, he was prepared to raise and to press the dreaded question of Conciliar supremacy, which was the cardinal principle of the Gallican Church. Once more, as in 1551, the fate of the Church lay in his hands. It was for him to decide. The defection of France in 1563 would be a wrench from which Rome might never recover, and he made it clear that he was not to be trifled with. His own government seconded him staunchly. Catherine invited the Emperor to stiffen his demands for "a good and complete reformation," and she suggested that the Cardinal himself pay a visit to the Emperor at Innsbruck. The Cardinal spent five days in secret conference with the Emperor. This visit caused the greatest uneasiness at Rome, and every effort was made, when he returned to Trent, to discover what had taken place. But he kept his counsel, reporting merely that the Emperor was highly incensed, that he declared that not one of his demands for reform had been so much as proposed for debate, that the Council was accomplishing nothing, and that the Pope was deceived either by the Council sitting at Trent or by his own Council sitting at Rome. He was evidently unwilling to assume the responsibility for an open breach with Rome alone; but he had already done enough to create a crisis.

It was at this moment that the news of the death of François de Guise reached Trent. The effect was catastrophic. The Cardinal collapsed; his spirit, his ambition, his principles, forsook him, and in his utter discouragement he proposed to return to France, to bury himself in his diocese, and to devote the remainder of his days to preaching and the care of his nephews.

But Charles de Guise made a brilliant recovery, reappearing in Trent in time to prevent the transfer of the Council to Bologna, where the Papal party proposed to spirit it away within reach of the Holy Ghost. His ardour was not dead, and he resumed the attack more vehemently than ever, denouncing the efforts of Rome to shirk reform with a tenacity which astounded his adversaries. Against so unyielding a spirit it was necessary to produce one yet more unbending. The Jesuit General Lainez now entered the arena. He proclaimed, in the most categorical manner, the absolute, arbitrary, and irresponsible authority of the Pope. One right alone he denied him, the right to limit his own power; he pushed omnipotence to its extreme conceivable point at which it became impotent to control its own being. The arbitrary and the absolute could go no further. Proclaiming the premiss, he proclaimed the conclusion: To the Pope alone belonged the right of reforming, if necessary, each of the Churches whose bishops composed the Council, and conversely, the bishops lacked the constitutional right of reforming the Church. The bishops had never heard so frank a declaration that they were nothing and could do nothing. Even the Italians, accustomed to their own nullity, nursed the illusion that collectively they amounted to something, and were manifestly shocked and chagrined, while the French and the Spanish were outraged and exasperated. Lainez himself realized, when he left the arena, that he had not only surpassed but over-reached himself. He sent a message to the Cardinal de Lorraine, in whose chambers the French delegation assembled to decide what step to take, offering to apologize. The Cardinal was deeply wounded, so deeply indeed that he was unable to rally.

From then on he began to yield ground. The forces of reaction, against which he had flung himself so strenuously, swept him swiftly back to Rome. Within a few months he was an honoured guest in the Vatican. When he returned to France, it was as the unequivocal champion of Rome, pledged to enforce the reactionary decrees of the Council of Trent.

At Court, he was coldly received and kept waiting two hours before his first audience with the King. Catherine declined to accept the findings or to execute the decrees of the Council, which, she insisted, would only upset the kingdom. He had failed her; and the penalty was a treatment which differed little from disgrace. Impotent to repress, impotent to reform, he was made to feel that his public role was over. He retired to private life and devoted himself to his ecclesiastical and family duties. One mission was left. The leadership of the Guises was not for him, not for any of his brothers: neither Mayenne, nor Elbeuf, nor the Cardinal Louis de Guise, nor the Grand Prieur was of sufficient stature to assume the position vacated by François de Guise. The inheritance of the hero belonged to his son; as Henri de Guise was a boy of thirteen, it would be many years before he could assume his heritage, and to train him for his destiny was a duty peculiarly congenial to the nature of Charles de Guise, who needed to live in another in order to realize himself. The impresario of the father became the guardian of the son. Of his trust he made a vocation, giving his pupil the benefit of his versatile abilities and his varied experience of life. One lesson he impressed on him constantly: that a man of spirit never lets himself be discouraged by a few reverses.

- 15 -

The Guises, as a family, inherited from their hero the nominal leadership of the Catholic cause. The actual initiative, however, after the close of the civil war, had already begun to pass, not to a rival family, but to the anonymous masses. The legacy of the civil war was a general unsettlement of social conditions, in which the passions kindled by the conflict continued to labour, and the impulse which had been originally given from above now came, diffused and contagious, from below. The religious question was no longer a convenience and a vehicle for the ambitions and interests of aristocratic champions, but a chaotic upheaval of popular passions and prejudices. As the agitation seeped down and saturated the whole social body, the leaders of yesterday waned, while those of the morrow were not yet mature; and in the interim, the heritage of the hero became public property.

The first conspicuous feature of this phase was the spontaneous formation, all over France, of provincial leagues for the repression of the Protestants. Especially in the south, where the Huguenots were numerous, one Catholic community after another organized local crusades and private armies for this purpose. These bodies derived a semblance of legality from the approbation of the local Parlements, the connivance of the royal officers, and the inclusion in their charters of a saving phrase—"subject to the pleasure of the King"—but their object and their functions, such as the levying of men, the laying of taxes, and the stocking of arms, were in flagrant violation of the law.

The character of the religious conflict as well was modified as it passed from one class to another. What made these associations fanatical was the fact that they were religious only because they were economic agglomerations under an assumed name. They were the coefficient of many factors which combined to produce the civil war and to perpetuate it, the focus of all the restless elements left over from the foreign wars, the rallying-point of the unemployed and the dispossessed, the refuge of the turbulent and the outcast, bred by and breeding the disorder on which they throve. There were also, merging with the shiftless and anti-social elements, the respectable and propertied middle classes of the community—magistrates, merchants, civil servants, professional people— who joined the leagues in self-protection to preserve public order through an association which took up the slack in unrest, which diverted it from themselves, and which employed dangerous public charges to bait and persecute the Protestants as the convenient prey of popular passion and prejudice.

The nucleus of these associations was provided by the commercial guilds, whose evolution had reached a crucial stage of development. For more than a century they had become closed corporations, controlled by a master class which monopolized and transformed them. The ruling groups, formed of families of wealth and political influence, adapted the guilds to their own purposes. In consequence, the distance between the upper and lower labouring classes widened, and disputes ensued between the master and the working class within the guild on the one hand and, on the other, between organized and free labour without it. Free labour comprised the home-craftsmen, or *chambrelans*, as they called themselves, who left the guilds and worked independently in their own quarters, selling their products where and as they could; and since they were not subject to the rates, regulations, and restrictions of the trade, they were regarded as illegitimate competitors by the guilds.

These conditions became a public question when, at the States-General of Orléans, the political Huguenots solicited a reform on the statutes of the guilds. Acting on their recommendation, the Chancellor included in the Ordinance of Orléans a regulation designed to curb the economic despotism of the guilds and to favour freer labouring conditions. He threw the influence of the Crown on the side of the industrial serfs by providing for governmental supervision of the guilds, which were ordered to disburse the bulk of their accumulated capital in support of schools, hospitals, and charitable institutions for the benefit of the community. Their wealth was not expropriated, but it was socialized. This legislation, had it been enforced, would eventually have destroyed the guilds. But it was not enforced. The guilds circumvented the government. Pleading that they were religious associations, they enlisted the support of the Church, whose property, locked up in mortmain, the Chancellor also proposed to secularize. Against the alliance of such entrenched interests the weight of the Crown was of nominal influence, and though the Chancellor instituted the official supervision which he had promised, he succeeded merely in producing the death and transfiguration of the guilds. Religious confraternities, as they now called themselves, they became the nuclei of those provincial leagues whose avowed purpose was the repression of the Protestants. Factious and illegal, the Government made repeated but futile efforts to suppress them; they were protected by the unsettled conditions which they created.

Nor was it merely the government which these groups ignored; it was all the late leaders of the Catholic cause. They were governed by a local and communal spirit; they might borrow the services of a government officer—a Montluc or a Monsieur de Candalle—but they controlled their *condottieri* and remained themselves nameless and autonomous. Individuals no longer mattered; the motives were social, the cause was collective; it had outgrown the champions who lent it princely prestige or a commanding personality. It was a period of transition and redistribution of power, and the Guises had lost contact with it. They had never had an ear for the nation, and now, living in retirement, nursing their pride and their feuds, they were more detached from it than ever.

- 16 -

A year after the conclusion of the civil war, the country had not yet disarmed. Peace, peace, and there is no peace: the complaint became chronic. Trusting to time to provide eventual relief, but anticipating it by her own methods, Catherine temporized. Daily she sat down to the same task. Daily she laboured over her vast correspondence, manufacturing calm. Her sedative industry was untiring. Patient and alert, she passed from report to report, applying to each, with the proper variations, the same familiar reply. For her resources would not have sufficed for her task, if she had not reduced them to a routine. When she sat down with her secretaries, she knew what to expect. There would be another communication from the Admiral, complaining of another violation of the edict, anticipating fresh troubles, recapitulating old outrages. There would be another memorandum from the Nuncio or the Spanish ambassador, complaining of the progress of the Protestants, of the fallacy of her policy, of the improvidence of the edict. To the one and the other her replies were interchangeable: she did what she could, not what she would. Having failed to secure a radical or a far-reaching cure, she was reduced to temporary makeshifts and expedients. All that she could do was to maintain, by continual adaptation, the shifting equilibrium of an unsatisfactory compromise. But to maintain her own balance was difficult: the continual adaptation required to counteract a double stress involved concessions and inconsistencies, and they were rarely made in favour of the Protestants, whom she could protect only by penalizing them.

Her system, in sum, was to gamble on circumstances. But she gambled on circumstances against the overwhelming odds of conditions; and as her normal methods were unequal to exceptional strains, she was constantly obliged to invent new ones. The most novel were also the oldest, like most acceptable innovations. She made a campaign of a maxim of François I, for whose memory she had a cult. Remembering, and treasuring as a piece of political wisdom, a remark which she had once heard him make, that to live in peace with the French and to maintain their loyalty to the Crown, two things were necessary, to amuse and to occupy them, she made amusement a basic part of her programme of government. Believing devoutly in the visible prestige of royalty and the political value of pomp and circumstance, she reconstituted the Court on the magnificent scale which she had known in the days of François I, organized a brilliant routine of pleasure, pageantry, luxury, spectacles, and sports, attracted the Protestant and Catholic leaders to Court, wooed them into the charmed circle, and exerted all her abilities to domesticate and to disgust them with war. Her famous "Flying Squadron" of thirty-five ladies, recruited from the first families of France, served her campaign, supplying such charms as she lacked. But her own were not negligible. The winning amenity of which she had made a vocation as a young girl, mellowed by maturity and self-possession, had become a confident, a regal affability. Even under the stress of care and fatigue, she retained her gracious good humour. A diplomat who observed her closely during the harassing experiences and hardening responsibilities of her first four years of government was amazed by her sanguine vitality and could not contain the admiration which he felt when he observed her "humanity," her "goodwill," her "patience in meeting everyone on his own level," and her "indefatigable constancy in receiving all manner of people, listening to their speeches, and treating them with so much courtesy that it would be impossible to ask for more consideration." Her goodwill lagged only when she was baffled by opinionation and bias, and then she betrayed it only by a lassitude which was the sole lapse from courtesy that she ever allowed herself. Her sophisticated simplicity, her poise and her sympathy, her genial vivacity and subtle reserve, and her conversational skill were great charms which everyone felt who associated with her. Her harshest critics recognized and were on their guard against them, and when she chose deliberately to exert her fascination, there was no one—neither a martinet like Montmorency nor a moralist like Bèze nor an inquisitor like the Spanish ambassador —who disputed it or who denied her personal ascendancy. But these charms were mature and, by reason of her position, impersonal. Hence the Flying Squadron.

So far as it went, this generalship was effective. For longer or shorter periods, together or in turn, the opponents of the civil war frequented the Court, fraternized in sham battles, balls, hunting, masques, and spectacles, posed for complimentary verses by Ronsard, and the French were occupied and amused, or at least the class that counted most considerably in the pacification of the country. The association at Court of the Bourbons, the Guises, the Châtillons, and the Montmorencys offered certain guarantees of public security, since it was through the *grands seigneurs* that the government controlled the provincial gentry. Although feudalism was legally extinct, the feudal spirit still lingered in the system which grouped the local families of each district about the *grand seigneur*, on whose patronage they depended for promotion in life. The nobility as a class were poor—ruined by war, by economic dislocation, by the partition or sale of their estates, by legal disqualification for trade—and having lost their economic security in a society transformed by commercial development, they were also losing their public spirit and were a potential source of disorder and a social liability. Compelled either to live on their lands, the revenues of which, due to the rising rates of exchange, were barely adequate for their subsistence, or to become pensioners of the Crown and to find a livelihood in one of the noble professions—the army, the Church, or the administration—through the favour of a protector close to the Throne, and being as prolific as they were poor, their first loyalty was to the *grand seigneur* to whom they were under past, present, or prospective obligation for a living. These numerous and compact clienteles of the great houses were a factor with which the government had continually to reckon. The Guises controlled the provinces of the east, the Bourbons those of the west and south-west, the Châtillons and the Montmorencys those of the north-west and the Ile-de-France. Because of the zones of influence they commanded, Catherine was obliged to manœuvre among rival families and creeds, manipulating, combining, adjusting, and balancing them, and it was this scientific play which underlay the frivolous occupations of the Court.

Nevertheless, she held the leaders, not the country. The troubles continued. Her authority, whether it was relayed through the co-operation of the *grands seigneurs*, or through the normal channels of the administration and the local Parlements, was so frequently stalled in transit that it was clear that her contact with the country was too remote to control it. Under exceptional strain, neither her accustomed methods nor the maxims of François I sufficed. A fresh departure was needed, a personal initiative. She conceived the idea of pacifying the country by touring it. This notion, original with herself but familiar to crowned heads, combined a number of advantages. She hoped to quicken the loyalty of the country and to re-establish the authority of the Crown by the personal appearance of the King. At fourteen he was a tall, thin lad, constantly unwell, frail, high-strung, of a retiring nature, and, like his father, guileless, good, melancholy, and mentally backward. The tour might be expected to quicken his mind and improve his health. Besides its educational value, it had a diplomatic attraction. Catherine proposed to realize her long-cherished ambition, to meet Philip II on the Spanish frontier, and to settle the neighbouring sources of internal disorder by informal conversations with her son-in-law. This was to be, in fact, the culminating point of the tour, to which everything else was but a long-drawn and roundabout approach. The consummation, at the same time, of a sentimental journey, it would allow her to spend a few weeks with her daughter Elisabeth. Finally, to be complete, the royal progress would require two years, and in that time the King would be so much more of a man: the ultimate goal of all her temporizing. It was, in short, an omnibus plan, capacious enough to contain or to meet somewhere with success.

Early in the spring of 1564, the expedition left Fontainebleau. Reduced for purposes of economy to eight hundred souls, the Court, the Royal Council, four companies of *gens d'armes*, a company of light horse, a regiment of French guards, and hundreds of lackeys, cooks, grooms, beaters, and their menials took to the road, travelling on horseback, in coaches, in litters, and on foot. Catherine herself chose a litter as the most convenient vehicle in which to carry on her correspondence, master her reports, and expedite affairs. Progress was slow. Though the journey was one of investigation and had been carefully planned to discover only what was already known, the harsh realization of what were merely statistical tables in official reports was a continual and shocking surprise.

As the Court travelled southward, however, she enjoyed a respite from public problems. At Salon, where her astrologer Nostradamus was living, she rested her cares among his quadrants and compasses. He consulted his science. The wise man saw no solution in the stars for a problem which disappeared under the aspect of eternity; and that was clearly the only cure for it. But he cast the King's horoscope. "He promises all manner of good to the King my son, and says that he will live as long as you," she wrote to Montmorency, "and that you will reach fourscore and ten. I hope that he is right," she added skeptically. Since the supernatural world offered no solace, she sought recreation in the natural magic of a landscape that became

steadily more entrancing as she approached the Mediterranean. Her spirits rose. At Narbonne, where she left the
Court to visit the frontier of Roussillon, Montmorency received a note from her, advising him that she was on her
way to Barcelona. Highly alarmed, he called a meeting of
the Royal Council to consider what steps to take, only to
learn that she had sent the message for the sheer pleasure
of mystifying him. She passed it on to Madrid, instructing
her ambassador to "tell the story to my daughter the
Queen, so that she may laugh over it." At Marseilles
again she startled everyone by appearing in a Turkish
costume. Since the death of her husband, she had never
broken mourning except for the coronation of her sons.
But she was in a holiday mood. The journey of pacification threatened to become an escapade. She lingered along
the Mediterranean, enjoying the Italian aroma of that
chromatic world. The palms, the pepper trees, the groves
of mimosa around Hyères, the exotic meres and flamingos
of Montpellier exhilarated her. But this interlude of happy
irresponsibility did not last long.

Beyond Marseilles the route lay through Provence, Languedoc, and Guyenne, the volcanic soil of meridional
fanaticism and the hotbed of the leagues. Dangerous for
the present, their real menace lay in the future, and was
far more threatening to the Crown than to the Protestants.
The leagues pledged themselves to serve the government
as long as it served them, but they were prepared to secede
as soon as it disregarded them. The whole problem of
pacifying the country and restoring the central authority
was contained and concentrated in the problem of controlling these spectral experiments. Catherine was not
blind to it and she appreciated it more clearly as she advanced into their territory. She was startled to learn from
Montluc that the Guises had made overtures to join the
League of Guyenne—overtures which, as an officer of
the Crown, he had discouraged. In the hands of the
Guises the shadowy shape assumed so potent a menace
that Catherine felt compelled to meet, once and for all, the
growing problem raised by this movement. She appealed
to Montluc for advice. He proposed the formation of a
Confederation of the King, which would abolish the others
by embracing and incorporating them. She objected at

first that this was equivalent to abdication, but after two days of reflection she accepted the suggestion. The semblance of authority was better than the certainty of impotence.

The suggestion of Montluc was masterly. For some time he had been in secret correspondence with Philip II, to whom he proposed the formation of a league of the Catholic powers, led by Rome and Madrid, to support the domestic associations which he sponsored and to co-operate with them in dictating the religious policy of the French Government. As a part of this project it was planned to abduct the Queen of Navarre, to hand her over to the Inquisition, and to occupy her States. To a proposition which combined the double attraction of quenching the hearth of heresy in France and of planting a Spanish outpost north of the Pyrenees, Philip II gave no encouragement. It was too aggressive. But he tempted Montluc to tempt him, and offered him an asylum in Spain in case his intrigues should miscarry. The French ambassador in Madrid caught wind of the plot in time to nip it. Though the full extent of the fuse was not disclosed, enough transpired to put Catherine on her guard against the possible ramifications of the leagues.

If she countenanced the leagues, it was because she was determined to present an appearance of domestic security when she arrived at Bayonne. The Spanish conference was the crucial, as it was the culminating, point of her tour. For six years she had solicited it; for six years Philip II had eluded it; her persistent ambition had become a settled obsession because he was the arbiter of her destiny. The prepotent influence which he exercised over France paralyzed all her efforts to pacify it, and she could not rest until she had neutralized it by personal contact. But Philip II understood too well the nature of his influence to risk a personal interview. It depended on invisibility. He determined, therefore, to be represented at Bayonne by two persons who doubled his identity and divided his obligations. One of these was her daughter. That exhausted his duty to humanity. The other was the Duke of Alva.

Disappointed in her original aim, Catherine was disconcerted but undiscouraged. The substitution of Alva re-

duced the conference to a formal visit of courtesy designed
to promote a better understanding between the two countries, but without any specific programme beyond a general exchange of views. Its diplomatic value became secondary, therefore, to its personal interest, and the meeting
with Elisabeth was henceforth her primary concern. But
as she was partial to personal diplomacy, the inclusion
of Elisabeth in the conference was a factor which affected
public opinion in France. The pressure of Spain charged
the political atmosphere as the Court approached the
Pyrenees. Philip II took exception to the presence of the
Protestants at the French Court and, in particular, of the
Admiral. Catherine wrote to her daughter, explaining that
there was no ground for concern. "Although the Admiral
remains at Court, he will be here as if he were dead, because, God willing, I shall not let myself be governed
either by one party or the other, having learned only
too well that they all love God, the King, and your mother
less than their profit, their greatness, and the satisfaction of
their ambition, and since they know that I will not let them
ruin the King and the kingdom, they love me only in
words, knowing that my only aim is to preserve the King,
the kingdom, and his brothers, and that I want only what
is useful to them; therefore I trust no one. I know also
that they try to turn the King your brother against me,
but, God willing, I shall prevent them, and I shall preserve
the lives of your brothers as the dearest thing in the world
to me." These explanations appeared to be satisfactory,
since they produced no reply. But the mental habits of
Philip were slow, and what seemed to be tacit consent
might always prove in the end to be merely the maturing
of another complaint. At Bordeaux she learned that her
daughter had left for the frontier but had been delayed.
She sent for the Spanish ambassador and questioned him.
He mentioned a decree published at Toulouse which
allowed some latitude in the observance of Lent. "I hope
that this will not be made a pretext to put off the meeting
at Bayonne," she said. The ambassador was reserved.
"There is too much liberty allowed to heresy," he remarked. Suspecting the worst, she pressed him to admit
it. "Do you know what has retarded my daughter's departure?" He referred to a rumour, which had reached

Madrid, that the Prince de Condé and the Queen of Navarre proposed to be present at Bayonne. His Catholic Majesty could not consent to expose his wife to the reproach of having conversed with heretics. Catherine pleaded that to dismiss Condé would whet the suspicions of the Protestants, who already believed that some sinister design against them inspired the conference. But as the scruples of Philip II were invincible, she yielded. In consequence, the Huguenots observed the conference from afar, without reliable information, and derived their knowledge of it from hearsay.

Having made this concession, of which she recognized the error, Catherine was doubly impatient for its recompense. Uncertain but unchallenged, Catherine pursued the appointed itinerary and left Saint-Jean-de-Luz, according to schedule, for a ford on the Bidassoa, where the Queen of Spain was to cross the border. Tents were pitched on the banks of the Bidassoa and bowers built against the glare. At last someone discerned a cloud of dust developing in the distance but blending so completely with the landscape and moving with so faint a motion that it required a touch of second sight to identify it. The King and the Court crossed the river and, several hours late, the scheduled ceremony took place. Alva introduced the Queen of Spain to her mother, but it was not until she held her securely in her arms that Catherine seemed to recover her sense of the finite world.

The first tears and embraces were followed by constraint and formality. In crossing the river, Catherine insisted on yielding the place of honour to Elisabeth, who insisted on declining it, reddened when she was overruled, and still demurred for a daughter's place; but her mother would not allow her to forget who she was. This caused a little stiffness at the start. That night, at Saint-Jean-de-Luz, there was a family reunion; Catherine, the King, the little Margot, and Elisabeth supped together and attempted to coax back the old intimacy, but after six years of separation it required time to renew their acquaintance, and there was none. No provision for privacy had been made in the schedule of festivities. The parade into Bayonne was a magnificent solemnity, marred by the nonchalance of the Spanish who, mounted on hacks and

mules, and riding with their portmanteaux, made a mortifying display of their poverty, which was mistaken for a
deliberate attempt to insult the prodigality of their hosts.
Such an impression could not be too promptly corrected.
Catherine gave a series of elaborate entertainments, balls,
banquets, masques, suppers *al fresco,* sham battles, picnics,
and promenades. Finally, Elisabeth attempted a confidential talk. Resigned to her official capacity, she approached
her mother on public affairs and ventured to explain the
sentiments of Philip II on the religious question. This
conversation ended badly. Catherine cut it short. "So your
husband suspects me? Do you know that his suspicions
will lead us straight to war?" Elisabeth protested. "What
makes you suppose, Madame, that the King suspects
Your Majesty? Only malicious people could give you such
an impression." "My dear daughter, you have become very
Spanish." "I am Spanish, I admit, it is my duty to be so,
but I am still your daughter, the same whom you sent to
Spain." Catherine made no comment. Where she expected
an ally, she found an alien, and she avoided the subject.

In the meanwhile, amid these diversions, the conference
began casually, surreptitiously. Alva sounded the most influential Catholics on their views. As the Court had been
purged for the occasion, this amounted to little more than
taking a census of the orthodox party, and their opinions
confirmed his own. Without exception, they took a pessimistic view of the situation. The consensus of opinion
among the French Catholics, he found, was not in favour
of extreme measures. Expulsion of the Protestant preachers, prohibition of Protestant worship, and the execution
of these measures by the individual governors of the various provinces of France were considered an adequate
remedy for the present. These ideas coincided with those
which he was authorized to propose, but his instructions
were that he was not to make the advances. The initiative
must come from France and the appearance of outside
pressure be scrupulously avoided. He was to go as far as,
and no further than, his support warranted.

Alva then approached the King. Touching on his favourite topic, the chase, he induced the shy young man
to talk freely and, one serious subject leading to another,
begged him earnestly to preserve his health, "since the wel

fare of Christendom depends on it." "I believe," he went on, "that God has guarded it in order to perform some great work by your hands, such as the castigation of the offences that exist in your kingdom." But the King, realizing that Alva was not interested in the chase, showed no interest in this mission and brought the examination to a close, observing that he had no intention of resorting to arms and ruining his kingdom, "as we began to do in the late war." Alva refused to admit that he had received a rebuff. "I perceived," he explained in his report, "that they keep him fettered, and so I passed to other subjects."

The interview with Catherine Alva left to the last, waiting for her to make the advances. As she showed no inclination to do so, however, he was finally compelled to take the initiative. He sent the Queen of Spain to sound her mother. But between the two women the religious question became personal: a lurking antagonism rose between them; they were too sensitive antagonists and Elisabeth shrank from a discussion which visibly estranged her mother. After a conscientious attempt, she begged the question. "Since you dread war so much," she pleaded, "why not avail yourself of the presence of the Duke and reach a settlement with him?" "Agreed," said Catherine. Her curt tone cut Elisabeth to the quick. She felt that she had offended her.

Catherine had deliberately avoided the interview with Alva, who represented all the risks of the conference and none of its advantages. Catherine was on the defensive; she had nothing to gain from dealing with Alva except to discover how far he was prepared to go. The conference, minus Philip II, was at best a formality and, at worst, a liability which she was anxious to bring to a harmless conclusion. The possibility of mutual understanding was excluded; but as she had set the mechanism in motion and could no longer extricate herself from it, her only object was to conceal the fact that she had none.

Alva found her unfathomable. He credited her with powers of concentrated dissimulation which in all his experience he had never seen equalled. "I have never known anywhere, in anyone, such circumspection," he declared in describing their interview. She began by talking at an "incredible speed, touching on one subject after another" and studying him with that disconcerting stare which she assumed when she dissociated her conversation from her thoughts. Then she halted abruptly. "I see," she said, "that you wish to come to religion." "I admit it, Madame. It is the whole point of our conversation." She resumed, but at a pace which he could follow, enumerating all the events which had occurred since the publication of the Edict of Pacification, and demonstrating the improvement in the situation and the hopeful prospects for the future, until he corrected her and stated his own version of the facts. "It is quite impossible for us," he explained, "not to require the most effective cure, since the cause is common to Spain: the disease will spread and my master does not wish to lose his Crown or, it may be, his life." "You diagnose the disease very well," she agreed. "I suggest that you specify the cure." "But, Madame, who knows it better than yourself? It is for you to say what you wish. I will undertake to transmit your wishes to my master." "Your master knows everything that occurs in this kingdom better than I do. That is why I consult him. What would he do in my position?" "Has religion gained or lost ground since the edict?" "It has gained." "I cannot agree, Madame." He produced evidence to the contrary and demonstrated that she was either deceiving herself or misleading him—in either case a serious error. No one could flatter himself that he was acquainted with actual conditions in France without being informed, he said, of a fact so pertinent to the present negotiations. Ignoring the impertinence, she came to the point. "Am I to understand that what you propose is war?" "For the moment, I see no need of it," he parried. "My master would not advise it, unless the need became more urgent." But she pressed him for his own opinion. "In my opinion," he said, "there is great need of curing these disorders promptly, since sooner or later, whatever you may wish, your enemies will take up arms and compel you to do the same, and perhaps under less favourable conditions, when it will be too late and of no effect. The plan which my master approves, and to which he gives constant attention, is to expel this wretched sect from France, to restore the former power of the French King, and to maintain your legitimate authority as Queen-Mother." Personal reflections Catherine always ignored, but she resented any imputation against the power or authority of the Crown. "My son the King publishes whatever edicts he pleases and is obeyed," she began, and would have continued if Elisabeth had not challenged her. "Then why," her daughter argued, "if he has so much authority over his subjects, does he not punish rebels against God and himself?" But it was as if she had not spoken, as if she had ceased to be. Catherine diverted the discussion, and brought the audience to a close.

Other interviews followed, which added no new arguments but which increased the pressure and exasperation of the debate. The fact that it was conducted by a minister who had a masterful personality and strong private opinions had a decisive bearing on the outcome. Without transgressing his instructions, studiously avoiding the appearance of pressure, he brought to bear on her, nevertheless, a hypnotic power of suggestion, instilling into her mind a numbing sense of helplessness, penetrating her defenses, and prompting her to propose of her free will the solution which of her free will she was determined to avoid. At one of their last interviews, she took the precaution to receive him in a small room, of which the doors stood open, and as the adjoining apartments were crowded with courtiers, it was impossible to discuss confidential topics, and extreme measures were adjourned to a final encounter. This time, avoiding close quarters, Catherine met him in a long, vacant gallery, at one end of which the curious gathered, within sight but out of hearing, observing and speculating on a significant dumb-show. Against the midsummer glare, the two figures passed, through zones of mottled light and shadow, pacing to and fro, Catherine at her usual brisk gait, Alva stalking her respectfully. Some snatches of their conversation were caught. At one turn Catherine became impatient: "I have said all that I have to say." "You appear to have grown colder, Madame, since we first discussed it." "You appear to misunderstand me, Monsieur. I am capable of doing justice myself." Then they passed out of range. When they returned, she was defending the Chancellor. "It is his personal enemies who accuse him of being a bad Catholic." "Can you deny that he is a Huguenot?" "I do not consider him one." "Then, Madame, you are the only person in France of that opinion." Alva appealed to Elisabeth, who followed the promenade and caught up with the conversation. "Even before I felt France, while my father was alive," she said, "Your Majesty knows that he had that reputation." She was urging his dismissal as they moved off again, but she was left far behind by her mother, who quickened her pace to escape her objections. When they returned, their tempers were shorter. "His Catholic Majesty wishes to know," Alva said, "whether you mean to remedy this religious trouble. Can he count on the King your son, or must he act by himself? This is the only reason your daughter has come to Bayonne." "I have said all that I have to say," Catherine repeated with finality. And they were off again. The next turn brought them to the Council of Trent. She refused to accept its decrees, and explained that she was about to call a Council of theologians to settle a number of questions which the Œcumenical Council had left unsolved, and she anticipated his objections: "These questions are not matters of divine law, but of political expediency." This excursion carried them far and it was long before they again passed within reach of eavesdroppers. "I recognize the danger of Councils, but my son the King is strong enough to confine the discussions to such subjects as he may designate," she said. "Was it so at Poissy?" he queried, in a paroxysm of patience. That, she insisted, was the fault of the Cardinal de Lorraine, who believed that he could convince the Calvinist ministers. And the monotonous round continued. The spectators themselves tired of it before the antagonists were finally exhausted.

Nothing remained but to bring the conference to a close; but to separate in a spirit of antagonism and mistrust was equivalent to a covert rupture. Alva wrote to Philip II that he had been unable to induce her to accept a single one of his proposals, and as a defeated Alva was dangerous, Catherine determined, at the very moment when she had worsted him, to retreat and to make at least some nominal concession. She sent for the Nuncio to negotiate an understanding with him. She undertook to accept the Tridentine decrees, subject to the approval of her proposed Council. Then, taking refuge in a meeting of the Royal Council, after Montmorency had defended her religious policy and emphasized the dangers of civil war, she offered Alva a verbal and general assurance that she would apply a prompt cure to the situation as soon as she concluded her tour. She made a similar pledge in private to her daughter, but she refused to commit it to writing. The deadlock was dissolved and the danger averted by the usual practice in such cases. The conference, which had been called to promote a better understanding, and which had created fresh antagonism, was saved by a successful misunderstanding.

The conference had lasted two weeks (June 15-July 2, 1565). The Spanish ambassador, who saw the last of it on the banks of the Bidassoa, watched the leavetakings in a sympathetic and protective mood. "The farewells of the Queen of Spain, the Queen-Mother, and the King were more heartrending than words can express," he wrote. "There were floods of tears. The Constable came into the King's room and told him that he must not cry, since foreigners as well as his own people would see him, and kings must never cry. The King thanked him but he could not stop crying. . . . I reminded the Queen-Mother of the great perils to which she and the King would be exposed, since the Protestants are convinced that it has been decided at this conference to punish them, and I told her to be on her guard, now that the good Catholics who were with them have gone. The Queen of Spain gave her the same advice." But at that moment his warning made no impression. The mother and daughter clung together, cautioning, caressing, bracing each other, concerned with only one peril. They had narrowly escaped a profound misunderstanding and estrangement. In the moment of leavetaking, they were completely united, and they prolonged it insatiably. When the last delay expired, Catherine decided to accompany her daughter a few miles further. She crossed the frontier and escorted her as far as Irun, and there, fading into the distance and the dust of Spain, she saw the last of Elisabeth. On her return to Saint-Jean-de-Luz, she dictated a circular, explaining the true nature of the conference: "Because the King my son wishes that the visit of the Catholic Queen my daughter should not excite suspicion among his people and lead them

to suppose that we intend in any way to alter his Edicts of
Pacification and Majority, and of the other declarations
which he has made since then, we have decided to send
this dispatch, etc. . . . The Queen my daughter left us
on the third of this month. During our interview we spoke
of nothing but pleasures, feasts, and pastimes, and, in general terms, of the desire which we both feel to maintain
friendship between their Majesties and to preserve peace
between their people." The fictitious importance of the
Conference of Bayonne was confirmed by Cardinal Granvelle. "The truth is," he said, "that it was merely the
meeting of a mother and daughter."

- 17 -

The secrecy in which the Conference was shrouded, the
exclusion of the Huguenots from Court, and the official
reassurances which followed it, suggested the blackest suspicions to the Protestants. Where the suspicion existed,
the evidence was bound to follow. The aims of the French
Catholics were no secret, those of Alva were barely veiled;
it was assumed that a secret pact had been drafted to ruin
the Religion, and to decimate its leaders—a recognizable
version of Alva's proposals—and these surmises, based on
plausible premisses but leading to unfounded conclusions,
were inflated by the sensational story told by the one
Huguenot whose presence was tolerated at Bayonne. The
young Henri de Navarre, a boy of twelve, studied his
lessons with the royal children, was petted by the Spaniards, and fascinated by Catherine, whom he followed
about in pursuit of an education. A normal boy, curious to
see and hear, he was present at one of her interviews with
Alva, and later told his mother a tale that chilled the marrow of the chosen people. He remembered a phrase used
by Alva to illustrate the best method of checking the
Huguenots, one of those happy comparisons which a boy
could understand: "The head of one salmon is worth a
thousand frogs." His mother immediately warned Condé
and Coligny. When the Protestant leaders again joined the
Court at Moulins, everyone discerned the war clouds on
the horizon. The Protestants arrived in force, convinced
that the summons which they had received was the as-

signation to a massacre. Circumstantial accounts of the plan circulated, and when nothing occurred the failure was imputed to their precaution and the pusillanimity of the Queen-Mother. These hallucinations were a measure of the swiftness with which the feverish drift toward war was already flowing, for the Protestant leaders had been summoned to Moulins, in January 1566, six months after the Conference of Bayonne, to attend an Assembly of Notables which Catherine had called to consult with her on the pacification of the country. The Assembly was six months too late. Instead of being an antidote to Bayonne it was an anticlimax.

Before proceeding to public business, Catherine induced, or provoked, a final reconciliation between Coligny and the Guises. The delay of three years exacted by the King having elapsed, Charles IX pronounced judgment in Council, completely exculpating the Admiral. Before taking this public and statutory step, the hazards of justice were duly weighed. Both parties were privately consulted, and when the risks of equity had been carefully discounted, a public formality was arranged. Coligny appeared before the Council, stated his case, and retired. The Cardinal de Lorraine then appeared on behalf of his family. Catherine made an address, dwelling on the necessity of quenching private feuds in order to restore public confidence, and the Cardinal replied by a piece of oratory which was a minor masterpiece of equivocal consent— impeccable in its reserve, unexceptionable in its submission, intangible in its resentment, and supple in its assurance. Then he withdrew. After a lapse of several days, the final formality was effected. In the presence of Catherine, the King, and the Council, Coligny and the Cardinal embraced. The Duchesse de Guise submitted to the same ceremony, but Henri de Guise abstained.

Shortly afterward, the Duchesse de Guise remarried and became Madame de Nemours.

At the same time, a formal reconciliation was effected between the Montmorencys and the Guises.

The way being cleared for public business, the Assembly began its sessions, and the first radical step toward the pacification of the country was taken, on the initiative of the Chancellor, with the publication of the memorable

Ordinances of Moulins. This programme of legislation, which laid the basis for a far-reaching and fundamental reform of the administration of justice, of police, of finance, of hospitals, benefices, trade-unions, and confraternities, was remarkable as a departure from superficial and time-serving expedients, as an attempt to deal with organic sources of disorder, and as a monument to the public spirit, enterprise, and vision of Michel de l'Hospital. It embraced and attacked a whole system of inveterate and ingrown abuses which impeded the proper functioning of public authority. The most urgent of these reforms affected the Parlements, whose stubborn resistance to every liberal edict abetted the lawlessness of the Catholic masses, and defeated the efforts of the government to enforce an impartial authority. The Parlements were a hard tumour in the public system, clogging and intoxicating it; and no progress could be made in regulating the religious question without attacking the constitutional privileges of the magistracy.

For the magistracy, though nominally the agents of the Crown, actually constituted a class which escaped its control, because it had acquired a vested interest in the State through the venality of public office. The rising middle class, ambitious to translate its purchasing power into social and political power, profited by the economic distress of both the upper class and the Crown. Feudal estates, public offices, everything was for sale; the noble parted with his patrimony, the King with the public power; and the prosperous bourgeois, seeking social advancement and a safe investment, placed his money either in land or in the law, buying an estate and a title, or acquiring a seat upon the bench and becoming a member of that upper middle class, the *gens de robe longue,* whose nickname was their title: *les robins.* The *robins* were recognized as a Fourth Order, and their importance warranted it, for it was through them that the moneyed class pushed its way into the feudal state and transformed it.

The consequences of this change were manifest in the public service. The purchaser of a public trust administered it as his personal property, transmitting it to his heirs, selling it to other aspirants, and exploiting it for his private profit. Between the Crown and the people a judicial bureaucracy had grown up like a wedge, and the subject and the prince lost contact with, and confidence in, each other.

If such was the normal condition, how much denser was the obstruction in an emergency such as the religious crisis created! Wedded to the established order on which it subsisted, the magistracy was consistently conservative, and its bias was capable of balancing or unbalancing the government. Defending the orthodox policies of the Crown, it opposed any lapse from them with a resistance none the less powerful for being passive, using and abusing the right of remonstrance, and justifying its opposition by claims which encroached upon the sovereign attributes. The principle was formulated that the King was responsible to the law, from which he derived his authority. In the eyes of the law, he became merely a creation of the law. And what was the law? What the judiciary defined it to be. The sovereign promulgated it, but the magistracy interpreted and administered it. These pretensions increased under the stress of the religious struggle, and the magistracy, confounding public spirit with its *esprit de corps*, developed a concept of the State as an entity composed of the functionaries of the State, distinct from and all but independent of the sovereign.

Catherine had encountered this spirit from the beginning of her Regency. Much that passed for weakness and timidity in her political conduct was due to the fact that, coming to power in a terrible internal crisis, she was balked by the passive resistance of her own functionaries and, unable to command, was compelled to negotiate with them. The royal power, absolute in principle, was actually, as L'Hospital said, "without hands or feet." A thoroughgoing reform was too ambitious; all that was possible was a degree of regulation. The measures adopted by L'Hospital curtailed the right of protest of the Parlements and, in what amounted to a *coup d'état* against the municipal magistrates, deprived them of civil jurisdiction, which was transferred to the officials of the Crown. This was a beginning and nothing more. At bottom, the obstacle remained the same: the sovereign was bound by contract, and was obliged either to buy back the offices which he had sold or to abolish them arbitrarily. The latter would have been too revolutionary a measure, which would have added another menace of upheaval to those by which the Crown was already beset; the former was impossible. To redeem the power of the Crown by purchase required a prolonged period of economy and peace; and the reform was launched at the very moment when the atmosphere of war was forming anew.

Under such circumstances, the result of a reform too prudent to be effective and too provocative not to alarm those whom it threatened could only be unsettling. Its political value was that of a pledge, a bid for confidence; but it increased the prevailing unrest and served merely to add to the unpopularity of the Chancellor. At Bayonne, Alva had demanded his dismissal; at Moulins, he was attacked in the Royal Council. The Parlement of Dijon had sent two of its members to Court to protest against an edict issued by the Chancellor, on his own authority, permitting the Protestants to hold private worship in their homes and to call in their ministers for the instruction of their children. Failing to obtain satisfaction from the Chancellor, or an audience from the King, the delegates complained to the Cardinal de Lorraine, who laid the matter before the Royal Council. Explanations were demanded, the edict was produced, the Cardinal de Bourbon threatened to resign, a violent altercation arose between L'Hospital and the cardinal de Lorraine, and it required all the address of the Queen-Mother, who reprimanded the Chancellor and revoked the offending edict, to check the incident.

The Assembly at Moulins was stillborn. While the war clouds gathered in France, relations with Spain became suddenly strained in consequence of the massacre by the Spanish of a French colony in Florida. To the sharp protests which Catherine addressed to Madrid, she received only evasive, indifferent, or provocative replies. This incident marked the culmination of a long series of colonial conflicts between France and Spain. Bitter as a challenge to the right of France to colonial expansion, it was aggravated by its bearing on the religious question. The colony in Florida was one of many sponsored by Coligny in the New World—in Brazil, in Newfoundland, in Florida—in an effort to find an outlet and a refuge beyond the seas for his co-religionist. That solution was henceforth eliminated.

Her tour was now drawing to a close, and she prolonged its final stages, lingering at Moulins for three months, on one pretext or another. First, it was the cold which forbade her return to Paris; then, the famine which gripped France and which forced her to reside in Moulins, because of the high cost of living elsewhere; but at last another impatience made itself felt. The country people complained of the burden of feeding the Court over so long a period, and when they presented a petition for relief, she resumed her journey.

- 18 -

The last stage of the great tour brought Catherine home two years older. She had completed the vicious circle, she was seasoned in experience, but she returned with her original principles intact. In June 1566, there was a Protestant outbreak in Pamiers, near Toulouse. The convents were attacked, the monks were killed, and the Catholics were expelled from town. Catherine took stringent measures to repress this mutiny. She was shocked by the excesses of Protestants—they were worse, she declared, than the Turks—she was alarmed by the leaven of war, and she welcomed the opportunity to prove to her critics in Madrid that her moderation was not to be mistaken for weakness. But, two months later, when the iconoclastic riots occurred in Antwerp, she welcomed the opportunity to moralize on them. She wrote to Philip II, recommending that he "take us as an example, for we have sufficiently shown, at our own cost, how others should govern themselves." Informed by some irresponsible person that the Spanish Government had determined to abate its severity in the Low Countries, she sent a note of congratulation to her ambassador in Madrid.

These congratulations were premature. If the troubles in Flanders proved anything, they proved the contention of Alva that the contagion of unrest between neighbouring States effaced their frontiers and made their problem a common one; where the issue was international, the cure could not be local. Far from following her example, Philip

II corrected it, and not by another of those futile notes which he had been writing for years, but by a demonstration more telling than words. He removed the Duchess of Parma, who had administered the Netherlands with relative moderation, and appointed the Duke of Alva in her stead. Preparations were made to raise an army and send it overland to Brussels—a lengthy operation which required careful international planning. The Duke of Alva approached the French Government with a request for permission to pass through French territory, and invited its co-operation in repressing the iconoclasts in Flanders. But he received no encouragement. Insisting that the Huguenots would rise, Catherine maintained an attitude of inimical neutrality, mobilized troops, and fortified the frontiers. These precautions annoyed Philip II and alarmed the Huguenots, who were convinced that they were a blind. That no immediate disturbance occurred was due in part to the prudence of Coligny and in part to the length of time which Alva required to complete his preparations.

By February 1567, the preliminaries were approved, and in May the march began. From Genoa, through Savoy and Franche-Comté, skirting the eastern frontier of France, it followed an itinerary which was a segment and a forcible reminder of the encircling span of empire, and which produced in France, but on a larger scale, the same furrows of concerns as had the domestic tour of the Court. At the last moment Catherine determined, as a further precaution, to engage six thousand Swiss. Coligny, consulted on this step, approved it, and the order was placed. The Spanish march was accomplished without mishap. In August, Alva reached Brussels, where he immediately erected the Tribunal of Troubles or, as it was popularly known, the Tribunal of Blood; and the demonstration began.

The example of his drastic methods was not lost on France. The terror in Flanders and the arrest in September of Counts Egmont and Horn excited another sympathetic reaction among the Huguenots, and when, amid this excitement, the Swiss battalions arrived, Condé wrote to Catherine, urging her to countermand them and warning her that he could not answer for the peace of the country unless she did. She assured him, in reply, that the edict would be inviolably observed, but insisted that the Swiss were required to secure the country against surprises. Condé and his colleagues discounted this explanation. The emergency was over; since there was no good reason for the presence of the Swiss, there could only be a bad one.

The Court was staying at Montceaux when the first warnings reached it. A troop of twelve or fifteen hundred horse was reported in the vicinity of the Admiral's estate at Châtillon-sur-Loing. Catherine attached little importance to the alarm, remaining at Montceaux, which was an unprotected manor in the open country. When the warnings were repeated, however, the Court moved to the town of Meaux, and hurried orders were sent to the Swiss, who were quartered at Château-Thierry, thirty miles away, to advance. Horsemen were sighted in the vicinity, and the seriousness of the situation could no longer be denied. The Council met, and the majority urged an immediate retreat to Paris. The Chancellor alone held out, arguing that to seek asylum amid the fanatical population of the capital would make all accommodation impossible. Fighting the immediate emergency to prevent a greater crisis, he made a stubborn stand to save his policies. But Catherine turned on him. "It is you and your advice that have brought us to this pass," she said hotly. The debate was cut short by the arrival of the Swiss. Under their escort, the Court left Meaux, at three in the morning, and after a laborious and ignominious flight of fifteen hours, harassed by sharp skirmishes with Condé's cavalry, reached Paris on the same night.

The attempt on Meaux marked the conclusion of the phase that began with the Tumult of Amboise. The rising of the Protestants, seven years before, started Catherine on her first groping efforts toward toleration; the repetition of it, seven years later, put an end to them. Her patience was exhausted. Her first reactions of amazement and indignation turned, in retrospect, to incredulity and outrage when she was safe in Paris. The humiliation of the King, who wept with rage during the flight and could not forget the memory of it, was an offence which she could not condone; the crime of lese-majesty placed the Protestants beyond the pale of compromise. Because of the conditions of the country, the balance, once broken, could no longer be restored, and she abandoned the attempt to master a problem which, insoluble by sanity, could be liquidated only in blood. Mastered by it at last, she let events take their course.

- 19 -

Henceforth the only balance possible was the shifting equation of force, alternating cycles of rabid war and vicious peace succeeding each other in convulsive stages of continuous conflict, maddening monotony, implacable repetition; the rest was redundancy without resolution. The struggle continued for seven years on the lines laid down at its outbreak: a triangular contest between the factions to control the Crown and between the Crown and the factions to maintain its independence; and through all the vicissitudes of the conflict—the ebb and flow of seasonal campaigns, the redundant battles, the fleeting truces, the baffled compromises, the precarious repairs, the recurrent explosions—it remained a dynamic deadlock. Unchanging, it developed, nevertheless, by decomposition. The strain of a long and fruitless struggle gradually exhausted the adversaries and the issues, and though the situation remained stationary, it was transformed by a lengthy process of erosion, disintegration, and decay. The sediment of civil war fertilized France for a social upheaval far exceeding the scope of the religious wars which, religious only in name, were a complex, turgid, confused phenomenon that embraced and hallowed social power and social protest in all its forms—the rivalry of princes, the impoverishment of peoples, personal ambitions, economic pressure, financial chaos, class friction, republican stirrings, reactionary repression—and these elements, coalescing with the religious principle, began by adulterating and ended by submerging and transmuting it. A corresponding development occurred in Catherine. Placed at the centre of the conflict, acted upon and reacting to it, counteracting it successfully but never succeeding in controlling it, she underwent the only possible development in her position: the long ordeal of foiling the contending forces neutralized her and their pressure converted her into a negative force. Of this double process

—the interaction of a personal and a public tragedy—
the main lines emerge in a summary and synoptic view.

When force came to the fore, Catherine was eclipsed
by it. Jostling figures, thronging masses, crowded her out
of the public eye during the periods of declared war. In
the intervals of opaque peace she reappeared and resumed
her sway, apparently unchanged, but a cloudier personality after each submersion.

The second civil war was a war of nervous improvisation. The dash on Meaux having failed, Condé galloped
headlong with his fifteen hundred horsemen into a blockade of Paris. Hostilities began, as usual, by peace parleys.
Catherine consented to negotiate, partly to avert war,
partly to gain time to prepare for it, and opposed the
military investment with a blockade of bargains. But both
parties were too embittered to bargain; she offered an
amnesty, Condé replied with a Bill of Rights, demanding
not only the restoration of the original edict, without
limitations, but a political programme as well. Realizing
that the fears which inspired the rising were not a legitimate excuse for it, he posed as a champion of political
grievances, and demanded the convocation of the States-
General, a diminution of taxes, and a sweeping financial
accounting. A month passed in negotiation and guerrilla
warfare, the attitude of the government steadily stiffen-
ing. The negotiations, which at first were entrusted to
three moderate Catholics, were concluded by the Constable, who rejected the terms of Condé *en bloc*. The reinforcements of the government were on the way. But they
constituted a hazard which Catherine was anxious to
limit. When Condé divided his forces to intercept the
Spanish reinforcements, the Constable recommended an
immediate engagement. While the Spanish were advancing, the battle of Saint-Denis was fought (November 10,
1567). The day ended in a draw. Three or four hundred
men fell on either side. One of these was the Constable,
who covered himself with glory and succumbed to it at
the age of seventy. The government made no attempt
to renew the attack, Condé retreated to a less exposed
position, and the blockade was broken.

Months of relaxation and delay followed. The dash, the

spirit, the endurance of the Huguenots were severely
tried by the sober, humdrum business of war, the drain
of a dragging campaign for which they were ill equipped,
and the difficulty of raising one hundred thousand crowns
to pay the *Reiters* sent them from Germany. Condé retraced his steps toward Paris and laid siege to Chartres.
The government reluctantly applied to Alva for fresh
reinforcements, but he made difficulties, he could not
spare a small detachment, and yielded only when he was
warned that peace would follow. The reinforcements
arrived, too late; Catherine anticipated them by negotiating with Condé. The high command having been vacated
by the Constable, the campaign had been conducted
under the nominal command of the Duc d'Anjou. At the
first mention of peace the Huguenot volunteers, who had
served for six months without pay and were restless and
homesick, began to desert in droves. By the Peace of
Longjumeau (March 23, 1568) the second civil war
ended on approximately the same conditions as the first.
The Edict of Toleration was restored without important
restrictions. But the situation, then and now, was completely reversed. In 1563 Catherine had capitulated willingly and had welcomed the restoration of the edict as a
personal vindication; in 1568 she submitted reluctantly
and reverted to her former policy under constraint; and
the treaty contained no guarantees against mental reservations. It provided for the disarming of both sides, and
Condé, abandoned by his volunteers and in debt to the
Reiters, fulfilled his obligations scrupulously. But the government remained under arms.

If the brevity of the war was due, on the Protestant
side, to the spirit of irresponsible panic and reckless discouragement in which it was undertaken, and which lent
it a character of levity, the inability to sustain it was, on
the side of the government, a fact of serious consequence.
The Venetian ambassador was struck by the abnormal
rapidity with which the government consumed its resources. But there was a bright side to the picture which
he did not fail to mention: the patience of the Queen-
Mother, her perseverance in seeking peace, her far-sighted
opportunism, her indomitable optimism. As he was the

representative of a neutral State, which had no stakes in the domestic troubles of France, she spoke to him a little more freely than to most of his colleagues. One day, when he sympathized with her, she expatiated on her difficulties and said that she would consider herself the most unfortunate woman in the world if she were the only one among the Queens of France to whom such troubles had befallen. But there were others. During the minority of French Kings, the nobles had always been rebellious. An ardent student of French history, she devoted much time to reading the Chronicles, and at Carcassonne, on her way to Bayonne, she had come into possession of a manuscript history of Blanche de Castille, the mother of Louis XI, whose Regency was in some respects a remarkable parallel to her own. The nobles had rebelled against her, as a woman and a foreigner; they had combined with the Albigensian heretics, who, like the Huguenots, were opposed to priests, monks, Masses, and images; they had called in the King of Aragon; there had been a pitched battle; Toulouse, their stronghold, had been dismantled; and finally peace had been made, through the influence of the Queen-Mother, granting many of their demands. In time, the King had grown stronger and, acting on the advice of his mother, he inflicted on the rebels the punishment they deserved. In some respects, which she pointed out, the parallel was remarkable: she too was a widow when she assumed the Regency, with a son eleven years old; the nobles had rebelled against her on the pretext of religion but in reality against her government; they had called in the Queen of England and the Germans; there had been war; Orléans had been taken and dismantled, like Toulouse; and peace had been made, by her advice, to the advantage of the Huguenots. He realized that she was talking of the First Civil War in order to apologize for it. She had made peace on terms advantageous to the Huguenots, she explained, in order to gain by time what she could not hope to obtain by arms without great bloodshed. He took up the Chronicle where she left off. "Madame," he said, "Your Majesty should take comfort from these events. They are not only a picture of your own day but a forecast of their final outcome." She laughed, and he concluded that she was pleased. But there was one respect in which the parallel did not hold. "I should not like anyone to know that I have been reading that Chronicle," she said. "They would say that I am imitating that good lady and Queen, Blanche de Castile." He recorded this conversation, among the memorabilia of the year 1567, as an example of her long suffering, her longanimity, and her long memory.

A formal peace, imposed on a hostile Church population, compressed and exasperated by it, could be only an armistice. The government, to maintain order, remained on a war footing. The country was an armed camp. Local regulations forbidding the Huguenots to meet after dark, to approach the walls or to leave the precincts of the town without police permits, condemned the homecoming soldiers to a life of galling probation. Interned, segregated, irritated, ostracized, in many provinces they took to the road again and lived by pillage, in such numbers that they were classed as rebels and bandits and hunted by the police of two hundred towns, acting on instructions from the King. The discharged Catholic soldiery, accustomed to the easy life of the camp, followed the same practices.

The edict aggravated these conditions. The incensed Parlements resisted it with a tension which was a direct incitement to popular violence. From Rouen, where crowds rioted, broke into the prisons, and massacred the Huguenots, and where troops had to be sent from Paris before the edict could be posted, to Toulouse, where the Parlement arrested the royal messenger, who was a Huguenot, tried him on a manufactured charge, and hanged him, and where the government sent merely a rebuke, the contagion spread in one manifestation after another of legal brutality and administrative sedition. The revolution so long foreseen as the outcome of the progress of heresy was actually gathering in the reactionary tension of rebellious orthodoxy. Where peace was officially in force and a state of war existed in fact, systematic assassination and private proscription became normal, and anarchy evolved its own law. The loose, diffused violence of the masses was legalized by the Parlements; the Parlements in turn were supported by the leagues, which multiplied rapidly during the peace, spawning in Berry, in Burgundy, in Champagne, in Languedoc, in Maine, protected by the provincial governors, and developing into a growing network of confederations prohibited by the Crown but supported by popular sympathy and official connivance and, to make the hierarchy of anarchy complete, patronized by Philip II.

Against these odds the King had given his word. Condé and Coligny, on whom fell the task of presenting the complaints of their co-religionists, appealed to it, as if he were the responsible as well as the nominal head of the State. From the base to the summit of the public system chronic irresponsibility was the outcome of the forced peace; but they protested on principle. The King did what he could. Investigations followed, whose findings were negative, and fresh crimes were committed, and the only satisfaction they obtained was the perpetration of fresh pledges by the King. But they believed in his goodwill, and they persisted in the hope of dissociating him from the influences by which he was surrounded. Coligny made it his duty to prove the common interests of the Crown and of his cause, which suffered equally from lawlessness, and every fresh outrage furnished him with a text for warning as well as complaint. Finally, the climax of a long series of provocations came when the money collected for the *Reiters* was seized by the garrison of Auxerre, the captain sent to claim it was assassinated, and the official investigation ended, as usual, in smoke. Coligny wrote one more letter of admonition to the King, but he also addressed a letter of biblical warning to Catherine. In view of so many tolerated atrocities, he wrote, "we can look for nothing but the imminent desolation and ruin of this State; for no one who has read sacred or profane history can deny that such things have always preceded the overthrow of monarchies and empires. . . . To satisfy my conscience and duty, besides all that I have said when I have spoken to Your Majesty, I must write you this one word more: it is well known that whatever is done today is done only to provoke and offend those of the religion, in order to make them lose patience, and to seize the occasion to attack and exterminate them; but I shall remind Your Majesty of what I have sometimes said before, that religious convictions cannot be removed by fire, nor by sword, and that they consider themselves highly favoured who can employ their lives in the service of God and His Glory; and, besides, there is nothing more natural than to defend one's honour, life, and property.

The imputation of bad faith, the warnings of revolution, the tone of revelation, she overlooked as the rhetoric of special pleading. "As for what you write me of what commonly occurs in the whole country," she replied easily, "and that there is no justice done for all murders committed in it, you will hear from Teligny how displeased the King is to be so badly obeyed, and if anyone were so ill-meaning as to renew the troubles on this account, he would allege what is not the will of the King. The King wishes justice to be done to all his subjects without discrimination, and he has sent orders to those who administer justice in the provinces, and I believe that his will would produce more effect if arms were not in the hands of those who should not have them rather than in his, which is why everyone resists and prevents him from being obeyed." That was all the satisfaction he obtained. It required a strained impartiality to measure her responsibility and to distinguish what was mere caution from what was sheer connivance in her conduct. Strictly fair himself, Coligny did her the justice to believe that her attitude was at least equivocal, and by a diplomatic fiction which was in fact a personal appeal he attributed the irresponsibility of the Crown to the influence of the reactionary party. The Cardinal de Lorraine had returned to power, and his titles to credit were above question. The greatest was his ability to raise money, where no one else could. But, besides his financial wizardry the credit of the Cardinal was based on the principle of government in which Catherine herself sought security. She continued to govern by coalition, and no coalition would have been complete from which the Guises had been absent. One of her countrymen criticized her one day for not employing the Machiavellian principles of statecraft common in Italy. "One cannot govern France like a little Italian State," she replied. "This kingdom is composed of a great nobility, which is accustomed to live very freely

and according to laws which it is not easy to change."
There was no possible comparison between the problems
of personal despotism in the petty States of the peninsula
and that presented by the social organization of a vast
semi-feudal State like France.

But the difference between statecraft and personal
stratagem became steadily narrower under the stress of
circumstances. The coalition was incomplete, since the
Protestants were absent from it. Condé and Coligny having retired from Court, their places were taken by a
group of moderate Catholics, led by the young Montmorency and L'Hospital, between whom and the ultra-
Catholics feeling ran high. The efforts of Catherine to
maintain a balance between them were hampered by the
fact that, while the King favoured the former, the Cardinal de Lorraine put forward the Duc d'Anjou as the
sponsor of his own party, and the jealousies in the royal
family were as acute as those in the Council. This division
and confusion of responsibilities in the government height-
ened the apprehension of the Protestants. When the government attempted to exact a loyalty oath from the
Protestants, binding them not to take arms under any
conditions unless authorized by the King, they protested
against what was not only an imputation on their loyalty
but obviously a blind and a fetter to prepare their destruction. They made their own preparations. Coligny
drafted a treaty with William of Orange in view of even-
tualities; volunteers poured into La Rochelle for its defence. The troops which the government had mobilized
for the reduction of La Rochelle were recalled to intercept those of William of Orange. A thousand French
Huguenots who attempted to slip into Flanders were
massacred by the order of the government. The strain of
six months of intolerable peace made the renewal of war
a relief for both sides, and as the tension increased, the
only question was which would anticipate the other.

In August 1568, the Governor of Burgundy, the Maréchal de Tavannes, received verbal instructions from Catherine to surprise the town of Noyers, where Condé and
Coligny were living. The agents who delivered the message were a secretary and a captain without official
standing. Tavannes replied that "the Queen is counselled

by passion rather than reason, the enterprise is dangerous, proposed by impassioned and inexperienced persons, he is not the proper person for surprises, and if he obeyed, the Prince and the Admiral, having good horses, would escape and leave him with the blame of having broken the peace." To cover himself, he wrote an official letter to the King, in which he declared that, "where it is a question of the commands of Your Majesty, of your State, and of the duties of my position, I am ready to undertake not only against Condé, but against my own father, if he were living." At the same time, he dispatched couriers, who were arrested, as he expected, in the vicinity of Noyers, with a message reading: "The stag is in the toils, the hunt is up." As a spy had been caught some weeks before, measuring the walls of Noyers, Condé and Coligny understood the code. They left at once for La Rochelle. But before leaving they wrote a pair of farewell letters. Condé addressed his to the King. Reviewing once more all the outrages they had endured, he concluded: "We lay everything to that sworn enemy of your State, the Cardinal de Lorraine, and his adherents and accomplices . . . who have forced you to violate your faith and public pledges, to serve as an example to your people and to all foreign nations never to trust your word: a thing very dangerous and pernicious for the preservation of a State." Coligny wrote to Catherine. He made a final effort to preserve the appearance which she had maintained throughout the opaque peace: "It must be admitted that, if you have goodwill, you have no power, and it may be said also that impunity and tolerance serve as an example. But what more can be said when, after so many promises made to Monsieur le Prince de Condé and myself, and after having driven us from our homes and put upon us every possible indignity, an attempt is now made to surprise and seize us, as happened yesterday, in order to satisfy the practices of the Cardinal de Lorraine? . . . But if we are constrained, in order to defend the liberty of our consciences, our honour, our lives, and our property, we shall show that we are not so easy to ruin as the Cardinal de Lorraine boasts every day. And as we can never expect reconciliation if once we take arms, I beg you to believe that you can expect

nothing but the certain devastation and ruin of the kingdom; and I beg you also, Madame, to consider what a
pitiable memory it will be for you and your posterity if
under your government such a misfortune should come
to pass. . . ." He still refused to recognize her first furtive
lapse from statecraft.

- 20 -

Of all the versatile talents which served the career of the
Cardinal de Lorraine, the one which finally returned him
to power was the most remarkable: his ability to raise
money was prodigious. His secret was simple. Money
which was normally non-existent could always be found
for war. If the government failed to obtain it, it was because no one believed in its intention to wage war seriously. It was this guarantee which the Cardinal furnished.
All devout Catholics were in his debt. Hence, whether at
the Hôtel de Ville of Paris or the Roman Curia, credit
which had been sealed to the King was reopened on the
collateral of the presence in the government of a man
who was determined on a war of extermination. The
wavering liberal, the eloquent latitudinarian, had grown
into a man of hard and unbending determination. Catherine found him unmanageable, but she used the Chancellor to check him, and the Chancellor, undoing in one
day what the Cardinal had been planning for months,
became the *bête noire* of a man overbearing by nature.
In the last months of the peace the Chancellor felt his
hold slipping and threatened to resign, and two weeks
after the flight of Condé and Coligny their friction came
to a head.

The Cardinal had obtained from the Curia a Papal bull
authorizing the alienation of ecclesiastical property in
France to the value of fifty thousand crowns. The bull,
which was read in the Royal Council, stated explicitly
that it was granted for the exclusive purpose of exter-
minating heresy and that the revenue thus obtained was
to be administered by a reliable person, such as the Cardinal de Lorraine. In this form the Chancellor refused to
countersign it, on the ground that it constituted a flagrant violation of the edict. The Cardinal, highly incensed,

called him a hypocrite. A violent altercation developed. The discussion took a personal turn. L'Hospital had begun life as a creature of the Guises. The Cardinal baited him on his antecedents and accused his wife and daughter of being Calvinists. "I come of as respectable stock as yourself," L'Hospital retorted. The Cardinal leaped to his feet, and would have assaulted him if the members of the Council had not intervened. Both appealed to Catherine, accusing each other of being the cause of all the troubles in France, and the altercation ended in the resignation of the Chancellor.

Ten days after the fall of the Chancellor, war was officially declared by the publication of two reactionary edicts, abolishing the Edict of Toleration, banishing the ministers within two weeks, and discharging all Protestants from public office. There was some disagreement in the Council as to the wisdom of publishing these edicts before the government was in a position to apply them. It was pointed out that they would merely "augment the strength of the enemy," and the strength of the enemy was not to be underestimated.

From the outset it was clear that the Third Civil War would be, on both sides, a war to death which would require and exhaust all their resources. In announcing the publication of the reactionary edicts to Philip II, Catherine emphasized the risks which the government incurred. All the measures recommended by Alva at Bayonne had now been applied, or attempted: the capture of the Huguenot leaders, the dismissal of the Chancellor, the proscription of heresy, the expulsion of the preachers, the purging of the administration; and she was uneasy. In complying so completely with the prescription of Philip II, she had sacrificed her independence and placed herself at his discretion. She depended on his support, she was reluctantly compelled to invoke it, and she was not certain of obtaining it. At this moment their most intimate tie snapped. Her letter announcing the decisive step which she had taken crossed in transit a letter from Madrid announcing the death of Elisabeth (October 3, 1568). The news was withheld from her for twenty-four hours by the King, who would allow no one to break it to her but himself. When he announced it in Council, she said nothing, rose, and retired to her room; the Council waited, and an hour later she reappeared, resumed her seat, and proceeded with business. She alluded to her loss with complete self-control and assured the Council that she would not swerve from the policy which she had adopted. "The Huguenots need not be too quick to rejoice in this death," she added, "or to conclude that the bond which united these two Crowns is in any way broken. The King of Spain can not remain a widower, and my one desire is that my daughter Marguerite should take the place of her sister." After a decent lapse of time, she broached the suggestion to her ambassador in Madrid. Her advances, however, were coldly received. Accustomed to rebuff, she was not discouraged. Again and again her letters repeated that he had as much stake as she in the war and that it was waged in his interests as much as in her own.

Under these handicaps, the preparations for war began on Italian financing, Venice, Florence, and Rome advancing the initial expenses. The autumn of 1568 was spent in mustering troops. A diversion by the Prince of Orange, who, out-manœuvred by Alva in Flanders, crossed the border, camped in Picardy, and threatened Paris, immobilized the government forces. When he was finally dislodged by a mutiny of his mercenaries and compelled to retreat to Strasbourg, the initial advantage of a rapid offensive against the Huguenots had been lost, and hostilities were deferred to the spring. During the winter months, there was a respite for second thoughts. The peace party, led by François de Montmorency, asserted itself with increasing insistence in the Council. After one of these meetings, Alava, the Spanish ambassador, met Catherine in the antechamber and, angling for information, advanced with a smile. She saw no occasion for amusement and said so. "Why do you smile?" "Will Your Majesty permit me to speak?" "Speak, speak." "Well, the eyes of Your Majesty are swollen with sleep: it is as if you had come out of a dream." "It is only too true," she agreed, and her eyes filled with tears. Taking him by the arm, she led him aside. "I have every reason to seem dazed," she explained. "I bear the whole weight of affairs alone. Return tomorrow, we will speak of all this in the presence of the Cardinals." But as she appeared to be on the verge of confidences, he preferred not to let her mood cool. "The Cardinals are here. Why does not Your Majesty send for them now?" "Very well." She sent for them. She was visibly troubled and aching to talk. "You would be amazed, if you knew what has just occurred," she continued. "I no longer know whom to trust. Those whom I thought most devoted to the King my son have turned about and oppose his wishes." "If Your Majesty would explain herself a little more clearly?" he prompted. After some discursive remarks on the danger of her situation and her fear that the Prince of Orange and the Queen of England were about to combine against her, she reminded him that the Duke of Alva had not yet sent her the aid he had promised her. He produced a letter from Alva, announcing that he would soon keep his engagements, and, apparently satisfied, she continued her confidences. "I am scandalized by the conduct of the members of the Council," she said. "They want me to make peace." At this point they were joined by the Cardinals de Bourbon and de Lorraine, to whom, at her request, he re-read Alva's letter. Both the Cardinals expressed their satisfaction, but in a conventional manner which implied no conviction. "You should know," the Cardinal de Bourbon said, "that it is the Queen alone who sustains the cause of religion. In the last session of the Council, it was she who replied to every objection." She could not repress her tears. The Cardinal de Lorraine took up the grateful theme and, when he concluded, the Cardinal de Bourbon resumed it. "You cannot imagine what an ordeal the poor Queen has passed through today. If the Catholic faith perishes in this kingdom," he concluded, "the King your master will soon feel the effect of it." Alava promised to write once more for reinforcements.

Although she was inflexible in her determination to prosecute the war, she had to overcome her misgivings, her judgment, her inveterate inclination for peace. She was in a dream of the impossible peace when Alava startled her with his smile. But she was not often surprised off her guard. She met the world, day by day, with an assumed confidence which won her a long appreciative portrait from the Venetian ambassador. "I will not say that the Queen is a sibyl and cannot make mistakes, or that Her Majesty does not trust too much to herself sometimes, but I will say that I do not know what prince, however wise and experienced, would not have lost the match, with a war on her hands in which it is difficult to discern friend from foe, and compelled, in order to provide for it, to rely on the advice of those about her, and knowing them to be all self-seeking and few of them loyal. I repeat that I do not know what prince, however prudent, would not have lost his way amid so many impediments, much less a foreign woman, without confidants, frightened, and who never hears a single truth. For my part, I wonder that she has not become completely confused and given herself wholly to one party or the other, which would be the total ruin of this kingdom. For she has preserved what little regal majesty may still be seen at this Court, and therefore I have rather pitied than blamed her. I have said so to her several times, and, weighing her difficulties, Her Majesty has agreed with me, and reminded me of it more than once. I know that she has been seen weeping in the privacy of her cabinet; then, mastering herself, and drying her eyes, she has appeared in public places with a cheerful expression, so that those who judge conditions by her countenance should not lose heart."

She inspired a confidence which she was far from feeling. Craving an impossible peace, she prepared for an inevitable war, without conviction, without consistency, without confidence. Her one hope was to press it to a swift and decisive conclusion or, better yet, to anticipate it by a short-cut, and though all the signs pointed to a long, relentless, unyielding struggle, the hope persisted, secret at first, then cryptic, and finally occult. She had attempted, and missed, such a short-cut when Condé and Coligny escaped, and though they were beyond her physical reach, they were not, perhaps, beyond the reach of hypnotic suggestion. She was tempted. She sent for an Italian who practised in Strasbourg, gave him a house in Paris, and commissioned him to experiment. The nature of the experiment required hermetic secrecy, as it involved a criminal stigma if it succeeded and the stigma of ridicule if it failed. Her superstition and her sanity were at odds. Half-believing, half-doubting, she experimented for the first time since she trafficked with the occult to cure the sterility of her womb; and she reverted to it for a kindred reason. The sterility of all her efforts foiled her like a fatality of which the secret was, perhaps, supernatural.

The winter wore away. With the approach of spring, and the resumption of the campaign, Catherine yielded the foreground to the generals, but she took an active part in the direction of the war, and she maintained her independence of the elbowing ambitions of the great by appointing her son Henri, the Duc d'Anjou, to the supreme command. A youth of seventeen, burning to distinguish himself, she supplemented his inexperience by the veteran advice of the Maréchal de Tavannes. They opened the campaign in the west, while she went to Metz to supervise the defence of the eastern frontiers against the forces which the Prince of Orange and the Duke of Zweibrücken were leading to the Huguenots.

During her stay in Metz, where an epidemic of influenza was raging, she fell seriously ill. Her condition became so critical that the members of the Council and her family—the King, her daughters Marguerite and Claude, and the Duc de Lorraine—were called to her bedside one night. On Marguerite that experience left an indelible impression. Listening in silence to the echoes of a dream in which the patient was labouring, they caught, at intervals, delirious reverberations of a great battle. They followed all its phases in the lucidity of her trance—a headlong flight, the victory of Anjou, his sudden fall, and the discovery of the body of Condé. At the time, they supposed, as Marguerite said, "that she was dreaming and, knowing that my brother Anjou was about to give battle, that she had nothing else on her mind." When, however, on the following day news was received of the battle of Jarnac, at which the Huguenots were routed, the Prince de Condé killed, and the Duc d'Anjou, after narrowly escaping injury, had won a brilliant victory, the coincidence startled everyone except Catherine herself. Roused from sleep, she greeted the messenger irritably. He expected a handsome gratuity. "You are annoying," she said, "to wake me for this: I knew it. Did I not see it yesterday?" Then, said her daughter: "We knew that it was not a fevered dream, but a personal intimation given by God to rare and illustrious persons."

The battle of Jarnac (March 13, 1569), the first great Catholic victory of the war, was a major, but not a decisive engagement. Coligny effected a successful retreat, and the Duc d'Anjou made no attempt to follow up his gains.

The tactics of Tavennes were responsible for the victory of Jarnac, and if his generalship was marred by the failure to follow it up, it was because military considerations were superseded by the personal glory of the Duc d'Anjou. That glory, in turn, was marred by gratuitous atrocities. Condé, who dashed into battle with a broken leg, fought gamely until his horse fell and pinioned him; when he surrendered he was shot in the back by an officer of the Duc d'Anjou, and as six other prisoners of mark were slaughtered in the same manner, it was believed that the accidents were systematic. The conduct of the Duc d'Anjou did not belie this impression. The body of Condé, brought into camp on an ass, was exposed before the quarters of the young commander, who proposed to erect a shrine on the spot where he had been shot. Older soldiers, however, equally zealous for his glory, dissuaded him from commemorating it so permanently. The temper which marked his début persisted throughout the campaign.

The war lasted for fifteen months longer and was as bitter, obstinate, and unrelenting as had been predicted. Through the heavy engagements, the laborious sieges, the protracted campaigns, the exorbitant exertions, which revealed the desperation of the struggle, another tendency that manifested its extremity became more and more marked. Whenever the conflict stalled, whenever the odds became overwhelming, whenever the pitch of collapse approached, the nimble intercession of the same element emerged. Latent at first, developing with the struggle, it lent to the third civil war the distinctive characteristics of a war by assassination.

A month after the battle of Jarnac, the royal armies were again at a standstill. Catherine, who was recuperating from her illness at Metz, deplored the fact one day in a conversation with Alava and asked his advice. Advice was all that she expected from Spain. He recommended "the *knell*, as they say in Italy, for the Admiral, Andelot, and La Rochefoucauld." She replied that "only three days ago she arranged for the knell by promising to pay fifty thousand crowns to anyone who would kill the Admiral and twenty to thirty thousand for the death of two others." Proscription was by its very nature a public act of which the secret was bound to transpire. It was not surprising, therefore, that when Andelot died a month later (May 7, 1569) rumours of foul play gathered. His brother, the Cardinal de Châtillon, who was a refugee in England, in a dispatch to Catherine describing the extraordinary precautions taken to protect Queen Elizabeth, pointed out the grave consequences of such unfounded rumours. Eventually the denial arrived in a belated dispatch from the King, ascribing the death of Andelot to an old wound. A little later Catherine corrected this account, having received more reliable information which established that he had died of a fever.

The discrepancies and the delay in the official replies were due to the fact that, while the King remained in Paris, Catherine followed the armies. She received her information slowly and was not certain herself what had occurred, but she accepted the version of fever as the most plausible and was too busy to give it further thought. "The news of the death of Monsieur d'Andelot," she wrote to her ambassador in Madrid in a hasty note mentioning a number of miscellaneous matters, "has given us great pleasure. I hope that God will give the others the treatment they deserve in time." It was a providential fever. With no overt prompting on her part, two of the capital enemies of the Crown had been removed. But the third remained; and the long arm of coincidence had been heavily taxed. About Coligny there was that which defied compromise, which made equivocation desperate: his very existence was, as it had always been, a personal challenge to her.

In June, the Duke of Zweibrücken, with William of Orange and Louis of Nassau and seventeen thousand *Reiters*, crossed the frontier unchecked and advanced to meet the Admiral. As the junction of the allies meant an indefinite prolongation of the war, and the armies stationed on the eastern frontier had not attempted to engage the Germans, Catherine, who was at Reims to supervise the conduct of the campaign and to maintain its morale, was extremely uneasy. In one of those consultations with Alava which had become common between them, she dwelt on the danger of the Germans' passing through Normandy and co-operating with the English. On that score, he reassured her. They would undoubtedly join the Admiral. But, in that case, he added, her son was in danger of losing the reputation he had acquired. She agreed. Then, nerving herself to face the situation, she mentioned Coligny. "I have learned from the Queen of England," she said, "that long before the death of the King my husband, the Admiral planned to have him killed at the hunt. That man is more cowardly than a woman." As they were interrupted, she was unable to continue and she changed the subject. When they reverted to the subject, several weeks later, it was under different circumstances.

The Germans effected their junction with the Admiral. The march across five hundred miles of hostile territory, over a difficult terrain, followed and harassed by the enemy, was a feat which the Huguenot bulletins celebrated as an Act of God. With a combined army of twenty-five thousand men, Coligny took the field, gained several rapid successes, and appeared before Poitiers, a city whose size and strategic importance made its fate the turning-point of the war. The siege began on the last day of July. Several days later Alava had an interview in Paris with the King and his mother. The assistance of Spain, so long promised, was at last forthcoming: four or five thousand men were on their way from Flanders; but, besides this, he brought moral support, and the interview led to a succession of revelations. His account of it was detailed: "I told them that I had in my lodgings a German who had just come from the camp of the Admiral, and that he gave a good account of what occurred there and said that the death of the Admiral had been settled. The mother and son approached me and made me pass into a little cabinet where we were alone, and they both said that I was not to speak of this, for the love of God, as they were hourly expecting good news: this was said with such joy that undoubtedly they seem to believe that his death has been determined. . . . They counted so much on this death, that I asked them whether he was to be killed by the Germans. Hush, was the reply, ask us nothing now, you will learn very soon. And they spoke with such precaution that their eyes never left the walls of the room, as if they were searching for some window or opening."

The siege of Poitiers lasted for seven weeks. It was raised by a diversion by the Duc d'Anjou which obliged the Admiral to divide his forces for the relief of Châttellerault. Before it was broken by military strategy, however, another attempt was made to conclude it by a short-cut. A white powder, found on the person of Dominique d'Alba, the personal valet of the Admiral, was analyzed as poison. The valet confessed at his trial that he had been suborned by officers of the Duc d'Anjou. The rapid multiplication of these plots defied discretion or secrecy. The Parlement of Paris performed a public service by bringing into the open what was lurking in the shadows and placing a price of 50,000 crowns on the Admiral's head. This measure had the merit, at least, of dignifying a practice by which the State delegated its right to kill private persons. There was a fresh crop of attempts, and though the Admiral escaped, one of his most trusted lieutenants, Monsieur de Mouy, was killed by Maurevel, a former client of the Guises. This hysteria of assassination reached its peak during the siege of Poitiers. It proved fruitless, and it was necessary again to fight a regular campaign.

A month later, the Admiral was swept away by a great reverse. The battle of Moncontour (October 3, 1569) was another brilliant victory for the Duc d'Anjou and the Maréchal de Tavannes and another defeat for the Protestants which might have been crushing had it been pursued. In this case the delay was due to strategic reasons, which were debatable, and to a personal factor, which was not—the intervention of the King. Coligny withdrew into the Huguenot fastnesses of the southwest and recuperated.

The King at the age of nineteen was a tall, stooping young man, with very slender legs, passionately fond of strenuous exercise, and particularly of the chase, but unable to sustain any prolonged exertion. Because of his feeble constitution, he was not permitted to take active part in the campaign, but he had a cult for military glory, and was bitterly jealous of his brother, as the latter was well aware. On one of his flying visits to Court, the Duc d'Anjou enlisted the services of his sister as an ally. Marguerite was a timid and green child of fifteen and was bewildered and flattered by the suggestions which he poured into her ear. He explained his position. His prospects depended entirely on the favour of their mother. The King, who was constantly with her, flattering her and catering to her in everything, was a man now, spirited and courageous, who might tire of the chase and wish to assume command of the army. In conclusion, he froze her blood by declaring that, sooner than accept such a fall, he would "elect a cruel death." He placed his life in her hands. What he needed was some dependable person to protect his interests, to live night and day with his mother, and to live for this end alone. Who could resist such an appeal? Not *la petite Margot*. At first she was dazed and frightened by it. But she accepted.

A week later, her service began. Catherine called her into her cabinet. "Your brother has told me of your conversation," she said. "He no longer considers you a child, and I shall not do so. It will be a great pleasure for me to talk to you as I would to your brother. Wait upon me, do not fear to speak to me freely. I wish it." This forbidding invitation might have chilled a timid child, but Marguerite was endowed, by her own confession, "with considerable self-confidence." Catherine conversed with her daily, often for two hours at a time, and always, of course, about her brother—a subject on which the fond mother lost all count of time, and on which they agreed so completely that Catherine soon conceived a high opinion of her daughter's intelligence. They began to discover each other—through a third person. For six months Marguerite basked in unclouded bliss: from the battle of Jarnac to the battle of Moncontour. Then came an abrupt change—with the siege of Saint-Jean-d'Angély.

The King insisted on joining the army and co-operating with his brother.

The Court moved into the trenches. For Marguerite it was the beginning of a cruel disillusionment. The manner of the Duc d'Anjou, when he met her in camp, was so cool that even her mother was surprised by it. Somewhat blindly, Catherine sang the praise of Marguerite and observed how well his sister had served him. He agreed, but he remarked that what was useful at one time might be harmful at another. "What do you mean?" Catherine asked. "She is becoming very pretty," he replied unpleasantly. Pressed to explain himself, he then stated that Henri de Guise fancied his sister, that his uncles favoured the match, that if she were to lose her heart, she could not be trusted to hold her tongue, that his mother knew the ambition of that family and how it had always crossed their own, and that it would be as well therefore not to be too familiar with his sister or to discuss public affairs with her.

Marguerite pleaded, denied that she had ever given a thought to the Duc de Guise, but in vain: her mother sat in judicial silence, and finally, infuriated, the young girl declared hotly that she would never forget the injury her brother had done her—an exhibition of spirit that incensed her mother. Catherine warned her sharply never to let him see her feelings. Marguerite promised, but the mischief was done. "From that day she continued to treat me with less and less favour, making *an idol* of her son!"

Impressionable and depressed, she caught a camp fever. "Being in this extremity, the Queen my mother, who knew a part at least of the cause of it, omitted nothing to help me, taking the trouble to visit me continually, in spite of the danger, which relieved my suffering a great deal; but the dissimulation of my brother aggravated it. For, after betraying me so greatly, and showing me such ingratitude, he never stirred from my bedside, night or day, serving me as officiously as if we had still been the greatest of friends. As for me, since my mouth was sealed

by my mother's command, I replied to his hypocrisy only
by sighs. . . ." In the course of these bedside visits, he
brought with him the young Duc de Guise, for whom he
showed the utmost affection, with the intention, she supposed, of leading her on. She refused to give him that
satisfaction. But was it surprising that, with temptation
thrust upon her, she should yield, if only from pique?
But it was not pique alone: she was ripe for love, her
affections had been abused and exploited, and Henri de
Guise valued them. In the months following her recovery,
a clandestine romance began, under the benevolent and
unromantic eye of the Cardinal de Lorraine.

The decision of the King to see active service was responsible, in part, for the siege of Saint-Jean-d'Angély.
The pursuit of the enemy involved hardships to which it
was unwise to expose him; siege operation offered an
easier apprenticeship to a military career. But there were
sound strategic reasons as well. The pursuit and extermination of the Huguenot armies required the reduction of
a long boulevard of fortresses, of which Saint-Jean-
d'Angély was the first. In spite of a series of victories,
the end of the war was not yet in sight. Catherine began
overtures for peace, which produced no satisfactory response from the Protestants, but which alarmed Alava.
Remonstrating with her one day, he rehearsed all the
familiar arguments against a premature and weak peace,
begging her to be on her guard and not to let herself be
deceived again.

While the tentative negotiations for peace were in
progress, Coligny, who had retired into the densely Huguenot district of the far southwest, Guyenne, Navarre,
and Bordeaux, began to execute the plan of campaign
which he had formulated after Moncontour, and which,
in its conception alone, testified to a power of recuperation which its execution did not belie. This was to drive
directly to Paris and there dictate terms to the Court.
Always defeated and never beaten, he already enjoyed
a reputation in the military world as a general who became stronger with every reverse. Undoubtedly he became
bolder, gradually overcoming his inclination for defen-

sive operations. The remarkable feat of a march of twelve hundred miles from the southwest to the mouth of the Rhône, up the central valley to the Loire, and into the vicinity of the capital, was successfully accomplished in the course of the spring and summer of 1570. By the end of July, Coligny was within a few hours of Paris and had set up his headquarters on his confiscated estate of Châtillon. The final stage of the campaign—the dictation of peace—was feebly contested by the Court. There was a final stand by the Nuncio, who had nothing but protests to present, and by Alava, who offered one thousand men and pledged his government to any conditions to avert peace, but even his own government had lost hope.

In the last weeks of the negotiations for peace, the clandestine correspondence of Marguerite and Henri de Guise was denounced by the Duc d'Anjou to his brother, who was incensed beyond measure by the presumption of the suitor and the misconduct of his sister. One night he appeared in his mother's room, in his nightshirt, and sent for his sister. She arrived with her governess, Madame de Retz. The governess was dismissed, the doors were closed, and the King and his mother beat her so thoroughly that "when she came from their hands, her clothes were so torn, and her hair was so dishevelled, that the Queen spent an hour in repairing her daughter's appearance." In the first transports of his anger the King ordered the assassination of the suitor. The Duc de Guise saved his life by announcing his engagement to another lady whom he was courting, and the Cardinal de Lorraine left abruptly for his diocese.

The Peace of Saint-Germain (August 1569) re-established the Edict of Tolerance, as it existed at the close of the First Civil War: freedom of public worship being accorded to the nobility on their estates, and to other classes in the suburbs of two towns in each province, with the exception of Paris and a zone of ten miles in the vicinity. The imputation of rebellion and all civil disabilities were removed, the Protestants receiving as a guarantee four towns of refuge for a term of two years. The treaty was a replica of that of 1563. After seven years of terrible travail, Catherine accepted her original principles, under compulsion. In return for the liberties which she had granted, she obtained the only one she had ever enjoyed—the liberty to capitulate.

- 21 -

The civil wars had proved the impossibility of setting the religious conflict by force, but every peace had proved the impossibility of settling it by compromise, and the deduction which Catherine drew from experience was that the co-existence of two religions in one State was impossible. One solution had not yet been attempted. Foreign war, as an alternative to civil war, a patriotic crusade, which would fuse the country, resolve its discords, and unite it at least temporarily, remained to be tried; and there was always one cause which could effect the miracle: the hatred of the hereditary enemy. The Protestants, who had been the victims of Spain ever since the Treaty of Cateau-Cambrésis—and but for that treaty who could say that the civil wars would have been fought? —were naturally the first to recognize that they could hope for no relief until the pressure of Spain, which had produced the compression of France and provoked its explosions, had been broken. To attack the problem at its root was to attack the preponderant neighbour, which weighed on the country like an incubus; and however desperate such an undertaking might appear, it was not hopeless, for the Spanish empire, a monstrous agglomeration of peoples cemented by force and, at the zenith of its power, already economically rotten, was vulnerable and ready to crumble of its own too-heavy weight, provided it were attacked at its base: in Flanders.

But such an undertaking, because it was desperate, required long and careful preparation, far-sighted planning, patient and systematic soundings. It was necessary to convert the King and his mother, to kindle and to encourage them, to lend them vision, to offer them guarantees, to find alliances, to reorient the whole foreign policy of France. An entire process of political re-education was required, and moral recuperation, and internal recovery; and the maturing of the plan consumed two years.

The first constructive steps were taken by the Cardinal

de Châtillon, who, together with other Huguenot refugees in London, approached Catherine with a proposal
to secure the alliance of England by a marriage between
Queen Elizabeth and the Duc d'Anjou. This was to take
Catherine by her weak side, and though she replied at
first with reserve and professed to regard such a match
as visionary, she weakened. The difficulty was to persuade
the two parties. The Duc d'Anjou objected because of
religious scruples, the disparity of age, and a liaison
which he was loath to break. Elizabeth was less difficult.
Willing to be courted, resolved not to marry, coy, non-
committal, she embarked on another of those protracted
diplomatic flirtations which had covered so many of her
suitors with ridicule. Her stale virginity was of serious
consequence at a time when the captivity of Mary Stuart
was the occasion of Catholic plots, and a powerful party
at the English Court espoused the French marriage. Negotiations were opened; letters and portraits and emissaries
passed to and fro across the Channel; advances and re-
treats ebbed and flowed back and forth and in fluctuating
suspense the uncertain courtship was sustained for a year.

The orthodox party, fearing his defection, plied Anjou
continually with appeals and inducements to stiffen his
morale, and periodically he balked, jeopardizing the negotiations by his obstinacy, bigotry, and prudery. At such
times he indulged in offensive reflections on the reputation of the English Queen, or announced that his religious
convictions were incompatible with hers. The English
marriage exasperated the jealousy of the two brothers.
Eager to rid himself of an obnoxious presence, the King
was bent on shipping his brother to London. It was the
only condition on which he could forgive the laurels
which Anjou had won in the late war. The obstinacy of
his brother, and his subsidized conscience, incensed him
beyond measure and drove him into murderous rages
which alarmed his mother. Normally so docile, Charles
was completely unmanageable when he was overcome by
a temper which, insane in its violence, insane in its transformation of his nature, was insane also in the suddenness
of its passing—a nervous storm over which he had no
control and which left him stunned and spent. While it
lasted, he was her master, and with a kind of methodical

madness he seemed deliberately to induce his despotic frenzy. It was like some hideous subconscious revenge which he inflicted on her, to his own injury. The English marriage, apart from every other consideration, was necessary to prevent an open breach between her sons, and after these latest encounters, she sent for Walsingham, the English ambassador, begged him not to mention the quarrel, and promised to send a new emissary to London. But it was not a new emissary that was needed, it was a new suitor. Anjou remained obdurate, and eventually she put forward a substitute in the person of her youngest son, the Duc d'Alençon: a solution which Elizabeth found equally satisfactory and which allowed the negotiations to continue.

The Flemish enterprise, narrowed down to a marital intrigue, was not dangerous. But the King was speculating on the political alliance as well. In the last months of the civil war he had begun to assert himself, and his influence in the conclusion of peace was sufficiently marked to identify the Treaty of Saint-Germain as *la paix du Roi*. In the subsequent months he revealed an ever-growing initiative, applying himself to public affairs, presiding at the Council, and giving audiences, in spite of the difficulty which he found in remembering the threads of a negotiation and his aversion to close personal contacts. Reserved and observant, he understood people at least and far better than they suspected.

The Huguenots pressed the Flemish project and sent Louis of Nassau, who had joined them at La Rochelle, to lay it officially before the King and his mother. A secret interview took place, in July 1571, at Lumigny-en-Brie, and was followed by another at Fontainebleau, where the Count of Nassau spent three days hidden in the porter's lodge. He presented his case skillfully. The Spanish had not more than four thousand men in Flanders; the people, irrespective of religion, were ready to rise; the combined French and Flemish fleets would control the seas, and the rewards would be generous. The Netherlands were willing to purchase their liberty at the price of national partition among their saviours: Flanders and Artois for the French; Brabant, Gelderland, and Luxembourg, for the Germans; Holland, Zeeland, and the islands for the English, if

Queen Elizabeth consented to join them. The King replied, in the presence of his mother, that he would embrace the enterprise, if he were assured of the support of England. Immediately after this conference, therefore, Louis of Nassau held another with Walsingham, who agreed to consult his government.

The conferences were not so muffled but that Alava was informed of them. He called upon the King and lodged a formal complaint, warning him that the outcome of these consultations would be war. After continuing the conversation on various subjects, the King replied: "As for your threat of war, it would be a great mistake to suppose that I can be intimidated. Each of us must do what he thinks best for his interests." Catherine, to whom Alava complained in turn, took the same tone. His suspicions had irritated her for some time. She had gone so far as to complain, in a strained note to Philip II, of his malicious misrepresentation, "for fear it may anger the King my son, who is young and not so long accustomed as I to be lied about." She was inclined to favour the Flemish project, provided the guarantee of English support could be secured.

When Philip II was informed by the French ambassador in Madrid that the King was about to meet the Admiral at Blois, he expressed no surprise, merely regret. To Alava he wrote, despondently: 'We cannot cease deploring that the King has let himself be persuaded to permit so wicked a man as the Admiral to appear in his presence, after he has sought their lives with the sword, unless it were to secure and behead him, which would be an act of great merit and honour, but I do not see that they have the resolution of the courage for it, and he is so shrewd that he must feel completely secure. We shall see what will come of this voyage." He accorded himself a delay.

The reconciliation with Coligny was the next step to be negotiated. Since the peace, the Admiral, the Queen of Navarre, her son Henri de Navarre, the young Prince de Condé, and their associates had retired to La Rochelle and were living in an armed camp from which they refused to emerge. The existence of an isolated community, organized under its own laws, within the kingdom but

divorced from it, was an inevitable consequence of the
bitterness and mistrust left by the late war, but it was
also an impediment to the recovery of confidence and a
return to normal conditions. It was essential for the pacification of the country to put an end to so abnormal a situation. The Flemish enterprise required, first of all, internal
confidence; and the first, the fundamental, preliminary
had been left to the last. Accordingly, when Coligny received an invitation from the King, who offered to meet
him half-way at Blois—the peace capital, as it was called,
in contradistinction to Paris—he accepted, in spite of the
misgivings of his associates, who had not forgotten the
repeated attempts on his life during the war.

When he arrived at Blois, in September 1571, the Admiral was received, at his request, without official recognition. What he exacted he obtained—a reception of
studied informality, an elaborate pretence that his return
was a normal occurrence. Catherine was ill for the occasion and the King received him in her room. The quick,
unforced cordiality of the young man did much to dispel
their constraint, although Coligny had so far contracted
the mental habits of a marked man that he was jarred, as
he later admitted, when the King said with a laugh: "We
have you now, *mon père,* we shall not let you go whenever you please." However innocently meant, it was familiarity with a stranger. Confidence could not be forced.
Catherine, who observed them closely, called the Admiral,
kissed him, and exchanged a few remarks which put her at
her ease. After some general and determined conversation, he withdrew. She was still watching him with her
unfocused eyes. The resurrection continued. He visited
the Duc d'Anjou, who was indisposed, but who received
him graciously. The apartments reserved for the Admiral
were on the ground floor, giving on the *basse-cour;* as
they were isolated and exposed, and no arrangements
had been made for his escort to be quartered with him,
fifty of his captains made up straw beds and camped in
the adjoining rooms.

Coligny remained at Court for five months. The initial
mistrust which he inspired and felt wore off very slowly
and never vanished completely. The King showed him
the most conspicuous favour, referring to him with respect-

ful familiarity, calling for him continually, and setting an example which the Court slowly followed. The Duc de Montpensier, one of the most influential and fanatical Catholics, took the lead by a frank public reconciliation. Nevertheless, it was Montpensier who, meeting the Admiral one day in the ill-lit passage, scolded him for his imprudence and insisted on accompanying him to the public rooms. "I am in the King's house," Coligny protested. "Yes, Monsieur," Montpensier replied, "where the King is not always master. Where are your men?"

As this was not a favourable atmosphere in which to begin the work of national unification, Coligny chose the first occasion to have a frank explanation with Catherine. "I know very well that you cannot trust us any more than we can trust you," she said, "since you have offended the King my son and borne arms against him. Continue to show yourself a good servant and a loyal subject, and I assure you that I shall show you all manner of favour." She wished him to return La Rochelle and the other towns of security to the government several months before the stipulated date, but he hedged. The more frankly they talked, the less they understood each other. What he wanted was understanding and confidence; what she offered was mistrust and a deal.

The favours followed. He received a grant of 100,000 livres from the King's private purse to indemnify him for his losses during the war; the revenues of his brother the Cardinal de Châtillon, who had recently died, were conferred upon him for a year; he resumed his seat in the Council and he presided over it in the King's absence. His relations with the King reminded old observers of those between Henri II and the Constable: the same affection and respect on the one side, the same paternal solicitude on the other. With age, the Admiral showed many traits of his uncle in his bluntness, his self-sufficiency, his independence. But the points of difference also were not few; age and stern experience accentuated the qualities which had always distinguished him: his disinterestedness, his disdain for personalities, his superiority to intrigue, qualities which would have set him apart and made him unapproachable and unpopular at Court under the most favourable circumstances. Familiar as his figure became,

the grizzled soldier remained an alien and a chilling presence in a world that reconciled itself to anything, but not
to an inaccessible character. The King alone was on familiar terms with him and, indeed, in their confidential discussions of the Flemish project, the Admiral was frequently obliged to check his intimacy. "*Mon père*," Charles
said one day, "there is one thing against which we must be
on our guard. My mother the Queen likes to nose into
everything, as you know; she must not be informed of this
enterprise, or at least not of its full scope; she will spoil
everything." "As you please, Sire," Coligny replied, "but
I consider her such a good mother and so devoted to the
welfare of your State that, when she learns of it, she will
not spoil anything; on the contrary, it seems to me that she
might be of great assistance to us, not to mention the fact
that I foresee great difficulty and trouble in concealing it
from her." "You are wrong, *mon père*, leave everything to
me," Charles insisted. "I see that you do not know my
mother; she is the greatest muddler in the world." But to
maintain a correct and impersonal relation became increasingly difficult. It was, after all, on this young man,
manly in purpose, puerile in impulse, webbed to his
mother, straining to liberate himself, and cowed by her
in spite of himself, that the success of the adventure ul-
timately depended. As between him and the old woman,
disillusioned in life, hardened by experience, fearful of
everything and everyone, who could doubt which was the
more reliable? The very nature of the case compelled
Coligny to trespass discreetly, to assume the role of a
mentor, and to attempt the crucial task of fathering,
moulding, and training the King, without alarming the
mother who had shielded him all his life from every influence but her own.

During the first weeks of his stay at Blois, the Flemish
project remained in abeyance. The battle of Lepanto
(October 1571) raised the prestige of Spain and the
spirits of the whole Catholic world. After the first shock
had passed, the discussions were resumed intermittently.
That the plan was not abandoned was due in large measure to the preponderant influence of Coligny. And it was
preponderant because it was prudent. Far from hurrying
the King into a precipitate adventure, he insisted on lay-

ing the foundations for it by long and patient preparations. The pacification of the country, the enforcement of the edict—to these essential prerequisites he confined himself during his stay at Blois.

Because it was slow progress, Catherine countenanced it. A period of prolonged preparation suited her exactly, and the Admiral laid his course to win her confidence. But he missed it—by a narrow margin. His circumspection, which equalled her own, deepened her distrust of him. It was a form of competition against which she could not defend herself. He defeated her in the most subtle and effective fashion: he made her superfluous. All her former rivals had opposed her; he forced her to agree with him; and she found him far more dangerous as a friend than as an enemy. Knowing that he knew of her attempts on his life, she could not believe in the possibility of reconciliation; the victim might forgive, the criminal could not; and it was the penalty of her uncommitted crimes that, when their collaboration was indispensable to the nation, and when he offered her the final solution of her problems, she was incapable of trusting the one man who was both willing and able to help her.

Coligny adopted the most sensible course under the circumstances: he retired from Court, leaving Catherine to reach by herself the solution which, when he urged it, she avoided. Their association for five months produced at least one result. He returned, not to La Rochelle, but to his estate at Châtillon. Morally, however, they were no nearer than when he arrived. Shortly before his departure, Catherine asked him to use his influence with the Queen of Navarre to induce her to come to Court for the discussion of the marriage pending between her son and Marguerite de Valois. She had been repeatedly invited, she had accepted, but she did not appear. He explained the difficulty. The Queen of Navarre had warned him to be on his guard when he came to Blois, and in her own case she was not likely to be less prudent. "We are too old, you and I, to deceive each other," Catherine replied. "It is you who should be on your guard rather than the Queen of Navarre. Whatever she may say or do, we do not admit that she has any right to feel such fears. Can she believe that the King would seek an alliance with her

son in order to do away with her?" The words with which
she sped the parting guest were almost a duplicate of those
with which she welcomed him.

The marriage in question was an integral part of the
Flemish project. It had been suggested, shortly after the
Treaty of Saint-Germain, by François de Montmorency
and the moderate Catholics as a means of consolidating
the peace and uniting the country, serving the same purpose internally as the alliance with Elizabeth abroad, and
supplementing it; and the negotiations for both marriages
had been carried on concurrently. Catherine, piqued by
her failure to secure the hand of Philip II or, because of
his veto, of the King of Portugal for her daughter, had
welcomed the proposal, in spite of the difficulties it
presented. A mixed marriage, transcending confessional
differences, was a patriotic project which could recommend itself only to dispassionate minds that placed secular
above religious interests, and it was suspect, of course, to
the extremists on both sides. Coligny was cool toward it,
the Queen of Navarre had conscientious scruples, and
it was to overcome them that she had been repeatedly
pressed to come to Court.

The explanation of her delay offered by the Admiral
was either unfounded or too frank. At all events, she disavowed it in a spirited letter to Catherine: "Madame, you
say that you desire to see us, and not in order to harm us.
Forgive me if I feel like smiling when I read your letters.
You allay fears that I have never felt. I do not suppose,
as the saying is, that you eat little children." And she accepted the invitation promptly. She declined, however, to
bring her son. In the late winter of 1572 she set out. On
the way she was overtaken by the Cardinal of Alessandria,
charged by the Pope to oppose the marriage and to reopen
negotiations for the Portuguese match. Travelling post-
haste, he succeeded in reaching Blois before her, and to
avoid an encounter with the Cardinal, Catherine met her
at Chenonceaux.

The Queen of Navarre was a woman of character, positive and pronounced. Her religious convictions were accentuated by the secluded life she led in Navarre. Provincial and unworldly, the true explanation of her reluctance

to come to Court was that she was not sure of herself. She dreaded being induced to consent to a marriage which appealed to her ambition as a mother but which excited her scruples as a Calvinist. She was afraid, also, of being snubbed. This was a consideration to which she was extremely sensitive. Although a member of the royal family and a sovereign in her own right, she had been treated all her life as a country cousin. On her arrival at Chenonceaux, Catherine received her, standing on the sill of her room; the etiquette was correct, but as the Queen of Navarre was looking for slights, she saw one. She was favourably impressed, however, by the bride. "I must tell you that Madame Marguerite showed me all possible honour and hospitality and told me frankly how much she liked you," she wrote to her son. "If she embraces our religion, I may say that we are the happiest persons in the world, and not only our family but the whole kingdom of France will share in our fortune. On the other hand, if she should remain obdurate in her faith, and they say that she is deeply devoted to it, then this marriage will be the ruin of our friends and our country . . ."

The negotiations lasted six weeks. The match was based on opposed calculations, each of the parties speculating on the conversion of the other; and what began as a mixed marriage ended as a muddled one: the usual result of blending irreconcilable ideas. After a long unequal struggle, the maternal ambition of the Queen of Navarre overcame her conscientious scruples.

Finally, the contract was signed, and the ceremony was set for an unspecified date, in Paris. The Queen of Navarre travelled to the capital to prepare for it. It was noticed— by a woman—that her appearance had changed: she was far from well, and she wore more pearls than ever before in her life.

Two weeks after the settlement of the Navarrese marriage, the inert Flemish project suddenly quickened. Louis of Nassau had accompanied the Queen of Navarre to Blois to press the enterprise but he failed to bring the King or Catherine to a decision; it had to be made for them.

The first impulse came from England. The discovery of

the Ridolfi plot, the most serious of all the conspiracies
fomented by Spain and Rome to assassinate Queen Elizabeth, was followed by the expulsion of the Spanish ambassador from London. The excitement which it created
threatened for a time to precipitate the intervention of
England in Flanders. Catherine, whose own decision
depended on that of England, observed the movements
of opinion across the Channel attentively.

It was not the Ridolfi plot, after all, which supplied the
impulsion. While the Spanish ambassador was expelled
by one door, the agents of Alva were admitted by another. Commercial relations between England and Flanders having been interrupted, and the economic inter-
dependence of two countries which subsisted on each other
being so close, Alva closed his eyes to the political scandal
and sent his agents to London to negotiate a new trade
treaty. The back door was opened. Elizabeth did more.
She expelled the Flemish rebels from her ports. With this
move a long train of events was set in motion. The vessels
of the "Gueux de la mer" set out to sea, uncertain where
to seek asylum—an emblem, as they tossed in mid-Chan-
nel, of the whole haphazard situation. As they cleared
Dover, a gale rose and swept them toward their own
coasts. Fleeing the contrary winds, they cast anchor at
Brill (April 1, 1572), The Spanish garrison had evacuated
the town to relieve Utrecht; the Gueux landed, and the
storm which hurled them on their own shores shook the
Netherlands. Flushing rose; they overran Zeeland, they
menaced the waterways, isolated Holland, Gelderland,
and Friesland, cut communications with the north,
threatened Amsterdam, and compelled Alva to fall back
on Antwerp and Ghent. This prolific accident produced
immediate repercussions abroad. In England the Flemish
refugees embarked to join their compatriots, the Anglican
ministers petitioned the Queen to declare war, sympathizers and volunteers began to enlist, and Elizabeth,
veering to the shifting wind, concluded a long-pending
military and naval alliance with France (April 29, 1572).

In France the effect was equally stirring. The storm
in the Channel cleared the air and broke the dead calm
of indecision. Louis of Nassau left for Paris to organize a
secret expedition, with a letter of credit from the King

and a promise of open support if he prospered. Catherine went so far as to approach Cosimo de' Medici for a loan of 200,000 livres. On his own initiative, and against her advice, the King took steps which he promptly communicated to Constantinople. "I have concluded a League with the Queen of England, which, with the *entente* I have with the Princes of Germany, puts the Spaniards into a wonderful jealousy. . . . I am assembling a marine army of ten or fifteen thousand men . . . on the pretext of protecting my harbours but in reality to keep the Catholic King on the alert and to encourage these Gueux of the Low Countries to stir and undertake, as they have already done with the capture of Zeeland and the shaking of Holland." The Sultan, as the traditional ally of France, was invited to co-operate in the Mediterranean. "All my hopes," he concluded, "are banded to oppose the greatness of the Spaniards, and I am studying how to do so most effectively." Philip II cancelled the sailing orders of the Spanish Armada assembled in the Mediterranean, and the fleet remained in Sicilian waters, awaiting further developments. From the east to the west a tentative blockade of the Spanish colossus began, on paper: the plan depended on the concerted action of the allies, whose co-operation was still in an experimental stage. The initiative rested with the Flemish rebels.

In May, Louis of Nassau left for Flanders with fifteen hundred men and occupied Mons and Valenciennes. A fortnight later the Gueux dispersed a Spanish fleet in the Sluis; in the Bay of Biscay, the fleet of Flushing scattered a Spanish squadron. Holland, with the exception of Amsterdam and Rotterdam, was in successful secession. These advances caused more concern in London, however, than in Brussels. "As for affairs in the Low Countries, we have cause to be jealous," Walsingham was informed. "While they remain in the hands of Spain we cannot safely trade there, and if the sea-ports fall into the hands of the French, they will control our trade in those parts, and the sovereignty of the Channel, which belongs to us, will be cramped and imperilled." One decision was taken: English volunteers filtered into Flanders, a first detachment occupying Flushing, a second landing in the first week of June, while a third was to follow and occupy the adjoining towns of the interior. Another decision was drafted and held in reserve: "If we are assured that the Duke of Alva is strong enough to resist all the attacks of the French, the best course in the interest of England would be to let them fight it out for a time among themselves. If, on the contrary, the French succeed in securing a part of these countries, it would be well secretly to inform the Duke of Alva that the Queen is inclined to assist the Catholic King by all honourable means in the defence of his hereditary possessions." Alva, in the meantime, had not been idle. Strenuous efforts were made to close the German market to English trade, in order to force the acceptance of the Anglo-Flemish commercial treaty. Informed that the treaty was on the point of conclusion, the French Government reissued its official disavowals of the enterprise of Louis of Nassau.

Although this was the only prudent course to pursue under the circumstances, it was both compromising and inglorious. Coligny now took the initiative. "Seeing matters in such a condition," he wrote to the King from Châtillon, "that Your Majesty must take a prompt but carefully considered decision, I humbly request you to give it thought and to believe that it is of such consequence that your greatness or your ruin depends upon it. And since it is a military question, and one which captains are qualified to judge, I humbly request Your Majesty to consult those whom you can summon promptly." Châtillon was only a few hours from Paris, but he received no summons. He was called to Paris, however, by the Queen of Navarre, who was dying, and it was by her bedside that he met the King. His return to Court, unsolicited and urgent, was generally recognized as an indication of the gravity of the situation. The situation was, in fact, critical and required extreme measures: Mons was besieged, and the King continued to temporize, though he allowed Coligny to plan, to organize, to prepare, to do everything short of acting. Coligny spent his days, and his energy, in convict labour, sentenced to one fruitless consultation after another. To launch the war was a greater struggle than to fight it. The coalition of influences against which he had to contend was formidable. There was, in the first place, England. He consulted Sir Henry Middlemore,

urging the necessity of joint action. Sir Henry replied
frankly that his government would never tolerate the
French occupation of Flanders. There was the opposition,
open and covert, of the Catholic faction at Court. And
finally there was the tragic argument which not one mentioned because it was present to everyone's mind: that not
to advance was to relapse into civil war. But the crucial
obstacle, as always, was Catherine. Dominating the King,
and dominated herself by a supreme indecision, she maintained the situation in suspense. Never was it so clear as
in these critical weeks, when the rising pressure of the
situation exposed the basic character of the parties involved in it, that the central figure on whom every influence converged, from whom every impulse radiated,
and who was its passive pivot, was constitutionally incapable of action.

By the end of June, the situation of Mons became desperate. Valenciennes had already fallen. Spurred by an
urgent appeal from Louis of Nassau, Coligny induced the
King to consent to a relief expedition. Alva was warned
of it by advices from France. On July 17, the relief expedition was surprised and exterminated on the road to
Mons. The consternation which this reverse created at
the French Court was out of all proportion to its importance. There was a muffled panic, and Catherine called
an abrupt halt to the enterprise.

Confident that she had the situation under control,
Catherine left for Châlons to meet her daughter the
Duchesse de Lorraine, who was on her way to Paris for
the approaching marriage of her sister, and who had fallen
ill. That this was an imprudence was evident. She had
hardly reached her destination before she was recalled
by letters from her Italian confidants, Birague and Retz,
informing her that the Admiral had profited by her absence to recover his ascendancy over the King, that recruiting was being carried on openly, and that not only her political control was at stake but her influence as a mother. At
the same time she received a report, which was as yet
only a rumour, that Elizabeth was recalling her troops
from Flanders. She did not question it; she saw herself on
the brink of a bottomless abyss, and she posted back at
a pace which killed her coach-horses. The King was at

Montpipeau for a few days' hunting. She arrived breathless from the long journey, went straight to his closet, and broke down. "You hide from me, from your own mother, to take counsel with your enemies!" But she did not break him. She requested permission to retire to her estates. The King faltered out excuses, but she would not listen, he had hurt her too deeply, she called for her coach, and left for Montceaux. He was free, but he did not believe it until he learned that she had actually gone and had refused to eat or to drink, when he became alarmed. He followed her to Montceaux, where she was waiting for him with Anjou, Tavannes, and Retz. He apologized, and there was a general reconciliation. The "tears of Montpipeau" became one of Tavannes's favourite stories.

But how long would the reconciliation last? No one who followed the continual oscillation of the situation or who knew the tenacity of the Admiral could doubt that the attempt would be repeated, or that Catherine anticipated it. Their conflict was too crucial to be checked. Alert for the little things by which diplomats drew their forecasts, the Florentine ambassador noticed the frequent interviews, at extraordinary hours, between Catherine and Madame de Nemours. Under ordinary circumstances this would have attracted no attention, but Madame de Nemours, in spite of her remarriage, still made a cult of the memory of François de Guise, and had recently revived the charge against Coligny, which had been legally settled in 1566. The Guises, who had been confined to their estates by the King, in consequence of a report that they planned to attack the Admiral, had again appeared in Paris—that is, Henri de Guise and his uncle the Duc d'Aumale.

As everyone expected, the Admiral made another attempt to repair his defeat. Despite his tenacity, his ability to convert reverses into victories would have failed him without the support of the King. Ashamed of his desertion, Charles denied it, insisted that nothing had changed, and explained that, after consulting his mother and brother, he wished to review the situation once more in Council, and begged the Admiral to submit his arguments again. "As well not discuss it at all," Coligny objected. "I do not

feel the courage to combat them, or to debate with them."
But the King insisted: he would eliminate the civilians,
he would reduce the Council to a picked group of military
experts—Montpensier, Nevers, Cossé, and one other—who
could be easily handled; and Coligny consented grimly,
without confidence in the outcome. It was a formality, but
he went through with it doggedly, repeating his arguments, with the expected result. The verdict was negative and it was unanimous. At the conclusion of the session, Coligny rose and addressed the King, regretting his
decision and announcing his intention of going in person
to the support of the Prince of Orange. Then, turning to
Catherine, he added: "Madame, the King has refused to
undertake war. God grant that he may not be overtaken
by another, from which it will not be in his power to withdraw." Catherine made no reply, and the meeting was
dismissed, but she cited his words later as if they were not
a warning, but a threat. The decision of the Council, in
closing one question, reopened the other. The phantom
of civil war, lurking in everyone's mind, reappeared in an
atmosphere that was sultry and congested with promiscuous fears. Throughout his stay in Paris, the Admiral had
received repeated warnings to provide for his safety.
When they became pressing, he replied impatiently that
he was "surfeited with fears"—"a man would never have
peace if he listened to every alarm"—"whatever happened, he had lived long enough." After his defeat in the
Council, they multiplied. But there were compelling reasons which forbade his withdrawal—accumulating complaints from the Protestant communities, which he had
undertaken to present to the King—the marriage of Henri
de Bourbon, set for the middle of August, which he was
bound to attend as an officer of the Court and the guardian
of the young King of Navarre—and, lastly, the fact that
the Flemish question was not closed. He was raising thirty
companies of infantry, not only with the consent but with
the encouragement of the King, who had supplied him
with an order on the Treasury, signed by his hand, and
entered on the accounts for an unspecified purpose. That
order was a draft upon destiny, and the signature of the
King was a pledge of his willingness to have his hand

forced. His place was in Paris. "Whatever the danger," he said, "I would rather be dragged through the mud than again see civil war in the land."

- 22 -

The marriage of Henri de Bourbon and Marguerite de Valois was set for August 18; until then a recess was called in public affairs. In the lull the pulpits of Paris began to resound with violent denunciations of the principle of mixed marriage. Public opinion, hitherto disregarded by the government, made itself heard. The license of the preachers was unbridled, and it was freely predicted that the marriage would never be celebrated or that, if it were, it would provoke trouble. The fanaticism of the capital was a hazard which had been duly weighed in planning the celebration of the marriage in Paris instead of at Blois, as originally proposed; but dignity demanded the ceremony in Notre Dame. Moreover, since the riot of the Croix de Gastines, the turbulence of the capital had subsided, and preliminary tests of the popular temper had proved reassuring. Trouble had been expected when the Admiral made his appearance in Paris, but none had developed, and the Huguenots themselves were convinced that the fanaticism of Paris was greatly exaggerated, or at least—what amounted to the same thing—that it was not spontaneous.

Nevertheless, because the populace was inflammable, the King was impatient for the conclusion of the marriage. One impediment still remained: the refusal of the Pope to grant a dispensation and the scruples of the Cardinal de Bourbon, who declined to perform the ceremony without it. Negotiations had been conducted with the Vatican for the past four months; thanks to the skill and perseverance of the French ambassador and the accession of a new Pope (Gregory XIII) they had been on the verge of success when the Cardinal de Lorraine reached Rome. Monsieur de Ferrals, the French ambassador, invited him, in accordance with instructions from the King, to use his influence with the new Pontiff, who was his personal friend, to facilitate the negotiation. The Cardinal replied that for the past two years "he had been sequestered from public affairs and had taken no part in them, and that he did not wish to begin now, since he had come abroad as a mere Cardinal to pay his respects to the Holy See and also for some purely private affairs." Among his Roman friends he disparaged Catherine and in encyclical conversations deplored the situation in France. It was not surprising, therefore, that, when he finally consented to intercede with the Pope, his eminent friend categorically refused to grant a dispensation. Catherine complained, but the difficulty was insuperable. She determined to dispense with the Papal sanction; the scruples of the Cardinal de Bourbon were silenced by a fabricated letter purporting to come from Monsieur de Ferrals and announcing the imminent dispatch of the dispensation; and orders were sent to Lyons to allow no couriers to or from Italy to pass until the day of the ceremony. On the Sunday preceding the marriage (August 10) there was another blast from the pulpits. During the following week popular feeling was so tense that the King decided to leave Paris at the earliest opportunity. His wife was expecting an heir, and her condition required the calm of Fontainebleau. The departure of the Court was set for Tuesday, August 26, two days after the completion of the festivities. Coligny was anxious to visit Châtillon for the same reason; his wife was about to give birth. A deputation of Protestants from the provinces, learning of his decision, called upon him and asked him not to leave Paris before he had presented their complaints to the King. He lost no time in approaching the King, who promised to return to public affairs three or four days after the wedding; until then business remained in abeyance.

On Sunday, the seventeenth, the betrothal was celebrated in the Louvre; a ball followed, and the bride was escorted to the episcopal palace adjoining Notre Dame, where she spent the night. On Monday, the eighteenth, the marriage was solemnized. A platform had been erected before the porch of the cathedral and fenced off from the crowd which witnessed the ceremonial solution of the problem of mixed marriage. There were no demonstrations. The spectacle silenced criticism, and enthusiasm was supplied by a band of trumpets. The bride approached from one side, a glittering idol in violet velvet, a wig of ambitious dimensions, and an imperial crown, accompanied by her mother, the King, the Marshals of France, and the Guises; the bridegroom advanced from the other side with a group of Huguenots, his cousin the young Prince de Condé, and the Admiral; the Cardinal de Bourbon placed himself between them and began to officiate. When he came to the binding question, the rite was halted for a moment by the failure of the bride to make any response, but the King tipped her head in assent. The formula finished, the couple parted. The King of Navarre and his company returned to the episcopal palace, while the bride and her family entered the church and heard Mass.

Among all observers there was a growing conviction that something was brewing, a fleeting premonition formed partly of rational expectations, partly of nervous contagion, a state of mind common to so many that it had a magnetic force of its own and assumed daily a more palpable density. But authentic information was lacking.

There was one person in a position to know. But it was not until much later that he confided to one of his intimates the secret of that vague general expectation and unrest. When he did so, however, it was with the most explicit and circumstantial detail. "My mother and I noticed, three or four times," the Duc d'Anjou recalled, "that when the Admiral had a private interview with the King (which happened frequently, the two of them holding long conferences alone), if we approached the King after the departure of the Admiral, to speak to him of affairs, even when they concerned only his pleasures, we found him strangely moody and impatient, harsh in his manner and more so in his replies, which were not such as he was accustomed to make to my mother, nor expressed with the respect and honour he showed her, nor as friendly as usual with me. This happened several times, and in my own case a little while before the Saint Bartholomew. I had left my lodgings to go to the King, and when I reached his apartments and inquired for him and was told that he was in his sturdy, which the Admiral had just left, I went in at

once as I was accustomed to do. As soon as the King saw
me, he began to stride to and fro furiously, without a
word but frequently eyeing me sidewise and with such
black looks, and handling his dagger so ominously, that I
expected him to take me by the throat and stab me. I was
on my guard. And as he continued to pace up and down,
with this peculiar expression, I greatly regretted having
come in, and thought of my danger and how to escape it.
When he turned his back, I retired quickly toward the
door, opened it, and with a shorter bow than at my entrance made my exit, almost without being seen, not
so swiftly, however, but that he flung me several angry
looks, although without saying or doing anything further,
and I closed the door softly, thanking my stars, as the
saying is, for such a narrow escape. I went to my mother
immediately and told her what had occurred. We consulted and, after comparing all our reports and observations and suspicions and past incidents with this one, we
were all but certain that it was the Admiral who had given
the King some sinister opinion of us, and we determined
then and there to be rid of him, and to arrange the means
with Madame de Nemours, the only person in whom we
thought we could confide because of her hatred of him.
Having sent for her and conferred with her, we summoned
a Gascon captain named —— to whom I said: 'Captain
So-and-So, the Queen and I have chosen you above our
most trusted servants, as a man of spirit and courage, to
execute a plan for us. It is merely a matter of lending us
a hand against someone whom we shall name to you. Tell
us whether you have the spirit for it; there will be a
reward worthy of the remarkable service we expect of you.'
But his promises were so prompt and so unconditional
that we saw at once that he was not the man for us. By
way of sport, we asked him to show us how he would set
about attacking the person we had in mind; and after
watching him closely, and all his movements, and his
words, and his expressions, which made us laugh and
gave us some amusement, we judged him too reckless and
loose (though very daring and courageous) to undertake
it. We dismissed him and decided immediately to use
Maurevel, as a more reliable person and more practised in

assassination, since he had done away with Monsieur de Mouy not long before."

The schedule of festivities was inexorable. On Monday, after the marriage, there was a banquet in the episcopal palace, followed by a reception in the Louvre for the municipality and the members of Parlement, and then a ball and mythological pageant, which lasted until the small hours of the morning. Coligny spent the evening quietly in the house which he had leased in the rue de Béthisy, within a few minutes' walk of the Louvre, writing to his wife at Châtillon, giving her a brief account of the marriage, explaining his delay, and concluding: "Let me know how the little man, or the little girl, is doing. Three days ago I had an attack of colic, partly wind, partly gravel, but, thank God, it lasted only eight or ten hours, and today I feel no effect of it, thanks be to God, and I promise you that I shall not be much in evidence during all these feasts and combats during the next few days." On Tuesday, the nineteenth, the King of Navarre entertained at dinner in the Hôtel d'Anjou, and in the afternoon there was a ball at the Louvre. The city was normal. On Wednesday, the twentieth, there was an elaborate entertainment in the Salle Bourbon, a sham battle between a Huguenot and a Catholic team which almost ended in a conflagration when the fireworks exploded. The King sent for Coligny to say that he had no confidence in the Guises and that he thought it advisable to call in a company of arquebusiers. The Admiral agreed. Twelve hundred men were marched into the city and distributed in the various quarters. On Thursday, the twenty-first, there was a great *course à bagues* in the courtyard of the Louvre, but as the match began late, only two or three entries were run, and it was adjourned until the next day. As it was the end of the political recess, however, the Council was called early on Friday, the twenty-second, to consider the petitions which the Admiral wished to present. The King was absent, the Duc d'Anjou presided, and he left before the end of the session. On the way out, Coligny met the King coming from chapel and accompanied him to the tennis-court. After a few minutes' chat, the Admiral left his son-in-law, Monsieur de Téligny, to play a match with the King and Monsieur de Guise, and went home to dinner, escorted by ten or twelve of his gentlemen. As he never wasted time, he read over a petition as they strolled along. They had passed the cloisters of Saint-Germain-l'Auxerrois and were almost in the rue de Béthisy when, incommoded by his large slippers, he turned aside to call his boy to remove them. The slight movement saved his life. At the same moment two shots rang out, one fractured the index finger of his right hand, the other lodged in his left fore-arm. He was able to point to the house from which they had come and to walk on, while his companions forced the door. They found the house empty except for two servants, whom they took into custody. Upstairs, behind a latticed window, they located the arquebus, still smoking, and loaded with a third bullet.

When the news was brought to the King, he flung down his racket with an exclamation of anger and discouragement. "Shall I never have peace? More trouble, more trouble!" He gave orders to close the gates of the Louvre, went to his room, and sent for his mother, Anjou, and the members of the Council. When the Protestants arrived to demand justice, the preliminary steps had already been taken. Highly excited, the King promised the most exemplary justice, and his mother vied with him. She left them nothing to say. The attempt was intolerable: no one was safe; if it were not punished today, it would be repeated tomorrow, in the Louvre, and the next day in her arms, in her bed. Téligny brought a request from the Admiral that they would visit him, and the King promised to do so after dinner.

Between two and three o'clock, Charles arrived at the rue de Béthisy, accompanied by his mother, Anjou, Alençon, Montpensier, the Cardinal de Bourbon, the Maréchaux de Damville, de Cossé, and de Tavannes, Monsieur de Retz, the Duc de Nevers, two of the Montmorencys, Messieurs de Thoré and de Méru, and a crowd of curious sympathizers. It was a large party to crowd into the small rooms of the Admiral's lodgings, already congested with the jostling throng of his followers; the atmosphere was unbreathable, and Anjou distinctly recalled the impression which the scene left on him. "Having missed our attempt and so narrowly, we considered our affair until after dinner when, the King wishing to visit him, my mother and I determined to accompany him and see the face of the Admiral. We saw him in bed, badly wounded, and after the King had given him good hope of recovery and exhorted him to have courage, assuring him that he would receive full justice on the party or parties who had wounded him, and all the authors and accomplices, and we had said the same, he made some reply and asked permission of the King to speak to him in private. The King made a motion to my mother and myself to withdraw, which we did, standing in the middle of the room during their private talk, which troubled us all the more because we saw ourselves surrounded by more than two hundred captains and gentlemen of the Admiral's party, who were in an anteroom, and who whispered among themselves, passing and repassing before and behind us, and not with so much respect as they should have, as we thought, and almost as if they suspected us of having a part in the wounding of the Admiral. However that may be, that is what we concluded, believing anything possible, and we were startled and alarmed to be enclosed there, as more than once my mother has admitted to me, saying that she has never been in a place where she had more reason to fear and from which she came out with more relief. This led us to break in on the speech which the Admiral was making. My mother approached the King and observed that it was not right to make Monsieur l'Amiral talk so long, his physicians disapproved of it, it was dangerous and enough to bring on his fever, and begged him to put off the rest of their conversation until another time, when Monsieur l'Amiral was better. This irritated the King extremely, but, as he was unable to contradict her, we drew him out of the house.

"My mother immediately asked the King what the Admiral had said. He refused to tell her, but at last, when we pressed him, in order to silence us, he told us shortly and angrily, swearing by *la mort Dieu* that what the Admiral had told him was true, that the management of all the affairs of State had subtly slipped into our hands, that our supervision might some day do great injury to the whole kingdom, and that he should be on his guard against it. By God, he said, since you wanted to know it, that is what the Admiral told me! and all this with such passion and fury that his words cut us to the heart. We concealed our feelings as well as we could, and excused ourselves, reasoning with him, and continuing the conversation from the lodging of the Admiral to the Louvre where, after leaving the King in his room, we retired to that of the Queen my mother, stung and outraged by the language of the Admiral and by the faith which the King seemed to put in it, and fearing lest this lead to some change in the management of the State. And, to be quite truthful, we were so bewildered that we could find no solution for the moment, and parted, deferring the matter until the next day."

At the suggestion of Retz, the King had offered to remove the Admiral to the Louvre and give him the rooms of his sister, the Duchesse de Lorraine; the physicians, however, objected, and Coligny declined. "Only a fool," he remarked later, "would trust himself within four walls." The King had also proposed to send a detachment of guards for his protection. This offer the Admiral also declined. Nevertheless, the detachment arrived to reinforce those already posted before the house and at both ends of the street, which was closed with chains to prevent the rumbling of carts in the loud August heat from disturbing the patient. These precautions, far from reassuring the Protestants, increased their sense of insecurity. At the suggestion of the King of Navarre and the Prince de Condé, they collected in an adjoining room to discuss what steps to take. The popular quarters were tense, the shops were closing. The Vidame de Chartres recommended removing the Admiral at once to Châtillon, insisting that the morning's work was "merely the beginning of the tragedy." Téligny, however, vouched for the good faith of his tennis partner, and the majority thought it imprudent to manifest any distrust of the King. The Vidame de Chartres, Montgomery, and several others moved to the faubourg Saint-Germain across the river.

In the Louvre, the King continued to take precautions. He dictated dispatches to the governors of the provinces, reiterating his determination to maintain the edict, and threatening to punish any violation of it with exemplary severity. To his ambassadors abroad he sent letters of the same tenor, stating explicitly that "this infamous act has its cause in the enmity existing between the Houses of Châtillon and Guise, but I shall take care that they do not embroil my subjects in their quarrels, as I wish my Edict of Peace to be observed in all points." Catherine worked by his side, dictating duplicates of these dispatches, bereft of decision, her waking mind blindly duplicating the directions of one son, her sleeping mind swayed by the mute prompting of the other, the medium of two wills which neutralized her own. Only the routine of work sustained her.

For a few hours the situation passed out of everyone's hands, drifting undirected. The ambassadors confined themselves to bare reports of the facts or to safe assumptions that "unless this great fury passes, we shall soon hear of some huge madness." The first to be informed of a mustering impulse was the Spanish ambassador. "It is to be hoped that the rascal lives," he wrote to Philip II, "for, if he lives, suspecting the King of this assassination, he will abandon his plans against Your Majesty and turn them against the man who consented to this attempt on his person. If he should die, I am afraid that those who survive will do more than the King will permit or command. If they have not yet declared themselves openly against Your Majesty, it may be because they fear that the Admiral with his heretics had more power than the King, as I have many times heard the Queen-Mother say." He added: "She has sent word to me that she cannot speak to me at this time for fear that I might be seen entering the palace, and that she does not wish even to write to Your Majesty, lest what she wishes to do be discovered, for letters can be intercepted, but that soon she will speak or write to me."

On the following morning, the Council met and examined several witnesses. The house from which the shots had been fired was the property of the Dowager Duchess of Guise, and it had been used by Madame de Nemours, during her recent stay in Paris, as a lodging for her dependants. It was usually occupied by Villemur, a former tutor of the Duc de Guise. The assassin was identified as Maurevel. Two of the Admiral's lieutenants, who sat out in pursuit of him, traced him as far as the country estate of a Monsieur de Chailly, a steward of the Royal Household. There the investigation was suspended. About eleven, when the Council had concluded its examination, the Duc de Guise, who had been missing for twenty-four hours, appeared with his uncle, the Duc d'Aumale, and requested permission to retire to his estates. The King replied that they might go where they pleased; if he needed them, he would have no difficulty in finding them. At Huguenot headquarters, the day began calmly. Bulletins were sent to the provinces, reassuring their followers, urging them to make no demonstrations, and reporting that the Admiral would recover. Throughout the morning the King sent repeatedly to inquire after his progress. The young queen of Navarre visited him. Montgomery and the Huguenots who had crossed the river sent a message, offering to take up their quarters with the Admiral, but Téligny replied that such precautions were superfluous. The guards were withdrawn. As the day wore on, however, anxiety revived. Since early morning the police had been making the rounds of all hostelries and lodging-houses, listing the names and quarters of the Huguenots, and the release of the Guises at the very moment when the evidence was accumulating against them did not pass unchallenged. Monsieur de Pardaillan, at the Queen's table, announced that, if the Huguenots did not receive justice, they would take the law into their own hands.

The morning passed in interminable suspense for Catherine and Anjou. The night had been sleepless, the dawn found them still groping in anguish. "I went to the Queen my mother, who had already risen. My brain was pounding, and so was hers; and we reached no decision for the time being except to finish the Admiral by whatever means we could find. And since we could no longer use stratagem, it had to be done openly; but for this purpose it was necessary to bring the King around to our resolution. We decided to go to him in his study, after dinner, and to send for Monsieur de Nevers, the Maréchaux de Tavannes and de Retz, and the Chancellor Birague, but merely to consult with them on the means of realizing what we had already decided, my mother and I." To pave the way, Retz was sent to the King. He told him the truth. To win everything he risked everything, admitting that not only Monsieur de Guise was involved, but Anjou and his mother, and explaining that her only aim had been to remove "that pest from the kingdom" but that "unfortunately, Maurevel had missed, and the Huguenots had become so desperate that they accused not only Guise but his mother and brother, and believed that the King himself had consented, and were preparing to rise that night." Having planted the mine, he withdrew. Then, and then only, did Catherine and her colleagues launch a concerted attack on the stunned mind, the aching nerves, and the cowed heart of the King. But in shaking him Retz shook himself. When Catherine had finished speaking, the mine exploded. "The King flew into rage and, as it were, a paroxysm of fury. At first, he would not consent that the Admiral should be touched; but finally, shaken by the danger which we had shaped, he wished to know whether there were no other remedy, and to have our counsel and advice, and that that each of us should pronounce an opinion. Now, the first to speak were all of the opinion that he should follow our plan. But when it came to the turn of the Maréchal de Retz, he disappointed us greatly, for we had not expected him to give an opinion completely contrary to ours. He answered us with so many and with such glaring reasons that he stunned us and deprived us of speech and even of the will to proceed, so completely did he convince us. But, as no one seconded him, when we recovered our senses, we all began to speak, battling against his opinion, and we prevailed, for at that very moment we noticed a sudden and extraordinary change in the King, who took our side and embraced our opinion, passing far beyond it and more criminally; where before he had been hard to persuade, now we had to restrain him; rising and pacing the floor and silencing us, he said, swearing by *la mort Dieu,* that since we wished the Admiral to be killed, he consented but that then every Huguenot in France must die, not one must remain to reproach him, and that we must give the command promptly. And, striding out furiously, he left us in his study, where we consulted for the rest of the day, the evening, and a good part of the night, on the best means of undertaking such a thing. We made sure of the

Provost of the Merchants, the captains of the wards, and other people whom we thought the most factious, dividing up the districts of the city, and designating certain persons to take charge of particular people. Monsieur de Guise was chosen to kill the Admiral."

The first person to be called in was Marcel, the ex-Provost of the Merchants, who had written to the King, six months before, complaining that the Huguenots were driving the wealth out of the country and warning him that the Catholics would no longer tolerate it. Summoned to the Louvre, he was asked how many men he could raise if the King needed to employ the people of Paris. That depended, he said, on the notice he was given. "In a month?" "One hundred thousand and more—as many more as the King wishes." "In a week?" "In proportion." "In a day?" "Twenty thousand or more." He was told to communicate with the captains of the wards and to be ready that night with one man in every house, armed and with a light. Monsieur de Guise was then summoned and given his instructions. Tavannes and Nevers were designated to kill La Rochefoucauld and the lieutenants of the Admiral.

The hasty improvisation of these arrangements created to a subdued stir in the city. About four in the afternoon Anjou and his natural brother Angoulême were seen posting about the streets in a coach. Toward evening the twelve hundred arquebusiers who had been summoned three days before for the preservation of order were distributed along the Seine and in the vicinity of the rue de Béthisy. The movement of so considerable a body of troops naturally attracted attention. With the oncoming of night, the Admiral's friends became uneasy. One of them went to the Louvre to request the King to detail four or five guards for the protection of the Admiral's lodging, in case of a general commotion. The King became very much excited and sent for his mother. "What is the matter? What does this mean?" he cried, when she came in. "He tells me that the people are rising and arming." "They are doing neither the one nor the other," she replied. "If you recall, you gave orders early this morning that everyone was to remain in his quarter, to avoid trouble." "That is true, but I forbade the bearing of arms," he said quickly. The messenger ventured to repeat his request, and Anjou, who had come in with his mother, approved it promptly. "You are right: take Cosseins and fifty guards." "Six archers of the guard," the messenger suggested, "will be sufficient; their authority will contain the crowd as well as if we had many more." "No, no," the King insisted, "take Cosseins; you could not find a better man." The messenger dared not insist. In the anteroom he met Monsieur de Thoré, Montmorency's brother, who observed: "They could not have given you a greater enemy to guard you." The other agreed. "But you heard how positively the King gave the command? We have trusted to his goodwill. You can testify to the answer I made when he first gave the order." Cosseins and his fifty guards took possession of two shops adjoining the Admiral's hotel. He was followed by the Royal Quartermaster, who ordered the Catholic gentlemen living in the quarter to evacuate their lodgings. The Huguenots were directed to move in, to be concentrated for greater security about the Admiral, and many hastened to obey, although on such short notice it was impossible for the majority to be informed or to make the necessary arrangements. By now night had set in. Another party meeting was called by the Admiral's staff. The Vidame de Chartres once more urged instant retreat, even if it were necessary to force their way out of Paris, but he was outvoted. The meeting broke up at a late hour, the leaders dispersing quietly, the King of Navarre and the Prince de Condé returning to the Louvre, and Téligny to his lodgings in the rue Saint-Honoré. With the Admiral there remained only four or five domestics, the pastor Merlin, the surgeon Ambroise Paré, and four or five familiars. For Swiss guards were left by the King of Navarre in the *basse-cour*.

The gentlemen who escorted Navarre to the Louvre were struck by the great number of lights burning at that late hour, since the scheduled festivities had been cancelled. The King retired early to kill time with La Rochefoucauld and a few intimate friends. For no one was the evening more trying than for the Queen of Navarre. Her recollections of married life began with that night. Since her wedding she belonged nowhere. "The Huguenots suspected me because I was a Catholic, and the Catholics because I had married the King of Navarre, so that no one told me anything until that evening. I was at the *coucher* of the Queen my mother, sitting on a chest with my sister of Lorraine, who was very depressed, when my mother noticed me and sent me to bed. As I was making my curtsy, my sister caught me by the sleeve and detained me. She began to weep and said: 'Mon Dieu, sister, you must not go.' This frightened me greatly. My mother, noticing it, called my sister and spoke to her sharply, forbidding her to tell me anything. My sister said that it was not right to send me away like that to be sacrificed and that, if they discovered anything, no doubt they would avenge themselves on me. My mother replied that, God willing, I would come to no harm; but in any case I must go, for fear of awaking their suspicions. I could see that they were arguing, though I did not catch the words. She commanded me sharply again to retire. My sister, melting into tears, bade me good-night, not daring to say anything further; and I left the room bewildered and dazed, without knowing what it was that I feared. No sooner had I reached my closet than I said my prayers, imploring God to take me under His wing and to guard me against what or whom I knew not. Then the King my husband, who was in bed, sent word to me that I should retire, which I did. I found his bed surrounded by some thirty or forty Huguenots, who were strangers to me as yet, as I had been married only a few days. All night long they talked of the accident to the Admiral, deciding to go to the King as soon as it were day and to demand justice on Monsieur de Guise, and if it were denied them, to take it into their own hands." Their loud talk, their rank odour—for, like her husband, they smelled highly—a raw, sweating, nervous, male stench and the heavy night, and her nameless alarm, kept her awake for hours; it was not until dawn that she finally dozed off.

At a late hour Charron, the acting Provost of the Merchants, was summoned to the Louvre and informed that a Huguenot conspiracy had been discovered that very evening and that, to anticipate it, certain measures were to be taken for the security of the city, the State, and he royal family. He was instructed to lock the city gates, to keep the keys at the Town Hall, to collect and chain all the river boats, to muster the entire police force and every citizen capable of bearing arms, to station squads in every district and at all cross-streets, to prepare the artillery on the Place de Grève and in the Town Hall, and to report hourly to the Louvre the progress of these arrangements. They were entered on the municipal records before midnight, and were swiftly executed on the understanding that they were defensive precautions.

The last of the Huguenots to leave the Louvre was La Rochefoucauld, and he left it without suspicion. Fat and genial, and a boon companion of the King, he remained with him until after eleven, whiling away the time. Then the tedium was too much for him. One of his servants caught their parting words. "We were waiting for him in the anteroom and, hearing the shuffling of slippers when one makes a bow, I approached the door and heard the King say to Monsieur le Comte: 'Foucauld, do not go, it is late, we will while away the rest of the night.' 'Impossible, we must sleep, we must to bed.' 'You can sleep here with my *valets de chambre.*' 'Their feet stink. *Adieu, mon petit maître!*'" And off he strolled. He looked in on the elder Madame de Condé, whose lover he was, then on the Queen and the King of Navarre, and finally, resigned to the necessity of going to bed, left for his lodgings in the rue Saint-Honoré. A little after midnight, Catherine entered the King's room, accompanied only by a maid. The risk of his relenting led her to invade his last solitude. After La Rochefoucauld she tried to while away the time for him. But the condemned are entitled to a last solitude, and he resented her presence. Feeling his restlessness, and fearing it, she went for Anjou, Retz, Tavannes, and Guise, and advanced the signal by an hour and a half, setting it by the bell of Saint-Germain-l'Auxerrois two blocks away instead of by the tocsin of the Palais in the city. Their conference lasted more than an hour; it was between one and two in the morning when they dispersed. Every precaution had now been taken except one. It had never occurred to Catherine that she herself might weaken. To relieve his restlessness, the King took up his station by a window and waited. She followed him with Anjou. Standing there, the woman who belonged to time was stalked by eternity and touched by compunction. Anjou was a wit-

ness to it. "Now, after resting two hours, when it began to
dawn, the King, my mother, and I went to the portal of
the Louvre near the tennis-courts, in a room commanding
the *place de la basse-cour*, to see the beginning of the
execution. We had not been there long and were meditating the consequences of so great an undertaking which, to
tell the truth, we had not considered clearly before, when
we heard a pistol shot; where it came from or whether it
hurt anyone I cannot say; but I do know that the sound
struck us all, stunning us with fear of the great disorders
which were to follow. We sent a gentleman in great haste
to Monsieur de Guise, commanding him expressly to return to his lodgings and on no account to undertake anything against the Admiral; this one order alone being
enough to check everything, since nothing was to begin in
the city until the Admiral had been killed. But a little later
the gentleman returned and said that Monsieur de Guise
had replied that the order arrived too late, that the Admiral was dead, and that execution had already begun
throughout the city. And so we let the enterprise run
its course."

The margin of time was a narrow one. The portal over-
looking the tennis-courts and the *basse-cour* was situated
at the angle between the river and the narrow rue d'Au-
triche leading to it; beyond it lay a long block of houses,
the Church of Saint-Germain-l'Auxerrois and its cloisters,
and, almost within call of the Louvre, the rue de Béthisy.
It was shortly before dawn when Guise, accompanied by
a crowd of his partisans, appeared in the rue de Béthisy,
and the bell of Saint-Germain-l'Auxerrois sounded. They
knocked at the Admiral's lodgings, demanding admittance
in the King's name. A man came to the door. Cosseins
stabbed him and pushed in with the archers. The five
Swiss guards sprang up, one of them was shot, the rest
fled to the stairs and closed the door leading to them.
The Admiral sent a servant to the roof to call Cosseins
and his guards. At the same time, he had himself lifted
out of bed, slipped on his dressing-gown, knelt, and asked
the pastor to pray. His ensign burst into the room, warning them that the house had been forced. Coligny urged
everyone to escape by the roof and, under cover of the
darkness, most of them were able to do so. One of his

servants remained with him. The lower door was forced, another of the Swiss guards was shot, Cosseins and his men clambered up the stairs over a barricade of boxes and furniture. The first to reach the Admiral was Besme, a German servant of François de Guise, and he took a moment to identify him. "Are you the Admiral?" "I am. You should respect my age and my weakness, young man, but you will not make my life any shorter." Someone thought that he also said: "If only a man had killed me, and not this blackguard. . . ." Besme ran him through the breast, struck him on the head, and the others fell on him. Guise was waiting in the courtyard below, on horseback, with Angoulême and Aumale. "Besme," he called out, "have you finished?" "It is done," Besme called back. "Monsieur le Chevalier will not believe it unless he sees it with his own eyes. Throw him out of the window." But the window was small and, as the body was pushed through, the hands—the tenacious, the reaching hands— clutched it and had to be pried loose before it fell. Guise dismounted, wiped the blood from the face with a handkerchief, and identified him. "It is he, I know him," he said, and kicked the face, and mounted, and rode off. Immediately afterward, the bell of the Palais was heard tolling. At what point in the carnage he received the message from the Louvre countermanding it, no one noticed. But he left his superiors no further time to reconsider; as he clattered off, he gave the signal, *"Tue! Tue!"*

At dawn the King of Navarre and his gentlemen went to the tennis-courts until the King should wake and they could present their ultimatum. It was the last they saw of each other. The King of Navarre was summoned before the Council. "Do not be afraid and do not take what you will hear to heart," the King said to him. "If I have sent for you, it is for your own safety." He informed him of the death of the Admiral and of the extermination which was to follow, and offered him his life if he renounced his religion. The Prince de Condé was also present for the same purpose. Navarre finally collected himself and replied prudently, but Condé flatly refused and, being a very young man, denounced the execrable crime. The King swore at him, threatened him, and gave him three days to reconsider. Then he conducted both princes to his room for safekeeping. The carnage had begun in the Louvre. Immediately afterward, the tocsin of the Palais was heard tolling.

After the departure of Navarre for the tennis-court, his wife ordered her nurse to lock the door and fell into an exhausted doze. "An hour later, when I was fast sleep, a man beats on the door with his hands and feet, crying, 'Navarre! Navarre!' My nurse, expecting my husband, runs to the door and opens. It was a gentleman named Monsieur de Leran, who had been wounded in the elbow by a sword and by a halberd on the arm, and who was pursued by four archers who followed him into the room. To save himself, he flung himself on my bed, and I, with that man holding me, rolled into the alley and he after me, still hugging my body. I did not know who he was nor whether he meant to outrage me nor whether it was him or myself whom the archers were pursuing. We both screamed and were equally terrified. But at last, as God would have it, Monsieur de Nançay, the captain of the guards, came in. Seeing me in that position, though he pitied me, he could not help laughing, and, turning angrily on the archers, he drove them out of the room and gave me the life of that poor man who was clinging to me. I had him laid in my closet and his wounds tended and kept him there until he recovered. While I was changing my shift, which was bloody, Monsieur de Nançay told me what was happening and assured me that the King my husband was in the King's room and that no harm would come to him. Wrapping me in a bed-robe, he led me to the apartment of my sister Madame de Lorraine, where I arrived more dead than alive. As I entered the ante-chamber, the doors of which were standing wide open, a gentleman named Bourse, running from the archers who were at his heels, was struck by a halberd not three feet away form me. I fell almost fainting into the arms of Monsieur de Nançay and thought that we had both been fleshed by that blow. As soon as I could recover, I ran into the little room where my sister slept. While I was there, Monsieur de Moissans, first gentleman to the King my husband, and Armagnac, his *valet de chambre*, came to beg me to save their lives. I went to the King and the Queen my mother and implored this favour on my knees, and they finally agreed."

The gentlemen who were sleeping in the anterooms of the King of Navarre or who were waiting for him in the tennis-court—those thirty or forty "strangers" whom Marguerite was destined never to know, and who passed through her life, voluble and blustering, on the eve of oblivion—were the pick of the Protestant party. They were rounded up by Monsieur de Nançay and the guards, disarmed, marched to the courtyard, and passed out between a double row of Swiss to be spitted in lusty contortions. What method there was in the madness that followed—the elimination of all past or possible leaders of civil war—was soon exhausted. Téligny, La Rochefoucauld, and the majority of the Huguenot staff, lodged in and around the rue de Béthisy, were butchered in their beds. Those who fled to the Seine or down the rue Saint-Honoré to the gate beyond the Tuileries were immediately trapped. The conspicuous names were accounted for within easy radius of the Louvre and in the small hours of the morning. But there were exceptions. Among the Huguenots living on the Left Bank, there were many veterans of strong calibre—Montgomery, the Vidame de Chartres, Fontenay, Beauvois, La Nocle, Caumont, Pardaillan Senior, and others. Marcel had been commissioned to raise one thousand men by midnight and to send them to the commissioner of the faubourg Saint-Germain to carry the massacre into this suburb. The man who at midnight could muster twenty thousand could not find one thousand by dawn; the commissioner overslept, connections were missed, and a fugitive swam the river and gave the alarm about five in the morning. Montgomery, Chartres, and their companions, believing the commotion to be a popular brawl, were about to go to the relief of their friends in the city and had assembled on the shore when they were sighted and shot at by a boatload of soldiers crossing from the Louvre. They fled. This was a little before seven. Marcel had not yet produced his men. Guise set out in pursuit with Angoulême. Crossing the river by the Pont Saint-Michel, they dashed to the Porte de Bussy, which gave onto the faubourg, only to find that they were provided with the wrong keys, and by the time a messenger returned with the right ones, the fugitives had gained a long start. Guise pursued them for eight miles before abandoning the chase. A dozen men, each capable of kindling a fresh civil war, thus slipped through the net.

As the hours wore on, and the massacre gained momentum, it outgrew and overpowered its authors, the original purpose blurred, and, as its scope broadened, system was lost in indiscriminate slaughter. Tavannes and Nevers and Montpensier rode through the city, inciting the crowds. By noon three thousand victims littered the streets. Of these only a fraction represented the "rebels," while of the ministers who, next to the military men, were the most systematically hunted, two names alone figured on the casualty lists sent in to the Louvre. The tumbrils made the rounds, collecting the corpses of men, women, and children who were dumped into the Seine under the common denomination of Huguenots.

About eleven in the morning the municipal authorities became alarmed and sent a delegation to the Louvre to protest. The instructions which they had received the night before and which they understood to be defensive measures to prevent a Protestant plot no longer applied to the promiscuous carnage and pillage in which the Royal Guards, the officers of the Court, and princes themselves took the lead. Orders were issued by the King to patrol the city with the entire municipal police force, to disarm the bourgeois who had been called to arms the night before, and to prevent the Royal Guards from committing any further excesses: orders so futile that they were constantly repeated, and so contradictory that they exasperated the mounting confusion; the municipal police were pitted against the officers of the Court, the populace was uncurbed, the massacre was gaining momentum hour by hour, the butchery had only begun. Three thousand victims were a mere morning's work; Paris was the most densely populated city in Europe, and the wealthiest and the poorest, and the spectators crowding to the windows of the Louvre began at last to consider when this would end, and where.

- 23 -

The weather was beautiful. "As I write, they are killing them all, they are stripping them naked, dragging them through the streets, plundering the houses, and sparing not even children. Blessed be God who has converted the French princes to His cause! May He inspire their hearts to continue as they have begun!" So wrote Cuniga, the Spanish ambassador, on the day that marked the triumph of Spain in France.

The streets were not safe for foreigners. The Duc de Nevers, making his rounds, came upon five Englishmen defending themselves against the crowd, and rescued them with difficulty. Mounted *en croupe* with his escort, they were obliged to make the rounds with him for the rest of the day and to witness atrocities which it was as much of a martyrdom to see as to suffer—an old bookseller half burned under his books before he was dragged to the river and drowned—an infant dragged about by a band of urchins little older than itself—a pregnant woman shot on the roofs, disembowelled in the gutter, and her embryo beaten to a pulp—glimpses of the abysmal savagery of the the Parisian underworld which made the history of humanity on Saint Bartholomew's Day a branch of demonology. The journey was interminable. In the course of the afternoon, they came to the Admiral's lodging. The carcass was still lying in the courtyard where the Duc de Guise had left it. Nevers pointed it out and asked them if they recognized it. The Englishman whom he addressed, having served under the Admiral in the civil wars, denied it. Nevers walked his horse about the body two or three times and observed sententiously: "*Sic transit gloria mundi.*" They rode on. Subsequently, the head was hacked off and later visitors saw only a torso basking in the August sun and a dirty dressing-gown over which the flies were humming.

The house had been gutted and sacked. The Admiral's papers were brought to the Louvre, where they were examined by the secret Council in a strenuous search for evidence to support the fiction of a Huguenot conspiracy. None was found. There was nevertheless an alarming revelation of the efficient organization of the Protestant party which the Council capitalized and divulged as proof that it constituted a State within the State.

A circular letter was sent to the governors of the provinces, under the date of the twenty-fourth of August, supplementing the instructions dispatched two days before, blaming the massacre on the commotion caused by the feud of the Admiral and the Guises and reiterating the determination of the King to maintain the Edict of Pacification. Such was the first impulse—to disavow, to contain, and to localize the disaster, and to prevent its repetition in the provinces; but another impulse supervened. Half-measures had been the ruin of France for the past ten years, the cause of all its civil wars, and the source of this final paroxysm; half-measures in massacre would be the climax of folly. Accordingly, verbal instructions accompanied or followed the circular letter, and the next morning the Venetian ambassador was informed that "the King sent couriers in the night to Orléans and other cities, to have the same thing done there as in Paris, and to Châtillon to seize the Admiral's children." The discrepancy between the written command to respect the edict and the verbal instructions to disregard it was allowed to stand. It served a strategic purpose: the former tending to reassure and blind the Protestants in the provinces, while the latter caught them unprepared for resistance. It served also another purpose: it allowed the King to disavow his responsibility and, if circumstances required, to change his mind again.

And, indeed, all the official acts and explanations of the day, whether they emanated from the actors or the spectators, were tentative and subject to change, depending on the turn which the crisis would take. about five in the afternoon, a proclamation was issued by the aldermen, and announced with trumpets in the King's name throughout the city, calling for a cessation of pillage and slaughter, and there was a lull in the massacre. The worst was over: the circular letter affirmed it positively. For a time indeed the situation had been out of control; the King admitted that the massacre had been "conducted with such fury that it was not possible to apply the remedy which might have been desired, having enough to do to employ my guards and other forces to maintain my superiority with my brothers in my castle of the Louvre, in order later to give orders throughout the city to appease the sedition, which has died down at this hour, thank God." His relief at least was sincere. What had threatened to become a sedition had proved to be, after all, only a riot. But it had been a narrow escape. Externally there was no sign of the convulsion that had been draining the city for over twelve hours, beyond a few bodies floating on the Seine and the lines of corpses laid out for identification in front of the Louvre. The appearance of Paris at the close of the day preoccupied all observers, and no one thought to report the appearance of the author of that stupendous purge. One diplomat alone had the curiosity to glance at her. He remarked that "she looks ten years younger and gives me the impression of a person emerging from a grave illness or who had just escaped from some great danger."

It was only natural that no one should have noticed Catherine at the most conspicuous moment of her life. If there had been any doubt of the criminal, her entire past would have pointed to her as the one person predestined to commit a crime which was the necessary consummation of her nature. Physically, morally, politically, her sterility reappeared; and the only progress which it was possible to trace in her life was the growing influence of continual frustration, gradually neutralizing and deadening her, until she became what she was destined to be, a completely negative nature. There her destiny might have ended, had her life been a private and passive one. But the designs of destiny were far-reaching: circumstances placed her for some ulterior purpose in a position of supreme public responsibility, at a period of revolutionary struggle, in which she was the focus upon which the most dynamic forces converged and upon whom their success or failure turned. For years she had checked and foiled them, by compromise, by evasion, by temporizing, by a tireless industry of indecision, by all the resources of negation; but those forces were too positive and their pressure was too overpowering for makeshifts and half-measures; and when their aggression compelled her at last to act, she reacted in the only possible way for a negative nature—by a blind act of destruction.

Character and circumstance combined to produce the

inevitable convulsion. The massacre was a paroxysm of sterility. The specific purpose for which she perpetrated it was merely the accidental expression of a latent force which possessed her and of which she was the unconscious agent. For her sterility was itself a force of infinite power, and it was only beginning to manifest itself. For years, however, it had been visible in her face. That face from which all personal life had faded had been slowly transformed into an impersonal mask. Blank and impassive, with the masses undefined, the lines effaced, the eyes like lenses in a mist, it was a model for some nebulous impressionist, moulded all in monotone, one neutral hue blending with another. It defied definitions; no mirror could focus it. Framed by the black widow's hood and set off by stiff gauzes, the colourless eyes, the faded hair, the sallow complexion, the drained mouth, seemed all to be wrought, wraithlike, out of nothing and to be mere modulations of the void made visible. And that marrowless mask appeared, conversely, to be possessed by an occult presence of which she was unconscious. Labouring always for life, she produced in spite of herself nothing but death. The massacre was her work, those thousands of bodies were her fruit, those shambles were her accomplishment. But the purpose she accomplished by that slaughter far transcended her own. From the day that her inert sterility was transformed into an active force of negation, she became a medium through which all the negative and destructive forces of life were free to work. Her development had been the slow unfolding, the gradual revelation, the growing enlargement, of a latent power that had now reached its final consummation. But was it final? In the night that followed the Saint Bartholomew, it was possible to see the figure of Catherine de' Medici in double exposure, as a person and a portent, looming in ever larger proportions, gaining in stature, losing in definition, and blending at last with the everlasting nonentity of nature, of which she personified in her lifetime the timeless purpose and the ultimate power to defeat and destroy all the positive and productive efforts of men.

On the following morning the massacre began anew. Monday was a day of recrudescent riots, of murderous second thoughts, of a systematic search for survivors, and of a morbid worrying of the dead. The headless trunk of the Admiral was hauled through the streets by a band of children who cut off the hands and the genitals and offered them for sale. At intervals during the day it was abandoned, on the banks of the Seine or at some street corner, only to reappear again elsewhere, until it was spirited away and came to rest finally, hanging by the feet, from the public gibbet at Montfaucon. Paris was a huge morgue where the quick and the dead mingled in normal promiscuity. For after the orgy of Sunday, Monday was devoted to industrious destruction, methodical plunder, and laborious workaday butchery. The crowds scouring the streets redoubled their crusade, ferreting out fresh fugitives before they were overtaken by the police, who were ordered to protect the lives and property of law-abiding Protestants and to place those whom they could locate in the dungeons of the Châtelet for protective custody. A number were thus saved. Their names were sent to the Louvre and carefully winnowed by the King in person. Those whom he sentenced were drowned in the course of the night in batches of fifteen or twenty at a time.

Monday was a day of second thoughts for the authors of the massacre as well. On his return from the pursuit of Montgomery, the Duc de Guise took no further part in the slaughter. On the contrary, he saved a number of victims, harbouring them in his house, treating them humanely, and studiously spreading the impression that, his personal quarrel with Coligny having been voided, he had no further scores to settle. The King called him sharply to account for his conduct, and even accused him of favouring the escape of Montgomery, reminding him that those whom he saved would later seek his life. But Guise was no sentimentalist, and his mercy was not misguided. The enormity of the massacre, and the odium which its authors would incur by it, dawned on him, as it did on his accomplices, only when it was too late to arrest it—they all suffered from the same lack of imagination, their common criminal trait—and on second thought he began discreetly to dissociate himself from his superiors and to limit his responsibility. Not only did he refuse to leave Paris and retire to his estates, as it had been originally agreed that he should do to lend colour to the official account of the assassination of Coligny as a purely private feud, but he insisted that the King should publicly avow his responsibility for the massacre. A meeting of the Privy Council was called to consider this demand. Catherine and Anjou seconded it. The King consented to assume the sole responsibility for the massacre. To sanction it as an arbitrary manifestation of absolute power was, however, too hazardous a step, and on second thought it was decided to explain it on the only less arbitrary theory of a Huguenot plot.

On Tuesday, emerging for the first time from the Louvre, the King proceeded with his mother, Anjou, Alençon, Navarre, and the Court, under heavy escort, to the houses of Parlement where he held a solemn *lit de justice* and read the required avowal. Rehearsing all the outrages which he had suffered, ever since childhood, at the hands of the Admiral and his associates, who had made religion a pretext for rebellion, he reminded his hearers of the many large concessions he had made and which they had so far abused as to conspire to kill himself, his mother, his brothers, and even the King of Navarre, with the intention of placing the Prince de Condé on the throne and eventually doing away with him as well in order to confer the crown upon Coligny himself. "I wish it to be known," he concluded, "that the severe executions of the past few days have been performed by my express command in order to prevent the results of this abominable conspiracy." Parlement, which had been for years the intractable critic and antagonist of the Crown, now echoed and applauded the royal address with fulsome servility. The President, Christophe de Thou, replied with a long speech of congratulation, lauding the prudence of the King and comparing it to that of his ancestor, Louis XI, whose apophthegm he cited: *Qui nescit dissimulare, nescit regnare.*[1] The details which remained to be discharged, and which occupied the Court for two months, were to place the late Admiral on trial, to declare his memory infamous, to degrade and outlaw his heirs, to demolish his residence at Châtillon, to sow the site with salt, to saw off the trees,

---

[1] He who knows not how to dissimulate, knows not how to reign.

to erect a commemorative pillar, to destroy all his portraits and statues, to drag his arms through the streets and destroy them, to drag his body if it could be found or, if not, his effigy through Paris and to hang it first in the Place de Grève and then on the public gibbet at Montfaucon. His confiscated property was conferred upon Alençon. At the close of the session, Pibrac ventured to suggest that the King might now wish to put an end to the pillage and slaughter. The King assented. On the return to the Louvre, a survivor insinuated himself into the escort and was recognized and killed by the crowd. Apprised of the disturbance, the King smiled and gave orders to proceed. "Would to God that this were the last one," he observed.

The end, however, was not yet in sight. Although there were relatively few casualties on Tuesday, the police were still unable to control the situation. If it was not to degenerate into chronic confusion, it was imperative to re-establish order and authority without delay; but it was clearly impossible to do so until the popular frenzy had spent itself. For this reason the Court was immobilized in Paris. Tuesday was the day originally set for the departure for Fontainebleau, where the young Queen Elisabeth was scheduled to bear her child. This was now out of the question. Her condition was alarming. The physical horror of the massacre, and the moral horror of discovering that her husband was responsible for it, had prostrated her. Hysterical fits of weeping were followed by agonized prayers and prolonged spells of exhaustion and gloom. These were hardly healthy conditions for the birth of an heir; but her health mattered little compared to the paramount necessity of remaning in Paris until the storm subsided. The sylvan calm of Fontainebleau was a prospect deferred to an indefinite future. For reports now reached Paris that massacres had begun in the neighbouring towns of Meaux and Orléans. The only prospect which was neither indefinite nor remote was the vast travail which had begun to shake the country. Charles recognized it. Since he could not prevent the course of events, he was determined to profit by it. Within twenty-four hours he had undergone a rapid and forced development. The pressure of Guise had compelled him to acknowledge the massacre in Paris; the spread of the massacre compelled him not only to sanction it in the country but to transform it into a systematic policy of wholesale extermination. But not openly: that reservation he still made. On the same day, the Duc d'Anjou wrote to the Governor of Saumur a letter relaying secret instructions. "Monsieur de Montsoreau, I have instructed the Sieur de Puygaillard to write to you respecting a matter that concerns the service of the King, my brother, as well as my own. You will not fail to believe and to do whatever he may tell you, just as if it were myself"—so ran the covering note, which the letter of Puygaillard amplified: *"Monsieur mon compagnon,* I will not fail to acquaint you with the fact that on Sunday morning the King caused a very great execution to be made against the Huguenots; so much so that the Admiral and all the Huguenots in this city were killed. And His Majesty's will is that the same be done wherever there are any to be found. Accordingly, if you desire ever to do a service that may be agreeable to the King and Monsieur, you must go to Saumur with the greatest possible number of your friends and put to death all the principal Huguenots whom you can find there. Having made this execution in Saumur, I beg you to go to Angers and to do the same there, with the assistance of the captain of the castle. And you must not expect to receive any other command from the King, nor from Monseigneur, for they will send you none, inasmuch as they depend upon what I write you. You must use diligence in this affair and lose as little time as possible."

Such was the resolution which, swept on by the momentum of the massacre, the King reached on Tuesday the twenty-sixth. On Wednesday the twenty-seventh, he reversed himself once more, writing to the provincial governor to prevent local disturbances and to protect the lives of peaceful and law-abiding Protestants; in confirmation of these orders, three days later he revoked his verbal instructions. The governors, perplexed and thrown on their own responsibility by constant relays of contradictory orders, acted according to their various prepossessions. The fanatical lost no time in inciting local massacres; the scrupulous connived at the excesses of the local populace; a few risked their position and refused to obey; the majority temporized. Thus, when the frenzy spread through the country, it was sporadic, blazing up here, damped out there, sputtering, fitful, haphazard, without the concerted force which alone could have made a movement of whole-sale extermination successful.

On Thursday the King led a religious procession through Paris, pausing at various stations to render public thanks for his preservation and that of his family, includ-ing the King of Navarre. The King of Navarre and the Prince de Condé had the courage to absent themselves from this ceremony. But their position was becoming pre-carious. Though they had both attended Mass on the day after the massacre, they were still struggling to preserve their consistency and to defer or evade their conversion. On the same day there was a violent scene of which the diplomatic world caught wind. "The Prince de Condé having refused to humble himself and having dared to say that he had five hundred gentlemen who were prepared to avenge this lamentable execution, the King in a fit of rage threatened him with his dagger and then, turning to the King of Navarre, said: 'As for you, show some goodwill, and I shall treat you well.'" The King of Navarre, being the more tractable of the two, was comparatively secure, but compartively only, for the favoured position which he enjoyed by his marriage was both a guarantee and a handi-cap. The conversion or elimination of the Princes of the Blood was obviously imperative to disarm the Protestants in the event of another civil war. Despite his pliability, the King of Navarre was in more danger than he realized. Another scene, of which the diplomatic world did not catch wind, was preserved by his wife as the final recollec-tion of her first fortnight of marriage. "Five or six days after the massacre, those who had begun it perceived that they had missed their main aim, and hating the Huguenots less than the Princes of the Blood, became impatient that the King my husband and the Prince de Condé had survived. And knowing that since he was my husband, no one would dare to attack him, they contrived another scheme. They went to my mother the Queen and persuaded her that I should be unmarried. In this resolu-tion, one day when we were to perform our devotions and I had gone to her *lever,* she makes me swear to tell her the truth and asks me whether the King my husband were a man, adding that, if he were not, she would be able to divorce me. I begged her to believe that I did not know what she meant . . . but that, since she had married me, I wished to remain so; for I suspected that they wished to separate me from him in order to do him a bad turn."

By the end of the week, the frenzy in Paris, after subsiding for several days, was revived by the repercussions of the upheavals in the provinces. The diplomats who now felt it necessary to supplement their accounts of the massacre by explaining its causes and outcome were baffled by the confusion and inconsistency which prevailed in the government. It was clear that the government was struggling to adapt itself to a crisis which had overtaken and submerged it: its explanations varied and its acts were revised from day to day. Hence the question which was paramount in everyone's mind remained unanswered. Was the massacre the result of premeditation or of an accident? There was only one authoritative source of information, and the diplomats now turned their attention once more to Catherine. But her explanations were guarded and official, varying with every interlocutor. The consensus was that it was an accident, and she did not contradict it. To a favoured few, however, she suggested that it was also premeditated. But these suggestions were discreet and tentative. It was clear that she meant to capitalize the accident for all that it was politically worth among the Catholic powers; but she did not press the suggestion because it was necessary to reckon with the political reactions of the Protestant powers. How would the public opinion of the world react to the massacre? By the end of the week, that question superseded all others.

- 24 -

On August 26, the secretary of the Governor of Lyons dispatched a courier to Rome with the first information of the massacre. The message was worth money, and by dint of furious riding the courier reached Rome on September 2. He was taken directly to the Cardinal de Lorraine, who paid him two hundred crowns, and then to the Pope, who added one thousand more. The Pope was overjoyed and would have given orders to illuminate Rome at once, had not the French ambassador, Monsieur de Ferrals, objected on the ground that the information was not yet official.

The Cardinal, it was noticed, received the news with elation but without surprise, and from the questions which he put to the courier those who were present inferred that he was fully prepared for it. It was recalled that he had told Cardinal Sermoneta, three months before, that he was hourly expecting what had now occurred. At all events, he lost no time in spreading the news on his own responsibility and in a version which aggravated it.

On September 3, a private letter received by the Cardinal d'Este mentioned the detention of the King of Navarre—a fact which caused immense satisfaction in Rome. There was still, however, no official news. That came only late the following night with the arrival of a courier from the Nuncio, Salviati, and, two hours later, of Monsieur de Beaulieu, the nephew of the ambassador, who brought an official but purely verbal account of the massacre. Both these reports contradicted the version already set in circulation by the Cardinal. The Cardinal solved the difficulty adroitly by attributing to Catherine the premediation which it was no longer possible to claim exclusively for his own family. But the theory of premeditation was contradicted by a letter from the Duc de Montpensier, mentioning the supposed Huguenot conspiracy. The whole question was still a subject for diplomatic guesswork.

But the explanations of the massacre were completely eclipsed by the confirmation of its execution. On September 5, the French ambassador announced it officially, and the jubilation of Rome burst forth without restraint. The Pope ordered a general illumination for the next three nights, anyone who failed to contribute to the celebration being automatically suspect. "Tell your master," he said to Monsieur de Ferrals, "that this event has caused me a hundred times more pleasure than fifty victories such as the League won last year over the Turk." A Jubilee was announced, and medals were struck commemorating the blessed event. Vasari was sent from Florence to paint the massacre on the walls of the Vatican. The canvas reserved for it was the antechamber to the Sistine Chapel.

Te Deum was sung in the Chapel of San Marco, and three days later the Pope proceeded in state to the Church of San Luigi dei Francesi for a solemn Mass of thanksgiving. The Cardinal de Lorraine received him at the door. Above it, in letters of gold, an inscription had been placed by his order, extolling Charles IX, who, "like a smiting angel divinely sent, had suddenly destroyed by a single slaughter almost all the heretics and enemies of his kingdom," and discreetly associating himself with his glory by a parenthetical phrase suggesting that this result had been attained by following the advice which had been given him.

The myth of premeditation died hard—so hard, indeed, as to suggest whether, like most myths, it did not contain an element of truth. The conduct of the Cardinal de Lorraine—his statements months before and immediately after the massacre, his prompt assumption that it was the work of his family, and the use which he made of it to discredit the Queen-Mother—suggest that some such plan may have been hatched by the Guises, without the knowledge of Catherine, and that it was her intervention which spoiled it. In that case his conduct became clear. The plan of the Guises was unwittingly anticipated and effaced by Catherine, who appropriated the invention and the profits for herself. There was no patent in massacres, and the role of the Guises became purely subordinate. They were merely the agents of her will, and nothing remained for the Cardinal, when he made this discovery, but to associate himself discreetly with the glory of the royal family by promoting the theory of premeditation. But even that explanation was discredited by the evidence of eyewitnesses and the exigencies of political dissimulation. Nothing remained of the abortive plan but the memory of a potential triumph which had miscarried. It was a sensation *manqué*. The excitement created by his first version fizzled out in some random jests at the expense of the Guises. Nor was this all. Catherine learned of his attempts to appropriate her credit. "The Cardinal de Lorraine," she said to the Florentine ambassador, who brought her the story, "knew no more about the massacre than you did. If it had not been for me, nothing more would have been done. I decided suddenly, because of certain information I received. Lorraine and the Admiral are on a par for lies, inventions, and malignity." This was explicit, and so was her reply when the ambassador suggested that "it might be well, since he has so restless a mind, to recall him to France." "Oh, no," she said quickly, "let us leave him there. If he were here, he would upset everything." Accordingly, word was sent to Rome that his return to France would be inopportune. The massacre extinguished, among other victims, Charles de Guise. His career was over.

The myth of premeditation died hard, not only for the Cardinal, but for the whole Roman world. If the massacre was an accident, it lost half its merit; and therefore, though the facts were known, every effort was made by the Pope and the Cardinal to represent it as at least an act of deliberate policy. Catherine was extolled in a full diapason of superlatives. The practical value of the act was, after all, of more consequence than its motive; and it was in this spirit that the Pope, in his letter of congratulation, recommended that she complete her holy work by revoking the edict and carrying out the extermination in the provinces. The effect of this letter was unexpected. No sooner had the Nuncio begun to read it to her than Catherine interrupted. Never had he seen her so furious. Was Rome not yet satisfied? Did the Pope propose to dictate the policy of France? She *wondered*— and to that word she could give the most withering force —she *wondered* at such designs and she was determined to tolerate no interference in the government of France. She and her son were Catholics from conviction and not from fear or influence; let the Pope be satisfied with that. The Nuncio had foreseen that the effect of the massacre would be to make the French government not more, but less, amenable to the influence of Rome; and this explosion was only the first of several shocks. A Papal Legate was on his way to France, but his journey was halted at the request of the government, and it was several weeks before he was allowed to approach Paris, so as not to compromise the government in the eyes of the German Princes. To these rebuffs the Pope accommodated himself readily. The afterthoughts of the massacre mattered no more than its premeditation; what mattered was the massacre itself, which had rendered so inestimable a service to Rome that in his gratitude the Pope overlooked every affront.

Much the same, and even more pronounced, was the effect in Spain. The French ambassador, Monsieur de Saint-Gouard, learned of the massacre not from his own government but from Philip II. He was in a difficult position. Taken completely by surprise, he was uncertain what attitude to adopt, but he conducted himself skillfully. On the following day he was received in audience by Philip II at the Convent of San Hieronimo on the outskirts of Madrid. Something unprecedented happened. Philip laughed. For the first time in his life he gave vent, in public, to a spontaneous expression of feeling and an impulse of joy. He declared that there was no king who could be compared to Charles IX in valour and prudence, that he more than deserved his title of *Très-Chrétien,* and that there was only one question in his mind, whether to extol the son for having such a mother or the mother for having such a son. The ambassador listened in amazement to these demonstrations so "contrary to his native temperament and custom," echoed them carefully, and had the presence of mind to observe, before he withdrew, that "you must confess, Sire, that you owe your Netherlands to His Majesty, the King of France." Even this remark failed to cool the excitement of Philip.

But certain qualifications soon began to appear. The same controversy sprang up in Madrid as in Rome over the theory of premeditation. Philip was informed of the facts by his ambassador in Paris: "The killing was not premeditated, it was an unconsidered act, they wanted nothing but the death of the Admiral and to give the impression that the Duc de Guise was the author of it; then, as the arquebus shot missed its mark and as the Admiral knew whence it came, they determined, in order to avert his vengeance, to do boldly what they did." This information leaked out and created a storm of protest. The theologians remonstrated indignantly against any attempt to minimize what was manifestly an Act of God. But of all the protests the most outraged were those of the French ambassador. On his own responsibility as a patriot he lodged a formal and emphatic complaint with Philip II.

But the zeal of the ambassador was wasted. Catherine herself, in writing to Philip II, represented the massacre as an act of self-defence taken at the very last moment, to save herself and her children from the machinations of the late Admiral. All that transpired from her account was her insatiable personal hatred of Coligny, whose death she described in order to disfigure it: when the assassins entered his room, she wrote, he simulated death, then begged for life, and was finally killed like a dog. This letter Philip filed with all those that confirmed it in the secret depots of his enormous correspondence.

Anxious though Catherine was to exploit the political value of the massacre, she made no attempt to suggest that she had perpetrated it deliberately to serve the interests of Spain. Such a claim was not only untenable but dangerous. The interests of Spain had been served too well, and she was uneasy, as she wrote to Saint-Gouard, the French ambassador in Madrid. "It is thought here that the fear they felt lest the King my son favour the troubles in Flanders was likely to induce them not only to maintain but strengthen their friendship with us; now, on account of this change, it is to be feared that they will no longer be so anxious to seek our friendship." Philip, on his side, was making precisely the same calculations with respect to France. Invited by Saint-Gouard to press Alva to capture Mons and put the garrison to the sword, Philip at first complied. "I desire," he wrote on the margin of his instructions, "if you have not already rid the world of them, that you should do so at once and let me know, for I see no reason for delay." But Alva was more far-sighted. He pointed out, in his reply, that the massacre had changed the international situation in a manner by no means favourable to Spain and that France, being delivered from internal dissension, was now a formidable neighbour. Hence he was not of the opinion that it was best to behead Genlis and the other French prisoners, as the King of France requested him to do. The French should know that Philip II had in his power men capable of causing them great trouble. Philip recognized the force of this argument. In reality, neither France nor Spain could afford the clear situation which the massacre created, and both craved and sought to re-create the old complications which, with their tissue of obligations and compromises, permitted each power to hold the other in check without recourse to the ultimate necessity of outright action. Coligny had perished because he threatened to upset this equivocal balance.

The conduct of Alva at this juncture was remarkable. His approbation was one of the few satisfactions on which Catherine counted unquestioningly. She made a deliberate bid for it. In an interview with his envoy, when he asked what message he should take back to his master, she delivered herself of a reply so elaborate that it was obviously composed for the occasion. "Am I so bad a Christian as Don Fernando de Alva claimed?" she asked with assurance. "I do not know what reply I can make except that which Jesus Christ made to the disciples of Saint John: 'Go and show John again those things which ye do hear and see: the blind receive their sight, and the lame walk, the lepers are cleansed, and the deaf hear, the dead are raised up, and the poor have the gospel preached to them.' And do not forget to say to the Duke of Alva: 'Blessed is he, whosoever shall not be offended in me.' " The satisfaction of confounding her inveterate critic was denied her, however. It was true that he ordered public celebrations in honour of the massacre, but it was also true that in private he declared that he himself would never have committed so base a deed. He was even more disgusted by the message of Charles IX, inviting him to kill his French prisoners. When he captured Mons, he allowed the French garrison to leave the city with flying colours as a deliberate rebuke to the King. Mercy itself was not too high a price to pay for the opportunity of humiliating him. This act of political clemency was dictated by other motives as well. His ruthless administration of the Netherlands had been a complete failure, and, by a supreme irony, at the very moment when the French Crown finally followed his example, he was about to adopt the temperate and conciliatory policy which he had criticized so bitterly when it was pursued in France.

Political calculations cheated Catherine of the benefit of her crime in Spain and Rome, the two great Catholic powers whose pressure was primarily responsible for it and to which it was most profitable. She dared not exploit it in the States where she was certain to profit by it, because she had yet to reckon with the States where she was equally certain to lose by it. The reaction of the Protestant powers was a foregone conclusion. Nowhere was the shock more profound and condemnation more outspoken than in England. On September 8, the French ambassador, Monsieur de la Mothe-Fénelon, was received in audience by Elizabeth at Woodstock. The solemnity of the occasion was deliberately emphasized. The entire Court was present and in mourning. When he entered, a sepulchral silence prevailed. Elizabeth led him aside into the embrasure of a window. "Are the rumours true?" she asked him abruptly. Her manner was peremptory. He repeated the official version of a Huguenot plot. Elizabeth disposed of his plea with regal address. "I would with all my heart," she said, "that the crimes laid to the Admiral and his partisans were greater than those wherewith they were formerly taxed, and that this conspiracy exceeded all those in the past, for I am jealous of the honour and reputation of the King, whom I love and esteem above all else in the world. At first, I undertook his defence and sought to justify him; but since I am informed that he has had all things approved by his Parliament, I no longer know what to think or to say. I pray God to avert from his head the evils I foresee!" The ambassador thanked her profusely, assured her that the massacre had not been premeditated, that religion was not involved, and that the edict would be maintained, and, emboldened by her tone, he ventured to hope that the negotiations for her marriage with Alençon might continue and that the Earl of Leicester would come to France, as he had planned. But she would not allow him to presume on her ironic lenience. To his last suggestion she replied sharply that she would not permit Leicester to risk his life by going to France. As for herself, "I shall regulate my conduct on that which I encounter." That was all. On the whole, the ambassador escaped easily; but he escaped from her presence only to find himself the butt of her ministers and courtiers, who, unhampered by the exigencies of royal etiquette, treated him unsparingly. The comparative moderation of the Queen was no indication of the general temper. His flimsy excuses were brushed aside, and he was baited, bullied, and badgered with reproaches of which he felt the force so keenly that in an unguarded moment he confessed that he was ashamed to be counted a Frenchman.

The first news of the massacre created not only a sensation but a panic in London. Among the populace there was a vague expectation that it might be repeated in England, as if it were an infection brought over with the French. These irrational fears extended to the highest quarters. The Bishop of London proposed, as a measure of retaliation, that Mary Stuart should be immediately beheaded, and addressed a petition to that effect to Burghley. Not only indignation, but alarm, prevailed in the government and orders were given to man the coasts against a possible aggression by the French fleet.

Walsingham, in Paris on the day after the massacre, sent a message to the Louvre asking for explanations. As the streets were still unsafe, an escort was sent for him and he was granted an audience. In the first interview, Catherine insisted that the edict would not be infringed. Subsequently, however, she reinterpreted this statement. "The King's meaning," she said, "is that the Huguenots shall enjoy liberty of conscience." "And the exercise of their religion too?" "No, my son will have the exercise of only one religion in this realm." He reminded her of her first promise of which he had already informed his government. How was he to account for the change? She replied evasively that certain matters had come to light, which made it necessary to abolish all exercise of the religion. "Why, Madame," he protested, "will you have them live without exercise of their religion?" She reminded him that the English Catholics under Elizabeth lived without the exercise of theirs. But there was, he insisted, an essential distinction. "My mistress never promised anything by edict; if she had, she would not have failed to perform it." To this retort Catherine found nothing to say except that "the Queen your mistress must direct the government of her country, and the King my son his own."

England baffled her, but braving obloquy and rebuke, she waited patiently for the storm of moral indignation, which she discounted, to subside and for the sanity of its political interests to reassert itself. Few things on earth were unchanging; but the character of English policy was one of them.

It was in Germany, however, that the reaction to the massacre revealed most clearly that it was not merely a crime but a blunder. Negotiations had been under way to conclude an offensive and defensive alliance between the French Crown and the Protestant Princes. The royal agent, Gaspard von Schomberg, had been empowered to promise that Charles IX would patronize the enterprise of William of Orange in Flanders to the same extent as his German backers, and on the strength of this assurance he was just beginning to make progress when the news of the Saint Bartholomew burst like a flood and effaced all that he had accomplished. Overwhelmed and engulfed by it, like all the diplomatic agents of the French Crown, he struggled in vain to repair the catastrophic impression it created. He could not "get it out of their heads" that the massacre had been preconcerted in order to allow Alva to crush the Prince of Orange, and that the negotiations which he had been conducting had been a blind for that purpose. Protestant Germany, the great reservoir of French soldiers and the indispensable ally of France against the Spanish dominance in Europe, was alienated if not irretrievably lost. Measures of common defence were taken by the Landgraf of Hesse and three Electors against what was believed to be the beginning of a war of general extermination launched by Rome and Spain, in pursuance of the decrees of the Council of Trent.

In Catholic Vienna there was no less antagonism to France. The Emperor Maximilian and the French Crown, after collaborating so long to maintain a common policy of moderation and to preserve a balance against the forces of reaction, now found themselves as the poles apart. The Emperor listened to the varying explanations of the French ambassador with a reserve that never varied and with comments that were mere repetitions of the same condemnation. When he was assured that the massacre was not premeditated, he cited the confidences of the Cardinal de Lorraine and the remark of someone in Rome, three weeks before the marriage, that "now that the birds were all in the cage, they could all be taken together." He was irreconcilable, not only because of his personal sentiments, but because the massacre served his political purposes. His son was a candidate for the Polish Crown, and he had every reason to foment the resentment it aroused in order to defeat the competition of the Duc d'Anjou.

This was, in fact, the most cruel consequence of the massacre for Catherine. Jean de Montluc, the Bishop of Valence, whom she had sent to Poland to support the candidacy of her son, and who was the ablest and the most trusted of her diplomats, was also the loudest in denouncing her ineptitude. The Protestant party in Poland was of a strength capable of deciding the election. All that he could suggest, to repair so colossal a blunder, was to back water at once and to publish an edict guaranteeing the Huguenots liberty of conscience. "If between this day and the day of election there were to come news of any cruelty, we could do nothing, not even if we had ten millions in gold with which to win votes. The King and the Duc d'Anjou will have to consider whether the satisfaction of revenge is worth more to them than the acquisition of a kingdom."

Across the border, in barbarous Russia, the voice of Ivan the Terrible became audible, denouncing the barbarities of the West.

The civilized world was not merely the non-Catholic world. In Catholic Venice, as in Catholic Vienna, the shock was profound. And this was of more than passing importance. For Venice was the financial brace of the French Crown, the ally on whose loans it had been subsisting for years. Opinion on the Rialto, therefore, was immediately reflected in France. And the opinion which Monsieur du Ferrier, the resident ambassador, had to report was calculated to cause a sinking of the heart in Paris.

The balance of public opinion was distinctly not in her favour. The repercussions of the massacre threatened to disrupt the whole structure of international relations upon which the security of France depended. The explosion rocked the continent, and in one night it seemed as if the labour of years had been wantonly lost. Yet within a few months the damage was repaired and, when the shock was absorbed, the international situation, in spite of the severe strain placed upon it, remained fundamentally unchanged. Never had Catherine's diplomacy been so successful. How had this remarkable result been achieved? By patience, by perseverance, by imperturbable poise, by cautious manœuvring, by lying with the minimum of mendacity, by maintaining against the censure of the civilized world a moderation so dignified and disarming that it seemed impossible to associate her with so brutal and deliberate a crime, but above all by inertia. She allowed the force of things to work for her. Within three months Elizabeth who, at first, had mobilized her fleets and sought a *rapprochement* with the Duke of Alva, had resumed the negotiations for her marriage with Alençon and consented to stand godmother to the daughter of Charles IX. The Prince of Orange, who had declared that Charles IX would never wash his hands of the blood of Saint Bartholomew, accepted a subsidy from him, while Louis of Nassau signed an engagement in his name both to resume the war in Flanders and to support the candidacy of the Duc d'Anjou in Poland. The reconciliation of the Flemish patriots, to which they submitted in self-preservation, was the pivotal success which swung the Protestant power of Europe back into the French orbit. The Protestant Princes of Germany, despite their abhorrence of the massacre, realized that it was necessary to preserve the French alliance as a bulwark against Spain and were mollified by the evident intention of the French Government to resume the policy of the Admiral. Philip II, who had supposed it destroyed for ever, saw the same coalition which menaced the Netherlands before Saint Bartholomew forming against him again. The hopes of the Pope that France would henceforth be amenable to his influence were deluded. The Legate, after attempting to persuade Charles IX to join the League against the Turk or at least to lend his name to it, and pressing for a complete extermination of the Huguenots, returned to Rome empty-handed; and Catherine repeated in public that henceforth she would not permit the Pope to interfere in the affairs of France. The lesser powers followed the lead of the greater, and Europe gradually settled back into the accustomed rut, the old perennial stalemate. Nothing had changed; the massacre might as well not have been committed. For all the horror it aroused, the bonds of self-in-

terest were stronger than the claims of humanity, and the
force of things, on the one hand, and the diplomacy of
Catherine, on the other, combined to restore the *status
quo ante*.

This remarkable recovery abroad was offset, however,
by the inevitable relapse into civil war at home.

- 25 -

No diplomacy could avert the outcome of the massacre in
France. After the massacre, the Huguenots rallied in scattered strongholds—La Rochelle on the west coast, Sancerre in the centre, Montauban, Nîmes, Milhau, Aubenas,
and other towns in the south—and refused to admit the
royal governors. The government attempted to subdue
them by negotiation, guaranteeing them full protection of
their religious rights and the maintenance of the edict. But
since August 24 such promises were not worth the paper
on which they were written. Finally, in December 1572,
a royal army laid siege to La Rochelle. The command was
taken over, two months later, by the Duc d'Anjou, who
came out escorted by an imposing staff, comprising his
brother the Duc d'Alençon, the Duc de Guise, the Duc
d'Aumale, the King of Navarre, the Prince de Condé, and
Montluc.

The siege dragged on for six months, consuming the resources of the besiegers without result. From a military
point of view it was a prolonged failure, and from a financial one a futile drain. Intrigue and jealousy divided the
staff. Want and disease and discouragement made such
inroads among the unpaid, ill-fed, and demoralized soldiers
that they were on the verge of mutiny when, in June, the
last of many desperate assaults was launched. It failed. At
this moment it was learned that the Duc d'Anjou had been
elected to the throne of Poland. The government, which
had only been waiting for a pretext to abandon the siege,
hastened to capitulate, granting the Huguenots of La
Rochelle all their demands, freedom of worship, exemption
from a royal garrison, and local autonomy.

The Polish election, so fortunate in its domestic effects,
was the final triumph of Catherine's recuperative policy
abroad. With only a limited amount of money to spend she

was able to outbid both Philip II, who spent 6000 crowns to defeat her, and the Emperor, who backed his son to a considerable figure. But she owed her success primarily to the skillful misrepresentation of Jean de Montluc, who amply redeemed her confidence in his diplomatic ability. Learning that the co-existence of two religions was perfectly practicable in Poland, he presented his candidate as a convert to that principle. What money he could raise he placed to good advantage, and what he could not, to even better. He gave the electors to understand that the Duc d'Anjou would spend all his French revenues in Poland and that he would assume the debts of the Crown. He would do more: he would extend the frontiers of Poland into Russia and lead its braves against the Turk. Henri de Valois was elected amid scenes of wild acclamation. A delegation of two thousand patriots dashed to Paris to welcome their new sovereign. They were disconcerted to meet a delicate young man with a pronounced taste for effeminacy in his dress. Nor was this their only surprise. In Paris the pledge to assume the debts of the Polish Crown was reinterpreted to apply only to those contracted by the late king, while the revenues of the Duke were admitted to be, for the moment, hypothetical. Nevertheless, these disappointments did not quench their enthusiasm.

To the royal family the Polish election brought as much relief as to France. Everyone was satisfied by it except the Duc d'Anjou. When Catherine first received the news, her tongue tarried and she wept for joy. The King was equally delighted: he was at last relieved of the presence of a brother of whom he was still sullenly jealous; and such also were the sentiments of the Duc d'Alençon. The Benjamin of the family, who was now a man of sixteen and still a nonentity, had made some fumbling attempts at the siege of La Rochelle to oust his brother from the supreme command, and now looked forward with confidence to filling the place which he vacated. Anjou vacated it reluctantly, however; he was loath to leave France for a land which Tavannes described as a "desert and worth nothing, not so large as they say and where the people are brutes." But his mother minimized these objections. Henri deferred his departure for several months, speculating on the King's health, which had been steadily declining for the past year.

Finally, in November 1573, he took the royal road of exile, accompanied as far as the eastern frontier by his family and the Court.

The remainder of his journey was a test of the success of Catherine's recuperative policy abroad. His itinerary lay through several of the German Protestant States, and though he was received with the proper respect by the local authorities, he was insulted more than once by the people, especially in places where Huguenot refugees had settled. The authorities were no more than correct, and not always that; pointed allusions to Saint Bartholomew were sometimes made in public addresses. A few days after his arrival in Cracow, homesick, depressed, lonely, detesting Poland, longing insanely for Paris, and unable to sleep, he called in one of his intimates and confided to him exactly what had occurred on the night of August 24, 1572.

After the departure from France of the Duc d'Anjou, Catherine and the King returned to the relentless chore of civil war. A truce had been published, and an Edict of Pacification, but the cities of the south were still in arms. At Villers-Cotterêts, they had been met by a Huguenot deputation bringing the demands of a general Protestant assembly held at Montauban. The re-enactment of the Edict of January, freedom of worship irrespective of place, restoration of civil rights, rehabilitation of the martyrs of Saint Bartholomew, punishment of the authors and instigators of the massacre, Protestant judges for Protestant cases, the retention of all the cities then in their possession, the repudiation of alliances with their enemies, the conclusion of an alliance with the Protestant powers of Europe—these were not the demands of a defeated party. A year after Saint Bartholomew, they were bolder than ever, as Catherine exclaimed. "If your Condé were alive and in the heart of the kingdom with twenty thousand horse and fifty thousand foot, and held the chief cities in his power, he would not make half so great demands!" Something had happened which startled her. She was still thinking in terms of men —of individuals and leaders—a Condé, a Coligny—and she could not yet conceive of the movement apart from them or realize that they had not so much conferred power on the party as derived strength from it. The extermination of the leaders had merely pruned and invigorated it. The limbs had been lopped off and the trunk was exposed, sound, indestructible, and swelling with organic vitality and fresh power of growth.

The impossibility henceforth of trusting any compact made with the King compelled the Protestants to constitute themselves permanently into an independent political body. The significant feature of that general assembly at Montauban, which the deputies represented, was the formation of a broad Huguenot confederation to assume direction of the war and the regulation of finances, civil administration, and religious protection. The province of Languedoc was divided, for purposes of administration, into two *assemblées de généralité,* having their seats in Nîmes and Montauban, under the authority of two noblemen, each assisted and controlled by a council which, in turn, was obliged to refer all matters of importance to local assemblies. Each of these assemblies was elective. This system was the translation into civil life of the religious organization of the Protestant movement and represented the armature of a democratic State, empowered to lay taxes, to administer justice, to make war and peace, and to carry on all the normal functions of autonomous government. The demands presented to the King at Villers-Cotterêts were, potentially, those of one independent power to another, and it was this which made them so astounding to Catherine. With her passion for personalities and her indifference to forces and ideas, it was only natural that she should scan the manifesto for the names of its signers—a long list of insignificant and obscure persons, among whom were a great number of titled people, however. The prominence of the local aristocracy in the confederation was also the manifestation of a force and an idea. The necessity of permanent self-defence revived the spirit of feudal independence among them and made them willing, in order to secure it, to join the democratic confederations of the towns, where the feudal tradition of communal autonomy was also reviving. Protestanism, which, in religion, had been a reversion to the past, showed the same tendency, in its political transformation, to seek the sanctions and the models of an earlier social organization. Here, then, was an incipient political experiment which, if expanded and perpetuated by civil war, was capable of becoming as decentralizing a force in France as the Catholic leagues, of which it was the Protestant counterpart.

Of the leagues, at least, Catherine had sufficient experience to recognize the affinity which this confederation bore to them. The King dismissed the delegation with the promise that he would take their demands under advisement and send them a reply after mature reflection.

It was time to reflect. The final and most far-reaching consequence of the massacre manifested itself neither in the field of foreign relations nor in that of domestic discord, but in the public domain of ideas. The civil war was accompanied by a polemical campaign against the Crown, conducted by Protestant pamphleteers, no longer on religious but on political grounds. Propaganda pouring from the presses of Switzerland, Germany, and Scotland, smuggled into France, circulated there with the same electrical effect as the religious polemics of the past, but which was charged now with far more subversive ideas.

Though the earliest of these productions consisted of factual accounts of the massacre and violent denunciations of its authors, in their conclusions they rose to a plane of general ideas. The denunciation of tyranny and the justification of tyrannicide led to an analysis of despotism, and this, in turn, to plans for municipal and democratic organization and appeals to the French to recover their liberty. These ideas were developed by subsequent writers, who, passing from persons to principles, made the crime of Charles IX the basis of an attack on the monarchy. The most influential of these tracts were the *Franco-Gallia* of François Hotman and the *Vindiciae contra Tyrannos* of "Junius Brutus." Hotman, the literary terrorist who led the polemical campaign against the Guises in 1560, was again in the vanguard of the agitation of 1572. His *De Furoribus Gallicis,* which appeared in Edinburgh in 1573, arraigned the King for the feudal crime of felony, which dissolved the bonds of sovereign and subject. The old sacrosanct fiction of attacking the King only in his ministers vanished, even his mother was ignored, and the King became the butt of a direct attack on the Throne. The mutual obligations and the respective rights of the ruler and the ruled became the subject of passionate and public debate. Hot-

man took the lead, in his *Franco-Gallia,* an historical review of the monarchy demonstrating that until recent times
it had been elective and controlled by the National Assembly. True to the Protestant respect for the primitive, he
went back to the origins. In ancient Gaul the King had
been merely an itinerant magistrate, elected and controlled
by a National Assembly, which persisted under various
names—Convention, Placite, Cour, Parlement—and which
still survived in a modified form, in the Parlements on the
one hand, and in the States-General on the other. The
parent body possessed and delegated all the sovereign functions—the choice or deposition of the king, the decision of
peace and war, appointment to government office, legislation, monetary measures; and the royal formula which had
become the brevet of absolutism, *car tel est notre plaisir,*
was merely the corruption of the original *bene-placet,*
which signified the general will. Of that aboriginal power
only a tradition and a fragment remained. Parlement, with
its right of registering the royal acts, was one relic, but
how changed and debased: a closed corporation devoted
to the rule not of law but of lawyers, whom he compared
to butchers, buying their meat wholesale from the King
and selling it retail to the country. The States-General were
another relic, capable of resuscitation, but smothered by
the monarchy, which consulted them only in emergency,
and which had forgotten them ever since 1560. In those
twelve years the absolute power of the Crown, founded by
Louis XI and fattened by Louis XII, François I, and Henri
II, had reached its culmination. Hotman had been for years
the stormy petrel of the Calvinist cause, an extravagant
and embarrassing journalist whose temerity shocked his
own party—he had been forced to leave Geneva for
Strasbourg—and it might have been expected that he
would push his thesis to extreme lengths. But his conclusions were moderate. He confined himself to invectives
against absolutism, the government of women, the magistrates who justified the twenty-fourth of August, and the
Parlements who prepared it by wrecking the Edict of
Toleration, and to insisting on the rights and privileges of
the provinces, for which he claimed precisely the form of
autonomy in effect in Languedoc. Yet he could write with
truth to a colleague: "This book is of great importance in

order to reconquer our government and restore to France its balance and true peace." As he explained to the Count Palatine: "The civil wars have been only the beginning of our afflictions; we must seek their cause further back, in our neglect of the ancient constitution of the kingdom, openly violated for a century." The book was permeated with an old and popular tradition which, in one passage, he stated explicitly: "A free man is not made to suffer the arbitrary will and the good pleasure [of the sovereign]; to the people alone belongs the right to elect and to depose kings." He stated the facts and allowed the public to draw the conclusion.

It was Théodore de Bèze who carried those implications one step further in a treatise *Du Droit des Magistrats sur les Sujets,* in which he attempted to reconcile the Calvinist principle of submission to the civil power with the exigencies of the times. On the right of the subject to resist oppression, he hedged; but he came out frankly with an affirmation of popular sovereignty and advocated the convocation of the States-General to enforce it. Another writer of the same school, unembarrassed by religious scruples, derived the right of revolt from the traditional institutions of France, as their logical consequence and necessary complement. Inspired by these works, and amplifying them, the *Vindiciae contra Tyrannos,* semi-religious and semi-secular, established the social contract as the only legitimate base of the monarchy.

All these productions were marked by an obvious reluctance to push their principles to extreme lengths. The authors, startled by their own deductions, took cover in the past to escape the future, but what they began could not be left unfinished. For the present, they compromised. Their common aim was a limited monarchy, based on an unwritten constitution, confined by the nobility, and responsible to the States-General. Even in this anodyne form, their propaganda, and particularly the *Franco-Gallia,* caused intense indignation at Court. Counter-pamphlets appeared, violent, prolific, and feeble, and the defence of the monarchy undermined it even more than the attack. The mere fact that the subject was debated was damaging. The Protestant agitators had succeeded in translating into politics the spirit which had made them so formidable in religion—the spirit of free inquiry, of scientific disregard for authority, and of independent judgment.

The *Franco-Gallia* of Hotman found friends not only among his fellow-believers. As the Huguenots developed from a purely religious into a quasi-political body, they approached that group of moderate Catholics who had always sought to dissociate religion from politics and who were now crystallized into a party known as the Politiques or Malcontents. The leaders of this party were the Montmorencys who believed that they had narrowly escaped extermination in the maelstrom of the Saint Bartholomew. This suggestion was one of the minor mysteries of the massacre. The political Malcontents, revolted by the massacre, and sympathetic to the Protestant polemics, were willing to meet them in a programme curbing the arbitrary power of the monarchy, and as a fusion of the two parties was of material advantage to the spread of the new ideas, efforts were made on both sides to bring about a coalition. These efforts were fruitful, though not conclusive. Among the Protestants, two elements resisted—the religious groups, which feared the adulteration of the party, and the democratic element, which dreaded any increase of the aristocratic affiliations. Both were submerged by the course of events.

Even a tentative understanding was of service to the Huguenots. The protection of a Montmorency, the Maréchal de Damville, who was Governor of Languedoc, which he had ruled for years with virtually sovereign independence, fostered the growth of the local Protestant government. When the King replied to the demands presented to him at Villers-Cotterêts, it was Damville who was charged to negotiate with the Huguenots of his province. The negotiations came to nothing. They were followed by another General Assembly of the Protestants at Milhau-en-Rouergue, at which plans were made to extend their confederation to the rest of France and to develop their embryonic government. Taking over and modifying the existing machinery of the royal government, they produced a charter, calling for the periodic convocation of a local States-General, composed of deputies from the Nobility and the Third Estate elected by the General

Assembly, in which popular sovereignty was invested, and to which belonged the right to appoint, depose, and control all executive officers, and in particular the military leaders. These regulations, inspired by an ardent hatred of absolutism, represented the first attempt to convert the theories of the propagandists into practice. The experiment was still in its infancy and might yet have been crushed, but for the goodwill of Damville, who not only connived at it, but later, under the impulsion of events, openly adhered to the movement.

To cement this experiment, all that was needed was the protracted isolation of war. Since the departure of Anjou for Poland, a truce had been in effect, renewed every few months, and a separate peace had been concluded with La Rochelle, by which the Court hoped to detach it from the cities in the south and to proceed against these piecemeal, by either negotiation or arms. But in December 1573, shortly after the Assembly at Milhau, a plot to capture La Rochelle by treachery was discovered; this fresh violation of the peace roused the city, and La Noue, the last of the great captains of the past, who had commanded the city during its siege, appealed to it to join the confederation of the south. Weary of war, the burghers hesitated; as a final inducement, he promised them the support of "a greater leader than any in the past," and this pledge, combined with the renewed evidence that no trust could be placed in the engagements of the Court, decided them to resume the war in conjunction with the confederation in Languedoc. La Noue planned a concerted uprising to begin in March 1574.

The leader so mysteriously named was Alençon. Through the Politiques the Prince had been approached with a proposal to escape from Court with the King of Navarre, to flee to Sedan and from there, under threat of heading the civil war, to dictate his terms to the King and obtain the Lieutenant-Generalship of the kingdom. Alençon, who suffered from an acute sense of inferiority, accepted. On the appointed day, a detachment of Huguenot cavalry was to repeat the exploit of Meaux in 1567, surprise the Court at Saint-Germain, and in the resulting confusion Alençon and Navarre were to make their escape. The plan miscarried, but it caused a panic at Court.

Alençon confessed and was hurried by his mother into her coach, with Navarre, and driven to Paris. The King, too ill to move, followed on the next day.

When the first alarm had subsided, the royal family made light of the incident, and the princes were pardoned. But they were held under such close surveillance as to be virtual prisoners, and they made a second attempt to escape. Arrested and examined, Alençon betrayed his confederates. The principals escaped—Condé and Monsieur de Thoré fleeing to Germany—and the brunt fell on two subordinates, Coconas and La Mole, who were tortured, tried, and executed. Montmorency, whose name was mentioned in the course of the examination, was sent to the Bastille. It was in consequence of this step, and of a surreptitious attempt to arrest him as well, that Damville openly joined the Protestants of Languedoc.

The abortive conspiracy of the Politiques forged the first living link between their party and the Protestants. This combination, which blended the malcontents of both faiths in a common aim to limit the monarchy, altered the whole character of the war, giving it a constitutional object beside which the sectarian issues of the previous civil wars paled in importance. Alençon admitted his affiliation with the Politiques, and though his examination disclosed little of their aims, it revealed clearly that he was the tool of persons of far greater capacity and experience than his own, who were exploiting his thwarted ambition and his princely position for their own purposes. This was enough to alarm Catherine, who saw in the conspiracy merely another intrigue, but a singularly formidable one at this juncture of affairs. From such evidence as she was able to gather, she suspected that one of their aims was to place Alençon on the throne in the event of the death of Charles IX. And that contingency was no longer a remote possibility.

Ever since the Saint Bartholomew, it was clear that the King carried death in him. His constitution, never robust, and constantly overtaxed, gave way and consumption set in. When he realized that his days were numbered, he began again to take a stubborn interest in public affairs. His sullen resentment of his mother rose in intermittent explosions. One day, during the trying months of the siege of La Rochelle, when he lost his temper with the huntsmen, *"Hé, mon fils,"* she rallied him, "you would do better to be angry with the Rochellois, who are killing so many of your good servants." He swung on her furiously. *"Hé, mon Dieu,* who but you are the cause of all this? *Mort Dieu,* you are the cause of it all!" And, speechless with rage, he left her. In recounting the scene to her women, "I always said that I had to deal with a madman," she moaned, "and that I should never make anything of him." Yet, though the bonds between them were strained, they remained unbroken. The massacre had riveted them, and he was too sick to emancipate himself. He worked at public affairs, he presided at the Council, he made decisions himself, but, always incapable of sustained effort, and now physically failing and morally ruined, he was too remote from the world to fix his attention upon it. It was as if he had exhausted the power which, in his famous line to the poet Ronsard, he recognized as his only sovereign attribute: *"Je puis donner la mort, toi l'immortalité."* [1] All that he had to give to the world, he gave utterly on the night of Saint Bartholomew, and he was spent. It was time to pass on.

In the autumn of 1573, his health declined rapidly. Any undue excitement was certain to hasten the end, and the conspiracy of the Politiques, which occurred six months later, was equivalent to an assassination. "If they had waited at least for my death," he said, as he was hurried from Saint-Germain. "Too much malice, too much malice . . ." He was on the verge of collapse when he reached Paris, and after resting in the house of Monsieur de Retz —he refused to return to the Louvre—he was removed to the Bois de Vincennes. Although mentally resigned to die, he lingered for three months, sinking, rallying, sinking again, waiting patiently, with no will to live, for the stubborn vitality of his body to subside.

The end came on May 30, 1574. Two hours before, he summoned the captains of his guard and begged them to take their orders from his mother until the arrival of his brother from Poland. A declaration had already been

---

[1] "I can give death, but you give immortality."

issued announcing her Regency. He was in extreme pain, and his bed was wet with blood, but he remained clear and coherent to the end. One of his last requests was for his brother. Alençon came. "Send for my brother," the King repeated. "He is here," Catherine said. "No, Madame, my brother . . . the King of Navarre." Navarre was summoned and when, after some delay, he arrived, uncertain of his reception, Charles embraced him feebly. "You are losing a good friend, brother," he said. "If I had believed all that I was told, you would not be alive. Do not trust . . ." Catherine interrupted. "Do not say that, Sire!" "I do say it, Madame, it is the truth." But he never explained himself. His mind wandered. He continued to speak from time to time, as if he felt it incumbent upon him to relieve the long wait, like a guest whose departure has been accidentally delayed. Finally, he dozed off and, as he slowly lapsed into oblivion, he was still trying to express himself. His last murmur was: ". . . *et ma mère*. . . ." What he meant no one divined, but she understood. "After God, he recognized no one," she said later, "but me."

CHAPTER VI

The Reign of

HENRI III

- 1 -

The death of Charles IX had been too long foreseen to produce a violent shock. Catherine had made every provision for it, including her own consolation. "Your brother is dead," she wrote on the following day to the King of Poland. "He received God in the morning. His last words were: '. . . and my mother!' It could not but be an extreme grief for me, and my only consolation will be to see you here soon, as your kingdom requires, and in sound health: for if I were to lose you, I should bury myself alive with you." Yet, though she had steeled herself for it, the actual experience prostrated her. But she did not abandon herself to despair, and both to brace herself and to dispel any posthumous jealousy, she repeated: "I am dying to see you, you know how much I love you, and when I think that you will never leave me again, that thought gives me patience."

No one believed that she assumed the Regency reluctantly. Her regret was accepted as a decent example of the dissimulation for which she was so notorious that she deceived no one except when she was sincere. But in this case she was sincere. During the last months of the reign of Charles IX the burden of responsibility began at last to weigh on her.

The vast burden of responsibility which she had borne patiently for thirteen years had become overpowering since the Saint Bartholomew. The consequences of the massacre, if not the massacre itself, demoralized her. The remorse which the King felt for it hastened his end. He rarely spoke of it, but it consumed him in silence. He admitted to his sister that he would never have consented if he had not believed that his life and the State were in danger. On the night before his death, he was overheard by his old nurse bemoaning the blood he had spilled and the advice he had followed. She consoled him with the assurance that it could not be held against him but against those who inspired him. For two years Catherine had borne his mute reproach patiently, but when he died in her arms, reconciled to her at last, she felt that her heart would break and longed for death herself.

But death was too easy. That crushing burden of responsibility she had still to carry and pass on to another son. The conditions of the country at the death of Charles IX were critical. The relapse into civil war, the growing disrepute of the monarchy, the spread of disaffection— these consequences of the massacre required the control of an expert hand during the difficult period of interregnum. How insecure Catherine herself felt, while there was no King in France, was illustrated by a remarkable incident. During the forty days of royal mourning, the body of Charles IX lay in state, his apartments remained open, the usual routine was observed, the table was laid, meals were served, his servants performed all their accustomed duties, as if he were still alive. When the body itself was removed, an immaculate dummy, simulating him to the life, replaced it, and the same ceremonial was continued. To such artifices did she resort to preserve a visible fac-simile of the royal presence. She dispatched the news of the King's death to Poland with an urgent appeal to Henri to speed his return; but as time would be required to arrange his affairs, it was clear that there would be a prolonged interim before she could resign her functions to the new sovereign.

The courier who brought the news of the King's death to Poland broke every record for speed, covering eight hundred miles in seventeen days. Henri had prepared for it for months and had waited for it for years, but when it arrived he had made no arrangements. On the following day he fled, pursued by the Poles, who overtook him at the Austrian frontier. He promised to return and pursued his journey to Vienna. To avoid passing through the States of Protestant Germany, he decided to travel by way of Venice, Turin, and the Mont-Cenis. He was magnificently entertained in Vienna and in Venice. The memorable fortnight which he spent in the Adriatic capital was the most provident act of his life. He crowded a lifetime of unalloyed bliss into those two weeks, shopping for perfumes and gems, frequenting the courtesans, posing for Tintoretto, complimenting Titian, attending banquets, dancing, experimenting with philosophic love, making speeches.

The Venetian interlude was a march which he stole on time. At Turin, he met and faced the stern realities of the situation to which he was returning. He had given much thought to it without reaching any conclusion. Both in Catholic Vienna and Catholic Venice he had been advised to inaugurate his reign by a policy of moderation and peace, and though his replies to the Emperor and the Doge were non-committal, he was inclined to follow their recommendations. At Turin, the same advice was given to him by the ultra-Catholic Duke of Savoy, while the Duchess induced Damville to come to Turin to discuss the possibility of peace. At the same time, Henri received a letter from his mother, laying down some general principles to guide him. "You must show yourself master," she wrote, "and not let people think, he is young, we can make him do whatever we please. . . . You must break the custom of giving in to anyone who braves you or who tries to convince you as an equal or a malcontent. Break this habit with two or three of the boldest, and the rest will come around." He was to beware, above all, of Damville and to state firmly that he would treat with the rebels only on his own terms, and of these the first should be the prohibition of the Protestant cult. Acting on this advice, Henri rejected the terms of Damville, who returned to Languedoc and signed a contract with the Huguenots, which converted their improvised alliance into a formal and political coalition.

The journey of homecoming lasted three months. Early in September 1574, the King reached Lyons, where his mother was waiting for him. Though the welcome which she arranged was not as magnificent as that which he received in Venice—that was peerless and unique—it was as sumptuous as she could manage, and she gratified his one remaining wish. During the state entry she sat beside him in a great coach, enjoying her share of the honours which he owed to her. But the French were not as sympathetic as the Italians: the crowd was large but there was a conspicuous absence of enthusiasm. Nor was this impression dispelled by the household arrangements which he made immediately after his arrival, and which were marked by a foreign formality. His six months in Cracow had been spent in homesickness and seclusion. The Poles were fascinated by him, but their mentality and their habits, their exuberance, their bibulousness, their boisterousness, and their flamboyance shocked him, and he shrank from their advances and caged himself behind a rigid barrier of etiquette, which increased their respect for him. These habits he brought home to France, where there seemed to be no reason for them; but, in reality, among his own countrymen, there was even greater occasion for them. The elaborate ceremonial with which he surrounded himself—his insistence upon being addressed at all times as a Majesty, his custom of eating his meals behind a balustrade—an innovation that annoyed courtiers who had always had access to the King at such times— was inspired by a determination to visualize the royal dignity and to exact the proper respect for it at a time when the monarchy was sinking into disrepute; but the effect of these regulations, which the French described as *mœurs Sarmates*, was to make the King remote and inaccessible at a time when communication and understanding with his subjects were of the utmost political importance. His mother perceived it and persuaded him to abandon these formalities. But first impressions are lasting.

Too proud to court popularity, he had none of the qualities which inspire it spontaneously. In private, he could be easy, unassuming, and affable, but he remained aloof. His disability was partly a matter of health. At twenty, his vigour was exhausted and with it his martial ambitions and his taste for physical exercise, an indispensable qualification for popularity with the upper classes. He began to lead an indolent, pleasure-loving, and effeminate life. His abnormal sexual proclivities increased his isolation.

The regal dignity, and its conservation, were the constant preoccupation of the *petit-maître* who now wore the crown of France. It was his one political principle. The Secretaries of State, who of recent years had assumed an undue independence, composing and signing dispatches and conducting public business on their own responsibility, were instructed that no official paper was valid without the royal signature and that all correspondence was to be submitted to him. Though this required long hours of labour, Henri worked with regularity and application, appending his signature in a small, fine, perpendicular hand—the calligraphy of a polished and painstaking character—to documents which he studied carefully and frequently drafted himself. Irksome as this routine was, he trained himself to perform all the duties of his station in person. He refused to delegate authority. He followed his mother's advice to the letter and he needed no urging. He was determined, as she wished him, to acquire the *main de maître*, and when he revoked her privilege of opening the diplomatic correspondence, she did not complain, though she was hurt. She murmured a little in private and submitted. Her influence remained. He listened to her advice, though he did not encourage her to offer it unless he solicited it. But, as someone said, "if the King wished to do otherwise, I do not know where he could turn for advice."

He brought home with him the friends who had lightened his exile in Poland, and he rewarded their devotion lavishly, but he drew a sharp line of demarcation between public and private favours. He made no attempt to place gilded youths in the State. A few of his older friends, who deserved promotion, he introduced into the Council, which became a composite of his creatures and Catherine's, but which remained the instrument which she had established. The great representative names of the past—the Guises, the Montmorencys, the Bourbons—the representatives of a feudal and factious aristocracy, were conspicuous by their absence. The King governed, no longer with the country, but against it. The Council of 1574 was her gift of accession to her son, an instrument of personal government which she had been evolving for years. Though three of its members—Pibrac, Foix, and Bellièvre—were ex-magistrates, they were thoroughly subdued and serviceable, while of the military men, whom she preferred only as a lesser evil, there was not one. The Council was composed entirely of trained diplomatists and bureaucrats, whose fortunes she had made, and who were wholly subservient to her will. It was a royal gift, the fruit of her lifework. "He can do whatever he will," she said, "provided he wishes to."

Now, this substitution of the personal creatures of the Crown for representative figures of the past, and the elimination of men of ideas, constituted a fact of peculiar importance at a period when the Crown was on the verge of a conflict which, while it was a continuation of the wars of the past, was already of a radically different character. For two months after the arrival of the King in Lyons, the Council consulted with him on the advisability of renewing the civil war. When Damville left Turin and joined the Huguenots in Languedoc, he brought an enormous accession of strength to his allies, swinging not only Languedoc but the adjoining provinces of Dauphiné and Guyenne into the Protestant orbit, and in those districts which had once been hotbeds of the Catholic leagues there now sprang up a political organization of a diametrically opposed character but which was equally capable of becoming a social dissolvent. The Huguenot government took over the machinery of the royal administration and transformed it, vesting all the sovereign functions—the rights of legislation and taxation, the administration of justice, the regulation of commerce, the determination of war and peace—in a representative body. The republican nature of this constitution was jealously safeguarded. The towns which composed the Protestant Union retained their local autonomy and were federated into a common body whose general interests were settled by a local States-General; and though the proportional representation of classes was simplified by the elimination of the clergy, as a precaution against the preponderance of the aristocracy, double representation was accorded to the Third Estate. Before the war had fairly begun, the national government was confronted by a *fait accompli*—the constitution of a State within the State, independent and autonomous, in which representative theories had been converted into practice, and which was no longer an experiment but an example to the country at large. The war was already a war of secession.

But this was not all. The conflict was launched by a campaign of propaganda. On November 4, Damville issued a manifesto defining the joint policy of the Protestant-Politique party, and following this ultimatum by convoking the local States-General at Montpellier. This double manœuvre, expertly timed to attract attention to the *fait accompli* in Languedoc, had the strategic effect of defining the war as a war for and against ideas. Carefully weeded out of the King's Council, they reappeared in the field, arrayed against him. The very military men were imbued with them. Damville styled himself the "Liberator of the Commonwealth" and the "Reformer of the King's Council." These two titles epitomized the claims of the manifesto. With shrewd political generalship, the Marshal emphasized the two points of the party programme best calculated to appeal to the country at large and to rally national sentiment to the cause. The first of these was the resuscitation of the States-General; the second, the elimination of Italians from the government. The latter was instantly effective. The country was suffering from acute poverty; all the great names of France were absent from the Royal Council; and it was easy to win support by focusing popular discontent on a group of aliens who enjoyed the profits and privileges of which Frenchmen found themselves despoiled. The group was not large, and there was more chauvinism than justice in the attack. Only one Italian sat in the Council—the Chancellor Birague—but the attack was levelled against all the aliens in the entourage of the King. Most of these could claim to be fully naturalized: the Italian colony had been in existence ever since François I, and the expatriates had served their adopted country long and faithfully. Nevertheless, the Italians were a convenient scapegoat for the sins of the Crown, and Birague, Retz, and Nevers were odious to the Protestants because they had promoted the Saint Bartholomew. And, whatever their individual merits or crimes, they paid for the vice of a system. The Italians were unpopular because they personified the parasitic grip which international finance had fastened on the government, and to which most of them owed their fortune.

The agitation against the Italians was an indirect attack upon Catherine herself. Since the Saint Bartholomew, she had been the object of a breathless hue and cry among the pamphleteers. The most violent of these libels, the *Discours merveilleux de la vie, action, et déportements de la reyne Catherine de Médicis*, by an anonymous Huguenot author, appeared in Lyons shortly before the arrival of Henri III. The slim little volume, which had a sensational vogue, the booksellers stocking their cellars with it and the Catholics buying it as eagerly as the Huguenots, was a compendium of founded and imaginary charges. The author stigmatized her as the instigator of the massacre, credited her with the death of every public person by whose removal she had profited in the course of her life, related her reign as a simple and sinister succession of intrigues, plots, and perfidies, and accused her of debauching her sons to sap their energy and stunt their intelligence. Lurid, hysterical, extravagant, the libel nevertheless satisfied the hatred of a public which found nothing too abominable to believe of her, and that public was no longer a faction. Sworn enemies of the Huguenots took it to heart, accepted it as their gospel, and vouched for its accuracy. The vogue of the *Vie de Sainte Catherine*, as it was vulgarly called, was symptomatic.

Of this literature Catherine was also an attentive reader. She made no attempt to censor or suppress it. Indifferent to public opinion and accountable to no one for her conduct—"I do not care," she said once, "who thinks it good or bad"—she read. She read for the same reason that she went to the studio of Corneille de Lyons, whenever she was in Lyons, to look over her old portraits, because she had a healthy interest in herself. But she recognized so little of herself in the vulgar caricature of the *Vie de Sainte Catherine* that it caused her inordinate amusement. If only the author had consulted her, she said, she could have supplied him with so much which he had overlooked that he might easily have swelled his slim volume. But there were some pamphlets which could not be dismissed with cheerful bravado or bantering contempt. There was, for instance, the *France-Turquie*, inspired by the Montmorencys, which appeared at the same time and which, equally splenetic, had an even greater success. Under the pseudonym of "a Florentine," a Politique purported to reveal a deep-laid scheme to convert France into an Oriental despotism by the elimination of the Nobility from the government. A public refutation of this pamphlet appeared, provoking plainer charges: the scheme was laid to the influence of the Italians, and patriots were exhorted to protect their country; the most effective measure, it was suggested, would be to refuse to pay taxes. These systematic attacks on the monarchy, on herself, and on the Italian financiers eventually convinced Catherine that she could not ignore public opinion.

This preliminary campaign of propaganda affected the deliberations of the Royal Council and precipitated its decision. Catherine, determined that the new reign should not begin weakly, forced the decision for war. It was impossible to dissociate the constitutional from the confessional issue; Damville demanded, together with political reforms, the liberty of the Protestant cult; the two were identified, and the religious conflict was already developing into a political struggle. At the session of the Council at which it was decided to prosecute the war, the speaker who concluded the discussion repeated the time-worn argument: "Either Your Majesty must perish, with the entire State, or the Protestants must be exterminated." But it had acquired a new meaning. The old fallacy was charged with pregnant reality. Four armies were put into the field, and it was decided that the main body should be led by the King in person.

The campaign was a long, miserable, desperate failure. In the conviction that by an abnormal exertion it might prove swift and conclusive, Catherine had assembled a large quota of troops which it was a severe strain on the financial resources of the government to maintain under arms for a prolonged period.

Success depended on a swift and decisive offensive, but a war of movement and pitched battles was out of the question: the Protestants, entrenched in walled towns, had to be attacked piecemeal, and siege warfare, in which they were experienced and spirited, consumed time. With one exception, the Protestant fortresses proved inexpugnable. After appearing at one siege and abandoning it in disgust, the King with his family and the Court descended the Rhône by boat, drifting through the enemy territory, as far as Avignon. Two months had passed, and nothing had been accomplished. Yet the time had not been wasted. Intelligent and impressionable, Henri had come into contact with hard realities and gained personal experience of problems which had hitherto been merely Cabinet questions—the desolation of a war-weary country, the ravages of endless civil war, the passing of royal authority, the progress of the separatist spirit, the independence and insolence of the Huguenot captains. The whole campaign, undertaken for prestige, was a succession of humiliations. When he reached Avignon, the King was profoundly dispirited. Daily, down the river he heard the cannon of Damville battering the walls of Saint-Gilles. He went no further.

Essentially a creature who thought with his senses, Henri was in a state of exasperated sensibility. Before leaving Lyons, he learned of the death of the Princesse de Condé, the one woman whom he sincerely loved. The announcement was slipped among his papers and, when he came upon it, he fainted. For a week he was lost to the world. Every memento of his mistress was removed by his mother, but it was impossible to efface her image from his heart. He reappeared, in an exquisite uniform embroidered with death's-heads, and when he started for the front, he was still suffering from shock. The depressing experiences of the campaign completed his disillusionment. He was, or he believed himself to be, world-weary. His spiritual director, the Jesuit Father Auger, turned his mind to religion and, knowing the impressionable nature of his patient, organized a parade of the Flagellant monks who were one of the sights of Avignon. The spectacle had the desired effect. In an ecstasy of self-mortification he discovered a new sensation and, shortly before Christmas, led the entire Court, wailing, through the streets of Avignon. The demonstration lasted all day, and by nightfall the tribal dance of devotion was in full swing.

These spiritual exercises cost one life. No one who valued his soul or his reputation was exempt from them. The Cardinal de Lorraine, at the age of forty-nine still in search of popularity or, failing that, of salvation, participated in the barefoot procession. The weather was raw and he limped home in a high fever. He hibernated in bed for a few days. On the day after Christmas, he died. His passing created no more impression than that of a country curate. His memory haunted Catherine. Several days later, and again at dinner, she perceived him so distinctly that she dropped her glass with a cry. For weeks she complained that she could not rid her mind of him, and her women noticed that she frequently woke at night in terror. Such was the posthumous career of that great prelate.

Above all, she could not rid her mind of a reflection which he had been in the habit of repeating to his nephews as a maxim of life. "For the least annoyance in the world," he would say, "to forsake one's duty and to desist is the true mark of a frivolous and inconstant man, easy to disgust, and in no wise fit to manage affairs of State." From that facile soul, so easily elated and so easily downcast, the observation came with the effect of a verdict on his own conduct. But it was not of him that she thought, it was of her son. His terrible facility of feeling, his nervous excitability, and his easy discouragement troubled her. He had undertaken the war, against his inclinations, on her advice, and at the first "annoyance" he was ready to desist. She was on the verge of discouragement herself.

By the end of December, Henri decided to negotiate. He made overtures to Damville, recognized the Protestant Confederacy, and invited the allies to present their terms to him in Paris. Leaving his generals in the field to continue the campaign, he hurried to Reims for his coronation

(February 11, 1575). A loan of 100,000 francs supplied by a Florentine merchant in Avignon enabled him to make the journey to Reims. The accommodation which allowed him to be crowned also allowed him to be married. The expenses were funded, and one ceremony followed the other. His bride was a young lady of modest extraction who reminded him of his mistress. His mother thought the choice arbitrary. The next problem was to reach Paris. Catherine appealed to the Parlement and the Châtelet. Word went around that *"le Roi n'a pas de quoi dîner";* [1] a collection was raised; and the royal family arrived somehow in the capital. The situation was intolerable. The wages of the household servants had not been paid for nine months, and to meet the salaries of the guards an assessment was levied on the gentlemen attending the Court. The King studied the problem of setting his house in order.

The insolvency of the Crown was, as it had always been, the basic obstacle to the re-establishment of the royal authority. The year 1575 was marked by another general financial crisis, the most acute since that of 1558, and money was tight abroad. Henri resorted to the usual expedients, negotiating with the Pope, with Venice, with Florence, with Savoy, for fresh loans, selling seats in the Council, dismembering the forest domain, farming out the *parties casuelles*, confiscating the temporalities of the clergy, but these were mere stop-gaps. With the courage of necessity and the recklessness of inexperience, he attempted one drastic measure and imposed a tax on capital, graduated to shift the weight from the pauperized people to the only prosperous classes, the clergy and the middle class. This experiment netted the Crown 3,000,000 livres and cost the King his popularity, and it remained an experiment. The agitation among the propertied classes, whose savings and whose privileges were attacked, rose to fever-heat; libels, diatribes, pamphlets, attacked the King with unmeasured violence; and after breasting the storm of obloquy he became discouraged by the magnitude of his difficulties.

To recoup his popularity, the King paraded his religious zeal, making pilgrimages, visiting monasteries, spending

---

[1] "The King has not the price of a dinner."

days in retreat, and leading penitential processions through the streets of Paris. Instead of mass hysteria he aroused the caustic wit of the Parisian masses and lost what little respect they still felt for him. Having been gouged by every other means, they refused to be fleeced of their last few pennies for alms: such was the response which rose in antiphony to the chants of the royal penitent, walking barefoot, telling his beads, through a multitude that was fanatically indifferent. "Brother Henri" was added to the other popular nicknames which belittled him, and of which a copious list appeared one day in a placard posted on the walls of Paris, beginning: "Henri de Valois, King of Poland and France by the grace of God and his mother, *concierge* of the Louvre, hairdresser-in-ordinary to his wife," and ending in those slang terms coined by the crowd to give a popular stamp to their ridicule.

It was in these conditions that the delegates of the Protestant Confederation arrived in Paris, early in April, to present their terms to the King. The deputation had previously journeyed to Basle to consult the Prince de Condé, who was mustering troops and diplomatic support in Switzerland and Germany. The outcome of this consultation was a Bill of Rights demanding the unrestricted exercise of religion, the establishment of Law Courts with equal representation of both faiths on the bench, the concession of towns of security, the liberation of Montmorency, the punishment of the authors of the Saint Bartholomew massacre, the rehabilitation of the victims, and the convocation of the States-General. When the bill was read to him, the King began by reprimanding the deputies for their presumption in presenting and ended by a sarcasm: "Well, what more do you want?" His mother was equally shocked but less superior. "I know that you Huguenots are like cats, you always light on your feet," she said, "but if you had fifty thousand men in the field, and the Admiral were alive and all the leaders, you could not talk more proudly than you do now." Nevertheless, times had changed, and, rapidly, the bill was discussed. Certain articles the King struck out on sight. A clause demanding the reduction of taxes to the scale prevailing a hundred years earlier revealed such economic innocence that he found it impossible to believe that it could be seriously formulated in the year 1575. Less than three years after the Saint Bartholomew, the punishment of the authors of the massacre was proposed to the King and his mother. The article was discussed on both sides with complete amenity. On behalf of the King, Monsieur de Morvilliers proposed a general amnesty. When the deputies insisted that the King owed it to his honour to clear himself not only of the crime but of the mere imputation of it, the King agreed with perfect urbanity. "That crime occurred contrary to my will, and I detest it heartily," he said. "Nor can it be imputed to my brother, King Charles." Catherine replied in the same sense, though a little more guardedly, admitting that grave errors had been committed, but suggesting that, when the faults of both sides had been weighed, the balance was even. The deputies disagreed emphatically and proceeded to distinguish. She preserved a severe silence which made it clear that she regarded the question as closed. And closed it remained. On the religious question, the King was inclined to bargain. The asperity with which the discussions began gave place, as they progressed, to a more and more amicable temper.

After a fortnight, the negotiations were broken off. The King offered liberal concessions, on one condition. "If I am not forced, I shall give you peace, and I shall see that it is observed." But the deputies had been instructed to be uncompromising: since the Saint Bartholomew it was all or nothing.

The war continued, desultory, dogged, indeterminate. The royal armies won some sporadic successes without affecting the course of the campaign. It was a war like all the others which had preceded it, but it differed from them in certain features which foreign observers recognized as extremely significant. The Venetian ambassador Michiele, who had witnessed the Saint Bartholomew, and who returned to France in 1575, was struck by the remarkable changes which three years had produced. He found it highly significant that the formation of a great new hybrid party had transformed the wars of religion into a war for the public good, as it was now called. He recognized the difficulty of quenching a conflict so profitable to the insurgents because, "while the King spends thousands in war, they spend nothing of their own, living on the property of the King or of others, and while he ruins himself, they prosper, and with peace they would lose all their following and authority." Another feature struck him: the enlistment of the ruined peasants who, having lost all livelihood but war, constituted a serious problem in the event of peace. Because the war was so embedded and diffused and was likely to smoulder, like a burning coal bed, indefinitely, he could not conceal his amazement at the imprudence with which the King had inaugurated his reign by a conflict which he was in no position to sustain.

- 2 -

"They were all bent on preparations for war, but these domestic discords tame them. It is a very hell among them, not one content with another, not mother with son, not brother with brother, not mother with daughter." Dr. Dale, the English ambassador, specialized in the private affairs of the royal family, and these, as it happened, had a more direct bearing on the outcome of the war than economic conditions. There was continual friction between the King and his brother and sister, and hence between them and their mother. Marguerite had never forgiven the King the deception in which their early friendship ended, nor his denunciation of her weakness for Henri de Guise. The King, whose effeminate habits included a weakness for backbiting and gossip, persecuted her in a number of small ways. He betrayed her love affairs not to her husband, who was indifferent to them, but to her mother, who had old-fashioned notions of honour and a hot temper. In retaliation, Marguerite befriended her younger brother, Alençon. Him the King despised. "Do not let that scamp come to the throne," he said one day, when he was seriously ill, to Navarre. Alençon was undersized, restless, and ambitious. In the autumn of 1575, these family jealousies fell into the public domain. Du Guast, the royal favourite, was found murdered. The King suspected his sister. This blow coincided with another in which he detected her hand. Alençon fled from Court and joined the insurgents.

The general dismay lent an extraordinary importance to the escapade of a dissatisfied younger son. In an audience with the King and his mother, Dr. Dale found them so crushed that they made no pretence, even in his presence, of spirit or self-possession. "They both spoke very lowly for their degree," he observed. What was grave in this incident was precisely its demoralizing effect: it was a shock that exposed the lassitude and discouragement that permeated the Court. The King, uncertain what to do, expected his troops to desert if he sent them against his brother. Alençon was an insignificant young man, without reputation or talent, but his name carried credit. At Dreux, where he published a manifesto embodying the demands of the Politiques, he was joined by over a thousand gentlemen. A few days later, an army of fifteen thousand *Reiters* crossed the frontier. The situation was by no means desperate but, in the state of dejection prevailing at Court, it seemed so. Catherine, who, a year before, had insisted on war at all costs, now veered about and became the most determined champion of peace. She set out at once in pursuit of the fugitive, overtook him at Chambord, and opened negotiations. Under cover of the general confusion, Navarre fled from Court and returned to his kingdom and his faith. The negotiations were long and arduous, the conditions of Alençon were exorbitant, but after five months Catherine capitulated. The Treaty of Beaulieu, or the "Paix de Monsieur," as it was commonly called, in honour of the Prince whose escapade brought the Fifth Civil War to a close, awarded Alençon an enormous apanage and restored peace to the royal family. The Protestants secured all the basic demands of the Bill of Rights—the unrestricted exercise of the cult, mixed representation in the Law Courts, full civic rights, eight towns of security, public repudiation of the Saint Bartholomew, rehabilitation of the memory of Coligny and his fellow-victims, full approval of all alliances contracted in defence of the Cause, and the recognition of the Protestant Confederacy in Languedoc, Guyenne, and Dauphiné. It was the most extensive charter ever granted to the Reformed Faith. Lastly, the Politiques obtained their demand for the convocation of the States-General, which the King bound himself to summon six months after the signature of the treaty (May 1576).

Throughout the negotiations, Catherine had written to the King repeatedly that he was lost unless he capitulated. Permeated by her despondency, he declared at one moment that he would give half his kingdom to have peace, but he did not expect her to take him at his word. Weak, confused, and discouraged, he yet had a jealous respect for the monarchy, and he was bitterly humiliated by the terms imposed on him. He signed the Treaty with tears in his eyes. The Paix de Monsieur was a turning-point both in his reign and in his relations with his mother. For two months he refused to see her. When she returned to the Louvre, he continued to treat her with every outward appearance of respect and consideration, but her position gradually changed from that of a partner to a minister, the agent and not the pilot of his will. But his will remained passive. He had lost confidence in her without gaining confidence in himself.

Ten years later, looking back on the first years of his reign, the King told one of his confidants that his capital mistake was that he had not followed his original purpose. On his return from Poland, he said, he had carefully considered the situation in France and had decided, without advice and contrary to his inclinations, to conclude peace at once and to convoke the States-General. Reviewing his troubled beginning with the insight of later experience, he regretted bitterly that he had lost an irreparable opportunity to do freely what he was compelled to do too late. The end might have been different.

But the end was already implicit in the beginning of his reign, and nothing could have altered its ineluctable development. The history of the next ten years was, on the surface, a succession of inconsequential, incoherent, and inconclusive incidents, without consistency or continuity. All the features which were visible at the opening of the reign—the transformation of the religious into a political struggle, the translation of the conflict to a new plane, the emergence of embryonic ideas, the weakening of the royal authority, the spread of decentralization, and the economic ruin which fostered these social growths—developed for a decade, in incessant complications and combinations, toward their appointed end.

The Paix de Monsieur, which accorded parity to the Protestants, was not only a profound humiliation to the monarchy; it was a challenge to Catholic France. The treaty was prefaced with the words: "In oblivion of the past." It resuscitated the past with provocative force. In Paris the publication of the peace excited less trouble than was expected. Though the preachers thundered professionally, the attitude of the people was one of passive resistance. Fatigue, disaffection, financial depression, tempered their normal fanaticism. The Canons of Notre Dame, who refused to celebrate the peace, were fined for insubordination by Parlement. Parlement itself was subdued. Anticipating its customary protest, the King appeared before it, escorted by the Princes of the Blood, commanded the registration of the Edict of Pacification in his presence, swore to observe it faithfully himself, and required the same oath of the members of Parlement and of the persons who accompanied him. There was no resistance, although it was noticed that the Duc de Guise, his brothers Mayenne and Aumale, and the Maréchal de Retz raised their hands reluctantly; but they raised them. Three weeks later, there was a movement of resistance in Parlement over the innovation of the *chambres mi-parties*, but it was cowed by another injunction from the King. When he appointed the Protestant President of the mixed tribunals, the magistrates made a stand and refused to seat him, but after repeated threats and commands from the Louvre, supplemented by private negotiation, the President obtained his place. These incidents were to be expected. But a change had come over the spirit of Parlement: the partisan temper that had made it so intransigent in the reign of Charles IX had abated.

Appearances were deceptive, however. The submission of Paris was due in large part to the presence of the *Reiters* on the Marne. By the terms of the peace treaty, the King had undertaken to pay them an indemnity of 3,000,000 livres: the pledge was fantastic, but until it was redeemed the *Reiters* were quartered on the Marne to

assure the execution of the treaty. The King forced a loan
by surrounding the capital with troops and threatening to
starve it into compliance; but he did not venture to repeat
this pressure. How long the occupation would have
continued would have been problematical had not a disturbance in the Rhineland recalled the *Reiters* in the middle of the summer.

With the departure of the *Reiters*, the Catholic reaction
began to stir. The example of the weakness of the King
on the one hand, and the power of organization on the
other, was not lost on the Catholics. The resurrection of
the Protestants was a proof of what could be accomplished
by federation, and a group of enterprising Catholics
adopted their methods in a counter-movement which appeared, a few weeks after the peace, in Picardy. The governor of the province, with one hundred and fifty of his
friends, formed a league for the preservation of the orthodox faith and the maintenance of the royal authority
and issued a manifesto, defining their aims, which was
remarkable in several respects. The Protestants were denounced not only as religious but as political heretics,
whose object was the introduction of a novel form of government. The League, nevertheless, appropriated their
principal demand—the convocation of the States-General
—and carried it one step further, proposing that the King
bind himself to respect the decisions of the States as inviolable. Posing as the champions of the Crown, the mani-
festants made their loyalty to the King conditional upon
his acceptance of this pledge. Another article, calling for
an extension of local franchises and provincial privileges,
and appealing to the same spirit of local autonomy and
feudal independence which had served the Protestants
so well in consolidating their Confederacy, revealed the
close study which the organizers of the League had made
of the experiments and the propaganda of their enemies.
Similar groups organized in Champagne, Burgundy, and
Poitou. The movement spread sporadically, gaining ground
in the country but making little headway in the cities.
Many peasants enlisted in the belief that they would
escape the payment of taxes, but the movement as a whole
was dominated by the nobles. Finding that the idea did
not spread as rapidly as they expected, they entrusted their

propaganda to the Jesuits and the Cordeliers, who carried the new gospel up and down the country. With a long memory of the Catholic leagues of 1565, and with ample evidence of the power of the Protestant federations, Catherine was alarmed by the revival of a movement which had already defeated her. The King was equally exercised. He took energetic measures to check the spread of this spirit of pseudo-loyalism by writing to the governors of the provinces on whose fidelity he could count, declaring that he would consider any move to form or to participate in these "sinister associations" an act of treason. But on how many provinces could he count?

The rise of the movement coincided with the publication of the summons for the meeting of the States-General at Blois, in December 1576, and it soon became clear that the League proposed to make the States an organ of publicity and propaganda for their cause. Throughout the autumn of 1576 the election of the deputies was conducted in an atmosphere of high tension, the League setting all its resources in motion to assure an exclusively Catholic representation in the Assembly. In the contested provinces the Protestant candidates were intimidated; and in cases where they won a majority, their election was set aside. Long before December, the outcome was so clear that the Protestants and the Politiques, seeing their demand for a National Assembly converted into a party manœuvre against them, decided to abstain altogether and declared the forthcoming session null and void.

While the original promoters of the States repudiated their achievement, they carried on a campaign, however, to expose the nature and aims of the League. Their most sensational stroke was the publication of the David mémoire. In the autumn of 1576, Nicolas David, a member of Parlement who had joined the League, died in Lyons, on his return from a journey to Rome in company with the Bishop of Paris. His trunk was opened, and among his papers was found the document which came into possession of the Protestants and which they rushed to press as a revelation of the ulterior motive of the movement. This paper purported to be a digest of plans to be laid before the Pope for his approval. The Paix de Monsieur, it stated, had proved the unfitness of the degenerate descendants of Hugh Capet to reign. The legitimate heirs of Charlemagne, on the contrary, were in their prime, and fully capable of retrieving the situation. For this purpose a comprehensive campaign was planned. The Catholic population was to be stirred up, by preaching, to oppose the public celebration of Protestant worship. The King was to be induced to appoint the Duc de Guise, as the head of the League, to suppress the ensuing disorders. Under his direction the parish priests were to recruit all men capable of bearing arms and issue instructions to them, in the confessional, respecting their service. The first move was to be made at the meeting of the States-General. The States, composed exclusively of staunch Catholics, would repeal the Paix de Monsieur, re-enact the edicts for the extirpation of heresy, declare the rights of succession of the heretical Princes of the Blood forfeited, and impeach the Duc d'Alençon for rebellion, for extorting an excessive apanage from the Crown, and for abetting heresy. Simultaneously, a portion of the parochial militia and other troops would place the Prince and his associates under arrest. With the remainder the Duc de Guise would take the field and subdue the rebellious provinces. Upon his return, he would provide for an exemplary punishment of Alençon and his accomplices and would permanently restore order, with the consent of the Pope, by imprisoning the King in a monastery. Having purged the kingdom of heresy, he would conclude his pious work by abolishing the liberties and privileges of the Gallican Church.

It was a large programme, even for the capacities of a legitimate descendant of Charlemagne, and accomplished with astounding ease on paper. Such was the general impression when the pamphlet appeared. Accepted as a forgery, it was discounted as a campaign trick of the Protestants. The King was of the same opinion, and he was not seriously disturbed until he received from his ambassador in Madrid a document which had been submitted to Philip II for his approval, and which proved to be a duplicate of the David *mémoire*.

The avowed aim of the League to renew the war was troubling enough, apart from such revelations. After making such heavy sacrifices to secure peace, the King was determined not to be forced into a repetition of the conflict. But as the partisans of the League were heavily represented among the deputies, and the King hoped to obtain a subsidy from the Assembly, he was not in a position to oppose the League openly. In this dilemma he conceived a plan to outwit the warmongers and satisfy the States by recognizing the League and assuming the leadership himself: an operation by which he proposed to emasculate it. The same inspiration occurred to Catherine. It had been suggested to her years ago by Montluc.

The deputies, on the other hand, were primarily concerned, apart from all questions of religious partisanship, in obtaining certain economic reforms from the King. This interplay of cross-purposes lent a shifting, complex, and incoherent character to the deliberations of the Assembly; and they were further complicated by turns which had been foreseen neither by the League nor the King nor the deputies themselves. The mere act of assembling the nation was sufficient to strike sparks and to generate forces which startled and foiled those who proposed to manipulate them.

Despite the pressure brought to bear on the elections, the League had not succeeded as completely as it expected, and its agitators, accordingly, conducted a final campaign among the deputies as they arrived in Blois, interviewing them individually and pressing them to subscribe the formula of the manifesto. The majority complied and informed the King that they would vote in favour of a single religion, but there was a substantial minority which maintained an attitude of reserve. Moreover, there was another factor with which the League failed to reckon: the impressionability of assemblies, the solution of the individual in the mass, all the more pronounced since the usual result of electoral pressure is to substitute for men of conviction pliable nonentities susceptible to the shifting temper of their colleagues. This was manifest at the outset.

The King pronounced the inaugural address, appealing to his audience to transcend partisanship, and expatiating on the distress of the people with an eloquence and a sympathy not common in the mouth of kings. A ready orator, he showed himself, at his début, a no less able parliamentarian. The deputies were surprised and stirred. The Chancellor followed with a speech in which he made a strong bid for the support of the Third Estate, recognizing that it carried an undue share of the burden of taxation, criticizing the immunities of an aristocracy which enjoyed the privileges without incurring the obligations of caste, and acknowledging the corruption and abuses which had crept into the government. This speech was received with so much satisfaction by the Third Estate and so much irritation by the Nobility, who were appeased only by a private apology from the Chancellor, that it accomplished its purpose, driving a wedge between the two Orders and relegating the question of the League to the background. The susceptibility of assemblies favoured the King for twenty-four hours.

On the following day the surprises began. The deputies settled down to the routine of business, and two remarkable movements of opinion developed. The first was the proposal, formulated by the manifesto of the League, that the King be bound to respect the inviolable resolutions of the Assembly. Broached simultaneously in the committee-rooms of each Order, it was discussed in a common consultation. The temerity of a measure which transformed the States from a consultative to a directing body, investing them with a legislative initiative incompatible with the royal authority, without even providing the King with the safeguard of a veto, shocked several speakers. The majority, however, argued that, unless the States assumed such authority, their function was superfluous: if it was confined to the presentation of grievances and the expression of advice, a messenger could render the same service. It was proposed therefore to petition the King to appoint a permanent commission of thirty-six members of the Assembly, whose unanimous decisions should have the force of law. The question then arose: what would occur when the decisions were not unanimous? None of the Orders was willing, in case of conflict, to accept the decision of the majority, least of all the Third Estate, which foresaw that it would invariably suffer, in case of a conflict with the privileged classes, if it were deprived of an arbiter. For this reason, it preferred to rally to the Crown. This disagreement crippled a measure of extraordinary con-

sequence to the monarchy. Nevertheless, so strong was
the feeling in favour of it, that it was decided to proceed
on the basis of the original motion. Thirty-six deputies presented it to the King. The orator of the Clergy, the Archbishop of Lyons, insisted on the necessity of according
a genuine authority to the States and requested that the
royal sanction be obligatory when their resolutions were
unanimous. The King replied that he could give no such
pledge beforehand, without limiting his authority, but he
reserved his answer. The date on which this move was
made was one of the crucial moments in the session of the
States-General. Though the move came to nothing because
of the attitude of the Third Estate, the mere fact that a
demand which would have been inconceivable under
Henri II could be formulated under Henri III was a measure of the distance which had been travelled.

The next question which engaged the deputies was the
religious problem—a problem only because, though they
were unanimous in voting for a single religion, they were
divided as to the advisability of renewing the war to
secure it. The moderate group was completely outnumbered, and when the question was put to the vote in the
committee-room, the unanimity of the three Orders was
such that nothing, it appeared, could prevent a declaration of war. This was the situation at the end of December
when, amid this rising war-fever, it was learned that the
Protestants had taken the initiative, reopened hostilities,
and captured two towns in Poitou. The King attempted
to cool the bellicose temper of the States by confronting
them once more with the financial question, and informed
them that if they voted for war, they would be obliged to
furnish the expenses. Until the moment when the question of finances was raised, complete unity had prevailed.
The pacific minority which hitherto had been unable to
make itself heard began to gain steadily in influence. On
the eve of the royal session, at which the issue was to be
decided, the Third Estate, which a fortnight before had
supported a belligerent policy, reversed itself and recommended the maintenance of a single religion in France
by every means short of war. The two other Orders, which
had counted on the financial support of the Third, were
in an embarrassing position. The Nobility declared them-

selves ready to give their lives for the King but "determined not to put their hands to the purse and the sword at once." The Clergy had made too many sacrifices to furnish any more. So soon as it was a question of prosecuting the war at the expense, not of the Crown, but of the nation, each class became temperate. Thus, from the mere assembling of the nation, the spirit of moderation triumphed, in spite of the League, in spite of the passions and prepossessions of the deputies themselves.

The King now bent all his efforts to inducing the States to vote some measures of relief for his intolerable financial situation. He plied the deputies with appeals, interviewed them individually, reduced his demands, bargained, begged, but without result. Any suggestion involving new taxes was rejected.

The obstinacy with which the Third Estate refused to supply him with funds—a stand unprecedented in the history of the States-General—caused the King increasing uneasiness. There were moments when it seemed as if he would be forced to throw himself into the League if only to derive a source of income from its members. He had directed the governors of the provinces to supply him with exact figures of the money which the association could command. But the figures were not encouraging. Though the association had spread with the announcement that it was authorized by the King, it continued to meet with rebuffs, especially in the towns. In Paris, where house-to-house visits were conducted to obtain subscriptions, the citizens either signed with restrictions or refused to have anything to do with it. Despite the zeal of the propagandists, the League made little progress against the apathy, the suspicion, or the outright hostility of the country at large.

In the meantime, the Protestants having mobilized, the King had sent emissaries to Damville, the Prince de Condé, and the King of Navarre to pacify them. They returned from their mission, just before the close of the sessions, with discouraging reports. The war party made a last stand in a meeting of the Royal Council. When the Duc de Nevers appealed to the zeal of the King and urged him to imitate the fervour of the Crusaders, a voice was raised which had not been heard for some time. Catherine made a little speech. "I am a Catholic and have as good a conscience as anyone else," she said. "I have no desire to gain credit among the Catholics by destroying this kingdom; my aim is to preserve it. If there are others who are indifferent to the loss of the State, provided they can say, I have maintained the Catholic religion, or who hope to profit by its ruin, I have nothing to say to them, but I do not wish to resemble them. I advise the King to preserve the State in his person, and God, I hope, will favour him so that one day he may unite the two religions in one." The King paid her the compliment of repeating her opinion, and she was so pleased with his approbation that she rallied Nevers gaily. "So, *mon cousin*, you would send us to Constantinople?"

At the close of the sessions, both the States and the King were in substantial agreement as to the necessity of maintaining peace. Yet war followed. The intransigent temper in which the sessions began and the menace of the League sufficed to mobilize the Protestants and to rekindle the conflict, and the King was compelled to take the field. The Sixth Civil War lasted only six months, and was completely adverse to the Protestants, who lost their allies, Damville and Alençon. The latter accepted the command of the royal armies against his late friends, won several resounding successes, and celebrated them by the butchery of thousands of captives. The Protestants were saved from disaster only by the intervention of the King, who was fighting for peace, and who checked his brother on the eve of a great engagement. The "Paix de Bergerac" (September 1577) confirmed the previous peace, with some modifications which eliminated the most provocative gains of the Huguenots, and substituted for the humiliating "Paix de Monsieur" the generous "Paix du Roi."

For the next two years there was an interval of relative calm, but a calm so troubled that Catherine set out in the summer of 1578 on a journey of pacification, which was, as it were, a roundabout way to reconciliation with her son, to the recovery of his confidence. Her travels lasted sixteen months and carried her into the heart of the

Huguenot country. Frequently the towns and manor houses closed their gates to her, but she pitched her camp wherever she could find quarters, set up a portrait of the King, convoked the notables of the district, and harangued them on their duties. Alarmed or indignant at the approach of "the new Jezebel," as they called her, the Huguenots came nevertheless to her summons, listened to her appeals, and were impressed in spite of themselves by her intrepidity. She was nowhere molested or insulted. She accomplished, it is true, very little, but that little consoled her.

Her greatest ordeal was to be separated for so long from her son. As she approached the end of her journey, and felicity was once more in sight, she ventured to congratulate herself. "I have finished my work and, in my humble opinion, I have made many people liars and accomplished what was considered impossible. . . . In ten days I shall be in my dear France and in the town where I shall see the dearest thing I have in this world." She claimed her reward and begged the King to meet her in Lyons.

The King had none of her love of travel or movement. He had settled in Paris for life. He was, moreover, engrossed in business, in suspicion, in cares, in disgust, in his daily laborious routine of disillusionment and doubt. Nevertheless, he paid her the tribute of suspending his affairs and his fears. "We must resign ourselves to going to Lyons," he wrote to his chargé d'affaires, "for the good woman wishes it, and she writes me too urgently to refuse. . . . Adieu. I am in bed with fatigue, having just come from a game of tennis." When Catherine reached Lyons, however, she learned that the King had been gravely ill and that his life had been despaired of, although the crisis was over. But the end of her journey was not to be such a mockery of all her efforts. On her return to Paris she found him fully restored to health and beginning to recover his confidence in her. That was the essential condition of health; he could not live without it. She looked forward to a new lease of life. On her arrival she was met by the Parlement and the people with demonstrations of gratitude and respect. People paid tribute to her conscientiousness, her public spirit, and her perseverance, but no one carried congratulation so far as to suggest that she had settled the troubles of the country.

The years of truce were, in fact, a period of gestation, of internal travail, and of preparation for a renewal of the struggle, but on a new and far more fundamental basis. The League, defeated by the States-General, the King, and the indifference of the country, recognized the necessity of broadening its appeal and agitating issues more vital than religion if it was to secure general support. Altering its tactics, it identified itself with the popular unrest, fomenting and exploiting it. Since the States-General, the demand for relief had begun to mount in all parts of the country. During the last weeks of her journey she learned of riots in Rouen and risings of the peasants in Lower Normandy. On her return she went to Normandy to investigate. She sent urgent warnings to her son: "I beg you emphatically to command your financiers to provide you with a fund for your assistance without crushing your people, for you are on the eve of a general revolt, and anyone who tells you the contrary tells you an untruth." This movement, spontaneous in origin, was promoted and exploited by the nobles and the League; but the people, once aroused, outgrew their control. The peasants, indoctrinated with the new principles of liberty and resistance, applied them not to the King, who was distant, but to the landowners, who were near. In Brittany, Auvergne, and Dauphiné, they attempted to form their own leagues.

This spreading unrest was reflected, intensified, and propagated by the pamphleteers. The ideas broached in 1574, premature and partisan then, were taken up after 1576 by a growing and miscellaneous group of writers, whose common aim was to demonstrate the necessary conflict between absolute power and the popular will. The public which they reached was also growing and miscellaneous. A dialogue demonstrating the theory of popular sovereignty was dedicated to Bellièvre, the Superintendent of Finance; and this literature was read at Court with the complaisance with which a doomed regime that has lost even the will to react reads the works that pave the way for its destruction. The King made no attempt to censor them, merely inspiring replies by his own pamphleteers, and carrying his indulgence so far that it was difficult to say where his liberalism ended and his weakness began. The avidity of the public for this literature was such that booksellers prepared lists of recommended reading; and the titles of the most popular pamphlets in these years of economic crisis and political ferment were an index to the times: a *Remonstrance to the States of Blois*, a *Secret of Finance*, a *Reply to the Maxims of Machiavelli* (the King was an ardent reader of Machiavelli), an *Ecclesiastical History*, a re-edition of the *Vindiciae contra Tyrannos*. But of all, the financial studies were the most eagerly written, bought, and discussed.

Never before had the contrast between abject poverty and insolent luxury been so glaring. This familiar phenomenon of decadence, steadily deepening the breach between the classes and increasing tension along the whole social scale, reached its culmination at Court. Condemned to chronic insolvency, the King squandered money defiantly, with the prodigality of the poor and the improvidence of the doomed. He spent from policy for pleasure, and for pleasure from despair, so that, to preserve appearances, his expenses attained ruinous proportions. A portion of this enormous outlay was devoted to public works: he embellished the Louvre, he built the Pont Neuf, he began the reconstruction of old Paris—a wilderness of squalor in which the *hôtels* of the great stood out in isolated grandeur—into a noble capital; but the bulk of his inflated fortune was lavished on favourites and dissipated in frivolities.

The financiers themselves were almost forgotten in the popular hatred of the "Mignons," who monopolized the royal bounty, and who represented a new type of parvenu. Of obscure extraction, some of them gently born, others of humble origin, glorying in their frizzled hair, their diminutive caps, their enormous starched ruffs, and looking, as one writer said, like the head of Saint John the Baptist on the charger or, as unlettered people preferred, like the *têtes de veaux* in the butcher shops, they were an inexhaustible theme for popular ridicule. Their passage through the streets was the signal for sly whistles and an impertinent peeping, a long jeering cry of *piou piou*, that heralded their comings and goings, and one day, at the

Foire Saint-Germain, the King and his friends found the students parodying them in paper ruffs borrowed from the butcher shop. Braving derision and courting contempt, they made a point of provoking everyone—the public which was fleeced to support them, the old nobles whom they superseded at Court, and even the royal family. Alençon, Marguerite, Catherine herself, preferred to avoid them. Friction, quarrels, insults, sudden death, were part of their code. Desperate duellists, combining extravagant daredevilry with piquant effeminacy, young, cynical, craving life and contemptuous of it, they consumed themselves in a meteoric flash: none lived to thirty, and most of them met violent ends. The King mourned them tenderly, erected costly monuments to their memory, preserved their locks, and replaced them with fresh faces. But the Mignons, ephemeral and fantastic, were a permanent phenomenon.

In 1579 another civil war—the seventh—flared up, blazed for six months, and flickered out in the "Paix de Fleix" (November 1580) which reaffirmed the previous peace. Contemporaries compared it to a straw fire. The Protestants refused to rise; the occasion of the war was so futile that the campaign was known as the "Guerre des Amoureux." The civil wars had become by now a periodic but unimportant disturbance compared to the fundamental travail which consumed the country. The issue was no longer the religious question but the relentless progress of political and social disintegration.

To that process seventeen years of civil war had contributed a fertile sediment, a rank subsoil. Chronic turmoil had created a class of permanent unemployables in the professional soldiers, the adventurous gentry, and the ruined peasantry, who could no longer be assimilated into normal life and who were a leaven of perpetual unrest. Ready to embrace, or provoke, any disorder, they rallied about every troublemaker; and in these years of ferment the principal troublemaker in the kingdom was the Duc d'Alençon. The youngest member of the royal family was the counterpart of those whom he led: they gravitated toward each other. Restless, dissatisfied, rootless, spoiled, he drifted from adventure to adventure, in aimless futility, drawing the dregs of the civil wars with him. In spite of his princely apanage, he fell out again with his brother, fled from Paris, instigated the seventh civil war, pacified it, and flung himself into Flanders as the champion of the insurgents there, captured two towns and disgusted his allies, returned to France and again became a liability to his family, returned to Flanders and resumed his hectic activities, varying them with a farcical courtship of Queen Elizabeth, and provoking the retaliation of Philip II in France. The international ambitions of the Duc d'Alençon finally culminated in a resounding collapse. After the failure of an attempt to capture Antwerp by treachery he returned to France and died at Château-Thierry in June 1584. His life had been a futile extravaganza; his death was a decisive calamity.

The King was childless. The heir presumptive to the throne was, therefore, the first Prince of the Blood, Henri de Bourbon. Sending for Duplessis-Mornay, the minister of the King of Navarre, the King took a step of extraordinary consequence. "Today," he said, "I recognize the King of Navarre as my sole and only heir. He is a prince of good birth and good parts. I have always been inclined to like him and I know that he likes me. He is a little sharp and choleric, but at bottom a good man. I feel certain that my disposition will please him and that we shall agree very well." This was not a confidential communication. Several days later, the King expressed himself even more positively to the Provost of the Merchants. "I am highly pleased with the conduct of my cousin of Navarre," he said. "There are those who are trying to supplant him, but I shall take good care to prevent them from succeeding. I find it very strange, moreover, that any dispute should arise as to who is to be my successor, as if it were a question admitting of doubt or dispute." These statements were made with full knowledge of the storm which they would arouse; nor was it long in coming.

The prospect of the succession passing to an heretical prince fanned the smouldering fanaticism of the Catholics into flame. But who were these fanatical Catholics? Perhaps the only pure zealots were the Jesuits. The shock-troops of the Papacy recognized that the hour for which they had been held in reserve had come. If France was to be retained, if the nation that held the balance of ecclesiastical power in Europe was not to be lost, if fifty years of pressure and subsidies were not to be wasted, a supreme exertion was required. Though its missionaries launched a crusade to resuscitate the League, they soon discovered that some issue more burning than religious zeal was needed to win the French masses.

The League had been abolished by royal decree in 1577. It succumbed, however, not to a decree, but to inanition. Defeated by the indifference of a country too war-weary for fanaticism, it subsided and blended with the economic and political unrest of the country, but only to find itself submerged and dissolved in a ferment too large and diffuse to be grasped and controlled. The task which the Jesuits now undertook was to harness and organize the vast motive power provided by this social unrest, to divert it into a new League, to amalgamate it with the religious issue, and to place it at the service of the Church. Singular anomaly, and yet perfectly normal in times of transition: the Jesuit became the apostle of liberty; the missionary of Papal autocracy became the fomenter of rebellion; the preacher of blind obedience became the champion of popular rights and democratic independence. To such a pass had the Church come that it could survive only by the tactics of self-contradiction, by grafting life upon death, and by yoking, in the monstrous alliance of a hybrid Holy League, the forces of reaction to the forces of revolution.

But if the Jesuits were the only pure zealots, there were other fanatical Catholics whose spirit was equally uncompromising but whose motives were more mixed. Three months after the death of the Duc d'Alençon, the first steps to organize the Catholic reaction were taken by a group of five persons—the Duc de Guise, his brothers the Duc de Mayenne and the Cardinal de Guise, an agent of the Cardinal de Bourbon, and Monsieur de Sennecey, who had been the President of the Nobility at Blois. They met at Nancy to lay the basis of a new league. The meeting was fruitful: it convinced them of the impossibility of reviving the League without broadening its scope and of

the futility of any movement exclusively confined to promoting the interests of the aristocracy and the clergy.

On the last day of the old year (December 31, 1584)
the Holy League was born. The same persons who had
met at Nancy a few months before assembled at Joinville
to incorporate themselves and to prepare a manifesto.
There was one important new member, the Spanish ambassador. The scope of the League was broadened to include the interests of Madrid. The extirpation of heresy
in France and Flanders, a guarantee that no enterprise
would be tolerated in France to the detriment of Spanish
trade with the Indies, and a pledge that the alliance of
the French Crown with the Porte would be renounced
were written into the articles of association, in return for
which Philip II pledged himself to bear the expenses of
a war to extirpate the Huguenots. The recognition of
Spain lent the League the dignity and the pretensions of
a sovereign power. The remaining articles, specifying
that the heretical Princes of the Blood were excluded
from the succession and recognizing the Cardinal de
Bourbon as the legitimate heir to the throne, implied the
same attribute. This private Franco-Spanish alliance was
incorporated in a secret treaty. Two months later, the
League published a manifesto in which it posed as the
champion not only of the Catholic faith but of a people
oppressed by taxation.

The King replied by a declaration which was an appeal
to public opinion. Although he condescended to argue,
the manœuvre was both politic and effective. He riddled
the logic and derided the public spirit of the League,
which complained of popular distress, on the one hand,
and demanded a renewal of war, on the other. He made
an eloquent plea for peace, pointing to the gains which
had been made since the last conflict. As the crowning
argument, he emphasized the fact that he had taken advantage of the peaceful condition of the past few years
to relieve the taxpayer of burdens amounting to 700,000
livres and had already begun on his own initiative the
reforms so urgently demanded. The tragedy of the situation was that this was true. With all his reckless extravagance, Henri had not been insensible to the signs of the

times and, in an access of economy, he had instituted, among many minor privations, one major reform of genuine public spirit—the abolition of the sale of public office. But the revenue which he sacrificed from this source had been recouped by the taxation of the clergy, which was one of the crying grievances of the League.

The force of this appeal to public opinion was immediately manifest. The League replied by taking up arms.

"My brother," the King wrote to Henri de Navarre, "this is to notify you that, whatever resistance I have made, I have not been able to prevent the mischievous designs of the Duc de Guise. He is in arms. Be on your guard, and make no move. I have heard that you are at Castres for the purpose of conferring with my cousin the Duc de Montmorency. I am very glad of this, so that you may provide for your affairs. I shall send a gentleman to Montauban to advise you of my will. Your good brother, Henri."

The mobilization of the league confirmed the friendly understanding between the King and Henri de Bourbon. The logical result of the crisis was that Henri III should turn to the Huguenots for support. He shrank, however, from a step which was repugnant to his religious convictions and which would infallibly precipitate the conflict he was resolved to avoid. Henri de Navarre realized that sooner or later their alliance would become necessary, and he made his preparations in expectation of the call. But the call never came.

Nevertheless, if the rise of the League produced no immediate change in the position of the Protestants, it affected the whole future development of the movement. The succession to the throne naturally made the King of Navarre more accommodating, and the party followed his lead. Henceforth it was to the interest of the Protestants to support, instead of opposing, the Crown, and the result was that their polemics, their agitation, their attacks on the monarchy subsided. Quietly, imperceptibly, a momentous reversal of position took place. The revolutionary principles which their agitators initiated in 1574 were allowed to lapse and, as they had already taken root in the thought of the time, they went by forfeit to their opponents and were appropriated by the League. While the Catholics became the subversive party, the Protestants developed into the staunchest supporters of the monarchy. In this they reverted to their original habit: Calvin had always preached submission to the civil power, and only the stress of circumstances had forced them to depart from his tenets. Circumstances compelled them to return to them, and the religious element triumphed over the political radicals in the party. The promise which had loomed so large, the pregnant impulse to transpose the spirit of free inquiry from religion to politics, the groping thought, the pioneer experiments, the capacities of evolution of the Protestant movement, were checked and withered by the appearance of the League; and this miscarriage was the major triumph of the Sainte Union.

The mobilization of the League revealed, with startling swiftness, the advanced state of disaffection of the country. When, in reply to the appeal of the King to public opinion, Guise began to assemble troops, to concentrate munitions, and to send for mercenaries in Switzerland and Germany, the verdict of public opinion was drowned in the din of arms. Normandy, Picardy, Brittany, and Burgundy rose, and the royal governors of Bourges, Orléans, and Lyons went over to the League. Guise seized Toul and Verdun and narrowly missed Metz. The event was upon it. The King, surprised and unprepared, applied himself with feverish activity to emergency measures. In Paris, where a house-to-house search was conducted to ascertain how many suspects had answered the call of the League, it was estimated that some six thousand artisans had responded. The police were overhauled, the district lieutenants were dismissed, and new men, chosen among property-holders who would have a personal interest in maintaining order, were sworn in. The King doubled his precautions for his personal safety. He was dismayed by the spread of defection even to his own household, and when one of his favourites insinuated that Catherine favoured the House of Lorraine, the attempt to shake his confidence in his mother affected him like a betrayal.

At the first hint of trouble, Catherine had taken to the road in search of the leaders of the League. They eluded her, pleaded excuses, avoided a meeting. She toiled after them until she was overcome by a complication of ailments—gout, cough, ear-ache, foot-ache, heart-ache. Barely able to stand and leaving her bed only long enough to have it remade, she would not admit, however, that she was ill. Her only ailment was her inability to negotiate. Finally, the Cardinal de Bourbon allowed himself to be inveigled into an interview. She embraced him and he broke down. With tears in his eyes, he admitted that he had embarked on an ill-considered adventure. Every man, he said, must commit one folly in his life, and this was his, but he had acted, he insisted, in pure zeal for religion. She drew him out, searching for his true intentions, but she discovered none. The Cardinal, like his brother, Antoine de Bourbon, was a nonentity, pliable to any influence, and for the moment so completely subject to hers that she regretted having an influence. The Duc de Guise followed the Cardinal, a harder antagonist, and one who immediately placed her on her mettle. His intentions were shrouded, shifty, and unfathomable. When she pressed him for explanations, he answered coldly or, as she expressed it, only half-talked; cornered, he made excuses; and on one occasion he admitted frankly that "he did not know what devil plunged him into this, and that he wished himself well out of it." She met the leaders of the League at a moment when their morale was wavering. Despite the first rapid blaze of revolt, they were uncertain of carrying the country with them, and they expected an alliance between the Protestants and the King.

But it was too late to draw back. Twenty-seven thousand men were concentrated at Châlons. The only solution was, by an overpowering demonstration of force, to compel the King to come promptly to terms. Accordingly, Guise worked on the fear of a mother defending a helpless son and imbued her with a sense of defeat, which she communicated to the King. Catherine negotiated for three months and finally capitulated. On July 7, 1585, the Treaty of Nemours was concluded. The terms imposed on the Crown by the League—the proscription of heresy, the repeal of all preceding edicts of pacification, the banishment within six months of all Protestants who refused conversion, the cession of cities of security to the League, and the payment of its troops by the Crown—were as humiliating as those dictated by the Protestants ten years before. Catherine regarded them merely as one more compromise, but the King declined to see her for three months.

The swift and sweeping triumph of the League might have been expected to cause unalloyed satisfaction in Rome. But a remarkable character now occupied the See of Saint Peter. When the League was first formed, Monsieur de Nevers was invited to join it. Although an ardent Catholic, he felt scruples about entering an association which involved a conflict between his loyalty to the Church and to the Crown. In this dilemma, he consulted the then reigning Pope, Gregory XIII. The reply was a memorandum which endorsed the League and encouraged Nevers to join it, but which eluded the crucial question— the right of bearing arms against the King. In private, however, the Holy Father confided to Father Mathieu, the courier of the League, a few observations which were transmitted to the Duc de Nevers for his guidance. "The Pope does not approve any attempt on the King's life, for that cannot be done with a good conscience. But if his person could be seized, and those removed from about him who are the cause of the ruin of the kingdom, and if other men could be assigned to keep him in check and to give him proper advice and compel him to follow it— this the Pope would approve. Countless evils might thus be avoided, which will materialize if the King continues in his present course and is so ill-advised as to take sides with the heretics in opposing the Catholic princes. This he seems intent upon doing, and in that case he will be followed by a good part of the Catholics." These verbal assurances failed to satisfy the Duc de Nevers, who applied to the Pope for a bull or brief expressly authorizing the proposed course of the League. Naturally, no such permission was forthcoming. The Duc de Nevers would not let the matter rest, and in the spring of 1585, while the negotiations between the League and the King were in progress, he travelled to Rome to consult the Pope in person. On his arrival, he met with a great change. Gregory XIII was dead, and his successor, Sixtus V, was a man of independent and unequivocal views and outspoken habits. The first audience which the Duke had with the new Pontiff occurred after the conclusion of the Treaty of Nemours. The Pope immediately brought up the question of the League. "I am convinced that conscience is your only rule of conduct," he said, "and that you have no regard for anything else than the glory of God and the preservation of the Catholic, Apostolic, and Roman Religion. But in what school did you learn to form parties against the will of your legitimate sovereign?" Nevers rose from his knees in astonishment. "Most Holy Father," he exclaimed, "whatever has been done has been with the King's consent." The Pope corrected him sharply. "You warm up very fast. I supposed that you had come to me to hear the voice of your father and to obtain his advice and to follow it. Instead, I see that you have the same temper as all the members of your association. You cannot endure correction. You condemn all who do not agree with you. Believe me, the King has never consented sincerely to your leagues and your bearing of arms. He may be compelled to dissemble, for fear of greater evils, but he is bound to consider you his enemies, and enemies more cruel and dangerous than the Huguenots. I greatly fear that matters will go so far that, Catholic though he is, the King will be compelled to turn to the heretics to free himself from the tyranny of the Catholics." Swept on by a subject which lay close to his heart, the Pope pursued it at great length. At one moment, he apostrophized his predecessor. "O Gregory XIII, O Gregory XIII," he exclaimed, "how much harm you have done in trying to do good! Your soul answers today before the bar of God for the desolation of France and all the blood which will be shed there." As for the religious zeal of the leaders of the League, that was mere cant: "Every one of them wishes to become, not a better Christian, but a greater power. A hundred ambitious men, all seeking to be kings, and since they cannot all rule so mighty a State as France, trying, at least, to tear it apart and find a fragment on which to settle and set themselves up as mimic kings. Poor France!" the Pope concluded. "Everyone has designs upon her, everyone racks his brains to ruin her. But I love France. The Holy See owes to her its splendour and its defence, and the Popes cannot be too watchful in seeing

to it that the first crown in Christendom remains intact
upon the head of those whom God has elected to wear it."

That the Pope should distinguish between secular and
ecclesiastical authority was undoubtedly a remarkable
precedent, but it was without consequences. The personal
views of Sixtus V, sane, conscientious, honest, and independent as they were, were powerless against that force
which compels every member of an institution to think
as the institution thinks. The League expressed the true
sense of that immutable organism more truly than the
Pope. The League was governed by the dictates of self-
preservation; and with the frenzied strength of the mad or
the dying, after imposing itself on the Crown, it bent the
Papacy as well to its will.

The Duc de Guise pressed his friends in Rome to solicit
the prompt publication of a bull, already promised by
Gregory XIII, excommunicating the King of Navarre and
the Prince de Condé. This measure had the support of a
majority in the Sacred College and, being aimed against
heretics, could not be reasonably refused by the Pope.
Guise expected much from it, as he explained to the
Spanish ambassador. Should the King attempt to repeal
the edict proscribing the Protestants, the Papal excommunication would legitimize an insurrection against him;
and thus, at one stroke, the King would be secured against
relapse and the Pope would be bound by his own precedent to countenance even the seditious activity of the
League. The calculation was shrewd but for one fact: it
assumed that a profound moral effect would be produced
by the excommunication. The bull appeared, in September 1585, signed by the Pope and twenty-five Cardinals
—a corporate act—and produced the shock of an anach-
ronism. There are terrors whose effect depends upon
their never being produced. Henri de Navarre held it up
to the ridicule of Europe by inspiring a counter-excom-
munication of the Pope, which appeared in Rome and
was placarded over the walls of the Eternal City. Sixtus
V was privately delighted, observing that he knew only
two persons in Europe who were fitted to rule, and they
were both under sentence of excommunication: Elizabeth
of England and Henri de Navarre.

Nevertheless, the bull had one serious consequence.

When the King sent it to Parlement for registration, Parlement protested against the exorbitance of the Papal pretensions. "The Court cannot deliberate on the bull," the King was informed, "unless the Pope first prove the right which he claims over kingdoms ordained and established by God before the name of pope was known to the world." The magistrates threatened to resign in a body rather than to admit such a precedent, and recommended that the bull be burned in the presence of the entire Gallican Church. Measures were taken to suppress the bull; it was forbidden to print it, and a printer who ignored the order was imprisoned, over the protest of the Nuncio and the League. Nor did the spirit of independence end there. At the same time the King presented for registration an edict confirming the Treaty of Nemours, which called for the confiscation of the property of all Protestants who had not yet left France and which curtailed the period of grace for those who remained from six months to fifteen days. Parlement, once the promoter of all reactionary legislation, denounced this edict as vigorously as the bull, and in a remonstrance the like of which had not been heard since the days of Anne du Bourg, a body completely Catholic undertook the defence, on civic grounds, of the heretics. "Were the entire Huguenot party reduced to one person, there is not among us one judge," the remonstrance read, "who would dare to render a sentence of death against it, unless its solemn trial had first been held. Though they had little hope of a favourable hearing from His Majesty, the magistrates declared that they presented this remonstrance as a matter of duty, in view of the licence shown by the enemies of the State to take advantage of the piety and devotion of the King in order to cover their own impiety and rebellion.

Thus, though the material triumph of the League was unquestionable, its moral victory was far from complete. The reaction of Parlement, the running criticism of the public, the loyalty of many provinces to the Crown, the apathy of others, indicated clearly that there was a considerable body of opinion, sane, moderate, enlightened

by experience or merely wearied by it, that repudiated the
fanatical policies imposed on the King by the Treaty of
Nemours. The far-sighted course of safety for the King,
as some of his friends recognized, was to cast himself on
the nation and to identify himself with the non-partisan
elements which represented its true sentiment. As these
elements were unorganized, however, they could be welded
into cohesion only by his leadership. The solution was
hypothetical.

- 3 -

The reactionary Treaty of Nemours created a situation of
acute inconsistency and confusion. It was a declaration
of war upon the Protestants—that much was clear—but
it was also clear that the King would not abide by it if
he could find any loophole of escape. Aware of the hostility of the responsible sections of public opinion, but
emboldened by its victory, the League forced the King
into war. The Huguenots, knowing that he was acting
under compulsion, subordinated military to political tactics
and confined themselves to a defensive demonstration of
resistance. The League alone was in an unequivocal position. There, at least, the will to war, and the driving
power to wage it effectively, should have been found.
But such was not the case. The League was crippled by
the duplicity of its aims. While Guise had obliged the
King to take up arms, he was personally jealous of the
credit which would accrue to him from a successful prosecution of the war and determined to prevent it. His strategy was dictated by his ambition to neutralize the King
and by the fact that he was in the employ of Spain.

After twenty years of struggle, Philip II had not yet
succeeded in subduing the Netherlands. One governor
had followed another—Alva, Requesens, Don Juan of
Austria, the Prince of Parma—one policy had followed
another—repression, compromise, temporizing, and a com-
pound of all of them—but the spirit of rebellion was still
unbroken. The Prince of Parma, however, benefiting by
the failure of his predecessors and the weariness of the
rebels, had a more favourable balance of power to show

than any of his forerunners, and it seemed as if one more effort might be decisive. At least, the position was sufficiently favourable to free the hands of Philip II for a concerted effort against the neighbouring powers whose intermittent intervention in the Netherlands kept the rebellion alive and prevented any lasting settlement. The problem could be solved only by attacking it as a whole, and the opportunity now presented itself to deal with France and England. The first manifestation of this attempt to cope with the Low Countries on an international scale was an abortive conspiracy, in 1583, to assassinate Elizabeth and invade England. Upon the discovery of the plot, the Spanish ambassador, Don Bernardino de Mendoza, was expelled from England and transferred by Philip II to France, where he arrived in 1584, just when the League was forming, and immediately assumed its direction. He financed it, and his house in Paris became its secret headquarters. Guise, the nominal leader, took his orders and received his pay from Mendoza and the Prince of Parma. Philip II employed the League to foment civil war and keep Henri III so occupied as to preclude any temptation to intervene in Flanders, but while he was determined to control and embarrass the French Crown, he had no intention of wrecking it for the benefit of the Guises: what he wanted was a war sufficient to maintain a continual ferment in France but not so effective as to produce a decisive resolution of the struggle, and he held Guise in check by doling out funds to him so meagrely and with so many delays that Guise was all but bankrupt with debt and never in a position sufficiently solvent to act independently of his employer.

Under these circumstances, it was not surprising that the first eighteen months of the war were spent in military demonstrations which produced no decisive results. The deadlock was broken by external events. The execution of Mary Stuart (February 8, 1587) put an end to the possibility of attacking England by the shortcut of domestic conspiracies, and Philip II now planned a combined naval and military offensive. In Flanders the Prince of Parma collected materials and men; in Lisbon the great Armada began to rear its towering bulk. In France, Mendoza prodded Guise to quicken his activity. After eighteen months of shamming, of skirmishes, of demonstrations, of marches and counter-marches, the war began in earnest.

To the campaign that followed, popular common sense gave the name of the "War of the Three Henris"—a nickname and an analysis. Behind the parade of principles, it was essentially a personal struggle for survival between Henri de Navarre, Henri de Valois, and Henri de Guise. The first move was made by the King, who sent an army under the Duc de Joyeuse against the King of Navarre. The latter avoided an engagement and beat a retreat to La Rochelle. Joyeuse captured a number of small towns and luxuriously committed atrocities, not because he was savage by nature, but in order to cater to the League, as he frankly admitted. The King of Navarre met him in the battle of Coutras (October 1587) and inflicted a crushing defeat on the royal army. Joyeuse himself was killed. At last, something had actually happened, inadvertently, it is true, but irretrievably. Faithful to his determination not to antagonize the King, Henri de Navarre made no attempt to follow up his victory, but so signal a victory compelled the King to co-operate actively with the League. He took the field with an army stationed on the Loire, while the Duc de Guise led another to the east to intercept the advance of the *Reiters*.

The march of the *Reiters* was the decisive factor in the campaign, the magnetic force which brought all its mutually repulsive elements into play. The Elector Palatine had mustered eight thousand horse and twenty thousand Swiss for the support of the King of Navarre. Crossing into France, the *Reiters* advanced slowly and ponderously, their progress impeded by the rivers which intersected their route and by the necessity of methodically plundering the districts through which they passed. Guise and Mayenne hung on their flanks, harassing them but shirking an engagement because of their superior numbers. Their junction with the King of Navarre involved a long and arduous journey through enemy territory; the only secure route was circuitous and difficult, and the Germans preferred the fat pastures of the Loire. Disregarding directions, warnings, advice, they pushed on deeper and deeper into a hazardous position and found

themselves hemmed in between the armies of the King
and of the League, whose combined forces were sufficient
to match them. Had there been any genuine co-operation
between Guise and the King, an engagement must have
followed, but when the King sent orders to Guise to join
him, the latter as usual eluded them. While he manœuvred,
the King circumvented him by bribing the *Reiters* to return to their own pastures. Guise attacked them on their
retreat, at Auneau, inflicting considerable damage upon
them, but the fruits of the victory were lost. Before he
could pursue them, a royal army under the Duc d'Epernon
escorted them to the frontier. The war ended, as it
began, in a stalemate.

A stalemate, not peace. When the armies broke up and
retired to winter quarters, a troubled period set in—the
turgid aftermath of general frustration, the sick disappointment of an inconclusive struggle. On December 23, 1587,
the King made a triumphal entry into Paris, amid celebrations and acclamations that seemed, in their enthusiasm,
to be a rehabilitation of his prestige. But the acclamations
were paid, the celebrations were those of a claque. The
populace was sullen, the preachers were insolent.

If moderation could have mollified the bitterness of
partisan passion, the patience of the King might have
appeased it. But it was maintained by an agent more inflammatory than the tirades of the preachers and the
instigation of the League. For two years the government
had been on a war footing, without military results but
with financial consequences such as the King had clearly
foreseen when he first appealed to public opinion against
the bellicose policies of the League. The League had overruled him, and the inevitable result had followed. His
fitful reforms had vanished, and all the old abuses had
been restored: the venality of office had been re-established, the *tailles* had been doubled, the currency had
been debased, taxes of every description had been multiplied, and the conditions which had brought the country
to the verge of revolt in 1584 were once more approaching the danger point. The preachers and propagandists
of the League, systematically exploiting every source of
discontent with the government, championed the popular
complaints and capitalized conditions for which the

League was responsible in order not to become the victims of them. It was this pressure that made the rancour
of partisan passion irreconcilable. Nothing could mollify it
but the economic relief of the country, and this was obviously impossible without peace, to which the League
was unalterably opposed. The King made advances to
Guise and attempted to reach a personal understanding
with him. But Guise remained irreconcilable.

The League was an international entity. Had it still
been the domestic coalition which it was at its inception,
the King might perhaps have succeeded in detaching
Guise from it, but the Holy Union was merely one cog
in the great war-machine which Philip II was preparing
to launch against England. His preparations were now
complete. The Armada was ready to sail; the Prince of
Parma had assembled thirty-five thousand men and three
hundred vessels, which were to cross the Channel as soon
as the Armada had forced the English ports. To protect
this movement it was necessary to secure the neutrality of
France and to obtain Boulogne or another of the French
Channel ports as a base or a refuge. This could be guar-
anteed only by the League, as the King was bound by
alliance to England and had offered Elizabeth, in case of
attack, double the number of troops stipulated in the
military treaty of 1574. Hitherto it had been sufficient to
kindle a slow and desultory war about the throne in order
to paralyze the King, but as the climax of the attack upon
England approached, more drastic measures were required.
Mendoza and Guise laid their plans accordingly. At the
proper moment—a fortnight or three weeks before the
sailing of the Armada—Guise was to descend upon Paris,
seize the King, and put it out of his power to supply
assistance to England or to hamper the Spanish invasion.
The Armada was to sail on June 1; the move was timed
for the first weeks in May; and the first steps were taken
in March.

The Duc d'Aumale, who had petitioned the King for
the government of Picardy and had been refused, occupied the province by force and placed League garrisons
in the principal towns. Guise moved to Soissons, between
Picardy and Paris, and established his headquarters there,
to block any attempt on the part of the King to deliver

the province. In the meantime, he continued to negotiate with the King. By the middle of April, however, the situation began to develop more rapidly than either Guise or Mendoza had foreseen. Writing to Philip II, Mendoza announced that Guise was about to advance upon Paris. This plan was also part of the general offensive. The appearance of Guise in Paris was to coincide with a popular insurrection, engineered by the clergy and the *Seize*, a committee of the local ringleaders of the League representing the sixteen districts of the city. But the preliminary organization had succeeded too well: Paris was over-ripe for revolt, and the plan was no sooner broached than it threatened to produce a premature explosion; hence the determination of the Seize to advance the date of the uprising by two weeks. Now, this was a detail of some consequence: two forces were at work, which were not completely synchronized or co-ordinated: the popular impulse working from below and the Spanish pressure acting from above. Their immediate object was the same, but their eventual aim, like their motives, had a different origin: Mendoza and the League planned a *coup d'état* for the benefit of the Armada, while the populace of Paris looked for relief from intolerable economic conditions and the overthrow of the government. For the moment, these two forces coincided, but their alliance was a fortuitous one, dictated by expediency, not by a community of interest.

Guise refused to precipitate the revolt prematurely. The difference of two weeks might not be of material importance; so Mendoza thought, and he was willing to unleash the Parisian populace at once. The Prince of Parma spurred Guise with offers of assistance. Yet Guise continued to delay. As the consummation of the plan approached, he was beset by qualms. He excelled in all the covert preliminaries of betrayal, in manœuvring, in blockading, in humiliating, in undermining the King; but at the crucial moment he shrank from the patent crime which was the inevitable outcome of those preliminaries. It was the weak strain in the Guises. Dreamers of unbounded ambition, they lacked the complete ruthlessness indispensable to the steeled man of destiny; and such men do more mischief, perhaps, than unprincipled climbers.

He had two weeks in which to determine his destiny. In the meantime, the temper of Paris was rising. The Duc d'Epernon had been attacked by a mob; the royal guard, in attempting to arrest three factious preachers, had been set upon by an armed crowd: mutiny, seething beneath the surface, was already breaking through. The King, finally aroused to his danger, took precautions. Epernon posted a regiment of Swiss at Lagny, on the Marne, commanding the approach to the capital from the north-east, and occupied Rouen to control communications from the west, attempting at the same time to suborn the League governor of Orléans in order to complete the encirclement of Paris from the south. These precautions created a panic in the city, and the Seize, fearing that the government would anticipate the outbreak, sent urgent appeals to Guise to delay no longer. He decided to move, but he remained at Soissons. Meanwhile, detachments of League militiamen—veterans of the Saint Bartholomew—were sent to Paris and smuggled into the convents and the homes of his partisans. However secretly conducted, these movements could not be concealed, and they were reported by the police. The King maintained his composure in public and showed no alarm even when he was informed that Château-Thierry, Meaux, and Melun had been occupied by the League, but his cramped and impotent rage rose when he was alone. He shrank into himself but only to find emptiness and desolation there too; and to escape himself he went through the regular routine of business—audiences, conferences, Council meetings— with unflagging industry, studiously preserving an appearance of confidence and normal activity. The Council met daily, as it had met for years—that is, a dozen officials gathered about the long table, while in a corner of the room Catherine and the King sat apart, transacting affairs by themselves. She laboured by his side, but she dared not advise him, her resources were exhausted; and when the session was over, she gathered up her papers and went home. She no longer lived in the Louvre, but in a small house of her own where, in little rooms plastered from the floor to the ceiling with portraits of people she had known, she spent her leisure making work for herself. She still hoped, though she did not know how, to avert a rupture with Guise, but matters had gone too far to make such a suggestion to the King. Her efforts to keep peace had already exposed her to cruel misunderstandings. Her instinct warned her, in this emergency, to leave him alone.

Left to himself, the King reached the conclusion which his mother lacked the courage to suggest. He resolved to negotiate. It was useless, but it was useless to do anything else. The tension in Paris had reached such a pitch that to introduce troops would precipitate an explosion. Accordingly, he sent Bellièvre to Soissons again, with a message forbidding Guise to approach Paris and holding him responsible for the "emotions" which would ensue if he disobeyed. At the same time the Seize sent word to Guise that if he continued to delay he would not have a partisan left in Paris. Bellièvre returned to the capital with an evasive answer. He entered the city early in the morning of May 9 and went directly to the Louvre. About three hours later, a small group of horsemen passed through the Porte Saint-Martin and mingled with the crowds in the populous quarters surrounding the Bastille. The leader wore his hat pushed down over his face, as if to avoid recognition, and would have passed unnoticed if one of the party had not leaned forward and lifted the hat. Immediately the cry rose, "*Vive Guise!*" travelling in hoarse gusts that swelled into a steady roar of enthusiasm. He was swept along by the surging multitude, smiling, bareheaded, glancing at those above, bowing to those below, distributing a word here, a gesture there. Leading or led, it was difficult to say which, as the press milled about him, following and guiding at once, like the impatient pack unleashed for the chase. He had started for his house, but the mob steered him toward the Louvre, and he followed his manifest destiny for half the length of the rue Saint-Denis when, suddenly swerving and shedding his escort, he plunged into the tortuous lanes about the Church of Saint-Eustache and made directly for the *hôtel* of the Queen-Mother.

A dwarf standing in the window gave the alarm. Catherine, working in her closet, was so startled that her self-possession completely forsook her. Her world wavered and broke, she was face to face at last with finality; and when Guise entered the room, she was still dazed. But so was he. Neither could find a word to say. Then she began to repeat the half-forgotten formulas of life. She was pleased to see him, she said, though she would have preferred to see him at some other time. He explained his presence in various ways, and she gathered that he wished her to chaperon him to the Louvre. While he turned aside to chat with her ladies, she sent her usher, Luigi Davila, to inform the King of what had occurred and to say that she would bring Guise to him.

The King was working in his closet with Bellièvre and several other officials. The message stunned him. He buried his face in his hands and remained for some time lost in thought. Then, after questioning Davila closely, he sent him back to Catherine with a message that she should detain Guise as long as possible. He asked for advice. Ornano, the captain of his Corsican guards, offered to kill Guise as he entered, and a prelate, the Abbé d'Elbène, seconded the suggestion and produced Scripture to sanction it. The apposite text occurred to him at once. The discussion was still in progress when the coach of the Queen-Mother rolled into the courtyard. Accompanied by the Duchesse d'Uzès, she led Guise up the great stairway, lined on either side by guards with drawn swords. He bowed and smiled, but no one acknowledged his greetings. The King met them in a room adjoining his cabinet, surrounded by his undecided advisers. Unsettled himself, he began peremptorily. "I told you not to come." Guise attempted several weak explanations, which incensed the King, and finally declared that he had come by the command of the Queen-Mother. Catherine hastened to confirm this excuse, explaining that she had sent for him in order to reconcile them and to "pacify everything." Baffled, but not hoodwinked, Henri hesitated. Catherine and Madame d'Uzès advanced, enveloped him, and, drawing him toward a window, showed him the waiting crowd below. Guise pleaded fatigue and hastily bowed himself out.

Days of tension followed. Guise returned to the Louvre on the following day with an escort of four hundred armed men. His tone was firmer. Catherine attempted to discuss the restitution of the towns in Picardy, but he insisted that the scope of the question far exceeded such details: his concern was the reform of the State. With the King he had an interview in which both assumed a tone of deadly cordiality and cutting banter. The Duke asked permission to call to Paris the Archbishop of Lyons, who was known as "the brains of the League," the King acceded, and Guise remarked with a smile that he was certain His Majesty would welcome the presence of a man whom he had so often attempted to suborn. "Love the master, love the dog," Henri flung back, with an answering smile. On the following day they were so far advanced that Guise took the liberty of seating himself in the royal presence. The King turned his back on him.

On the night of May 11, Epernon's Swiss troops and a regiment of French guards marched into the city, with drums rolling and the fuses of their arquebuses glowing. Immediately the alarm spread. For weeks Paris had been listening for the tramp of marching feet; for weeks rumours had been flying that the King was in league with the Huguenots, that the son of the Admiral was approaching, that a Saint Bartholomew of the Catholics was planned. Stampeded by a nightmare, the city woke to the boom of the tocsin. The bells of Saint-Benoît and Saint-Séverin filled the dawn with the clang of aerial buoys. By five o'clock in the morning the Seize were directing the revolt. Swarms of students poured out of the Quartier Latin, scurrying to their posts. The Cité, the Université, the Evêché, the Palais de Justice, the Innocents, teemed with people building barricades. Volunteers, multiplying from moment to moment, tore up the pavements, chained the streets, piled up casks, furniture, tumbrils, sandbags, with a discipline and celerity that revealed long preparation. Crome, one of the Seize, gave the credit for the efficiency of the crowd to the preachers who had prepared the Day of the Barricades for over a year. The royal troops, in the meantime, had occupied the strategic points—the Bastille, the Arsenal, and the bridges. The Place Maubert, between the Cité and the Université, in the heart of the most turbulent quarter, was the last to be occupied—a capital error: when the troops reached it, they found themselves surrounded on three sides by a crowd entrenching itself under the direction of an experienced captain, Monsieur

de Brissac, and of Crucé, a veteran of the Saint Bartholomew. Even then it would not have been too late to disperse the crowd by a charge, but the regiment was under
orders not to attack, and for six hours it held its position
while the siege-works rose about it.

Who could sleep amid this turmoil? None but the
master of it: that Olympian feat was performed by Guise.
At his normal hour of rising he appeared at the window
of his mansion, in undress, and nonchalantly asked the
crowd what they were about. *"Eh, que fait-on donc?"* he
said drowsily, leaning out to chat with his humble neighbours with that easy familiarity which had endeared him
to the hearts of the Parisians. The crowd laughed, rising
promptly to the humour of his assumed surprise, and went
on with its work. But his surprise was only half assumed.
His own plans had remained shifting and impromptu, as
usual, and ready to be modified by circumstances, though
he had decided that, if extreme measures became necessary, the bell of Saint-Jacques de la Boucherie should be
rung as a signal to give the city over to the sword. Such
measures, however, were superfluous: the barricades
served the purpose as well; and he was glad to follow
the popular lead. Early in the morning he received the
visit of Luigi Davila, sent by Catherine as a scout with
a complimentary message. A little later, Bellièvre arrived
from the Louvre with the compliments of the King, who
desired Monsieur de Guise to understand that the presence
of the Swiss in Paris implied "no hostile intentions against
him." Bellièvre had no sooner concluded his tour of in-
spection and been shown out by the wicket gate than
Catherine herself arrived. Her delay in appearing was due
to circumstances entirely beyond her control: it had required two hours to make the crossing from her residence
to the Hôtel de Guise in a chair, for any other means of
conveyance was out of the question. Halted at every street
corner, she had been bumping from barricade to barricade,
in an agony of patience; but she was relieved to find
Monsieur de Guise in undress. With imperturbable amenity, she dwelt on the displeasure which this commotion
would cause the King and begged him to restore order.
He replied blandly that he knew nothing of what was
occurring beyond what some bourgeois had told him, and

he was after all neither a colonel nor a captain, the people had taken arms without consulting him, and to disarm them was the function of the municipal authorities. She returned to the Louvre, seemingly undiscouraged.

Even on the Day of the Barricades, even with the monarchy tottering, with her life-work crumbling about her, it was necessary to dine. She ate, in a daze, poring over her plate, studying her life. To this it had come . . . nibbling and listening, listening and nibbling . . . But the very finality of the situation stiffened her spirit. She determined to return again to Monsieur de Guise. By now, however, this was impossible. At noon the attack on the Place Maubert had begun. The royal troops had been forced to evacuate it and to fall back, first on the Marché-Neuf, then on the Petit-Châtelet, then on the Palais de Justice, then on the Cité, and finally to cross the bridges. At two o'clock the King sent Monsieur d'O with orders to recall the troops to the Louvre. There, if necessary, the last stand would be made, on the great staircase, with the Swiss performing an historic service to the monarchy and beating back the unbridled hordes of revolutionary Paris. But when Monsieur d'O reached them, they were hemmed in on all sides and their retreat was cut off by the barricades which had sprung up behind them and which were spreading under the very windows of the Louvre. Trapped, the Swiss stood their ground. Snipers shot at them from the roofs, cobblestones were hurled at them from the windows, and, as they fell, the futility of a massacre which might immortalize their loyalty but which could render no service whatsoever to the sovereign overwhelmed them. They flung down their arms and brandished their rosaries, crying in broken French: "*Bonne France!*"—"*Vive Guise!*"—"*Miséricorde!*"—"*Bons Catholiques!*"—whatever catchword came into their heads. Informed of their fate, the King sent the Maréchal de Biron to Guise to beg him to intervene and rescue the Swiss. Guise consented and, about four o'clock, unarmed and carrying only a riding-crop in his hand, he sauntered forth on his errand of mercy. Nevertheless, he reached his destination in time to save Monsieur d'O, who was about to be hanged by the crowd, and to rescue the Swiss. Their arms were restored to them, and they were marched

back to the Louvre. It was a measure of his popularity
that this act, far from infuriating the crowds, thrilled them
and redoubled his apotheosis. Toward nightfall, the situation was sufficiently under control for Catherine to accomplish her mission. Once more she worried her way
across Paris and deposited herself at the Hôtel de Guise.
The Duke was in a mood more exacting than his generous
act of a few hours before had led her to expect, as if he
regretted his rash chivalry and were determined to put
in a stiff bill for it. Before she could bargain or plead, he
presented her with an ultimatum: the exclusion from the
succession of the heretical Bourbons; the Lieutenant-Generalship for himself, to be confirmed by the States-General
meeting in Paris; the Admiralty for Mayenne; Picardy for
Aumale; Lyons for Nemours; Normandy for Elbœuf; the
dismissal of Epernon, Retz, Biron, O, and Ornano; the
abolition of the King's private bodyguard; the cession of
six cities of security; and a reduction of taxes. Though she
argued, remonstrated, and discussed, she was unable to
abate these terms; but at least they were specific terms,
not vague terrors, and she agreed to sleep on them.

The night passed in a nervous truce. There were restless brawls and much "pavement bravery," but no general
riots. After twenty-four hours of furious activity, the outcome was still uncertain, and the mobs bivouacked about
the barricades. Missing the accustomed warmth of their
beds, they were irritated by the prospect of another undecided day. The same temper troubled the lieutenants
of Guise. The release of the Swiss was a magnificent and
perhaps a politic gesture but it was a rash one, and they
determined, without consulting him, to secure the strategic
points still held by the royal troops. At dawn they drove
off the guards from the gates, seized the keys of the city,
and occupied the Arsenal and the Hôtel de Ville. The
Bastille they left unmolested. In the ecclesiastical quarter
a battalion of eight hundred seminarists and four hundred monks assembled to march on the Louvre and "fetch
Brother Henri."

It was not the panorama of Paris, glowing with thousands of campfires, patrolled by a population of insurgents, and congested with unlet blood, that offered the
most impressive evidence of the magnitude of the victory:

it was the desolation that reigned within the blockaded Louvre. The King spent the night sleeping fitfully.

The one person who was not crushed by the overpowering sense of approaching calamity was Catherine. At five in the morning, according to her usual routine, she went to early Mass at the Sainte-Chapelle; and with her remarkable facility for adapting herself to any situation, she met the barricades, on the second day, as if they were familiar acquaintances. Custom had robbed them of their terror and twenty-four hours had given them a traditional standing, and, though they were still a cause of inconvenience, she accommodated herself to them as a matter of course. She descended from her chair and edged through the narrow openings which were made for her, and the bystanders were amazed to see that "she showed a smiling and assured face, without being astonished by anything." The mob allowed her to pass, respecting her age, her fortitude, and the fact that she was the mother of a man who was about to be murdered. But her courage failed her when she was once more in the privacy of her home. She wept wearily throughout dinner. In the afternoon, the Council met at the Louvre. While the members unanimously favoured the flight of the King, she alone held out against it. "Yesterday," she said, "I gathered from the words of Monsieur de Guise that he was ready to reason: I shall return to him now and I am sure that I shall make him quiet this trouble." Accompanied by the Secretary Pinart, she traversed once more the succession of pens into which Paris was transformed by the barricades. She invited Guise to return with her to the Louvre, but as he declined, she sat down to the arguments of the night before. He cut her short. When she attempted to dicker, he referred her to the social upheaval. The mob, he said, were "mad bulls whom it was difficult to restrain." Turning to the Secretary Pinart, she whispered in his ear and sent him back to the Louvre, while she pursued the discussion with impotent tenacity.

The message which Pinart brought to the Louvre had already been anticipated. About five o'clock, the King sauntered out into the gardens of the Tuileries for a stroll which led him as far as the stables. There he mounted and with a small group of friends cantered to the Porte

Neuve, at the head of the rue Saint-Honoré, and adjoining the Tuileries gardens. The position of the palace, contiguous to the city walls at this point, and with a clear stretch of open country beyond, was his salvation. The Porte Neuve was the only one of the gates of Paris which the League had neglected to secure. The party rode through, broke into a gallop, crossed the bridge of Saint-Cloud, reached Rambouillet that night, and in the morning was safely established at Chartres.

It was two hours before the flight was discovered. Catherine and Guise were still in conference when Monsieur de Maineville entered the room and broke the news to him in a whisper. "Ah, Madame," Guise exclaimed, "I am assassinated. While Your Majesty has been holding me off here, the King has left to make me more trouble." Murmuring her surprise, she excused herself into her chair and jogged back to the Louvre. The failure to secure the Porte Neuve was a remarkable oversight. Had Guise sought to provide the King with a means of escape, he could not have done more. After the first shock of dismay, he recovered his sang-froid. He had narrowly escaped a criminal success. While Henri was strolling in the Tuileries, a crowd was on the march, led by a fiery little lawyer who swept the barricades with the cry, *"Allons chercher ce bougre dans son Louvre."* When once that mob, which Guise himself compared to a herd of maddened bulls, had broken its pens, his triumph would have been irretrievable, his destiny indelible. Was it some unconscious prompting, perhaps, which led him to neglect the Porte Neuve? However that might be, he was in a difficult situation. He was answerable to the crowd for the flight of the King. It was a severe test of his popularity. He made the rounds of the city, ordering down the barricades, and almost everywhere they came down like a pack of cards. His commands were unquestioned, and he was met everywhere by demonstrations of enthusiasm.

The ease with which Guise quelled the storm he had raised caused Catherine profound relief. What had seemed in the morning to be a revolution proved, by nightfall, to be merely a revolt which he could raise and lay at will. The world was normal again. She announced immediately that the King had left her full power to represent him

in his absence. Whatever else it accomplished, the Day
of the Barricades restored her to power.

- 4 -

Power—the power of a proxy—the power to represent
the impotence of her son—such was the final phase of
sovereignty which the flight of the King—or the flight
of life—conferred upon Catherine. Actual power had
passed, in Paris at least, to the League, and her presence
there served merely to commemorate the fact, not to
contest it. Yet she was sanguine. She remained in Paris
in order to mediate between the League and the King,
to serve as a buffer between them, muffling and deadening their friction, and to salvage what she could of the
royal authority. Hopeless as the task seemed, it was not
impossible. The turn of events had invested her with
bargaining-power. The King was at large; that is, he was
at liberty to combine with the Huguenots, the Politiques,
and the loyal elements in the country, and in that case the
League could accomplish its object only by civil war and
avowed sedition. While many elements in the League
were ready for this step, and the revolt had progressed
too far in fact to avoid it, Guise himself still shrank from
it. His peculiar scruples, his equivocal mentality, his determination to legitimize his conduct, were her salvation.
To avoid a final rupture, he was obliged to revert to
diplomacy. Here was her opportunity to neutralize his
triumph.

To any accommodation with the King, the pacification
of Paris was an indispensable preliminary. In spite of the
ease with which the barricades collapsed at the command
of Guise, the city was still heaving in the throes of an
abortive rebellion. The mobs of Paris were determined to
root out the last nests of royalism in the city. The Seize
organized a house-to-house hunt for loyalists and heretics,
terms which by now had become synonymous. The Parlement was too imposing to be attacked directly, but it was
flanked by the capture of other strongholds of the *ci-
devant* government. The Bastille surrendered by pre-
arrangement, the commander sending the keys to Monsieur de Guise, and it was promptly filled with suspects

of all stripes. The haul included some odd prizes. Among
them was Michel de Montaigne, whose mishap it was,
after a lifetime of philosophic aloofness from public affairs, to find himself in Paris on the Day of the Barricades.
After several days of detention he was released through
the intercession of the Queen-Mother, who remembered
that the King had found merit in his Essays. She was less
successful in the case of Monsieur de Pereuze, the Provost
of the Merchants, who was hurried to the Bastille by the
mob and whom Guise, at her request, promised to release.
Days passed without result—days of turmoil and transition, which witnessed a remarkable shifting and dislocation of power in Paris. The Seize constituted themselves
into a revolutionary government and summoned a General
Assembly of the People—that is, of the Catholic bourgeoisie—to elect a new Provost and various municipal
officers by popular acclamation. The success of this experiment inflamed Paris and led to its extension to every
branch of the municipal administration. At a mass meeting of the people of the sixteen districts the officers of the
Garde Bourgeoise, appointed by the King from the personnel of Parlement, were voted out and replaced by
partisans of the League, drawn not only from the ranks
of the bourgeoisie—the respectable and legally recognized
People—but from the proletariat proper. The latter car
ried so little weight, however, that the electors themselves derided them and regarded the proceedings as a
farce. In the Halles, where they were celebrated by their
trade names, they were guyed as gaily as by the bourgeois who found an inexhaustible source of merriment in
the designation by the title of *Sire*, hitherto reserved for
wealthy merchants, of tavern-keepers, *cabaretiers*, and the
like. Nevertheless, beneath the self-conscious and embarrassed raillery of a people not yet accustomed to emancipation, incredulous of it, and bewildered by the rapid
changes which they found themselves free to produce,
something serious was happening. The civil administration and the armed forces of the city came into their
hands. Though Parlement still held out in august disapproval, the subsidiary courts of justice were captured by
the Commune. Monsieur de Séguier, the Lieutenant of
the Châtelet, was forced by threats to resign his post to

a Leaguer and to join the emigration of the royalists to Chartres. The control of the police courts was celebrated as a major victory by the underworld. This democratic movement came as a surprise to Guise, who had not founded the League in order to beget mob rule, but it was too swift and strong to be checked, and he recognized the necessity, if Paris was to be pacified, of amusing the crowd with a show of popular liberty, and he lent himself to it in order to control it. He received the oaths of the new magistrates and chose the occasion to recommend them to keep the people firmly in check. At the same time, to legitimize these encroachments and to cover his own responsibility, he called upon Catherine and requested her to confirm the popular election of the Provost of the Merchants and the *échevins*. After some argument, she consented, but with obvious reluctance, and when he suggested that she herself should receive the oaths of the officers of the Garde Bourgeoise, she flatly refused. She replied with dignity that she could not endorse the nominations: the people were not made to command. "Madame," he said, "we cannot help it. These people are our masters." She stared at him, uncertain whether he were serious. If not, he was making a mistake; she at least took these revolutionary manifestations seriously and she expected him to curb them. "You promised me," she said, "that you would save Monsieur de Pereuze, if I wished it, and that you would drag him out of prison in spite of the people." "True, Madame," he replied, "and if you wish I shall go and fetch him and lead him by the hand to you, but he is better off there than in his own house." His teasing tone nettled her, and she dropped the subject. She could not determine whether he was unable or unwilling to curb the situation, but his irresponsibility shocked her. Where was this to end?

Precisely. The Duc de Guise seemed neither to know nor to care. But, besides Catherine, there were other guardians of the royal authority who were alarmed by the encroachment of the Commune. The Parlement, which was in frequent communication with Chartres, impressed on the King the gravity of these developments. A week after his flight, he made overtures of peace to Paris, offer-

ing to forget the revolt and to reform the government,
provided the city returned to its allegiance; and as an
earnest of his sincerity, he revoked thirty-six financial
edicts which had caused continuous protest in the past. As
an attempt to cut the ground from under Guise and satisfy
his popular following, this move met with some success.
The Seize wrote to the King, assuring him of their loyalty
and devotion. But their submission was contingent upon
certain conditions—the disgrace of Epernon, the renewal
of war upon the Huguenots, the lieutenant-generalship
for Guise, and the recognition of the revolutionary municipality in Paris. Guise had been quick to take advantage
of the moral impression created by the Commune and had
grafted his demands upon theirs. The King, however, distinguished: while he was willing to discuss the demands
of the Guises, which were purely personal and political,
he could not bring himself to sanction the Commune,
which menaced the principle of sovereignty. On basic
questions he was too jealous of the interests of the monarchy to compromise. He parried adroitly. The delegations
sent to Chartres by the Seize returned to Paris elated with
success. They brought a letter from the King instinct with
public spirit and contrition. He recognized and deplored
the troubles which had brought about the revolt, he admitted the mismanagement of the finances, he suffered
with his people and for them. "The people are over-
burdened with taxes," he wrote, "and as only the State can
remedy the evils from which the State suffers we have resolved to summon the States-General at Blois so that,
without injuring the rights and the authority attached to
the royal majesty, we may proceed freely, according to the
custom of the nation, to seek the means of relieving the
people, by re-establishing the government on its ancient
basis, and by reforming the abuses which have crept into
it: declaring our intention that what is decided there shall
be inviolably observed and executed hereafter, with no
possibility of altering it for any reason whatsoever. . . ."
In this counter-proposal, the King advanced the only
possible compromise, the solution which safeguarded the
principle of the monarchy at whatever cost it might involve for himself. If he were compelled to surrender any

portion of his power, he was determined that it should be neither to the Guises nor to the Commune that he would abdicate, but to the nation.

In this manœuvre, the King acted on his own initiative, although in accordance with the advice of Catherine. She laboured incessantly to reduce the demands of the League and to induce the King to meet them. So soon as the King made concessions, however, Guise raised his conditions, and in recognition of the service which the Seize had rendered him, he included compensation for them: the control of the police, the razing of the Bastille or its custody by the city, immunity from garrisoning—in short, the Commune without the name. Henri still refused to barter his birthright, and on this point he was at variance with his mother. His birthright! She had spent her life in protecting it, but now, at the end of her days, she saw no possibility of saving it except by mortgaging it. Living not in the isolation and security of Chartres, but in the thick of the turmoil in Paris, she was nervously susceptible to its pressure, and she communicated her fears to the King. She lived in continual dread of the day when what he would not yield willingly would be taken from him by force.

Against the defeatist influence of his mother, the King opposed the only resistance he could muster, a stubborn power of inertia. Encouraged by the success of Epernon, who occupied Boulogne in time to save it from an army under Mayenne, he maintained his passive resistance for six weeks, from the end of May until the middle of July. Then another influence supervened. After long being delayed by adverse winds, the Armada left Lisbon, beat up the Bay of Biscay, and surged toward its destination, hugging the coasts of France. Even at a safe distance its passage created a disturbance in the political atmosphere of France—for what distance was safe? Catherine redoubled her appeals to the King to conclude an accord with the League as a precaution against the possibility of a Spanish invasion. If he refused, and gave Guise a pretext for calling in the hereditary enemy, he was lost. He believed it his duty to yield, and on July 21 he signed the Pact of Union with the League. By this treaty he obtained one guarantee: the League pledged itself, in return for official recognition, to renounce all foreign alliances; but in the remaining articles the King capitulated completely to its demands: he accepted the exclusion of Navarre from the succession, the recognition of the Cardinal de Bourbon as his nearest relative, the lieutenant-generalship for Guise, emoluments for his family and friends, the disgrace of Epernon, the renewal of war on the Huguenots, the acceptance of the decrees of the Council of Trent, and the convocation of the States-General. The question of the Commune remained unsettled. So far as Guise was concerned, it had served its purpose.

Deeply relieved, Catherine was not satisfied. She urged the King to return to Paris, but this he declined to do. He loved Paris, but he would not return to the city that had betrayed him. His refusal hurt her like a reproach, and failing to persuade him by letter, she set out in pursuit of him. He had moved to Rouen and Mantes to be close to the coasts beyond which the Armada was filing. She argued, she pleaded. Did he not understand the position in which he placed her? "What will people say of me, my son?" she complained, with tears in her eyes. "What will they suppose when they see that your mother means so little to you? Is it possible that your nature has changed? You were always so ready to forgive." "It cannot be helped, *ma mère*," he replied with a rueful smile. "It is that bad Epernon who has spoiled me." That was the only satisfaction she could obtain from him—a bruised smile, a callous rebuff. Realizing how deeply he was hurt, she dared not be offended herself. She returned to Paris, uncertain whether his resentment embraced her as well, and fearful of fathoming him further.

But it was not for sentimental motives, nor because of her dread of what the world would say, that she insisted on wooing the King back to Paris: his return to the capital was imperative to heal the breach and recover prestige; and she induced the Duc de Guise to repeat the attempt. He met the King at Chartres and failed. But there was a dinner of reconciliation, at which the guest and the host vied with each other in acid cordiality. Conversation was nervous and unflagging, and at times their wits crossed with a long-drawn grating sound. "Cousin, to whom do we drink?" the King challenged. "That is for Your Majesty to determine," Guise replied. "Well, then," the King laughed, "drink to our good friends the Huguenots." "Well said, Sire"—and Guise laughed easily. The entire table roared with appreciation when, above the din, the voice of the King rose, hilarious and harrowing: "And to our good friends the Barricaders of Paris!" But someone with an eye for nuances noted that "at that Monsieur de Guise began to smile, but the laugh stuck in his throat, and he retired soon afterwards, brooding and nettled. He was jarred by the novel notion of the King in associating the Huguenots and the Barricaders." He had his pride, if the King had none; and the peculiar humour of the King —that high rattling laughter of the damned—lay beyond his ken.

Obviously, there could be no reconciliation between them. The Pact of Union was a stop-gap. Guise regretted, as he admitted to Mendoza, that he had not given rein to the populace on the Day of the Barricades and pursued his original plans. But Mendoza was satisfied. So far as the interests of Spain were concerned, the abortive revolt had served its purpose: France had been paralyzed for the passage of the Armada, and there was no need to precipitate a revolution.

Lurching out of the Atlantic, the Armada loomed into the Channel late in July. For eleven days the lumbering herd surged through the sea-lanes, cruising within sight of the chalk cliffs. On July 30, the battle of the century began. It was merely a prolonged skirmish. The fleet English craft blew over the sea, involving the huge formation in confusion by their very inferiority. Floundering formidably, the great abdominal galleons manœuvred in vain to locate them. One of them foundered, carrying a thousand souls crusading into the depths of the sea. Medina Sidonia reassembled the rest and sailed into Dunkirk. There, huddled into port, it might have seemed that the mighty Armada had at least found security; but there, five days later, the enemy found it out with fire. Explosions rocked the port, the conflagration rose in rhapsodical spirals, and the Armada staggered out to sea. Raked by the fire of the English, it rallied, and sailed for Gravesend. Then the skies darkened, the hurricane came up out of the west, the Atlantic itself lurched into the Channel, and for months after, phantom vessels were sighted off the coast of Ireland, of Scotland, of Denmark, roaming aimlessly in search of a Spain that had vanished in general vertigo.

When the news reached France, the King sent for Mendoza, who had already composed an account of the victory and commanded a service to celebrate it, and handed him a dispatch from Calais describing the disaster. Mendoza did his duty—he denied it. Leading him into an adjoining gallery, the King introduced him nonchalantly to a group of three hundred Turkish galley-slaves who had been cast up on the French coast. This was more than even Mendoza could dispel with a gesture, but he maintained his composure and claimed them as subjects of his master. Henri corrected him quietly. They were subjects of his ally, the Sultan, and having been cast up on French soil, they had recovered their liberty. It was his way of informing Mendoza that he proposed to resume his own freedom of action. The Armada had passed.

The Armada had passed, and with it that incubus of fear—of phantom fears—which had weighed on France so long and precipitated so many disasters. Relieved and invigorated, the King began to assert himself. He dismissed his Council. The veterans of the past—Cheverny, Bellièvre, Pinart, Villeroy, Brulart—were discharged and replaced by unknown men whom he chose for their reputation of integrity. The significance of this move was apparent only to the practised eye. Catherine felt it immediately. All the men through whom she could influence him were gone. It was as if she herself had been dismissed. It never occurred to her that she herself might be to blame for it. Henri, in fact, had never forgiven her for persuading him to capitulate to the League. She had wronged him too deeply. He was surfeited with failure, and she had nothing else to offer. In self-preservation, his first move was to drop the pilot, whose course had consistently misled him, because it was consistently negative.

- 5 -

A change of Council might mean little in itself, but it was a political gesture, a token of reform. The retiring officials had so long been associated with the corruption of the Crown that they had become identified with it in the public mind; and in cleaning his house the King was preparing it for the imminent meeting of the States-General. If the nation was not to invade the house as master, it was essential to welcome it as an ally, and in the weeks preceding the convention Henri went to great lengths to secure its confidence. The fortunes of the monarchy were in the balance: the embryonic revolution hatched in Paris might be nursed or stifled by the States, and in either case reform would decide the issue. To anticipate it, he bound himself in his letters of convocation to observe inviolably the decisions of the deputies. The same pledge, however, had been made to the States of 1576, and nothing had come of it but a monumental accumulation of voluminous *cahiers*, which had been shelved and forgotten. The country was disgusted. The League, in the meantime, launched a campaign to carry the elections and control the Assembly. In 1588 it was in a far better position to succeed than in 1576, for in twelve years it had identified itself with the movement for political and financial reform, and had something approaching a programme to offer the country. The race between the King and the League to dominate the Assembly lent uncommon importance to a body which had already shown signs, in 1576, of asserting its own authority and limiting that of the sovereign. It was now in a position to arbitrate.

The opening session, on October 16, in the great hall of the château of Blois, was an occasion, therefore, of peculiar gravity. A pregnant sense of responsibility, and not the pomp and circumstance that accompanied the confrontation of the Crown, the League, and the nation, lent the occasion its uncommon solemnity. But the pomp and circumstance visualized the dramatic impact of the meeting. At the royal session, it was not the King who was the focus of attention but the Duc de Guise, who as his Grand Master sat directly below the throne, surveying the assembly and conducting it like a maestro. The King, seated above him with his wife and his mother, was a secondary figure. But there was a third protagonist, more important because impersonal, marshalled in the background—the shadowy mass of deputies, rising tier upon tier, awaiting their opportunity to mould the history of France and weighing their responsibility to the future for what, in that pregnant session of 1588, they did or left undone.

The King made the first advances. He stated his own position. "This session of the Estates," he said, "is a remedy to cure the maladies which long lapse of time and neglect of the ordinances of the kingdom have allowed to take root in it, and to re-establish the legitimate authority of the sovereign, instead of shaking or diminishing it, as certain ill-advised or ill-willed persons, disguising the truth, have attempted to make you believe." As the great majority of his audience were partisans of the League, he reaffirmed his intention of observing the Pact of Union and his determination to exclude the heretical princes from the succession. His next statement created a sensation. "By my holy Edict of Union," he continued, "all other Leagues cannot be tolerated under my authority and are formally contrary to it: for all leagues, associations, practices, schemes, intelligences, raising of men or money or acceptance of the same, either within or without the kingdom, are acts of the King and, in all well-regulated monarchies, crimes of lese-majesty, without the permission of the sovereign. Certain great personages of my kingdom have made such leagues and associations, but, manifesting my accustomed goodness, I consent to overlook the past; but as I am bound, and all of you as well, to preserve the royal dignity, I declare here and now for the future, after the conclusion of the laws which I shall have decreed in my Estates, that those of my subjects who do not abandon such leagues or who participate in them without my permission shall be attainted and convicted of the crime of lese-majesty." The Duc de Guise paled. The attack was as unexpected as it was abrupt, and it was with difficulty that he controlled himself until the end of the session. Ignoring the commotion he created, the King addressed himself to the nation. "I wish to bind myself by solemn oath, on the four Gospels, and all the princes, seigneurs, and gentlemen assisting me in this office, and all the deputies of my Estates, to observe whatever I shall have decreed in this Assembly as sacred laws, without reserving to myself the right to depart from them in the future for any cause, pretext, or occasion whatsoever. . . . If it seem that in so doing I submit too willingly to the laws of which I am the author, and which in themselves dispense me from obeying them, and that by this act I render the royal dignity more narrow and limited than my predecessors, it is in this that the generosity of the good prince appears . . . and it will suffice me to reply with that king to whom it was objected that he would leave the monarchy to his successors lesser than he received it from his fathers, that he would leave it much more durable and assured."

The speech from the throne created a favourable impression on the Assembly—an added reason why the Duc de Guise could not allow the attack on the League to pass. At the conclusion of the session, he consulted his brother the Cardinal de Guise and the Cardinal de Bourbon. The printer, who had already received the royal address, was ordered to delay setting it in type. On the following day the Cardinal de Guise and the Archbishop of Lyons called on the King and urged him to delete the offensive passage. They represented the danger of publishing so impolitic a speech, which had already outraged the Leaguers in Blois, and which would create an even worse impression in Paris. They threatened him with the withdrawal of a portion of the deputies, and precisely the most important portion, the deputation from Paris. They indicated what that meant. The deputation from Paris was solidly pro-League and contained many veterans of the Barricades. The Seize were prepared for any extremes. Had they not already appealed to the other cities of France to set up municipal governments and threatened those who refused with a rupture of commercial relations? Had they not prepared a programme for the States designed to secure a more popular form of government? That programme contained some very inconvenient questions. "Is it not the States that give to the Kings whatever power and authority they have?—Why should what we resolve and decide in this assembly be controlled by the Council of the King?—

The Parliament of England, the Estates of Sweden, of Poland, and of all the neighbouring countries being assembled, what they resolve and decide, their Kings are bound to observe without changing anything. Why should the French not have the same privilege?" Was it wise to antagonize the men who could not only frame such questions but support them with barricades? Catherine, who was present at the interview, advised the King to yield. He followed her advice, and the speech appeared emasculated of any disrespectful allusion to the League.

To obliterate the unfortunate impression, the King administered the oath of allegiance to the Pact of Union to the Assembly as a whole. As a corollary to it, the deputies demanded a united pledge by the King and the Assembly to exclude Navarre from the succession. The King agreed in principle, but he requested a delay "to warn the King of Navarre of his duty, so that he may not complain of having been condemned without a hearing." This subterfuge infuriated the fanaticism of the deputies, and when a rumour spread that the King was only waiting for a vote on subsidies to dismiss the Estates, the emotion of the Assembly took a menacing form. The fundamental, the constitutional question, was discussed *in camera,* "whether they should approach the King with resolutions or appeals: that is to say, whether he should be compelled to pass whatever they resolved, or whether, following the ancient form which had always been observed, they should employ humble remonstrances." The Third Estate formulated the question, whether the Assembly should constitute itself the legislative power in the kingdom and transform the Crown into a limited monarchy, and submitted it to the two privileged Orders, along with the programme of the Seize as evidence that the question was not academic but could be enforced. The fact that the proposal originated in the Third Estate and had a distinctly democratic character prejudiced it in the eyes of the Clergy and the Nobility. Though they considered it, they recommended postponing the question, since the King had voluntarily bound himself to observe the decisions of the Assembly, and reserving it in case of need. This opinion prevailed and it prevented the major issue of the authority of the States from being debated and decided by an Assembly which was profoundly penetrated by the sense of its own organic power.

This was the most critical moment of the session. The domination of the Assembly by the League had precipitated a crisis only to adjourn it. The basic constitutional issue was useful to the League as a means of bringing popular pressure to bear on the King, but the upper classes had no intention of satisfying the demands of their popular following. United in religious fanaticism, they were profoundly separated in political aims. Nevertheless, the question had been raised, and as political pressure it welded the Assembly in promoting the aims of Guise and the aristocratic element in the League. The Assembly unanimously demanded the resumption of war on the Huguenots. The King temporized and manœuvred, in vain. At this juncture the Duke of Savoy attacked the Marquisate of Saluzzo, the last Italian possession of France, and Henri appealed to the patriotism of the Estates and attempted to divert their bellicose ardour from a domestic to a foreign war; but Guise unmasked the manœuvre and frustrated it. The whole latent revolutionary pressure of the League, disseminated throughout the Assembly and legalized by it, was brought to bear on the King to force a new civil war. As a last resource, he fell back on the financial question. He accepted the war, provided the Estates paid for it. Once more, as in 1576, he produced a stalemate which altered the whole situation.

Dominated by the fanatical influence of the League, the deputies at first maintained a stubborn and irrational opposition, the absurdity of which Catherine pointed out to them in an interview with their leading spokesman. "You have asked for war to exterminate heresy," she said. "If now you will give nothing to pursue it, it is as if you gave with one hand and held back with the other." The deputies finally consented to vote credits but not until certain pressing financial reforms had been conceded by the King. The first of these was a reduction of the *tailles*. There was a long deadlock. The King bargained, made concessions which failed to satisfy the Assembly, and the deadlock continued. Finally, in the first weeks of December, the Duc de Guise became alarmed. Elated at first by the obstinacy with which the deputies opposed the

King, he was now uneasy lest their stubbornness end by
defeating his own plans. He felt it necessary to intervene.
At a supper given by the Provost of the Merchants, he
approached them informally, painted a pathetic picture
of the poverty of the King, and begged them to relent;
but he produced no impression. The next day he repeated
the attempt and this time he pleaded not for the King
but frankly for himself. "Rupture of the States is imminent," he said. "The deputies have threatened the
King with it, and the King is himself ready for it. This
measure would be the most fatal of all. The Huguenots
alone would benefit by it; it is precisely what they want.
We must not push matters to extremes, for this would be
the most certain way to leave the Edict of Union un-
realized." But his audience remained unmoved. The deadlock continued. Suddenly the King broke it. Summoning
the deputies to the château, after a feeling speech on the
distress of the country, he said abruptly: "I grant your
requests." He was unable to finish: acclamations broke
out, cries of *Vive le Roi!* which he had not heard for
years, a din of unbounded enthusiasm. The news caused
a greater sensation in the Assembly than his attack on the
League, and a revulsion of feeling in his favour set in. So
little was needed. He prided himself on a concession which
had won him a welcome popularity. "It is true," he said,
discussing it with the delegates, "that some of my Council
are not of my opinion, and say that this is to model myself
on the Doge of Venice and to make my State half democratic. But I shall do it. . . . I believe that I shall gain
by not continuing these taxes." He hoped, at least, to gain
a respite from reform. But having obtained one, the Assembly demanded another, and a more fruitful one than
the first: the creation of a Court of Commission to investigate all the financiers, favourites, and administrators who
had handled public money, with powers to confiscate
their fortunes for the benefit of the Exchequer. After long
hesitation, the King consented.

These concessions had been made by the King in order
to obtain a subsidy from the States. The Assembly, however, continued to defer the expected compensation. It had
discovered that, without raising the issue of its authority,
it could impose its will on the King and wrest one reform

after another from him by reserving the vote on credits, and it settled down to the business of repairing the worn edifice of State with a zeal which was as indifferent to the anxiety of Guise as to that of the King. The Third Estate proposed to claim the right of armed resistance to the collection of taxes of any description, which had not been authorized by the States themselves. How far this movement of reform, gaining momentum with every concession, penetrating more and more deeply into the unsteady structure of the State, igniting more and more combustible matter, might carry the Assembly was still uncertain when, at the end of December, it was suddenly arrested.

While the public competition between the Crown, the League, and the States developed in the foreground, another conflict went on in the background. The personal relations of Guise and the King, under an outward appearance of caustic cordiality, were severely strained. Precisely when the Assembly was outgrowing the control of Guise and pursuing its own political course, the King saw in the concessions which it wrung from him only the partisan influence of the League. Since the League had dominated the Assembly and Guise had manipulated it in the beginning, the inference was inevitable that all its works were prompted, not by public, but by party spirit. The King had hoped by conciliation and concessions to make an ally of the States and a means of re-establishing his authority; instead he found them the servile instrument of an implacable rival. A treasonable movement had been legalized, in despite of the sovereign, and the King was henceforth at his mercy. His humiliation was complete and, despite his powers of dissimulation, his impotent hatred transpired. Guise was well aware of it. He had been warned, before coming to Blois, to beware of an attempt on his life, and at intervals throughout the sessions the alarm was revived, but he ignored these warnings with easy bravado, though he took his precautions. Both were on their guard, smiling, mistrustful, bland.

Here was a situation which demanded the mediation of Catherine. She went to great lengths to placate Guise. She became his confidante, she associated with him con-

tinually, she called him the staff of her old age, and she
showed him an affection which the world believed was
not altogether assumed. She was accustomed to that
slander, and she ignored it. To protect her son, there were
no lengths to which she would not go, even at the risk of
incurring a cruel misinterpretation of her motives. But
that was not the only risk which she incurred. Because
she feared Guise, she was fascinated by him. She could
not help comparing him to her son. For all her devotion to
Henri, she had reached an age at which she could judge
him impersonally, and she saw in the last survivor of her
race a congenital failure, from whom she turned with
relief to the rising sun. When she won his confidence, she
was flattered; when he treated her familiarly, she was relieved; and when he accepted her friendship with something like filial devotion, she was disarmed. Insensibly,
her feelings changed. . . . Suddenly she realized what
was happening. She saw herself on the brink of an incredible betrayal. Of all the wrongs which the Guises
had done her, this was the greatest. If the hereditary
enemy of her race could steal her affections, then his triumph was complete. But it was not too late to arrest that
calamity. She was recalled sharply to her senses when she
learned one day that the King had said that he wished to
retire and leave the government to Guise and his mother.
She was hurt. Was it possible that even Henri misunderstood her? Or—worse—that he understood? She did not
rest until she had brought about the formal reconciliation
between Guise and the King.

The reconciliation of the sick and the sound—what result could that have? A bruising embrace, obviously,
breeding fresh infection. The situation had gone too far;
the only solution was the elimination of the one or the
other. This was apparent not only at Blois, but in the
outside world. A pamphlet which appeared in the last
months of 1588 and which found its way to Court printed
what was already being said there. The author, a grandson
of L'Hospital, after analyzing the situation, blamed the
King for not being obeyed. "Nothing should be so pre-
ciously preserved by a prince as the fear and respect due
to his Majesty, for once lost, they can never be recovered

except by such things as create fear, that is, by violence and cruelty." At Blois, the same predictions were freely made. The Leaguers, when they came to the opening of the sessions, suspected an ambush and expected the States-General to be merely a trap for their extermination. But these prognostics took no account of the soul-sickness of the King. Violence and cruelty were not foreign to his nature, but they had been sated by the Saint Bartholomew. The crime of his youth belonged to another life, which he had put behind him. For fifteen years he had reigned with a moderation which had atoned for his false start in life, and it was one of the crimes of the League that its provocation pushed him to relapse into a past which he had outlived. The triumph of the League in the States left him no legitimate means of crushing it; the only alternative was violence. Yet he was too soul-sick, too demoralized by failure, too cowed by intimidation, and too passive by nature, to muster the necessary resolution. The idea haunted his mind, tempting but vain.

Guise had also begun to realize that the only solution of the situation was the elimination of the King or of himself. The warnings of plots against his life, though he made light of them, impressed him. Pressed by his friends, he mustered his resolution; but having made the decision, he relapsed into his habitual hesitation and continued to procrastinate.

It thus became a race between two men equally driven by circumstances and equally infirm of purpose as to which would anticipate the other. The suspicion, the nervousness, the friction, caused by their common state of mind, were sufficient to precipitate the catastrophe. A succession of warnings was relayed to the King. A person who had applied to the secretary of the Duc de Guise for a passport had received a remarkably indiscreet reply. "If there is no great haste," the secretary said, "I advise you to wait a little. We shall soon have changed our title and quality." An Italian actor who served the King as an informer was present at a dinner given by the Cardinal de Guise, at which a toast had been drunk to the Duke as the next King of France. Even the Duc de Mayenne sent almost daily warnings to the King that his brother was about to proceed to extremities. To the latter Henri gave at first little credit, because of the source from which they came. He suspected a brutal form of humour, characteristic of the Guises, an attempt to play on his nerves, to bully him into betraying his fears, or to provoke him perhaps into a misstep which they could turn to account. But the accumulation of warnings, and their coincidence, finally decided him to risk the indignity of self-defence. On December 18, while his mother gave a dinner to the Court, he slipped into his study and consulted three of his familiars. One of them, a magistrate, advised the immediate arrest and trial of the Duc de Guise on a charge of treason. This the King dismissed with curt common sense and a commiserating smile. Where were the guards, the judges, the witnesses, for such a farce? The Maréchal d'Aumont and Ornano, the captain of the Corsican guards, proposed assassination. The King sent for Crillon, the captain of the Royal Guards, and offered him the commission. Crillon declined it, though he volunteered to challenge Guise to a duel. Having stooped to the indignity of self-defence, the King adjourned the decision. The next day, the secret was out. Guise prided himself on the professional system of espionage with which, as Grand Master of the Household, he had surrounded the King. His friends were highly alarmed, but he attached no importance to an incident, which was a purely routine alarm. Besides, he flattered himself that he knew the King to the core of his being and could count on his cowardice. "I know him better than you do," he told the Archbishop of Lyons, who was alarmed by the hectoring tone which he assumed with the King. "The only way to hold him is by braving him. He is a King who wants frightening." His military psychology was simple, but it had served him so far very successfully in every situation in life. Life was simple, provided one were not sick-minded, and no one could suspect him of that. Mentally, morally, physically sure of himself, he did nothing. He continued to fraternize with the King, and the King was never more cordial, more carefree, more affectionate.

On the twenty-first, they paid a visit together to the Queen-Mother, who was ill in bed, chatted, exchanged sweetmeats, and cheered her by the evidence of their reconciliation. "He is a good man," Guise remarked to his

brother the Cardinal afterwards; "he has not a bad heart."
Contempt could go no further. That evening the King sent
for him and requested the keys of the castle, since he was
to leave the next day for a pavilion in the park where he
proposed to spend the Christmas holidays. He added that
there would be a Council meeting at which he begged
him to be present, early the next morning. Guise agreed
genially. At supper he found, tucked into his napkin,
an anonymous note with another and more urgent warning. He read it aloud, scribbled on it four words—the pith
of his system—"He would not dare"—and tossed it aside.
At eight in the morning, he was promptly in his seat in the
Council. He was summoned to the King's study. As he entered the passage leading to the study, he saw the King's
bodyguards. For a moment he hesitated—an old habit, immediately suppressed in the hour of his destiny—and advanced. At the door of the study he turned to look back.
A blow in the chest, a man on his legs, a knife in his loins,
made him exclaim: "*Eh, mes amis!*" He staggered, and
recovered, but another and another fell on him. "*Ah, Messieurs! Ah, Messieurs!*" He was unarmed, but his strength
was prodigious, and he kept his feet, wrestling, dodging,
gasping steadily: "What treachery! Treachery!" The King
appeared in the doorway in time to see him fall. The body
was searched. One article of value was found, an unfinished letter beginning: "To sustain civil war in France,
700,000 livres will be needed every month. . . ." It
summed up his history.

The sound of the scuffle was heard in the Council
Chamber, and the Cardinal de Guise leapt to his feet,
crying that they were killing his brother, but he was overpowered by the Maréchaux de Retz and d'Aumont, placed
under arrest, and imprisoned with the Archbishop of
Lyons. The apartments of Catherine were directly beneath
those of the King, but she slept through the uproar, un-
disturbed. With his customary consideration, the King
had reminded the assassins that she was ill and urged
them to work quietly. Early that morning she had been
awakened by a request for audience from the Duc de
Guise, but she pleaded fatigue and begged to be excused
for the day. The day was cold and gloomy, the rain was
falling in torrents, and she returned to her nap. When she

opened her eyes again, she saw the King consulting Dr. Cavriana, and heard the physician assure him that she was doing well and had taken her medicine. Seeing that she was awake, the King turned to her. "How do you feel, Madame?" he asked. "Oh, my son, fairly, fairly." She was not as sanguine as the physician. She had contracted the valetudinarian habit of mind, and she discouraged an optimism which might deprive her of sympathy. But it was not sympathy that he gave her. "As for me, Madame, I am extremely well. Excuse me. Monsieur de Guise is dead. He will be heard of no more. I have had him killed." She stared at him, without a word, and he raced on, volubly explaining himself. He could no longer bear the Duke's insolence, he said; he had forgiven one offence after another, the thirteenth of May, and all the repeated outrages that followed it, but learning that Guise was again planning to sap and undermine his authority, his life, and his State, after long hesitation, he determined to anticipate him. God had inspired him, and he was on his way now to Mass to thank Him. Any man who spoke of joining the League would meet the same fate. He was determined to relieve the burdens of the people; he would continue to hold the States; but he was equally determined that they should speak according to their station, and not with the tone of kings, as they had done. He meant to be King and not a captive and slave, as he had been since the thirteenth of May. He had imprisoned the Cardinal de Guise, the Archbishop of Lyons, and the Cardinal de Bourbon. He would renew the war on the Huguenots; he was resolved to exterminate them. The speech ran on and on. She listened in silence, wondering why he made it to her. He might have been addressing the States. He was not accountable to her, he was his own master, he had not consulted her. She no longer had any part in his life. When the flood of his speech subsided, she began to abuse him, and asked whether he had well ordered his affairs, because Monsieur de Guise had many friends. He assured her that he had. She remarked that she prayed to God that all would turn out well, and re-lapsed into silence. He left the room, as he entered it, with a buoyant composure which amazed Dr. Cavriana, who lost no time in setting down the scene for his weekly letter. As a physician, he was particularly struck by the beneficial effect of revenge on the body: the King was rejuvenated by it. He neglected to observe, however, its effect on his patient.

The States-General were in session, on that morning of December 23, and a deputy was reading a report on the alienation of ecclesiastical property, when the President of the Third Estate was informed that there was "some noise and commotion in the château, that the bridges had been raised, and that the soldiers were on guard." One of the deputies proposed to dismiss the meeting, but the Assembly voted that it was inviolable and decided "not to move from a place which was the shelter and security and a part of the body of France." A few minutes later the door opened and a crowd of soldiers invaded the hall, shouting: "Kill, kill!" crying that a plot against the life of the King had been discovered and that the guilty were in the Assembly. Some of the members fled; others protested in the name of the States. The officer in command read the names of those whom he was under order to arrest, and the five whom he designated advanced and surrendered. Among them was La Chapelle-Marteau, the President of the Third Estate, who was also the Provost of the Merchants of revolutionary Paris and the representative of the Seize. The prisoners were led out, in spite of the clamour of the deputies who attempted to accompany them, as a protest, *en masse*, but who were beaten back by the soldiers. After debating whether to leave the premises and risk being locked out on their return, the deputies dispersed.

On the next day they reassembled at the command of the King. They were met by a member of his Council who informed them that they were not to leave Blois until they had completed their labours and that the arrests did not imply any diminution of the liberty of the Estates. The Third Estate immediately resolved to test this assertion and invited the two other Orders to join it in a delegation to the King to request the liberation of their colleagues. On Christmas morning the deputation arrived at the château, but was not admitted to the King. When the Clergy insisted, an answer was sent out that it was useless to plead for their President, the Cardinal de Cuise. He was dead. The delegates of the Third Estate, fearing for the lives of their colleagues, were silenced.

The assembly continued its session, at the command of the King, but the presence of hostages in his hands sterilized its labours and arrested that movement of reform, initiative, and self-assertion which had been steadily creeping forward and encroaching with slow but sure progress on the royal prerogative. The King profited by the assassination of the Guises to cow the States by a *coup d'état* which compelled them, as he said to his mother, to speak according to their station and not with the pretensions of a sovereign body. He exploited his crime far more cleverly than Catherine had capitalized the Saint Bartholomew, and more economically: two deaths and the mere unuttered threat of others sufficed for his purpose. Fearing to jeopardize the lives of their colleagues, the deputies abandoned those decisive measures which, however meagre in themselves, were the manifestation of a new spirit, a revolutionary consciousness lurking in the Assembly, and relinquished the opportunity to mould the history of France in 1588.

Nevertheless, their spirit was not fully broken. Though their deliberations were marked by an almost servile moderation, their acts betrayed their indignation and resentment. To speed their labours, which had lasted two months without producing the credits for which the King was impatient, His Majesty commanded them to appoint four of their number to draw up their *cahiers* in conjunction with his own Council. At the same time, he suggested that it would be appropriate, at a time when some of his subjects had conspired against his authority, to insert certain clauses in their *cahiers* explicitly defining the crime of lese-majesty, in order to spread a salutary terror among those who might be tempted to forget it. The Procuror-General read this communication to the States. The Assembly listened in mournful silence, embarrassed by this public allusion to the crime of the King, and indignant that it should be asked to associate itself with it and to sanction it. As a result, the States unanimously rejected both proposals. They refused to collaborate with the Royal Council, where they were outnumbered, and maintained the principle of their independence; and they repudiated the crime of the King by refusing his suggestion, on the plea that the purpose of their *cahiers* was to present the complaints of the people. The King did not insist: he reserved himself for a major question—the grant of the subsidy. On this question the States adopted an attitude of passive resistance. When the Maréchal de Retz presented the demand of the King for a vote of 3,000,000 crowns, Bernard, one of the ablest diplomats in the Assembly, intimated on what condition it might be obtained. The Assembly, he said, was in a difficult position either to honour or refuse such a demand, since those of its members who were most qualified in finance were no longer among them. For two days the deadlock continued. Then the King lost patience. He sent another spokesman to the States who, in a speech of brutal violence, declared that their function was not to present complaints, but to vote subsidies, that they had wasted two months, and that it was high time that they discharged their duty— so glaring a revelation of the despotic spirit of the King and his cynical contempt for the nation that the Assembly was profoundly shocked and incensed. The antagonism between the Crown and the country was seen to be inherent and irreconcilable, the smouldering anger of the Assembly rose, and with it the unbroken spirit of its self-consciousness and responsibility; but the only way in which it could express it was to employ its one substantial power and refuse all financial assistance to the King. This course it adopted, and it adhered to it steadily to the close of the sessions, which it forced. At the conclusion of the States-General of 1588, the bitterness of the deputies was deeper than ever, because of the promise with which the sessions began, the progress with which they continued, and the failure in which they ended through the *coup d'état*. Yet, at the end, moderation prevailed. The valedictory was pronounced by Bernard, and his parting words were a reminder of the ruin of a country, crushed by arbitrary taxation: "If, at least, these innovations had been of some profit to Your Majesty, our complaints would be neither just nor reasonable. But, Sire, we know that the army is without munitions, the soldiers without pay, the wages of your officials cancelled or reduced, the pensions due, the *rentes* unpaid, the domain mortgaged, and the finances completely dissipated and yet it is proposed to scrape new subsidies and crops of pennies, from whom, Sire? From a poor naked vagrant, who had been waylaid and stripped of his shirt. For so one must speak of your people." An appeal, it was also a warning. There were limits beyond which the patience of the people could not be strained. The revolutionary spirit had been stifled in the Assembly; it had only begun to stir in the nation.

- 6 -

On the day after the closing session of the States, the deputies held a farewell reunion in the Hôtel de Ville. No business was discussed; it was purely an occasion of sentiment. In three months of association they had developed a sense of solidarity, a feeling of fraternity which, for the moment at least, transcended the distinctions of party, of class, of profession, which normally divided them. The feeling might be transitory but, in the moment of parting, it was intense. They felt themselves members of a common and indivisible body which had been violated, but which could not be dissolved so long as they preserved its spirit, and because the spirit was new-born and needed nursing, they met once more to prolong it, to exchange impressions, to talk for the last time of what was and what might have been. Many parted with tears in their eyes. The common impression which they carried away was, as one of them said, a sense of bitter regret "for what was past and apprehension of the perils and troubles to come."

That premonition was not peculiar to the deputies. It pervaded the atmosphere of Blois. The uneasy conviction that all was not over, that the assassination of the Guises, like a surgical operation that had miscarried, was bound to breed fresh complications, haunted the Court as well with apprehension of perils, shapeless as yet but certain to follow. No one was more vulnerable to such suggestions than the invalid, lying inactive and helpless, with nothing to do but to brood. She would not talk to her familiars, who treated her as a sick woman and irritated her with professional consolation. On Christmas Day, she received the visit of a Capuchin father, and with a stranger she felt free to ease her mind. She spoke of her son. *"Ah, le malheureux!"* she said. *"Ah, le malheureux!* What has he done? Pray for him, he needs it more than ever. I see him falling headlong to his ruin, and I fear that he will lose body and soul and his kingdom." But the Capuchin also had only professional consolation to offer. There was no consolation, and she knew it. Dr. Cavriana was concerned about her condition. All his skill and sympathy were powerless against her troubled mind. "She is agitated," he wrote in his report of December 31, "and although very prudent and experienced in the things of this world, she does not know what cure to provide for so many present ills, nor how to avert those to come." She was baffled. Peering, straining, to discover the shape of things to come, she saw nothing ahead but finality. She had spent her life in putting it off and off and off, and now it was upon her. She had lived too long.

On New Year's Day, against the advice of her physician, she had herself carried to the prison of the Cardinal de Bourbon to announce his liberation by the King. It was an imprudence. The weather was raw and blustering, the prison damp and cold, and anyone else could have performed the office. But she wished to perform the errand of mercy herself. She was rudely received. The Cardinal was bitter, senile, and irreconcilable. "Ah, Madame, Madame," he cried, "these are your tricks. If you had not deceived us and brought us here with fine words and a thousand guarantees of safety, two of us would not be dead, and I should be free." She became highly agitated and protested vehemently against so unjust an accusation, but she could not convince him. "I cannot bear it any longer!" she complained, as she left him. She took to her bed at once. The excitement and the exposure prostrated her, pneumonia developed. On the morning of January 5, 1589, she dictated her will in the presence and with the help of the King, and sank into coma. At one-thirty she was no more.

But had she ever been? Her death passed almost unnoticed. The body was buried provisionally in Blois, awaiting an opportunity to transfer it to Saint-Denis, where she had built a superb mausoleum for her husband and herself. The Seize threatened to drag the body through the streets or to throw it into the Seine if it appeared in Paris. The League preachers, and there were no others in Paris, were too busy abusing the son to notice the mother. Her obituaries returned the indifference which she always displayed for public opinion. So far as private judgment was concerned, she was mourned by three or four persons who actually witnessed her death—the King, her granddaughter Christine of Lorraine, the Grand Duke of Tuscany, Francesco de' Medici, and Dr. Cavriana. Henri wrote more feelingly of her in his official letters of announcement than is customary in such documents, acknowledging that he owed her not only the common due of nature but all the joy that he had ever known on earth. But it was Dr. Cavriana who mourned her as she would have wished to be mourned, that is, less for herself than for what she left behind her. "She died with great repentance for her sins against God," he wrote. "We all remain without light, or counsel, or consolation, and to tell the truth, with her died what kept us alive. From now on we must turn our thoughts elsewhere and find some other support. The kingdom will suffer more than is believed, and the King remains without the most faithful and necessary support that he had. God help him."

God help him. It was her last thought, and she died of it. She disappeared punctually, at the appointed moment when her saving influence lost its virtue. On the day after her death, a sinister demonstration occurred in Paris. Twelve hundred seminarists and students marched through the streets, shouting the *Dies Irae*, and brandishing torches which they overturned and solemnly extinguished when they reached Notre Dame, intoning in unison, "So perish the race of the Valois!" While the mob spent its fury in the destruction of every visible trace of her son, wrecking the tombs of the Mignons, dismantling the royal arms, smearing the royal effigies with excrement, the Seize proceeded to serious measures, constituted themselves a Committee of Public Safety, and initiated a reign of terror. The Sorbonne pronounced the French free—free, that is, of their allegiance to a sovereign who was henceforth deposed because of his violation of public faith and "the natural liberty of the Three Estates of the Kingdom." The Pact of Union itself was denounced as invalid, having been contracted with a perjurer. These academic sanctions of revolt were peremptorily enforced by the Seize. On the sixteenth, the governor of the Bastille, Bussy Le Clerc, followed by a crowd of volunteers, invaded Parlement, deposed the President, arrested the loyalist members, and led them away. The entire body rose as one man and accompanied the prisoners in protest. A spectacle yet more extraordinary than the procession of the sacred battalion filled the streets of Paris: a long parade of venerable magistrates marching, two and two, from the Cité to voluntary imprisonment in the Bastille. Charenton and Saint-Cloud were garrisoned; the artillery was brought out to reduce the Château de Vincennes; and a systematic persecution of all internal opposition began. Persons suspected of being Royalists, or Protestants, or Politiques, were tracked down in a house-to-house hunt and arrested. The royal seals were broken, in token of the renunciation of the royal authority.

Hatred of the monarch, hatred of the monarchy: they were not the same, but the transition was easy. Was the rising pressure of Paris to convert a revolt into a revolution? That question still remained in suspense. The royal seals were broken, they were replaced by new ones bearing a simple reference to the kingdom of France. The future was open. Who would mould it? Besides Mendoza, who hastened to Paris to observe and manipulate events, there were three associated but distinct claimants of power. The Sorbonne sanctioned the revolt, and deposed the King, because of the violation of the liberty of the Three Estates of the kingdom. In theory, therefore, the kingdom was opposed to the King, and the revolt derived its authority from the constitutional freedom of the National Assembly. In principle, the three Orders combined to legitimize it in the name of France as a whole; in practice, they combined to exploit it for their interests. The Nobility, which had sponsored the beginning of the movement, naturally expected to control its outcome. One by one, the Guises appeared on the scene. The widowed Duchess, with her new-born son, became the object of a cult. The "Sainte Veuve," as she was called, was greeted with ovations whenever she appeared at her window, showing the people her child; and as she made a practice of sitting there, laughing at the great ladies on their way to the Bastille to visit their husbands, her window became a shrine of popular pilgrimage. The Duchesse de Nemours followed. Then came the sister, the lame Duchesse de Montpensier—the "Fury of the League"—to limp through the streets in religious processions, to agitate, to intrigue, and to organize the situation for her family. She brought in first the Duc d'Aumale, a nonentity, then the Duc de Mayenne, who assumed command of Paris with the title of Lieutenant-General of the Royal Estate and governed with a Council of Forty, made up of nobles, clerics, and bourgeois. But this Guise government was a mere shadow. The Seize refused to resign to the Forty. They continued to rule Paris, preserving their power by terror but using it to cater to the middle classes and the masses and to satisfy those popular demands which the aristocrats and the clerics had employed as a demagogic appeal, but which the Seize, staking their survival on the people, applied in earnest. The tithes were reduced by a quarter, tenants were dispensed from paying their rent, the *rentes* of the clergy were suspended. The clergy, forced into a bankruptcy which they had foreseen for years, made a desperate attempt to recover control of the revolt. They went to extremes. They became religious. They organized parades, they multiplied demonstrations to exploit the revolutionary excitement of the people and to lash it into religious frenzy. They went further. They became disinterested. They championed the cause of the people. The preachers outbid the Seize in their compassion for the masses and their execration of the King. And they excelled them in publicity: they had the pulpit and they had the press. Of demagoguery, and scurrility, and casuistry, there were no lengths to which the clerical press did not go to win popular favour. And, indeed, the three competitors for power had one point in common: they all addressed themselves to the people as arbiter.

From this seething, inchoate, turgid mass, fused only by confusion, what would emerge? Who would mould it? What direction would it take? The pressure continued to swell, and if pressure alone could have produced revolution, the accumulated power of intolerable misery, exasperation, and need would have sufficed to beget it. But this force remained merely negative without an aim to guide it and could produce only destruction. What was needed to transform the revolt into revolution was a constructive vision. And this was still wanting. Ripe as conditions were for a violent change, the eruption, when it came, was yet premature, because there had been no conscious preparation for it. The ideas which might have developed it were embryonic, vague, and immature. A beginning had been made, but no more. The Protestants had broached and abandoned them; the League had adopted only to pervert them to its purpose. And it was the League, which fathered the revolt, that made the revolution miscarry. It could not develop, because there was no progress within it. How could it be otherwise? A revolution led by reaction was a contradiction in terms, and could produce nothing but confusion in fact. What emerged from the clouded mass was disintegration and chaos.

The reign of chaos lasted for five years. Paris gave the signal, the provinces followed. Forced into alliance with the Protestants, the King marched upon Paris with Henri de Navarre in the summer of 1589. At Saint-Cloud, on August 1, the knife of the assassin, nerved by the preachers and Madame de Montpensier, slit the life of the last of the Valois. The next five years were spent by Henri de Bourbon in wresting his heritage from all the powers that disputed it—from Spain, from the League, from the Catholic Church, and above all from chronic chaos—the rank sediment of that pseudo-revolution which, sterilized by its own inner contradiction, unable to advance or retreat, static, destructive, without purpose, without policy, without leaders, without the generous emotion of justice which might have supplied them, degenerated into morbid anarchy. The end was exhaustion, and a compromise. Henri IV renounced his religion and the country renounced its dissensions. Weary of fruitless disorder, vanquished by that lassitude which led the peasants to revolt and to inscribe on their banner three words, their whole programme—*Nous sommes las*—France craved a return to

order at all costs. And the cost was high. The powers of
reaction triumphed. With the blessings of order, Henri IV
restored those of absolutism. Worn and scarred by the
victory, he appreciated the experience of his predecessors
by whose compromises and crimes he benefited. One day
the name of Catherine de' Medici was mentioned in his
presence. Someone accused her of causing all the evils
from which the country was slowly recuperating. But the
King defended her. "What could the poor woman do," he
said, "with five little children on her arms, after the death
of her husband, and two families in France, ours and the
Guises, attempting to encroach on the Crown? Was she
not forced to play strange parts to deceive the one and the
other and yet, as she did, to protect her children, who
reigned in succession by the wisdom of a woman so able?
I wonder that she did not do worse!"

The powers of reaction triumphed. The Catholic
Church, after a century of struggle with its own revolution, its hold breaking, weathered the last crisis and,
clinging to the French Crown, rode out the storm. But it
was battered and worn. The old spirit was tamed. It acquiesced in the Edict of Nantes, which finally secured
toleration for the Huguenots on the same terms as those
granted by Henri III in 1577. Time and exhaustion had
accomplished what reason could not. But time had worse
reverses in store. The day was to come when religion itself, and not merely the quarrel of creeds, would wither
away, and the stakes for which men had suffered so bitterly would no longer have any meaning for the world.
Then, and then only, could the underlying political issues
which the religious question had masked and misled in
the sixteenth century emerge. The abortive revolution of
1589, though it was lost, bred a revolutionary consciousness which matured for two hundred years. Two hundred
years later France and the world were ripe for the revolution of 1789. But again one oppression passes to be replaced by another. Political democracy is seen to be nothing without economic democracy. It has remained for
our own day to attack the fundamental question which,
had it been the first instead of the last to be reached,
might have spared the world the other two. Lurking in

the sixteenth century, swelling in the eighteenth, it embraces the world today. But of our own revolution who will say that it is the last? Nothing endures, nothing is certain but change. Who knew that better than Catherine de' Medici? And her anguish has long since turned to indifference. The peacemaker has found peace, sleeping in the bosom of the whirling sphere, deep in the dust and the certitude of everlasting negation.

Bibliography

ACTON, LORD. "The Massacre of St. Bartholomew's Eve." *North British Review*. 1869.

Archives Curieuses de l'Histoire de France. Cimber et Anjou. Paris. 1834.

BAIRD, HENRY M. *History of the Huguenots in France*. New York. 1879.

The Huguenots and Henri de Navarre. New York. 1886.

BASCHET, ARMAND. *Relations de la Diplomatie Vénitienne*.

BATUT, GUY DE LA. *Henri III*. Paris. 1931.

BERSIER, EUGÈNE. *Coligny*. London. 1884.

BOUCHOT, HENRI. *Catherine de Médicis*.

BUNGENER, L. F. *History of the Council of Trent*. New York. 1885.

Calendar of State Papers. Foreign Series. Public Record Office.

CATHERINE DE MÉDICIS, *Lettres de*. Edited by M. le Comte Baguenault de la Puchesse and M. le Comte Hector de la Ferrière.

CHÉRUEL. *Marie Stuart et Catherine de Médicis*. Paris. 1858.

CUNNINGHAM, W. *Christianity and Economic Science*. London. 1914.

D'AUBIGNÉ, J. H. MERLE. *History of the Great Reformation of the Sixteenth Century*.

DELABORDE, JULES, M. LE COMTE. *Vie de Coligny*.

DESJARDINS, ALBERT. *Les Sentiments Moraux au Seizième Siècle*. Paris. 1887.

ENGELS, FRIEDRICH. *The Peasant War in Germany*.

ERLANGER, PHILIP. *Henri III*.

GOULART, SIMON. *Mémoires de l'Etat de France sous Charles IX*.

GUILLEMIN, J. J. *Le Cardinal de Lorraine*. Paris. 1847.

HATON, CLAUDE. *Mémoires de* (1535-82).

HENRI·III. *Discours de, à un Personnage d'Honneur.* (*Mémoire de l'Etat de Villeroy.*)

Journal d'un Curé Ligueur.

L'ESTOILE, PIERRE DE. *Journal de.*

MACKINTOSH, SIR JAMES. *History of England.*

MARGUERITE DE VALOIS. *Mémoires.*

MARIÉJOL, JEAN-H. *Catherine de Médicis.* Paris. 1922.

MAULDE LA CLAVIÈRE, R. *Les Origines de la Révolution Française au Commencement du XVIe Siècle.*

PICOT. *Histoire des Etats-Généraux.*

Relazioni degli Ambasciatori Veneti al Senato. Edite da Eugenio Alberi. Firenze. 1839.

ROMIER, LUCIEN. *Les Origines Politiques des Guerres de Religion.* Paris. 1913.

Jacques d'Albon de Saint-André. Paris. 1909.

La Conjuration d'Amboise. Paris. 1923.

Catholiques et Huguenots à la Cour de Charles IX. Paris. 1924.

"La Saint-Barthélemy, les événements de Rome et la préméditation du massacre." *Revue du XVIe siècle*, t. I. 1913.

SICHEL, EDITH. *The Later Years of Catherine de' Medici.* 1908.

TAVANNES, *Mémoires du Maréchal de,* by his son Guillaume de Saulx, Seigneur de Tavannes.

TAWNEY, R. H. *Religion and the Rise of Capitalism.* London. 1926.

THOMPSON, J. W. *The Wars of Religion in France.*

VITET, L. *La Ligue.*

WEILL, GEORGES. *La Théorie du Pouvoir Royal en France.*

I wish to make especial acknowledgment of my indebtedness to the remarkable series of works on this period by M. Lucien Romier, who has brought order out of chaos and restored verisimilitude and clarity to the events and the characters of an age that has suffered with posterity, as it did at the time, from confusion and distortion. But for his guidance, this survey could never have been written; and if it serves to direct attention to its source, it will have been written to some purpose.

Chronological Table of
Principal Events

1513.   Election of Pope Leo X (March 11).

1515.   Battle of Marignano, September 12. Meeting of the Pope and François I at Bologna. At this conference the terms of the Concordat of 1515 or, as it is sometimes known, the Concordat of 1516 (it was published in August of that year in Rome) were established.

1516.   Death of Giuliano de' Medici, the Duc de Nemours, the younger brother of Pope Leo X.

1517.   Capture of Urbino by the Papal troops under the command of Lorenzo de' Medici, who becomes Duke of Urbino (March 30). Posting of the Ninety-Five Theses of Luther at Wittenberg (October).

1518.   Marriage of Lorenzo de' Medici, at Amboise, to Madeleine de la Tour d'Auvergne, Comtesse de Boulogne (March 2). They return to Florence in September.

1519.   Birth of Catherine de' Medici (April 13). Death of her mother (April 28); death of her father (May 4). Debate of Luther and Dr. Eck at Leipzig on the primacy of the Pope (June 29-July 14).

1520.   Election of Charles V (June 28). Luther publishes his *Appeal to the Christian Nobility of Germany* (June 25). The Papal Bull of Excommunication is burned at Wittenberg (December).

1521.   Luther appears at the Diet of Worms (April). Luther is in the Wartburg from May 4, 1521, to March 1, 1522. Pope Leo X dies (December 2).

1523.   Election of Pope Clement VII (November 19).

1524-5. The Peasants' War in Germany. The Battle of Pavia (February 1525). Capture of François I.

1527. The Sack of Rome (May 6). Revolt in Florence and restoration of the Republic (May 16).

1529. The Siege of Florence begins (October).

1530. Florence capitulates (August). The Lutherans present their Confession of Faith at the Diet of Augsburg.

1531. Catherine de' Medici is betrothed to Henri, Duc d'Orléans, by secret contract (June 9).

1533. Catherine de' Medici is married to Henri, Duc d'Orléans, at Marseilles (October 28).

1536. The death of the Dauphin François (August).

1545. The Council of Trent opens.

1546. Death of Luther.

1547. Death of François I (March 31). Accession of Henri II.

1548. Revolt against the *gabelle* in Guyenne and Poitou.

1549. Capture of Boulogne.

1551. The War of Parma.

1552. The Siege of Metz. The Siennese embrace French protection.

1553. Piero Strozzi is sent to Italy as Lieutenant-General of the King of France.

1554. Piero Strozzi is defeated at the Battle of Marciano.

1555. Abdication of Charles V (October).

1556. The Truce of Vaucelles (February). François de Guise leaves for Italy (December). The Neapolitan campaign begins.

1557. Henri II countermands the Neapolitan expedition (May). The Battle of Saint-Quentin (August 10). The town falls (August 27). Guise is recalled from Italy.

1558. Capture of Calais (January). Marriage of Mary Stuart to the Dauphin (April). The incidents of the Pré-aux-Clercs (May). Peace negotiations at Cercamps (October).

1559. Marriage of Claude de Valois to Charles, Duc de Lorraine (January 22). Peace of Cateau-Cambrésis signed (April 3). The *mercuriale* of Parlement (June 10). Marriage by proxy of Elisabeth de Valois to Philip II (June 22-23). Wounding of Henri II in the tourney (June 30). Marriage of Marguerite de Berry to Philibert-Emmanuel of Savoy (July 9). Death of Henri II (July 10). Accession of François II.

1560. The Conspiracy of Amboise (March). The Edict of Amboise (March 8) suspends persecution. It is supplemented by the Edict of Romorantin (May). Assembly of Notables at Fontainebleau (August). New conspiracy by the Bourbons. Arrival of Antoine de

Bourbon and the Prince de Condé at Orléans and arrest of Condé (October). Death of François II (December 5). Accession of Charles IX. Opening of the States-General of Orléans (December 13). The Council of Trent is reopened by a Papal Bull (November).

1561. The States-General in session until January 31. Release of Condé (January 20). The Assembly of the Prévôté de Paris (March 15). Formation of the Triumvirate (March-April). Coronation of Charles IX at Reims (May 15). Publication of the Edict of July (July 30). Colloquy of Poissy (September 9-October 14).

1562. Publication of the Edict of January (January 17). Interviews of François and Charles de Guise with the Duke of Württemberg at Saverna (February 15-18). Massacre of Vassy (March 1). Condé mobilizes his followers in Paris. The Triumvirs enter Paris (March 16). The royal family conducted to Paris by the Triumvirs (April). Outbreak of the first civil war. Siege of Rouen (September-October). Death of Antoine de Bourbon. Battle of Dreux (December 19). Death of Saint-André, capture of Condé, capture of the Constable.

1563. Death of François de Guise at the Siege of Orléans (February 24). Peace of Amboise (March 19). Closing of the Council of Trent (December).

1564. Catherine begins the journey of pacification (March 1564-May 1566).

1565. The Conference of Bayonne (June 15-July 2).

1566. Publication of the Ordinances of Moulins (February).

1567. March of Alva to Brussels. Arrival of Alva in Brussels (August). Attempt on Meaux (September). Outbreak of the second civil war. Battle of Saint-Denis (November 10). Death of the Constable Montmorency.

1568. The Peace of Longjumeau (March 23). Attempt on Condé and Coligny and their flight to La Rochelle (August). Outbreak of the third civil war. Fall of L'Hospital. Death of Elisabeth de Valois.

1569. Battle of Jarnac and death of Condé (March 13). Death of Andelot (May). Battle of Moncontour (October).

1570. The Peace of Saint-Germain (August). Marriage of Charles IX to Elisabeth, the second daughter of the Emperor Maximilian II.

1572. Tentative intervention of the French in Flanders (May-August). Marriage of Marguerite de Valois to Henri de Bourbon, King of Navarre (August 18). The Massacre of the Saint Bartholomew (August 24).

1573. The fourth civil war. The Siege of La Rochelle (November 1572-July 1573). The Duc d'Anjou is elected King of Poland (May). Edict of Boulogne accords a truce.

1574. The Conspiracy of the Politiques (March). Death of Charles IX (May 30). Return from Poland of Henri III (September). The fifth civil war begins in October. Death of the Cardinal de Lorraine (December 26).

1576. The Paix de Monsieur (April). The States-General at Blois (December). The sixth civil war breaks out.

1577. The sixth civil war closes with the Paix de Bergerac, or Paix du Roi, confirmed by the Edict of Poitiers.

1578. Catherine undertakes her journey of pacification (August 1578 to November 1579).

1580. The seventh civil war (La Guerre des Amoureux). The Paix de Fleix (November).

1582-3. Activities of the Duc d'Alençon in the Netherlands.

1584. Death of the Duc d'Alençon (June). Formation of the Holy League.

1585. Treaty of Nemours between the King and the League (July).

1587. The eighth civil war (La Guerre des Trois Henri).

1588. The Insurrection of Paris. The Day of the Barricades (May 12). Flight of the King to Chartres (May 13). Pact of Union between the King and the League (July). Dispersal of the Armada (August). Meeting of the States-General at Blois (December-January).

1589. Death of Catherine de' Medici (January 5). The League government in Paris. Henri III joins the King of Navarre. They march on Paris. Henri III is assassinated at Saint-Cloud (August).

Relationships of the Principal Figures Who Appear in This Study

THE GUISES

Claude de Lorraine (1496-1550), second son of René II, Duc de Lorraine, was the first Duc de Guise, married Antoinette de Bourbon, and had the following children:

Marie (1515-1560) married the Duc de Longueville in 1534. Married James V of Scotland in 1538.

François (1519-1563), Comte and then Duc d'Aumale, Duc de Guise on the death of his father. Married Anna d'Este, the second daughter of Ercole II of Ferrara and Renée de France, the daughter of Louis XII of France.

Charles (1524-1574) Archbishop of Reims, later Cardinal de Guise (1547), later Cardinal de Lorraine, on the death of his uncle, the first Cardinal de Lorraine (1550).

Claude, Marquis de Mayenne, later Duc d'Aumale.

Louis, Cardinal de Guise.

François, Grand Prieur de France.

René, Marquis d'Elbœuf.

François de Lorraine, Duc de Guise, had the following children:

Henri (1550-1588) Prince de Joinville, later Duc de Guise.

Catherine, married to the Duc de Montpensier.

Charles, Duc de Mayenne.

Louis, Cardinal de Guise.

THE BOURBONS

ANTOINE DE BOURBON, Duc de Vendôme, First Prince of the Blood, King of Navarre by his marriage in 1548 to Jeanne d'Albret, the heiress of Navarre.

CHARLES DE BOURBON, Cardinal de Bourbon, his brother, later the League pretender to the French throne (Charles X).

LOUIS DE BOURBON, Prince de Condé, his brother. Married Eléonore de Roye, the niece of Coligny.

THE MONTMORENCYS

ANNE DE MONTMORENCY, THE CONSTABLE OF FRANCE.
His sons:
> FRANÇOIS, later the Maréchal de Montmorency, married Diane de France, the illegitimate daughter of Henri II, after the death of her husband, Orazio Farnese, the Duc de Castro.
> HENRI, the Maréchal Damville.
> GUILLAUME, the Comte de Thoré.
> GABRIEL.
> CHARLES, the Comte de Méru.

His nephews, by his sister Louise de Montmorency:
> ODET, the Cardinal de Châtillon.
> GASPARD DE CHÂTILLON, the Sieur de Coligny, Admiral of France.
> FRANÇOIS DE CHÂTILLON, the Sieur d'Andelot.

CONTEMPORARY POPES

LEO X (Giovanni de' Medici), 1513-1521
ADRIAN VI (Adrian Dedel), 1522-1523
CLEMENT VII (Giulio de' Medici), 1523-1534
PAUL III (Alessandro Farnese), 1534-1549
JULIUS III, 1550-1555
MARCELLUS II, 1555-1555
PAUL IV (Giovanni Pietro Carafa), 1555-1559
PIUS IV, 1559-1565
PIUS V, 1566-1572
GREGORY XIII, 1572-1585
SIXTUS V, 1585-1590

Genealogy

GENEALOGY OF THE MEDICI

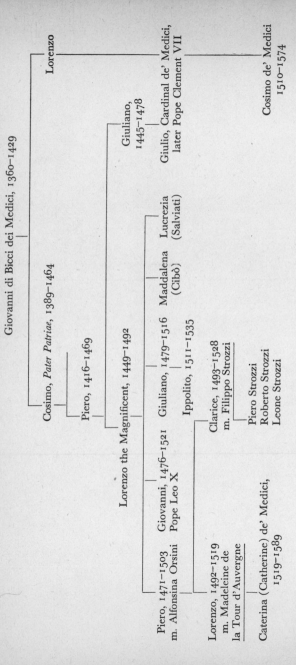

Lorenzo

Giovanni di Bicci dei Medici, 1360-1429

Cosimo, *Pater Patriae*, 1389-1464

Piero, 1416-1469

Lorenzo the Magnificent, 1449-1492

Giuliano, 1445-1478

Giulio, Cardinal de' Medici, later Pope Clement VII

Piero, 1471-1503
m. Alfonsina Orsini

Giovanni, 1476-1521
Pope Leo X

Giuliano, 1479-1516

Maddalena
(Cibò)

Lucrezia
(Salviati)

Ippolito, 1511-1535

Lorenzo, 1492-1519
m. Madeleine de
la Tour d'Auvergne

Clarice, 1493-1528
m. Filippo Strozzi

Cosimo de' Medici
1510-1574

Caterina (Catherine) de' Medici,
1519-1589

Piero Strozzi
Roberto Strozzi
Leone Strozzi

GENEALOGY OF THE VALOIS-ANGOULÊME

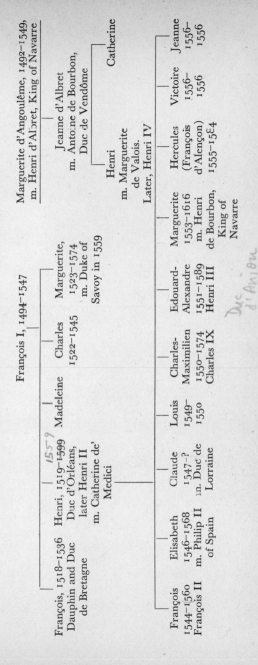

François I, 1494–1547

m. Marguerite d'Angoulême, 1492–1549,
m. Henri d'Albret, King of Navarre

François, 1518–1536
Dauphin and Duc
de Bretagne

Henri, 1519–1599 1559
Duc d'Orléans,
later Henri II
m. Catherine de'
Medici

Madeleine

Charles
1522–1545

Marguerite,
1523–1574
m. Duke of
Savoy in 1559

Jeanne d'Albret
m. Antoine de Bourbon,
Duc de Vendôme

Catherine

Henri
m. Marguerite
de Valois.
Later, Henri IV

François
1544–1560
François II

Elisabeth
1546–1568
m. Philip II
of Spain

Claude
1547–?
m. Duc de
Lorraine

Louis
1549–
1550

Charles-
Maximilien
1550–1574
Charles IX

Edouard-
Alexandre
1551–1589
Henri III

Marguerite
1553–1616
m. Henri
de Bourbon,
King of
Navarre

Hercules
(François
d'Alençon)
1555–1584

Victoire
1556–
1556

Jeanne
1556–
1556

Duc
d'Anjou

PUBLISHERS' NOTE

Since this book is not intended as a work of reference, it has been thought unnecessary to supply a comprehensive Index. The following is offered to assist readers who may wish to refer to certain figures and events which might not easily be found in their context.

Index

ALENÇON DUC D' (Hercules de Valois, alias François), 118; connection with Politiques, 387-8; joins insurgents, 405; returns to royal troops, 416; death, 421

Alva, Duke of, at Conference of Bayonne, 282-91; minister to Netherlands, 297; the Tribunal of Blood, 297

Andelot, François d', 51; siege of Saint-Quentin, 89-91; arrest for Protestantism, 99-102; government of Picardy, 108; death, 315

Assembly of Notables, 292-5

BÈZE, THÉODORE DE, at Colloquy of Poissy, 232-6; position at Court, 239

Boulogne, War of, 65-6

Bourbon, Cardinal de, named heir-presumptive, 423

Bourbon Conspiracy, the, 142-5; Tumult of Amboise follows, 152ff.

CALAIS, capture of, 91; treaty, 109

Calvin, John, 96; message to Huguenot deputies of States-General, 192; Catherine's attitude toward, 228

Catherine de' Medici (Queen of France, Caterina Maria Romola dei Medici), birth, 11; marriage, 24-32; birth of first child, 39; regency for the King, 75-8; Tuscan Campaign, 78-82; attitude to Protestants, 139-42; Edicts of Amboise and Romorantin, 163; takes hold of government, 158-9; regency for Charles IX, 181, 186-99; Edict of July, 227; Edict of Toleration, 244-6; conference at Bayonne, 280-91; Saint Bartholomew Massacre, 358; regency for Henri III, 389-90; Council of 1574, 396; mediates between League and Henri III, 450; death, 470

Charles V, Emperor (Charles of Spain), 15; abdication, 82

Charles IX (Charles-Maximilien de Valois), 73; regency, 186ff.; coronation, 223-4; majority proclaimed, 266;

Saint Bartholomew Massacre, 358; death, 389-90

Châtillon, Cardinal de (Odet de Coligny), 51; as Protestant leader, 239

Coligny, Admiral Gaspard de, 51; in War of Boulogne, 65-6; Treaty of Vaucelles, 83; Saint-Quentin, 89-91; Calais, 91; retires, 249; colonies in the New World, 295; treaty with William of Orange, 306; in Flemish War, 324ff.; assassination, 340-54

Colloquy of Poissy, the, 229-36

Concordat of 1515, the, 14; the Gallican question, 42; protest against, 61

Condé, the Prince de (Louis de Condé, Bourbon Prince of the Blood), at Court of François II, 131; Bourbon conspiracy, 142-5; in First Civil War, 251ff.; death, 313

DAUPHIN, the, Spanish captivity, 30; death, 34

EDICT OF JANUARY (Edict of Toleration), 244-6; edict restored, 263

Eighth Civil War, the, 425; Treaty of Nemours, 426-7

Elisabeth, Queen of Spain (Elisabeth de Valois, "Isabella de la Paz"), birth, 45; marriage, 124; at Conference of Bayonne, 282-91; death, 309-10

Elizabeth, Queen of England, in Bourbon conspiracy, 143; negotiations during civil wars, 261, 323, 332, 378

FARNESE, OTTAVIO, 72; regains Parma, 72

Fifth Civil War, 387ff.; Protestant-Politique party, 397; Treaty of Beaulieu or Paix de Monsieur, 406

First Civil War, 251-7; brought on by Massacre of Vassy and march on Paris, 251-7; Peace of Amboise, 263

Flemish Project, the, 324ff.

Florence, fall of, 21-4

Fourth Civil War, 379ff.; Edict of Pacification, 381; Pamphleteers, 383

François I, Battle of Pavia, 20; attitude toward Reformation, 43-5; Treaty of Crépy (1544), 47; death, 48

François II (François de Valois), birth, 39; marriage, 92; Bourbon and Protestant contest over regency of, 133ff.; coronation, 145; death, 185

Fuorusciti, the, Catherine's interest in, 57-9; in War of Boulogne, 65-6

GABELLE, revolt against the, 64-5

Gallican Question, the, 42-3; in the Italian War, 69-72

Guilds, Medici control of, 5; change in nature of, 5-6; development of Leagues from, 274-6

Guise, Duc de (Comte d'Aumale, François de Guise), 37; relation to Montmorency, 51-3; revolt against the gabelle, 64; marriage, 65; War of Boulogne, 65-6; siege of Metz, 78; invasion of Naples, 86-8; capture of Calais, 91; fall from favour, 104; war office, 129-33; Condé conspiracy against him, and the Tumult of Amboise, 142ff.; the Triumvirate, 218; Massacre of Vassy, 251; assassination, 263

Guise, Duc de, the younger (Henri de Guise), 117; head of League, 411; lieutenant-general, 451; assassination, 464-5

HENRI II (Henri de Valois, Duc d'Orléans), 26-9; Spanish captivity, 30; Gallican Question and War of Parma, 69-72; seige of Metz, 78-82; capture of Calais, 91; the Protestant situation, 94-103; campaign against heresy, 120-4; death, 128

Henri III (Edouard-Alexandre de Valois, Duc d'Anjou), 116; King of Poland, 379-80; coronation and marriage, 401-2; Pact with the League, 450-1; assassination, 474

Henri IV (King of Navarre, Henri de Bourbon), 117; at Conference of Bayonne, 291; marriage, 338-40; fight for the throne, 474

Heresy, campaign against, 120-4

Holy League, 423; attitude of Pope Gregory XIII, 427; attitude of Pope Sixtus V, 427-8

JULIUS III (Cardinal del Monte), elected Pope, 68; second Council of Trent, 69; the Gallican Question and the War of Parma, 69-72; death, 82

LA RENAUDIE, SIEUR DE (Jean du Barry), Bourbon conspiracy, 142ff.; death, 153

Leagues, anti-Protestant (Confederations), outgrowth of Guilds, 274-6; menace to Crown, 281

Leo X (Giovanni de' Medici), elected Pope, 5; recaptures State, 7; death, 15

L'Hospital, Chancellor Michel de, 166; speech to States-General, 192-7; Ordinances of Moulins, 292-3; resignation, 309

Lorraine, Cardinal de (Archbishop of Reims, Charles de Guise), 37; relation to Montmorency, 51-3; made Cardinal, 60; Parma War, 59-62; Guise and Loyola, 68-9; the Truce at Cercamps, 103-5; resigns, 108; campaign against heresy, 120-4; return to power, 129-33; the Triumvirate, 218; at Council of Trent, 268-73; death, 401

Lorraine, Duchesse de (Claude de Valois), marriage, 109

Loyola, and Society of Jesus, 68-72

Luther, Martin, the Ninety-Five Theses of, 9; the Diet of Worms, 15

MARGUERITE, Queen of Navarre (Marguerite de Valois, la p'tite Margot), 117-18; marriage, 338-40

Mary, Queen of Scotland (Queen of France, Mary Stuart), 65; marriage, 92; execution, 432

Medici, Alessandro de' (Duke of Florence), 12

Medici, Cosimo de' (Pater Patriae), banishment, 5-6

Medici, Giuliano de', 8; marriage and death, 10

Medici, Giulio de' (Pope Clement VII), 11-12; elected Pope, 16; death, 32

Medici, Ippolito de', 12; favoured by Catherine, 25

Medici, Lorenzo de', 6-7

Medici, Lorenzo de', the younger, birth, 7; expedition into Urbino, 10; marriage, 10; death, 11

Medici, Piero de', 6-7

Mendoza, Spanish Ambassador, 432ff.

Montluc, Blaise de, Confederation of the King, 281-2

Montmorency, Constable Anne de (Grand Master of the Household), 31; nephews of, 51; in revolt against the *gabelle*, 64; siege of Saint-Quentin, 89; Truce at Cercamps, 103-5; the Triumvirate, 218; death, 300

NAPLES, expedition against (third Italian War), 86-8

Navarre, King of (Pretender, first Prince of the Blood, Due de Vendôme, Antoine de Bourbon), 97; fight for regency of François II, 134ff.; Lieutenant-General of Army, 214; death, 262

ORDINANCES OF MOULINS, 293

PARMA, War of (first Italian War), 70-2

Paul III (Pope), attempt at Franco-Papal alliance, 59; in Œcumenical Council, 61; death, 67

Pavia, the Battle of, 20

Peasants' War, the, 18

Philip of Spain, siege of Saint-Quentin, 89; connection with the Leagues, 282; use of Holy League, 432; great offensive, 432

Poitiers, Diane de (Madame de Valentinois, the Grande Seneschale), 31; relations with Henri II, 35-6, 45, 54-6; attitude toward Catherine, 75; dismissal, 132

Politiques (Malcontents), 386ff.

Prévôté of Paris, the, 217

SACK OF ROME, the, 21ff.

Saint-André, Maréchal de, 31; Truce at Cercamps, 103-5; forms Triumvirate, 217; killed, 262

Saint Bartholomew Massacre, 358ff.

Saint-Quentin, siege of, 88-91

Savoy, Duke of (Philibert-Emmanuel), marriage, 105, 124; siege of Saint-Quentin, 88-91

Second Civil War, 298ff.; attempt on Meaux, 298; blockade of Paris, 300; Condé's Bill of Rights, 300; Battle of Saint-Denis, 300; Peace of Longjumeau, 301

Seventh Civil War, the ("Guerre des Amoureux"), 420; Paix de Fleix, 420

Sixth Civil War, the, 416; Paix de Bergerac, 416

Spanish Armada, the, built, 432, 435; sailed, 450; defeated, 452-3

THIRD CIVIL WAR, the, 313ff.; Duc d'Anjou in command of army, 313; Battle of Jarnac, 314; siege of Poitiers, 317; Peace of Saint-Germain, 321

Treaty of Cateau-Cambrésis ("The Prisoners' Peace"), 109-14

Treaty of Vaucelles, 83-5

Triumvirate, the, 218

Truce at Cercamps, 103-5

Tuscan Campaign, the (second Italian War), 79-82

Tuscany, Grand Duke of (Duke of Florence, Cosimo de' Medici, the younger), attempts relations with the Court, 53; defeat in Tuscan campaign, 79-81

Valois, Jeanne de, 118
Valois, Louis de, 73
Valois, Victoire de, 118

"War of the Three Henris," 433-4

RALPH ROEDER was born in New York City in 1890, and educated at Columbia University and at Harvard, where he graduated in 1911. Interested in the theater, after graduation he joined the Washington Square Players, later he worked in Paris for Jacques Copeau as a stage manager and again in Manhattan performing mostly in Greek tragedies. He drove an ambulance for the Italian Army before America's entrance into the First World War. Subsequently he worked on an American newspaper in Rome and in New York for Brentano's publishing company. Mr. Roeder's books include *Savonarola* (1930), *Man of the Renaissance* (1933), *Catherine de' Medici* (1937), and *Juarez and his Mexico* (1947). He now lives in Mexico, where he is working on a history of that country.

THE TEXT of this book is set in CALEDONIA, a Linotype face designed by W. A. Dwiggins. Caledonia belongs to the family of printing types called "modern face" by printers —a term used to mark the change in style of type-letters that occurred about 1800. Caledonia borders on the general design of Scotch Modern, but is more freely drawn than that letter. Composed, printed, and bound by THE COLONIAL PRESS INC., Clinton, Mass.

VINTAGE HISTORY—EUROPEAN

V-44	Brinton, Crane	THE ANATOMY OF REVOLUTION
V-250	Burckhardt, C. J.	RICHELIEU: HIS RISE TO POWER
V-67	Curtius, Ernst R.	THE CIVILIZATION OF FRANCE
V-704	Deutscher, Isaac	STALIN: *A Political Biography*
V-707	Fischer, Louis	SOVIETS IN WORLD AFFAIRS
V-114	Hauser, Arnold through V-117	THE SOCIAL HISTORY OF ART *(Four Volumes)*
V-201	Hughes, H. Stuart	CONSCIOUSNESS AND SOCIETY
V-50	Kelly, Amy	ELEANOR OF AQUITAINE AND THE FOUR KINGS
V-728	Klyuchevsky, V.	PETER THE GREAT
V-246	Knowles, David	EVOLUTION OF MEDIEVAL THOUGHT
V-83	Kronenberger, Louis	KINGS AND DESPERATE MEN
V-43	Lefebvre, Georges	THE COMING OF THE FRENCH REVOLUTION
V-92	Mattingly, Garrett	CATHERINE OF ARAGON
V-703	Mosely, Philip E.	THE KREMLIN AND WORLD POLITICS: *Studies in Soviet Policy and Action*
V-733	Pares, Sir Bernard	THE FALL OF THE RUSSIAN MONARCHY
V-719	Reed, John	TEN DAYS THAT SHOOK THE WORLD
V-724	Wallace, Sir D. M.	RUSSIA: *On the Eve of War and Revolution*
V-729	Weidlé, W.	RUSSIA: ABSENT AND PRESENT
V-122	Wilenski, R. H.	MODERN FRENCH PAINTERS, Volume I (1863-1903)
V-123	Wilenski, R. H.	MODERN FRENCH PAINTERS, Volume II (1904-1938)
V-106	Winston, Richard	CHARLEMAGNE: *From the Hammer to the Cross*

VINTAGE POLITICAL SCIENCE
AND SOCIAL CRITICISM

V-198	Bardolph, Richard	THE NEGRO VANGUARD
V-185	Barnett, A. Doak	COMMUNIST CHINA AND ASIA
V-87	Barzun, Jacques	GOD'S COUNTRY AND MINE
V-705	Bauer, Inkeles, and Kluckhohn	HOW THE SOVIET SYSTEM WORKS
V-42	Beard, Charles A.	THE ECONOMIC BASIS OF POLITICS *and Related Writings*
V-60	Becker, Carl L.	DECLARATION OF INDEPENDENCE
V-17	Becker, Carl L.	FREEDOM AND RESPONSIBILITY IN THE AMERICAN WAY OF LIFE
V-228	Beloff, Max	THE UNITED STATES AND THE UNITY OF EUROPE
V-199	Berman, H. J. (ed.)	TALKS ON AMERICAN LAW
V-211	Binkley, Wilfred E.	PRESIDENT AND CONGRESS
V-44	Brinton, Crane	THE ANATOMY OF REVOLUTION
V-37	Brogan, D. W.	THE AMERICAN CHARACTER
V-234	Bruner, Jerome	THE PROCESS OF EDUCATION
V-196	Bryson, L., *et al.*	SOCIAL CHANGE IN LATIN AMERICA TODAY
V-30	Camus, Albert	THE REBEL
V 98	Cash, W. J.	THE MIND OF THE SOUTH
V-67	Curtius, Ernst R.	THE CIVILIZATION OF FRANCE
V-234 V-235	Daniels, R. V.	A DOCUMENTARY HISTORY OF COMMUNISM (*Two volumes*)
V-237	Daniels, Robert V.	THE NATURE OF COMMUNISM
V-252	David, *et al.*	THE POLITICS OF NATIONAL PARTY CONVENTIONS
V-704	Deutscher, Isaac	STALIN: A *Poltical Biography*
V-225	Fischer, Louis (ed.)	THE ESSENTIAL GANDHI
V-707	Fischer, Louis	SOVIETS IN WORLD AFFAIRS
V-224	Freyre, Gilberto	NEW WORLD IN THE TROPICS
V-264	Fulbright, J. William	MYTHS AND REALITIES IN AMERICAN FOREIGN POLICY AND DOMESTIC AFFAIRS
V-174	Goodman, P. & P.	COMMUNITAS
V-32	Goodman, Paul	GROWING UP ABSURD
V-247	Goodman, Paul	UTOPIAN ESSAYS AND PRACTICAL PROPOSALS
V-248	Grunebaum, G. E., von	MODERN ISLAM: *The Search for Cultural Identity*
V-69	Hand, Learned	THE SPIRIT OF LIBERTY
V-95	Hofstadter, Richard	THE AGE OF REFORM
V-9	Hofstadter, Richard	THE AMERICAN POLITICAL TRADITION
V-201	Hughes, H. Stuart	CONSCIOUSNESS AND SOCIETY
V-104	Huxley, Aldous	BEYOND THE MEXQUE BAY
V-241	Jacobs, Jane	DEATH & LIFE OF GREAT AMERICAN CITIES

VG-1	Lewis, Oscar	THE CHILDREN OF SANCHEZ
V-193	Malraux, André	TEMPTATION OF THE WEST
V-726	Marcuse, Herbert	SOVIET MARXISM
V-102	Meyers, Marvin	THE JACKSONIAN PERSUASION
V-19	Milosz, Czeslaw	THE CAPTIVE MIND
V-101	Moos, Malcolm (ed.)	H. L. MENCKEN ON POLITICS
V-192	Morgenstern, O.	QUESTION OF NATIONAL DEFENSE
V-251	Morgenthau, Hans J.	PURPOSE OF AMERICAN POLITICS
V-703	Mosely, Philip E.	THE KREMLIN AND WORLD POLITICS: *Studies in Soviet Policy and Action* (*Vintage Original*)
V-46	Philipson, M. (ed.)	AUTOMATION: *Implications for the Future* (*Vintage Original*)
V-258	Piel, Gerard	SCIENCE IN THE CAUSE OF MAN
V-128	Plato	THE REPUBLIC
V-719	Reed, John	TEN DAYS THAT SHOOK THE WORLD
V-212	Rossiter, Clinton	CONSERVATISM IN AMERICA
V-220	Shonfield, Andrew	ATTACK ON WORLD POVERTY
V-253	Stampp, Kenneth	THE PECULIAR INSTITUTION
V-179	Stebbins, Richard P.	U. S. IN WORLD AFFAIRS, 1959
V-204	Stebbins, Richard P.	U. S. IN WORLD AFFAIRS, 1960
V-222	Stebbins, Richard P.	U. S. IN WORLD AFFAIRS, 1961
V-244	Stebbins, Richard P.	U. S. IN WORLD AFFAIRS, 1962
V-53	Synge, J. M.	THE ARAN ISLANDS *and Other Writings*
V-231	Tannenbaum, Frank	SLAVE & CITIZEN: *The Negro in the Americas*
V-206	Wallerstein, Immanuel	AFRICA: THE POLITICS OF INDEPENDENCE (*Vintage Original*)
V-145	Warren, Robert Penn	SEGREGATION
V-729	Weidlé, W.	RUSSIA: ABSENT & PRESENT
V-249	Wiedner, Donald L.	A HISTORY OF AFRICA: *South of the Sahara*
V-208	Woodward, C. Vann	BURDEN OF SOUTHERN HISTORY

VINTAGE HISTORY AND CRITICISM OF LITERATURE, MUSIC, AND ART

V-22	Barzun, Jacques	THE ENERGIES OF ART
V-93	Bennett, Joan	FOUR METAPHYSICAL POETS
V-57	Bodkin, Maud	ARCHETYPAL PATTERNS IN POETRY
V-259	Buckley, Jerome H.	THE VICTORIAN TEMPER
V-51	Burke, Kenneth	THE PHILOSOPHY OF LITERARY FORM
V-75	Camus, Albert	THE MYTH OF SISYPHUS
V-171	Cruttwell, Patrick	THE SHAKESPEAREAN MOMENT
V-4	Einstein, Alfred	A SHORT HISTORY OF MUSIC
V-261	Ellis-Fermor, Una	JACOBEAN DRAMA: An Interpretation
V-177	Fuller, Edmund	MAN IN MODERN FICTION
V-13	Gilbert, Stuart	JAMES JOYCE'S "ULYSSES"
V-56	Graves, Robert	THE WHITE GODDESS
V-175	Haggin, Bernard	MUSIC FOR THE MAN WHO ENJOYS "HAMLET"
V-114	Hauser, Arnold	SOCIAL HISTORY OF ART, v. I
V-115	Hauser, Arnold	SOCIAL HISTORY OF ART, v. II
V-116	Hauser, Arnold	SOCIAL HISTORY OF ART, v. III
V-117	Hauser, Arnold	SOCIAL HISTORY OF ART, v. IV
V-20	Hyman, S. E.	THE ARMED VISION
V-38	Hyman, S. E. (ed.)	THE CRITICAL PERFORMANCE
V-41	James, Henry	THE FUTURE OF THE NOVEL
V-12	Jarrell, Randall	POETRY AND THE AGE
V-88	Kerman, Joseph	OPERA AS DRAMA
V-260	Kermode, Frank	THE ROMANTIC IMAGE
V-83	Kronenberger, Louis	KINGS AND DESPERATE MEN
V-167	La Rochefoucauld	MAXIMS
V-90	Levin, Harry	THE POWER OF BLACKNESS
V-81	Lowes, John L.	THE ROAD TO XANADU
V-55	Mann, Thomas	ESSAYS
V-720	Mirsky, D. S.	A HISTORY OF RUSSIAN LITERATURE
V-77	Mizener, Arthur	THE FAR SIDE OF PARADISE: A Biography of F. Scott Fitzgerald
V-47	Murray, Gilbert	THE CLASSICAL TRADITION IN POETRY
V-118	Newman, Ernest	GREAT OPERAS, Volume I
V-119	Newman, Ernest	GREAT OPERAS, Volume II
V-107	Newman, Ernest	WAGNER AS MAN AND ARTIST
V-161	Picasso, Pablo	PICASSO & the HUMAN COMEDY
V-24	Ransom, John Crowe	POEMS AND ESSAYS
V-89	Schorer, Mark	WILLIAM BLAKE
V-108	Shahn, Ben	THE SHAPE OF CONTENT
V-186	Steiner, George	TOLSTOY OR DOSTOEVSKY
V-39	Stravinsky, Igor	THE POETICS OF MUSIC

V-100	Sullivan, J. W. N.	BEETHOVEN: *His Spiritual Development*
V-243	Sypher, Wylie (ed.)	ART HISTORY: *An Anthology of Modern Criticism*
V-266	Sypher, Wylie	LOSS OF THE SELF
V-229	Sypher, Wylie	ROCOCO TO CUBISM
V-166	Sze, Mai-Mai	THE WAY OF CHINESE PAINTING
V-214	Thomson, Virgil	THE STATE OF MUSIC
V-162	Tillyard, E. M. W.	ELIZABETHAN WORLD PICTURE
V-35	Tindall, William York	FORCES IN MODERN BRITISH LITERATURE
V-82	Toye, Francis	VERDI: *His Life and Works*
V-62	Turnell, Martin	THE NOVEL IN FRANCE
V-194	Valéry, Paul	THE ART OF POETRY
V-122	Wilenski, R. H.	MODERN FRENCH PAINTERS, Volume I (1863-1903)
V-123	Wilenski, R. H.	MODERN FRENCH PAINTERS, Volume II (1904-1938)
V-218	Wilson, Edmund	CLASSICS & COMMERCIALS
V-181	Wilson, Edmund	THE SHORES OF LIGHT

A free catalogue of VINTAGE BOOKS will be sent at your request. Write to Vintage Books, 457 Madison Avenue, New York, New York 10022.

V-219	Frisch, Max	I'M NOT STILLER
V-8	Gide, André	THE IMMORALIST
V-96	Gide, André	LAFCADIO'S ADVENTURES
V-27	Gide, André	STRAIT IS THE GATE
V-66	Gide, André	TWO LEGENDS
V-182	Graves, Robert	I, CLAUDIUS
V-217	Graves, Robert	SERGEANT LAMB'S AMERICA
V-717	Guerney, B. G. (ed.)	AN ANTHOLOGY OF RUSSIAN LITERATURE *in the Soviet Period*
V-255	Hammett, Dashiell	THE MALTESE FALCON *and* THE THIN MAN
V-15	Hawthorne, Nathaniel	SHORT STORIES
V-227	Howes, Barbara (ed.)	23 MODERN STORIES
V-727	Ilf and Petrov	THE TWELVE CHAIRS
V-716	Kamen, Isai (ed.)	GREAT RUSSIAN STORIES
V-134	Lagerkvist, Pär	BARABBAS
V-240	Lagerkvist, Pär	THE SIBYL
V-23	Lawrence, D. H.	THE PLUMED SERPENT
V-71	Lawrence, D. H.	ST. MAWR *and* THE MAN WHO DIED
V-706	Leonov, Leonid	THE THIEF
V-176	Lowell, Robert	LIFE STUDIES
V-59	Lowry, Malcolm	UNDER THE VOLCANO
V-170	Malamud, Bernard	THE MAGIC BARREL
V-136	Malraux, André	THE ROYAL WAY
V-180	Mann, Thomas	BUDDENBROOKS
V-3	Mann, Thomas	DEATH IN VENICE
V-86	Mann, Thomas	THE TRANSPOSED HEADS
V-36	Mansfield, Katherine	STORIES
V-137	Maugham, Somerset	OF HUMAN BONDAGE
V-78	Maxwell, William	THE FOLDED LEAF
V-91	Maxwell, William	THEY CAME LIKE SWALLOWS
V-221	Maxwell, William	TIME WILL DARKEN IT
V-730	McLean & Vickery (eds.)	THE YEAR OF PROTEST, 1956
V-144	Mitford, Nancy	THE PURSUIT OF LOVE
V-197	Morgan, F. (ed.)	HUDSON REVIEW ANTHOLOGY
V-718	Nabokov, V. (tr.)	THE SONG OF IGOR'S CAMPAIGN
V-29	O'Connor, Frank	STORIES
V-49	O'Hara, John	BUTTERFIELD 8
V-18	O'Neill, Eugene	THE ICEMAN COMETH
V-165	O'Neill, Eugene	THREE PLAYS: *Desire Under the Elms, Strange Interlude, and Mourning Becomes Electra*
V-125	O'Neill & Oates (eds.)	SEVEN FAMOUS GREEK PLAYS
V-714	Pushkin, Alexander	THE CAPTAIN'S DAUGHTER
V-24	Ransom, John Crowe	POEMS AND ESSAYS
V-731	Reeve, F. (ed.)	RUSSIAN PLAYS, VOLUME I
V-732	Reeve, F. (ed.)	RUSSIAN PLAYS, VOLUME II
V-16	Sartre, Jean-Paul	No EXIT *and Three Other Plays*

V-708	Aksakov, Sergey	YEARS OF CHILDHOOD
V-715	Andreyev, Leonid	THE SEVEN THAT WERE HANGED *and Other Stories*
V-705	Bauer, Inkeles, and Kluckhohn	HOW THE SOVIET SYSTEM WORKS
V-740	Berman, Harold J.	JUSTICE IN THE U.S.S.R.
V-738	Black, Cyril (ed.)	REWRITING RUSSIAN HISTORY
V-743	Bunin, Ivan	THE GENTLEMAN FROM SAN FRANCISCO *and Other Stories*
V-725	Carr, E. H.	MICHAEL BAKUNIN
V-723	Chernyshevsky, N. G.	WHAT IS TO BE DONE? *a novel*
V-734 V-735	Daniels, R. V.	A DOCUMENTARY HISTORY OF COMMUNISM (Two volumes)
V-704	Deutscher, Isaac	STALIN: *A Political Biography*
V-722	Dostoyevsky, Fyodor	THE BROTHERS KARAMAZOV
V-721	Dostoyevsky, Fyodor	CRIME AND PUNISHMENT
V-739	Fainsod, Merle	SMOLENSK UNDER SOVIET RULE
V-709	Fedin, Konstantin	EARLY JOYS, *a novel*
V-707	Fischer, Louis	SOVIETS IN WORLD AFFAIRS
V-717	Guerney, B. G. (ed.)	AN ANTHOLOGY OF RUSSIAN LITERATURE *in the Soviet Period*
V-742	Hare, Richard	PIONEERS OF RUSSIAN SOCIAL THOUGHT
V-727	Ilf and Petrov	THE TWELVE CHAIRS
V-716	Kamen, Isai (ed.)	GREAT RUSSIAN STORIES
V-728	Klyuchevsky, V.	PETER THE GREAT
V-710	Kohn, Hans	PAN-SLAVISM: *Its History and Ideology*
V-706	Leonov, Leonid	THE THIEF, *a novel*
V-726	Marcuse, Herbert	SOVIET MARXISM
V-730	McLean & Vickery (eds.)	THE YEAR OF PROTEST, 1956
V-720	Mirsky, D. S.	A HISTORY OF RUSSIAN LITERATURE *to 1900*
V-703	Mosely, Philip E.	THE KREMLIN AND WORLD POLITICS: *Studies in Soviet Policy and Action (Vintage Original)*
V-718	Nabokov, V. (tr.)	THE SONG OF IGOR'S CAMPAIGN
V-733	Pares, Sir Bernard	THE FALL OF THE RUSSIAN MONARCHY
V-737	Potapova, Nina	LEARNING RUSSIAN
V-714	Pushkin, Alexander	THE CAPTAIN'S DAUGHTER *and Other Great Stories*
V-719	Reed, John	TEN DAYS THAT SHOOK THE WORLD
V-731	Reeve, F. (ed.)	RUSSIAN PLAYS, Volume I
V-732	Reeve, F. (ed.)	RUSSIAN PLAYS, Volume II
V-741	Rubin & Stillman (eds.)	A RUSSIAN SONG BOOK

V-745	Schapiro, Leonard	THE COMMUNIST PARTY OF THE SOVIET UNION
V-736	Simmons, Ernest J.	DOSTOEVSKY: *The Making of a Novelist*
V-701	Simmons, Ernest J.	LEO TOLSTOY, Volume I
V-702	Simmons, Ernest J.	LEO TOLSTOY, Volume II
V-744	Simmons, Ernest J.	ALEXANDER PUSHKIN
V-713	Tolstoy, Leo	THE KREUTZER SONATA, *a novel*
V-711	Turgenev, Ivan	THE VINTAGE TURGENEV Volume I: SMOKE, FATHERS AND SONS, FIRST LOVE
V-712	Turgenev, Ivan	Volume II: ON THE EVE, RUDIN, A QUIET SPOT, DIARY OF A SUPERFLUOUS MAN
V-724	Wallace, Sir D. M.	RUSSIA: *On the Eve of War and Revolution*
V-729	Weidlé, W.	RUSSIA: ABSENT & PRESENT

V-715	Andreyev, Leonid	THE SEVEN THAT WERE HANGED *and Other Stories*
V-158	Auden, W. H., & Isherwood, C.	TWO PLAYS: *The Dog Beneath the Skin* and *The Ascent of F6*
V-80	Beerbohm, Max	SEVEN MEN *and* TWO OTHERS
V-93	Bennett, Joan	FOUR METAPHYSICAL POETS
V-21	Bowen, Elizabeth	THE DEATH OF THE HEART
V-48	Bowen, Elizabeth	THE HOUSE IN PARIS
V-79	Bowen, Elizabeth	STORIES
V-743	Bunin, Ivan	THE GENTLEMAN FROM SAN FRANCISCO *and Other Stories*
V-207	Camus, Albert	CALIGULA & 3 *Other plays*
V-2	Camus, Albert	THE STRANGER
V-223	Camus, Albert	THE FALL
V-245	Camus, Albert	THE POSSESSED, *a play*
V-28	Cather, Willa	FIVE STORIES
V-200	Cather, Willa	MY MORTAL ENEMY
V-140	Cerf, Bennett (ed.)	FAMOUS GHOST STORIES
V-203	Cerf, Bennett (ed.)	FOUR CONTEMPORARY AMERICAN PLAYS
V-127	Cerf, Bennett (ed.)	GREAT MODERN SHORT STORIES
V-142	Chaucer, Geoffrey	TROILUS AND CRESSIDA
V-723	Chernyshevsky, N. G.	WHAT IS TO BE DONE?
V-146	Clark, Walter Van T.	THE OX-BOW INCIDENT
V-155	Conrad, Joseph	THREE GREAT TALES: THE NIGGER OF THE NARCISSUS, HEART OF DARKNESS, YOUTH
V-138	Cozzens, James Gould	S.S. SAN PEDRO *and* CASTAWAY
V-10	Crane, Stephen	STORIES AND TALES
V-205	Dinesen, Isak	WINTER'S TALES
V-722	Dostoyevsky, Fyodor	THE BROTHERS KARAMAZOV
V-721	Dostoyevsky, Fyodor	CRIME AND PUNISHMENT
V-188	Eschenbach, W. von	PARZIVAL
V-254	Faulkner, William	AS I LAY DYING
V-139	Faulkner, William	THE HAMLET
V-5	Faulkner, William	THE SOUND AND THE FURY
V-184	Faulkner, William	THE TOWN
V-262	Faulkner, William	THE WILD PALMS
V-149	Faulkner, William	THREE FAMOUS SHORT NOVELS: SPOTTED HORSES, OLD MAN, THE BEAR
V-709	Fedin, Konstantin	EARLY JOYS
V-130	Fielding, Henry	TOM JONES
V-45	Ford, Ford Madox	THE GOOD SOLDIER
V-187	Forster, E. M.	A ROOM WITH A VIEW
V-7	Forster, E. M.	HOWARDS END
V-40	Forster, E. M.	THE LONGEST JOURNEY
V-61	Forster, E. M.	WHERE ANGELS FEAR TO TREAD

V-85	Sartre, Jean-Paul	THE DEVIL & THE GOOD LORD and Two Other Plays
V-238	Sartre, Jean-Paul	THE CONDEMNED OF ALTONA
V-85	Stevens, Wallace	POEMS
V-141	Styron, William	THE LONG MARCH
V-63	Svevo, Italo	CONFESSIONS OF ZENO
V-178	Synge, J. M.	COMPLETE PLAYS
V-131	Thackeray, W. M.	VANITY FAIR
V-713	Tolstoy, Leo	THE KREUTZER SONATA
V-154	Tracy, Honor	STRAIGHT AND NARROW PATH
V-202	Turgenev, Ivan	TORRENTS OF SPRING
V-711	Turgenev, Ivan	THE VINTAGE TURGENEV Volume I: SMOKE, FATHERS AND SONS, FIRST LOVE
V-712	Turgenev, Ivan	Volume II: ON THE EVE, RUDIN, A QUIET SPOT, DIARY OF A SUPERFLUOUS MAN
V-257	Updike, John	OLINGER STORIES: A Selecti
V-152	Waugh, Evelyn	THE LOVED ONE

VINTAGE BIOGRAPHY AND AUTOBI

V-708	Aksakov, Sergey	YEARS OF CHILDHOOD
V-159	Behrman, S. N.	DUVEEN
V-250	Burckhardt, C. J.	RICHELIEU: HIS RISE TO POWER
V-725	Carr, E. H.	MICHAEL BAKUNIN
V-704	Deutscher, Isaac	STALIN: *A Polticial Biography*
V-225	Fischer, L. (ed.)	THE ESSENTIAL GANDHI
V-147	Gide, André	IF IT DIE
V-742	Hare, Richard	PIONEERS OF RUSSIAN SOCIAL THOUGHT
V-50	Kelly, Amy	ELEANOR OF AQUITAINE AND THE FOUR KINGS
V-728	Klyuchevsky, V.	PETER THE GREAT
VG-1	Lewis, Oscar	CHILDREN OF SANCHEZ
V-34	Lowenthal, M. (ed.)	AUTOBIOGRAPHY OF MICHEL DE MONTAIGNE
V-92	Mattingly, Garrett	CATHERINE OF ARAGON
V-77	Mizener, Arthur	THE FAR SIDE OF PARADISE: A *Biography of F. Scott Fitzgerald*
V-107	Newman, Ernest	WAGNER AS MAN AND ARTIST
V-744	Simmons, Ernest J.	ALEXANDER PUSHKIN
V-701	Simmons, Ernest J.	LEO TOLSTOY, Volume I
V-702	Simmons, Ernest J.	LEO TOLSTOY, Volume II
V-736	Simmons, Ernest J.	DOSTOEVSKY: *The Making of a Novelist*
V-263	Roeder, Ralph	CATHERINE DE' MEDICI *and the Lost Revolution*
V-133	Stein, Gertrude	THE AUTOBIOGRAPHY OF ALICE B. TOKLAS
V-100	Sullivan, J. W. N.	BEETHOVEN: *His Spiritual Development*
V-82	Toye, Francis	VERDI: *His Life and Works*
V-256	Wilde, Oscar	DE PROFUNDIS (*Unexpurgated*)
V-122	Wilenski, R. H.	MODERN FRENCH PAINTERS, Volume I (1863-1903)
V-123	Wilenski, R. H.	MODERN FRENCH PAINTERS, Volume II (1904-1938)
V-106	Winston, Richard	CHARLEMAGNE: *From the Hammer to the Cross*